Month-By-Month™

WHAT TO DO EACH MONTH TO HAVE A BEAUTIFUL GARDEN ALL YEAR

GARDENING
I IN DAHO

D1614200

Library of Congress Cataloging-in-Publication Data is available.
ISBN: 1-59186-386-4
EAN: 978-1-59186-386-1

Published by Cool Springs Press, 101 Forrest Crossing Boulevard, Suite 100, Franklin, Tennessee, 37064

First printing 2007

Printed in the United States of America

Managing Editor: Mary Buckner
Cover Design: Marc Pewitt
Horticulture Editor: Troy Marden
Illustrator: Bill Kersey, Kersey Graphics
Production Design: S.E. Anderson

On the cover: Bitterroot

Month-By-Month™
WHAT TO DO EACH MONTH TO HAVE A BEAUTIFUL GARDEN ALL YEAR

GARDENING
IN DAHO

JOHN CRETTI

COOL SPRINGS PRESS

Franklin, Tennessee
www.coolspringspress.net

DEDICATION

To the volunteer Master Gardeners for their untiring efforts to provide helpful information to gardeners throughout the region.

ACKNOWLEDGEMENTS

Developing and putting together this book has taken the combined inspirations, experiences, talents, and efforts of many behind-the-scenes folks. Many of you, who have asked the thousands of questions throughout my media outreach, are responsible for much of the content of the book. No question is too dumb. It is my wish that you employ sustainable gardening techniques that will steadily improve soil tilth and our natural environment. May your landscape grow and prosper wherever you may garden!

I am grateful to many of my colleagues (past and present) from Colorado State University, throughout the Rocky Mountain region, and across the country with their voluminous knowledge of plants and gardening techniques, a few of whom are: George Kelly, Chuck Drage, Herb Gundell, "Bob" Holley, Jim Feucht, Whitney Cranshaw, Barbara Hyde, Jim Klett, Kelly Grummons, Panayoti Kelaidis, Karen Panter, 'Mick' Paulino, Patt Dorsey, Bob Polomski, Liz Ball, Felder Rushing, Brent and Becky Heath, Michael Dirr, Don Schlup, David Winger, Dee Lovisone, and Jo Kendzerski.

I am especially grateful to my Italian family (past and present) who taught me to respect and appreciate the simplicity of life and who inspired me to garden by following the wisdom of Nature.

My heartfelt thanks go to my family and friends who encouraged and supported me throughout the duration of "the project".

Finally, I recognize all those at Cool Springs Press who have made this book possible.

I thank you all!

CONTENTS

INTRODUCTION

Whether you are new to gardening or a seasoned gardener in Idaho, you'll quickly discover that gardening success relies on knowing not only **how** to do certain tasks, but **when** to do them. You'd like to create a landscape that draws attention from neighbors and reflects your personal gardening style. It's wonderful to plant trees, shrubs, vines, ground covers, and flowers and to brighten your indoors with colorful houseplants. But caring for the plants requires a plan. A schedule helps you keep track of what you need to do and when.

Month-by-Month Gardening in Idaho will help you with all these elements, guiding you throughout the year. This book describes 10 categories of plants, presented in a calendar format. Each chapter is designed to take you month-by-month through a year of growing for these plants with reminders, "how to" items, and helpful hints on "gardening with an ALTITUDE."

KEEPING A GARDEN JOURNAL

Though you can write in the margins of this book and add bookmarks, I strongly encourage you to keep a separate gardening notebook or journal. Most of us respond to such a suggestion with: Why add to the already busy schedule of garden activities? It seems like too much trouble, and for what?

One of the best reasons for keeping records may not be obvious at first, but sooner or later, the information you jot down can keep your memories fresh and help you avoid repeating the same gardening mistakes. It can help you plan on what will work best in specific areas of your landscape, since there may be various microclimates just in your own garden.

Despite our best intentions, we forget. Remember when you planted that beautiful peony last year and then sliced into the shoots during the autumn while planting hardy spring-flowering bulbs? Placing labels in the garden can help identify spots where perennials are located to avoid this mishap. You can even sketch a simple drawing to mark plant locations.

Keeping tabs on where you bought what, how much you spent, and how the plants performed helps develop a personal reference source. In a sense, record keeping is like writing your own garden book, specific to your property, your needs, and your gardening style. Over the years, as your garden matures and your gardening skills improve, you will know predictably the succession of bloom in your garden, when pests and diseases arrive, and how to be ready to cope with specific problems.

Don't forget to take pictures, either conventional or digital photos, to show the "before and after" of what's happening in your landscape. You don't need to be a rocket scientist to maintain a journal or garden notebook. I often use a 100-page, college-ruled composition notebook to record specific information such as weather conditions, the first and last freezes of the gardening year, the dates plants were installed, names and varieties of vegetables, herbs, flowers, shrubs, trees, vines, ground covers, and other plants that I'm attempting to grow. Keep notes about fertilizer applications and pest problems. When you visit other gardeners in your area, jot down interesting techniques or tips that may help you become more successful with your gardening endeavors. A journal is a tool, just like a spading fork or a good set of hand pruners.

INTRODUCTION

YEAR-ROUND GARDENING

Like any other aspect of life, gardening in our region will need some fine-tuning. The seasons do not always arrive here when expected. There are drought years (some droughts last for several years), water restrictions, and pest or disease problems. As your landscape matures, there are "microclimates"—areas that are more or less protected from the open parts of the landscape—that will allow you to grow more unusual plants or to experiment with plants not in your hardiness zone.

Every season in Idaho presents some kind of gardening opportunity. As host of "The Winter Gardener" on HGTV and the "Gardening with an ALTITUDE" radio program since 1981, I encourage you to keep gardening year-round, even in the winter, as the landscape can display some of its more interesting characteristics when frost and snow blanket the ground.

Prolonged periods of drought in fall and winter are no time to hang up the gardening tools and hibernate. Important tasks need to be done to ensure that your plants will stay alive and maintain their vigor and health. Decorate empty exterior containers with pine cones. Start cuttings indoors. Check your stored bulbs every week through the winter. Renovate a damaged lawn in late spring or early fall. Though you can gamble on doing certain tasks in the garden, knowing the when and how to catch the right month or season makes your efforts less risky, more fun, and ultimately easier.

GARDENING CONDITIONS IN IDAHO

Idaho has a diverse range of gardening conditions and challenges. The Rockies are separated from oceans and seas by huge expanses of plains, deserts, and other mountains ranges. You will find moist areas generally at the higher elevations or along the widely separated river or creek drainages. A drought can occur almost any-where in the region at almost any time of year. Soils can vary from acidic in the high country to extreme alkaline in the lower elevations. Soil structure can range from crushed granite to sand or heavy clay. Rapid temperature fluctuations are the norm in winter and early spring.

Despite all this, our region is rich in plant species, and I encourage you to collect seed and experiment with growing some native plants that will enrich your landscape with attractive blooms, plant forms, and habit. The very diversity of the state is one of the obstacles to growing non-native plants from other parts of the world. Fortunately, with the proper planning and soil preparation, plants can be adapted for growth in far different climates.

PLANT HARDINESS ZONES AND MICROCLIMATES

Idaho's climate in the Rocky Mountain region is truly unique. The low-water, high-pH, cold-winter-and-hot-summer conditions that characterize much of Idaho are some of the nation's most daunting. Despite all this, Idaho is world famous for its potatoes and a national leader in producing various other vegetables and seeds for many vegetable crops. The diverse climate and soils provide gardeners throughout the state with opportunities to grow healthy and functional landscapes. Successful gardening starts in part with understanding your growing area. Generally speaking, Idaho covers four zones, 2–6. These zones are based on average minimum temperatures and basically serve as guidelines for selecting the right plants for the right locations. To be safe, consider using plants rated at one temperature zone lower than the specific USDA hardiness zone shown for your area. For example, in Moscow you should plant zone 4 species, even though is shown to be zone 5. This is to compensate for below average temperatures that will often occur in winter.

These guidelines do not consider microclimates due to changes in elevation over short distances and location relative to structures or other landscape features. With the right planning and siting of plants, you can experiment and grow a wide variety of landscape plants that reflect your gardening lifestyle.

You can grow plants "out of zone" because of microclimates—those nooks or pockets in the landscape where environmental conditions differ from the norm. Buildings, large stones, retaining walls, nearby structures, or trees can sometimes block the sun and focus wind sheers to create very cold winter conditions, or conversely, they can block the wind and retain solar heat to create warmer south-facing areas. Remember, however, that even though microclimates may exist in your landscape, it is best to pay attention to the hardiness information when selecting plants. This will keep your garden safe for an "average" winter, whatever that may be.

PLANNING THE LANDSCAPE AND GARDENS

Whether you are creating an entirely new landscape or renovating an existing one, plan the landscape or garden area on paper first. It does not have to be a fancy design, unless that's what you desire. You will need a pencil, ruled graph paper, and tracing paper. If you have house plans or a plat map in your files, get them out, too.

• Create a base map. This is simply a plan of your property drawn to scale on graph paper. It shows the placement of the house, its orientation to the sun, other buildings and structures on the site, and existing plants. A base map helps you visualize your ideas and plan for the kinds of plants and hardscaping you will add.

• Using the graph paper, trace the outline of the house from a plat map, or simply measure the house and grounds. Next, measure the landscape area. Measure at right angles from a house corner to the property lines, and from the corner of the road to establish where your house sits within your property. Also, measure from fixed points of the house to the driveway, deck, patio, and any walkways. Draw in any existing trees, shrubs, retaining walls, boulders, and flower beds. Identify north on the plan. Plot all these measurements to scale on a large sheet of graph paper ($1/4$-inch grid allows for a scale of 1 inch = 4 feet).

• Analyze the land to familiarize yourself with the growing conditions within your property. Lay a sheet of tracing paper over the base map, and title it "Site Analysis." Make notes about sun exposure, shade patterns (morning sun, afternoon sun, full sun, full shade), wind exposure, topography, and water drainage.

• Look for and identify any microclimates—areas with atypical environmental conditions. For example, a microclimate could exist on a south-facing slope protected between two large boulders, which may be warmer in winter and hotter in summer than the open area surrounding it. A microclimate could also exist where water drains from the roof or collects in low spots.

• Examine drainage patterns and mark them on your map. Also take note of structural limitations such as overhead power lines and underground utilities.

• Consider which plants you want to keep, and list factors that will affect the selection of new plants. Does your site require plants that will tolerate the cold temperatures, full sun, shade, drought conditions, occasional flooding, or browsing from deer?

• Use another sheet of tracing paper over the base plan and site analysis to sketch out a landscape plan. Draw in trees where you want them and add shrubs, ground covers, or flowering plants. Remember to keep plants about 4 to 5 feet from the foundation to allow for growth and to make house maintenance easier. Be aware of the ultimate height and spread of the plants in various areas. Note whether you want plants that attract wildlife, birds, hummingbirds, or butterflies.

INTRODUCTION

Group the plants based on their watering needs so you can water more efficiently.

• If you are planning to irrigate, add the sprinkler or drip irrigation system to your plan. In-ground watering systems are not always needed in every landscape, particularly if you choose to create a water-thrifty or "xeric" garden. While plants are becoming established in the first growing season, however, it is very desirable to have a drip system or soaker hoses.

• Now you're ready to select plants for your landscape and gardening style. Be mindful of their maintenance requirements under the conditions at your site. Write the common name and the scientific name (genus and species) on your plan. Common names are less specific than scientific names and can be confusing when you are shopping for plants. At this step you should also consider landscape materials for pathways, mulch, edging, and borders.

• Purchase quality plants, and follow proper planting techniques to ensure rapid and healthy establishment and long-term survival. If you were overly ambitious and planned for an incredible design, remember you don't have to build it all at one time. Break the project into phases as your time and budget allow.

• Care for your plantings with proper watering, fertilizing, mulching, pruning, and other maintenance as described in this month-by-month book. By following the above steps, you will avoid most later maintenance headaches and surprises.

• Take photographs of your landscape as it progresses. Learn from your experiences and share your knowledge with fellow gardeners.

BUILD A HEALTHY SOIL

The secret to successful gardening is in the soil. We often get caught up in the beauty of plants in magazines and books without remembering that the foundation for any healthy and pest-free garden, landscape, or lawn is the soil. A good soil allows air, water, and nutrients to be absorbed by plant roots and lets the root system roam freely.

How do you build a healthy soil? Begin with a soil test through your state, university or local Cooperative Extension Office. The test will tell you the pH level of the soil and the level of nutrients available to plants.

Stated in numbers, pH is a measurement of acidity or alkalinity of the soil. On a scale of 0 to 14, a pH of 7 is neutral. Numbers below 7 indicate acid conditions and readings above 7 are basic or alkaline. Soil pH affects not only plant health but also the availability of nutrients. If the soil is too acidic or too alkaline, minerals such as nitrogen, phosphorus, potassium, calcium, and magnesium can be "tied-up" and unavailable to plants. Adding more fertilizer will not help. The soil pH will have to be corrected by mixing in the recommended amendment: sulfur to lower the pH; organic matter to raise pH. Limestone at the recommended rates will also raise pH or "sweeten" the soil, but this is rarely needed in our region.

Knowing which nutrients are already present will save you money and time. If your soil test shows your soil already has high levels of phosphorus and potassium, there's no need to add a fertilizer containing these two nutrients.

Organic matter such as compost, sphagnum peat moss, and aged manure is an important component to soil building. It improves the soil tilth—the physical condition or structure of the soil. When added to clay soils, organic amendments hold the clay particles apart, improving air and water movement in the soil. This is essential for healthy root growth and translates to deeper, more extensive root development as well as drought endurance.

The kind of organic matter you add to your soil is your choice, but I recommend weed-free materials such as compost, sphagnum peat moss, or well aged or rotted manure. My Italian grandmother, aunts and uncles liked to use chicken and cow manure. They would add these in the autumn, mixing to a depth of 6 inches or more and leaving the garden in a rough state. The alternate freezing and thawing would then break down the clods, and the organics made the soil mellow for spring planting.

Cover crops or "green manure" such as crimson clover or annual ryegrass are relatively inexpensive sources of organic matter. Sow these crops in the early fall, and then turn them under in the spring to enrich the soil.

Organic fertilizers derived from naturally occurring sources are my favorite alternative to synthetic plant fertilizers. They include composted animal manures, cottonseed meal, and bloodmeal, among many others. Although they contain relatively low concentrations of actual nutrients compared to synthetic fertilizers, they help to increase the organic content of the soil and ultimately improve the soil structure.

To avoid damaging soil structure, never dig or cultivate when the soil is too wet or too dry. Follow this simple test: if the soil sticks to your shovel or spading fork, the soil is too wet. Postpone digging until the soil dries out.

Coarse-textured, sandy, or granite soils provide excellent drainage but hold little water. Add organic matter to them to increase fertility and water retention.

Sand has often been touted as the perfect fix for improving drainage in clay soils. Unless you add it at the rate of at least 6 inches of sand per 8 inches of clay soil, your soil will be better suited for making adobe bricks than growing plants.

PLANTING AND WATERING YOUR GARDEN

Plant properly. The health and long-term survival of plants that you select for your landscape are affected by how they are planted. You can find step-by-step instructions in *My Rocky Mountain Gardener's Guide.*

Anyone can water a garden; what's more challenging is to meet the water demands of the plants while conserving water. This requires attention to details. Each chapter in this book provides information on when and how often to water. The aim is to avoid the common mistakes of over- or underwatering, the two practices most often associated with injuring or killing plants.

Water needs depend on both the plant and the soil. Moisture-loving plants require more frequent watering than plants adapted to dry conditions. Newly-set plants, even drought-tolerant ones, will need more water at first to become established. Generally, after the first growing season, they may not require supplemental watering even during the hot, dry summer months. Mulching will help conserve moisture and suppress weed invasions that compete for moisture. Some trees, shrubs, and ground covers are quite drought-tolerant and can withstand long periods without rain or irrigation. Soil also affects watering in several ways. For instance, plants growing in moisture-retentive clay soils need less frequent watering than plants growing in faster-draining sandy soils.

So whether you use a garden hose or an automatic below-ground sprinkler system, think about water conservation, and learn to water wisely.

"FEEDING" YOUR PLANTS

Fertilizing plants is often the least understood gardening practice, filled with all kinds of confusion. Just take a look at the different kinds of fertilizers available. In addition to knowing when, how often, and how much to fertilize, the choices of brands and mixtures seem endless. Should you choose a fast- or slow-release nitrogen fertilizer? Would your plants prefer a diet of organic or inorganic nutrients? What do those numbers on the bag mean? Dry or liquid fertilizer? Before making an application, realize that fertilizing should be guided by your soil test results, the appearance of the plants, and the purpose of fertilizing.

Fertilizers add minerals to soil, minerals which plants take up as nutrients. The three most important are nitrogen, phosphorus, and potassium. They are represented by three numbers on the fertilizer bag or package. For example, 5-10-5 gives the percentage by weight of nitrogen (N), phosphate (P), and potash (K). In this case, nitrogen makes up 5 percent of the total weight, phosphate, which supplies phosphorus, accounts for 10 percent, and potash, a source of potassium, makes up 5 percent. The remaining weight (the total must add up to 100 percent) comprises a nutrient carrier.

A fertilizer containing all three nutrients, such as 10-10-10, is referred to as a "complete" fertilizer. If your soil test indicates high levels of phosphorus and potassium but inadequate nitrogen, then apply an "incomplete" fertilizer, one that supplies only nitrogen, such as 21-0-0.

In addition to the primary elements (N-P-K), the fertilizer may contain secondary plant nutrients such as calcium, magnesium, sulfur, or minor nutrients such as manganese, zinc, copper, iron, or molybdenum. Apply these nutrients if dictated by soil test results or plant appearance.

Your choice of dry or liquid fertilizers depends on your needs. Dry fertilizers are applied to the ground around your plants. They are available in fast- or slow-release nitrogen forms. Fast- or quick-release nitrogen fertilizers dissolve readily in water and are almost immediately available to plants. They can also be quickly leached out of the root zone in fast-draining soils such as sand or crushed granite.

Liquid fertilizers can be absorbed through the foliage of plants as well as the roots. These have to be applied more frequently than granular types, usually every two to three weeks.

My favorite fertilizers are slow-release types. They are available to the plants for an extended period up to 6 months. While more expensive than conventional granular forms, they reduce the need for supplemental applications and the likelihood of fertilizer burn. Select a slow-release fertilizer that has a least one-half of the total nitrogen listed as "water-insoluble nitrogen".

A slow-release fertilizer is a good choice especially in sandy soils or crushed granite which tend to leach, or for heavy clay soils where runoff can be a problem. If the soil has been properly prepared at the onset of gardening, supplemental fertilization may not be necessary for several years after planting.

When fertilizing your perennials, let their growth rate and leaf color guide you. Rely on soil test results to help you make the right choices if you are not familiar with the plant symptoms of nutrient deficiency. If the garden is already highly fertile, the soil test will save you from overfertilizing, which will encourage a lot of leafy growth at the expense of flowers or fruit.

THE ART AND SCIENCE OF PRUNING

Pruning helps improve the health and appearance of plants. It can be as simple as pinching the spent or faded flowers from your annuals and perennials, called "deadheading." Or it may involve removing a large limb or smaller branches from a shade tree or evergreen. In the following chapters, read the step-by-step instructions for pruning trees, roses, shrubs, evergreens, and houseplants.

You should prune carefully and selectively with a purpose in mind. Pruning can be done to encourage more flowers on perennials, to reduce the height of plants, or to create a strong structure of trunk and limbs to support future growth in young trees.

SOLVING GARDEN PROBLEMS

You are bound to confront the three major pests in

INTRODUCTION

your garden: insects, diseases, and weeds. Deer, elk, voles, pocket gophers, meadow mice, and rabbits can also be viewed as pests and are addressed in the chapters.

Deal with pests sensibly. Just because you see one aphid on your rose bush, you don't have to get out the pesticide to kill the bug. There are many beneficial insects in the garden that will help keep insect pests at bay.

I like to recommend the **Integrated Pest Management (IPM)** program. It is a common-sense approach to managing and dealing with pests that brings Nature into the battle on the gardener's side. It combines smart plant selection with good planting and maintenance practices, and an understanding of pests and their life cycles. It starts with planning and proper planting to produce strong, healthy plants that, by themselves, can grow and prosper with minimal help from you. As in Nature, an acceptable level of pests is accommodated. Control is the goal, rather than elimination. Several techniques can be used in the garden and landscape IPM approach.

IPM CULTURAL PRACTICES

• **Proper soil management:** Maintain the appropriate soil pH for plants by having your soil tested every three years. Add generous amounts of organic matter to build and maintain soil fertility.

• **Plant Selection:** Match plants suited to the soil and climate of your area, and select species and cultivars that are resistant to pests. These plants are resistant—not immune—to damage. Expect them to exhibit less insect or disease injury than susceptible varieties growing in the same environment.

• **Watering:** Water late at night or early in the morning. Avoid watering in early evening because the leaves may remain wet for an extended period of time. This often favors fungus

and other disease infections.

• **Mulching:** Apply a shallow layer of mulch such as compost, shredded leaves, bark shavings, pole peelings, pine needles, or other organic materials to conserve moisture, suppress weed growth, and supply nutrients as they decompose.

• **Sanitation:** Remove dead, damaged, diseased, or insect-infested leaves, shoots, stems, or branches whenever you spot them.

IPM MECHANICAL CONTROLS

• **Handpicking:** Remove insect pests by hand, or knock them off with a strong spray of water from the hose.

• **Exclusion:** Physically block insects from attacking your plants. Aluminum foil collars can be placed around seedlings to prevent cutworms from attacking the tender plant stems. Plants can be covered with cheesecloth or spun-bonded polyester to keep out the insects.

IPM BIOLOGICAL CONTROLS

• **Predators and parasites:** Some bugs and spiders are on our side. Known as beneficial insects or natural enemies of the "bad bugs," they fall into two main categories: predators and parasites. Predators hunt and feed on other insects. They include spiders, praying mantises, lady beetles, and green lacewings. Parasites, such as braconid wasps and *Trichogramma* wasps, hatch from eggs deposited on or in another insect, and eat their host insect as they develop.

• Releasing beneficial insects into your garden may offer some benefit, but it is better to conserve the beneficial insects already there. Learn to identify the beneficial insects in your yard. Avoid broad-spectrum insecticides that will kill beneficial insects. Use my homemade remedies to control pest problems (see page 283).

• **Botanical pesticides and insecticidal soap sprays:** These naturally occurring pesticides are derived from plants. Two common botanicals include pyrethrins, insecticidal chemicals extracted from the pyrethrum flower (*Tanacetum cinerarifolium*), and Neem, a botanical insecticide from the tropical neem tree (*Azadirachta indica*), which contains the active ingredient azadirachtin. Insecticidal soaps have been formulated specifically for their ability to control insects. Soaps are effective only against those insects that come into direct contact with sprays before they dry. These natural pesticides break down rapidly when exposed to sunlight, air, heat, and moisture. They are less likely to kill beneficial insects than insecticides that have longer residual activity, and they are not as harmful to birds and other wildlife.

• **Microbial insecticides:** These are microscopic living organisms such as viruses, bacteria, fungi, protozoa, or nematodes, that combat insects. Although they may seem out of the ordinary, they can be applied in ordinary ways such as sprays, dusts, or granules. The bacterium *Bacillus thuringiensis* (Bt) is the most popular pathogen. Formulations from *Bacillus thuringiensis* var. *Kurstaki* (BtK) are the most widely used to control caterpillars, the larvae of butterflies and moths.

• **Horticultural oils:** When applied to plants, these highly refined oils smother insects, mites, and their eggs. Typically, horticultural oils are derived from highly refined petroleum products that are specifically manufactured to control pests on plants. Studies have shown that horticultural oils derived from vegetable oils such as cottonseed and soybean oil also exhibit insecticidal properties. Dormant applications generally control aphid eggs, the egg stages of mites, scale insects, and caterpillars such as leafrollers and tent caterpillars. Summer applications control adelgids, aphids, mealybugs, scale insects, spider mites, and whiteflies. Oils have limited effects on beneficial insects, especially when applied during the dormant season. Insects and mites have not been reported to develop resistance to petroleum and vegetable oils.

• **Traditional synthetic pesticides:** Synthetic pesticides should be your last resort when confronted by damaging pest levels. Use them sparingly to control the targeted pest. **When buying any pesticide, read the label and follow all the directions and precautions before mixing and applying to plants. Store and dispose of the product properly.** Specific names of pesticides are avoided in this book because products and their labels change rapidly along with pesticide registration and use process.

FURTHER HELP
Many other sources of help are available to answer your questions about gardening in your specific area. Check with local arboreta, botanical gardens, other public gardens, garden clubs, and societies.

USDA COLD HARDINESS ZONES

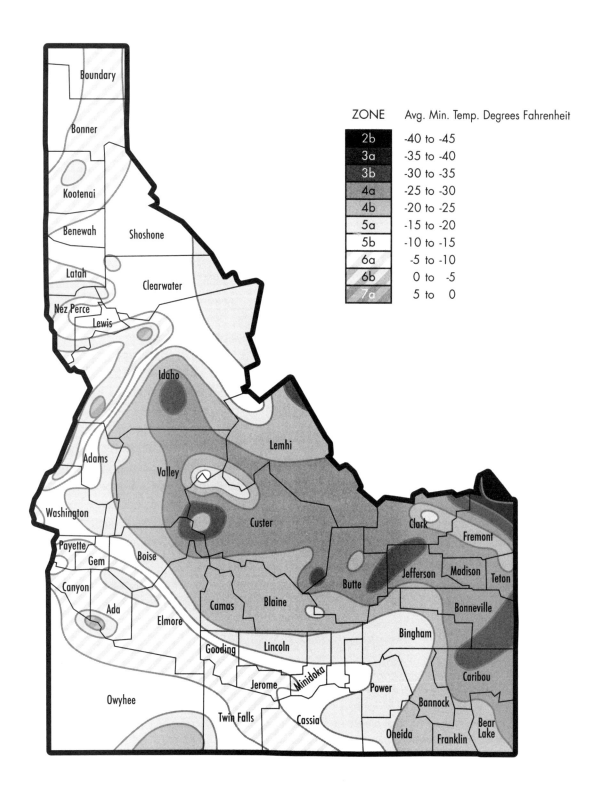

ZONE	Avg. Min. Temp. Degrees Fahrenheit
2b	-40 to -45
3a	-35 to -40
3b	-30 to -35
4a	-25 to -30
4b	-20 to -25
5a	-15 to -20
5b	-10 to -15
6a	-5 to -10
6b	0 to -5
7a	5 to 0

ANNUALS

Annuals are the heart of the summer garden. Their presence adorns the landscape with bright and cheerful colors. Flowering annuals begin to bloom in late spring and continue until they are killed by autumn frost. This long season of display makes them popular to fill in the bare spots in the landscape, since most of us want plants that will bloom and provide continuous color.

Plant hybridizers have developed a vast assortment of annuals that are prolific and disease-resistant. They can fit almost any situation in your garden, including shady areas, if you select the right kinds. Annuals can be used for edging, accents, background effects, a cutting garden, perennial garden fillers, containers, and window boxes. Like watercolors that run on wet paper, annual flowers that reseed themselves will paint the garden wildly and differently every season.

DESIGNING ANNUAL ACCENTS

Plan your annual flower garden carefully by sketching a plan to scale on a piece of graph paper. Check the seed packets or information tags of transplants for proper spacing. This will help you in determining how many plants to purchase for your specific garden area.

Use large splashes of color for the most impact. When annuals are planted en masse, you create a bolder and more noticeable display. Try to avoid planting in single rows along the driveway or sidewalk where the plants will look like toy soldiers, detracting from, rather than adding to, the allure of your landscape.

For shady areas where little else can grow, plant coleus, begonias, browallia, or impatiens. These annuals are adapted to shady areas and will provide a splash of welcome color.

Pink, rose and white cosmos (*Cosmos bipinnatus*) with its classic, daisy- like flowers, offset well against the deep, ruby leaves of New Zealand spinach or red orach (*Atriplex hortensis* 'Rubra') in a spectacular display from July to frost.

Like a jar of spilled gumdrops, moss rose (*Portulaca grandiflora*) reseeds readily along and through a gravel driveway or path year after year.

GARDENING WITH AN ALTITUDE TIPS
Annuals for Idaho

- Calendula, *Calendula officinalis*
- Cleome, *Cleome hassleriana*
- Cosmos, *Cosmos bipinnatus*
- Dusty Miller, *Senecio cineraria*
- Flowering Kale, *Brassica oleracea*
- Four-o-Clock, *Mirabilis jalapa*
- Geranium, *Pelargonium* x *hortorum*
- Impatiens, *Impatiens walleriana*
- Larkspur, *Consolida ambigua*

- Love-in-a-Mist, *Nigella damascena*
- Marigold, *Tagetes* spp.
- Morning Glory, *Ipomoea purpurea*
- Moss Rose, *Portulaca grandiflora*
- Pansy, *Viola* x *wittrockiana*
- Petunia, *Petunia* x *hybrida*
- Snapdragon, *Antirrhinum majus*
- Sunflower, *Helianthus annuus*
- Zinnia, *Zinnia* spp.

GARDENING WITH AN ALTITUDE TIPS
Starting Your Own Annuals from Seed

• Transplant seedlings into individual containers or cell-packs, the same kind that commercial growers use.

• Keep the artificial lights just above the plant tops to make them grow sturdy and strong. Apply a soluble fertilizer after the plants start to grow.

• Set the plants in the garden when frost no longer threatens them.

• Prepare the soil in the annual garden well before planting, preferably in the autumn after the frost has killed the previous season's annuals.

• Add compost or other organic matter. Spade or till the organic matter to a depth of 6 inches or more. Break up any clods or clumps to make a more uniform, fine soil.

• Set the plants at the proper spacing and at the same depth they grew in their transplant containers. If the root systems are rootbound, lightly score the rootball with a knife to encourage new roots to grow outward into your prepared garden soil.

• Apply a 1- to 2-inch layer of mulch around annuals after they are planted to help suppress weed growth. Pull or hoe weeds out as soon as you see them germinate.

• Remove annuals once the frost kills them back so the soil can be weeded and prepared for next spring's planting. This is much easier than weeding plants already in place.

Its 2-inch-wide, brilliantly colored succulent flowers are striking as they collide with scented sweet alyssum (*Lobularia maritima*).

For a delicious combination in the dryland garden, sow handfuls of the golden orange California poppy (*Eschscholzia californica*) with the royal blue desert bluebell (*Phacelia campanulata*), a few dwarf blue bachelor's-buttons (*Centaurea cyanea* 'Baby Blue') and the desert tickseed (*Coreopsis tinctoria*). You'll enjoy the flow of gold and blue strewn generously along a dry streambed in the garden.

For a cool, enchanted garden, mingle moonlily (*Datura meteloides*) with its angelic white trumpets and the tissue-paper flowers of opium poppy (*Papaver somniferum*) and false Queen Anne's lace (*Ammi majus*) for months of eye-calming pleasure.

Reseeding annual flowers need not feel unwelcome in the perennial garden, either. They can be quite useful in painting bare spots as the perennials fade from the picture.

FINDING ANNUALS

Look for reseeding annuals from seed suppliers, but don't forget about the neighbor just down the road and the lady who lives behind the grocery store.

Annuals are available at your local garden center, supermarkets, hardware stores, and nurseries. For the best selection, check with garden retailers who grow their own annuals from seed early in the season.

If you have the space, time, and experience, you can grow your own annuals from seed. The limiting factors include providing the proper light, temperature, and care to assure you get healthy and vigorous transplants.

JANUARY
ANNUALS

PLANNING

January is the time to begin planning your garden of annuals. Most mail-order catalogs and websites will offer you lots of help with plant selection and planning, too. Even if you don't order via mail, these seed and nursery catalogs provide helpful information. Use them as a resource to learn about new varieties being introduced. The All-America Selections (AAS) are highlighted by the companies that offer them. These are good plants to try since they have been grown in various trial gardens throughout the country, but their success depends upon your particular garden site and area.

Some things to do for January planning:

1. Once your list is completed, place your order early to beat the rush and to guarantee that you get the choices you selected.

2. Consider growing your own seedlings indoors if you have the space and time.

3. Plan on building a plant stand to start seeds indoors, particularly if you lack adequate bright light to grow strong seedlings.

4. Consult your garden notebook, calendar, or journal to refresh your memory of the annuals that performed best in your landscape last season. Note specific varieties you'd like to grow again, and experiment by growing some new ones.

5. Sterilize old containers and pots by scrubbing off old soil and debris with a scouring pad. Soak in a solution of bleach and warm water (1 part liquid chlorine bleach to 10 parts water) for a half-hour or so. Then, rinse with clear water.

PLANTING

Seeds of cool-tolerant annuals such as **pansies, primrose,** and **violas** need a longer growing period and can be started toward the end of the month. Read instructions on seed packets to determine how far in advance to start seeds indoors before you intend to transplant them outdoors. Look up the average last spring frost in your area to aid in your decision. Then mark your calendar.

Before planting seeds indoors, you will need to purchase or construct a sturdy plant stand to ensure success (see page 99 illustration for an example). The plant stand can be placed in a basement or unused room and will free up valuable counter space elsewhere.

To build a plant stand:

• Use a workbench or secure boards over sawhorses to make a stand that is about 4 feet long and 20 inches wide. This can accommodate several flats or pots.

• Construct a frame to hold simple lighting fixtures above the growing shelf. An inexpensive shop light that holds two 40-watt fluorescent shop lights will work well. Use two light fixtures to provide enough light to the growing surface. Use one cool white tube and one warm white tube in each light fixture.

• Hang the lighting setup so that the light fixtures can be suspended over the shelf or growing bench. The fixtures can be attached to chains that can be easily adjusted for height with pulleys. Most seedlings do best with the light source 2 to 3 inches above the tips of the young seedlings as they grow.

If you are rooting cuttings from last year's annuals, transplant them into a sterilized growing mixture for healthy, vigorous root growth. Place in bright light for optimum growth.

CARE

Annuals that have been growing indoors need bright light in the winter months to grow healthy, pest-free foliage and to set flower buds. Since the days are shorter, you may want to supplement natural light with artificial lights. Use fluorescent lights that are specially designed as plant lights. Suspend artificial lights within a few inches of the seedlings and leave the lights on for 16 to 18 hours out of every 24. To save time, plug in a timer to regulate the lighting time.

 WATERING

Routinely check potted annual cuttings for moisture. If your home is warm and dry, the potting mix may dry out more rapidly. Water when the growing mix feels dry to the touch. Newly sown seed will need proper moisture to ensure good germination. Do not waterlog the growing mixture, however. Cover the plant trays with plastic, but as soon as the seeds have germinated, remove the plastic cover to protect the seedlings from damping-off disease (caused by a pathogen in soil which is aggravated by keeping the growing mix too wet).

Once the seeds have germinated, remove the plastic cover. Water the growing mixture when it begins to dry out slightly or the seedlings begin to look droopy. Use a mister or watering can. It is better to underwater than to overwater, as the former reduces the onset of diseases.

 FERTILIZING

If you did not use a slow-release granular fertilizer in the potting mixture of overwintering annuals or new cuttings, apply a water-soluble plant fertilizer at half strength at every other watering. Plants that are not forming flower buds or those not blooming do not require very much fertilizer.

 GROOMING

Indoor annuals naturally stretch to reach for more light. This leggy growth can be limited by pinching back the terminals to encourage more lateral buds and compact growth. Place plants that need high light in a southern exposure or underneath artificial light sources.

 PROBLEMS

Hot, dry air from the furnace can lower the humidity in the house, a condition that favors spider mites. Be on the watch for aphids and spider mites on indoor annuals. When you detect pests and their eggs, wash them off with tepid water. Look for mottled or yellowing foliage, and fine webs between stems and leaves. Washing the foliage with water or applying a homemade soap spray can control the mites (see page 283).

Fungus gnat larvae live in the potting soil of indoor annuals. Keep the soil surface clean of debris and let the potting mixture dry out between waterings.

NOTES

_____
_____
_____
_____
_____
_____
_____
_____
_____
_____
_____

FEBRUARY
ANNUALS

 PLANNING

Place your annuals orders as soon as possible. Garden retailers are beginning to stock their seed racks, so look for special buys locally. Some annuals are started from seed several weeks before the last spring frost in your area, so it's not too early. Some mail-order catalogs offer annuals and biennials that are already young transplants. If you plan to purchase them, get your order in early to be sure the company will have your first choice. The young plants will be delivered at the appropriate planting time for your area.

Annuals that can tolerate cool weather such as **pansies, violas,** and **calendulas** can be started indoors six weeks before the last spring frost. Check the back of the seed packet for specific timing for planting indoors.

 PLANTING

Growing your own transplants from seed offers you a wide choice of varieties that are usually not available at garden retailers. However, you will need adequate light and time to care for the seedlings (See January to learn how to make a plant stand).

There are a couple of ways of growing your own transplants from seed. In the one-step method, sow the seeds directly into individual containers or cell-packs. These can be transplanted directly outdoors when they are ready and frost has passed.

The two-step method involves sowing the seeds in trays or flats and allowing them to grow until the "true leaves" emerge. Then, the seedlings are transplanted into individual pots for further growth before moving to their permanent homes outdoors.

 CARE

When the seeds have sprouted, **remove the plastic covering** and put them in bright light or under artificial light. A combination of one 40-watt cool white and one 40-watt warm white fluorescent light is very effective and inexpensive. Set the containers or seed-starting tray on your light stand and adjust the lights so they're just a few inches above the leaves. Keep the light on 16 hours each day. An automatic timer will help save time.

As the seedlings grow, raise the lights accordingly. The temperature can be between 60 to 70 degrees Fahrenheit, five degrees lower at night. Tape aluminum foil to the back and sides of the light stand to concentrate even more light on the seedlings.

 WATERING

Keep young seedlings moist, but not waterlogged. Water the young plants by spraying the growing mix with a fine mist or water from below. Water young potted plants when the growing mixture feels dry about an inch down. Do not overwater, as this can encourage fungus gnats.

 FERTILIZING

Young sprouts will not need fertilizer for a few weeks. It is easiest to add a granular, slow-release fertilizer to the growing mixture prior to transplanting. Follow the label directions on the package. Otherwise, use a water-soluble fertilizer diluted to half strength.

 GROOMING

Pinch back the leggy growth of annuals as they stretch for more light. You can take cuttings from this process and root more plants. This is a good time to root **geranium, impatiens, begonia,** and **coleus** cuttings.

GARDENING WITH AN ALTITUDE TIPS
Sowing Seeds Indoors

1. Moisten a quality soilless, sterile seed-starting mixture, and fill the containers or pots to within $1/4$ inch of the top.

2. For very tiny seed, mix with vermiculite or sharp sand and pour the mixture into the center of a folded sheet of paper. Tap the folded paper gently over the growing medium to sow the seeds.

3. If planting in individual pots, make a hole in the growing mixture with a pencil point or "wooden dibble." Plant the seeds no deeper than recommended on the packet label. A general rule is to cover the seeds to a depth equal to twice their diameter. Drop two seeds in each hole.

4. When sowing larger seeds in the two-step method, use the end of the pencil to create little furrows about 1 to 2 inches apart and about $1/8$ to $1/4$ inch deep across the surface of the growing mixture. Sow the seeds in rows for easier labeling and transplanting.

5. Press extremely fine seeds including **petunia, begonia, snapdragon, impatiens, pansies,** and **violas** lightly into the growing mixture or water them in with a fine mist spray. **Cover the seed if light is not required** for germination. Use a thin layer of vermiculite. Otherwise, leave the seed uncovered, exposed to light.

6. Label the containers or flat with the names of the annuals and the date planted. Refer to the seed packet and make a note of the expected germination date so you will know when to look for sprouting seedlings.

7. Spray mist the seeds with tepid water to settle them in. If watering from the top may dislodge the seeds, place the containers into a tub, sink, or shallow bucket containing a few inches of tepid water. After the growing mix is saturated, set it aside to drain.

8. Cover the containers or seed-starting tray with clear plastic wrap, or put them in a plastic bag secured at the top to create a mini-greenhouse effect. Don't water until the plastic wrap is removed.

9. Unless the seeds require cool temperatures to germinate, move them to a location between 65 to 75 degrees Fahrenheit in bright light, but not direct sun. Germination can be hastened by providing bottom heat with heating cables or mats, or by placing the seed starting tray on top of the refrigerator.

10. When the soil thaws and can be worked, you can direct sow seeds of **larkspur, sweet alyssum, California** and **Iceland poppies** toward the end of the month. Sprinkle the seeds on a roughly raked soil surface and gently water in. In high elevations, wait to direct sow in mid- to late March.

PROBLEMS

Continue to monitor plants for attacks by aphids, whiteflies, and mites. Spray persistent pests with a soap spray or commercial insecticidal soap, following label directions. Whiteflies can be trapped with yellow sticky boards.

Watch out for damping-off disease (see January Problems). Always use a sterile, soilless growing medium to reduce this problem. Maintain good light and air circulation to avoid making the plants more susceptible.

MARCH
ANNUALS

 PLANNING

The signs of spring are all around and this can be a busy month. The soil outdoors is beginning to become more workable. If you didn't add organic matter to flower beds last fall, plan to do so this month, at least several weeks before planting outdoors.

If you don't have room for starting seeds indoors, consider a cold frame. Many kinds are available through mail-order catalogs or you can make your own. Many seeds of annuals can be started in a cold frame. Add a heating cable or heating mat for seeds that require bottom heat for germination.

An easy-to-construct cold frame can be made by using straw bales to make three sides of a square, with the open side facing south. Put an old storm door or window on top and close the open edge with another piece of glass or Plexiglass set at an angle. Remove the front glass on sunny warm days so the plants won't cook.

 PLANTING

Some annuals can be directly sown in the garden even though the soil temperatures are still cold. If the soil has been worked previously, **sweet peas, snapdragon, pansy,** and **viola** are a few that can be directly sown outdoors. Their seeds need cool conditions for proper germination. Check the seed packets for more specific information and timing.

By midmonth, it's time to sow indoors seeds of warm-season annuals that need six to eight weeks lead time before transplanting. Determine the last frost date for your area in spring and count back the number of weeks indicated on the seed packet. (You will be planting after the last frost.)

If you did not transplant seedlings into larger pots last month, now is a good time to do so. If there is no granular, slow-release fertilizer incorporated into the potting mixture, add some prior to transplanting. This will save time for fertilizing later. Otherwise, use a water-soluble fertilizer at half the recommended strength. Apply to a moistened potting mixture every other watering.

Transplant overwintering **geraniums, begonias, impatiens, coleus** and other annuals that were in the basement or porch. Use a quality sterile potting mixture. Cut tall leggy plants back to balance them in their containers. Water in well.

 CARE

Annuals that you started from cuttings last fall should be thriving with the increased daylight hours as spring approaches. They may need to be repotted into larger containers before you actually set them outside. This is a good time to refresh the soil and cut back some of the leggy growth.

Continue to adjust the light over young annual seedlings as they grow to provide optimal growing conditions. Keep the lights a few inches above the terminals to encourage strong, sturdy growth. If seedlings are being grown in a windowsill, rotate the containers every few days so that light falls on every side. This will keep the plants from leaning too much and encourage sturdy stem growth.

Gently brushing over the tops of seedlings a couple of times daily with your fingertips or an open hand will also encourage the development of sturdier stems.

 ## WATERING

Keep potted annuals watered as the potting mixture dries out. Poke your finger down about an inch; if it feels dry, it's time to water the plant. Don't overwater.

New seedlings and transplants should be kept moist, but do not keep the soil too wet. It is okay to allow the growing mixture to dry out slightly between waterings.

Water plants with tepid water rather than water directly from the cold- water faucet.

 ## FERTILIZING

In the milder parts of the region, you may be able to get outdoors and work some fertilizer into annual flower beds. Check the soil first by taking a handful and squeezing it. If it forms a sticky ball, it is too wet to work. If it has dried out and crumbles, then it is okay to add slow-release fertilizer into the beds prior to planting season. Follow label directions for the amount to add. Slow-acting nutrients will provide transplants a long-term, consistent nutrition and saves your valuable time of having to apply liquid fertilizers.

 ## GROOMING

You can keep annuals from getting too leggy and tall by regularly pinching back the tips of their stems periodically. This will stimulate the plant to grow more lateral stems and compact foliage. You can do some pinching of annuals purchased at the garden store as well. This will get rid of the lanky growth if the light conditions have been poor.

PROBLEMS

Be on the watch for spider mites on annuals indoors. You will notice symptoms of mottled foliage, a "salt and pepper" look to the leaves, or fine webbing on the underside of the leaves. Wash the plant in tepid water from the faucet or in a bathtub to remove the mites and their eggs. You can also spray with a home-made soap solution and rinse off the foliage in the sink or tub.

If leggy stems are a problem on seedlings, this is an indication of insufficient light. Lower the artificial lights closer to the seedlings.

Damping-off disease can threaten seedlings that are too wet or have poor air circulation.

In the outdoor garden, be on the look out for weeds starting to pop up. Pull them or cultivate the soil to get them while they're still young. Spread mulch over the soil if needed to discourage weed seeds from germinating.

 ## NOTES

_____
_____
_____
_____
_____
_____
_____
_____
_____
_____
_____
_____
_____
_____

APRIL
ANNUALS

PLANNING

It's time to get outside and do some planting. Plan to plant **sweet peas** if you did not sow them in mid-March. They germinate best with cool soil conditions. Visit your local garden centers and nurseries for the early arrivals of **pansies, primroses,** seeds, and other supplies you will need for the annual garden.

• Plan to clean up hanging pots and other outdoor containers prior to adding new plants.

• Use a scouring pad to remove old potting mixture or soluble salt accumulations on the rims of the pots. Disinfect the pots if needed.

• Check the annual flower beds and remove any debris that may have blown in with the winter winds.

• Think about planting an annual garden that features flowers for cutting. Some of my favorites are old-fashioned varieties, such as **cosmos, dahlias, strawflowers, China asters, snapdragons, marigolds,** and **zinnias.** These are easy to sow directly outdoors and will germinate quickly.

• Sketch out a garden plan before you plant so you can designate areas for specific annuals. You don't need to be a landscape architect to draw or sketch a garden plan. This plan will also help you determine how many plants of each kind you will need for the size area you intend to plant.

PLANTING

To fill in the gaps when spring-flowering bulbs are finishing up their bloom cycle, interplant with **pansies** and **violas.** They are an ideal temporary early ground cover among **daffodils, tulips,** and other bulbs. If you have window boxes and other empty outdoor planters, grow some **pansies** now to brighten the scene.

Sow seeds of hardy annuals including **cleome, cosmos, four o'clocks, nigella (love-in-a-mist), portulaca,** and **sweet alyssum.** They can be sown directly in a prepared flower bed where you want them to grow.

Do not disturb the areas where self-sowing annuals went to seed last fall. There will be new sprouts appearing soon.

CARE

As the soil dries out from spring rains and snow, clean up any planting areas that need tidying. Pull out weeds and any dead plants and remove winter debris that may have blown in.

Young transplants that are thriving in a cold frame should gradually be exposed to outside temperatures, both day and night. This will harden them off before they are set outside permanently. Prop open the glass cover on hot days so that the plants don't cook in the heat. If temperatures are predicted to go below freezing, close the cover at night.

As the end of the month approaches, many of the transplants indoors should be readied to be set outdoors. Set them outside in a semi-sunny spot daily for increasingly longer times to adjust to the outside weather. Bring them in at night until it is mild enough for planting. This is called the "hardening off" process that gets plants acclimatized to the outside so they experience less transplant shock when they are finally planted in the garden.

Be ever vigilant of fluctuations in the weather, as we can experience several warm days in a row, only to be followed by a spring snow and freezing temperatures when a cold front rolls in.

 WATERING

If it's a good year, Nature should provide adequate moisture with rain and spring snows to keep the soil moist. If there is a prolonged dry spell, you will need to water newly planted annuals as the soil begins to dry out. Plants that have been mulched will need less frequent watering.

In areas where seed has been sown, lightly moisten the soil down an inch or so to help germination. You don't need to water deeply yet.

If you have biennials growing in the flower garden from last season, water them deeply, as they do have a more extensive and deep root system. This includes **foxglove, money plant,** and **forget-me-not.**

 FERTILIZING

When the soil is dry enough to be easily worked, this is the time to prepare the annual beds for new plants. Rototill or dig and turn over shovelfuls of soil to loosen the bed. Mix in slow-release granular fertilizer as you prepare the soil. Follow label directions on the fertilizer package.

If you did not incorporate organic matter such as compost, aged manure or sphagnum peat moss into the soil last autumn, do so now. Organic amendments will help to improve drainage, retain nutrients, and aid in moisture retention.

 GROOMING

Pinch back leggy stems of seedlings as they mature. Plants growing in pots or those retained from last year will benefit from a light pruning as well. This will make them grow out more lateral stems thereby creating a more sturdy and compact plant.

Pick bouquets of **pansies** and **violas** and put in a decorative drinking glass or bowl to add color indoors. This will encourage these plants to form more blossoms.

Remove yellow leaves from transplants as they adjust to the outside conditions. Just snip them off with a pair of scissors.

 PROBLEMS

It's time for weeds to pop up throughout the annual flower garden, too. Lightly cultivating the soil will bring their roots to the surface and make them meet their demise. Winter annual weeds will need to be dug or pulled out, as they have already developed a deeper and stronger root system.

As you set out new transplants, deer, elk, birds, rabbits, chipmunks, squirrels and other critters may find it enticing to nibble on the young plants. Protect the new plants by placing netting over them temporarily to discourage wildlife or construct a fence around plantings. If you prefer, spray a homemade critter repellent on the foliage. Repeat as needed.

MAY
ANNUALS

 PLANNING

Now is the time that annual bedding plants are available at garden retailers. Some are already in bloom so you can pick and choose your favorite colors and combinations. Plan where you will put all the plants you purchase. A garden plan done in advance will save you time and money.

If you're not around to enjoy your flower garden during daylight hours, create an "evening garden" with annuals that display best in the evening hours. **Petunias** open by day and release their scent at night. **Four o'clocks** brighten in the waning sun and provide a last stop for hummingbirds and hawk moths.

If you've grown annuals indoors, harden them off before planting them directly into the garden. Place plants outdoors in a semi-sunny exposure during the day and leave outdoors at night when temperatures remain above freezing. If frost is predicted, bring plants indoors. Do this for two weeks to acclimatize the plants.

 PLANTING

Sow hardy and half-hardy annuals directly in the ground whenever the soil can be worked. Some good choices include **larkspur, sweet alyssum, California poppy, spider flower, morning glory,** and **sweet peas.** Wait to sow tender annuals such as **marigolds, zinnias,** and **moss rose** until later in the month when the soil has warmed up and danger of hard frosts has passed.

Plant cool-season transplants such as **pansies, violas,** and **primroses** in the early part of the month since they will tolerate cool nights. Wait to plant warm-season annuals until around mid- to late-May, allowing the soil to warm up.

Transplants that have been hardened off can be planted directly to the garden.

Interplant annuals among spring flowering bulbs to camouflage the bulbs' foliage and fill in empty gaps. Be careful not to dig too deep so you won't injure the bulbs when planting.

 CARE

As cool-season annuals begin to decline with the onset of heat, remove them and replace with warm-season annuals including **geraniums, petunias, marigolds,** and **dahlias**. Thin out direct- seeded annuals to avoid crowding and to allow for good air circulation which reduces powdery mildew disease. Provide support for taller-growing annuals for protection from winds. Use bamboo stakes, peony cages, or tomato cages. As the foliage grows and fills in it will hide the supports.

 WATERING

Keep new transplants watered regularly to avoid stress. Check the soil to a depth of 2 to 3 inches and water as it begins to dry out. Keep the foliage dry, especially at night, to avoid the spread of foliar diseases.

 FERTILIZING

If you've already added a slow-release fertilizer to the flower bed when preparing the soil, you don't need to fertilize again. If you didn't add nutrients, add a granular 5-10-5 at the time of planting. A light scattering around the root zone will help transplants get an extra boost to become established.

If you prefer to use liquid-soluble plant food, it's best to be conservative and dilute to one-half the recommended rate. **Too much nitrogen promotes excessive foliage growth,** which can make plants floppy and often attracts aphids and other pests.

 GROOMING

Pinch young transplants after planting, even if it means removing some of the flowers. This helps the plants to become stockier and bushier. Annuals such as **coleus, petunia, cosmos, marigold, salvia,** and **sweet pea** benefit from pinching. Use your thumb and forefinger to nip out the growing tip of the main stem just above a leaf or pair of leaves.

Deadhead or remove spent flowers from annuals that bloom in flushes. This includes **petunias, geraniums, marigolds,** and **California poppies.** This promotes healthier growth and more blooms.

 PROBLEMS

Aphids, flea beetles, and slugs can become a problem on newly planted annuals. See page 283 for environmentally friendly homemade repellents.

Cutworms that live in the soil will sever plants at the base of the stem. You can protect transplants with a stiff collar made out of a plastic yogurt cup with the bottom cut out. Push the container 2 inches into the soil with about 2 inches remaining above ground.

Bt or Bacillus thuringiensis is a biological insecticide that is very effective against the larvae of moths and butterflies (Lepidoptera classification of insects).

Weeds are opportunistic and will compete with annuals since the soil was disturbed by planting. Get rid of them "the cowboy way" or by hand-digging or pulling as soon as they start to appear. Mulch the soil when annual transplants are 4 to 6 inches tall. This will smother out tiny weed seedlings.

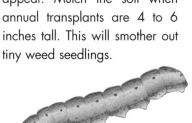

Cutworm Larvae

Keep newly transplanted annuals healthy, stress-free, and disease-free by proper watering. Water every few days or as the soil dries out to avoid plant stress. Water from below to reduce the spread of leaf diseases. Space or thin annuals to allow for good air circulation, which discourages fungus diseases.

Tender plants will need some quick protection from late spring frost. Monitor the weather report for predictions of freezing temperatures, and keep a few old blankets, cardboard boxes, or large plastic pots handy. When frost is predicted, cover vulnerable plants.

Record the dates you planted various annuals, including when you direct seeded them into the garden, so you can track how well they germinated and developed. This can prove helpful in future years for timing your planting and achieving the best results.

JUNE
ANNUALS

PLANNING

Annuals really show off their beauty as warm weather settles in this month. It's helpful to keep a journal or notebook to record information on how well your plants are performing in the garden. This will help you to evaluate which plants look and do best. If you need to redesign your garden, notes will come in handy for reference.

As cool-weather **pansies** begin to give out, have a few new transplants ready to replace waning plants. Also, use annuals to fill in the gaps left from some of the perennials that begin to die back such as **bleeding heart** and **Oriental poppies.**

If you're planning a vacation, make arrangements with a neighbor or friend to take care of your garden while you're away.

PLANTING

If you didn't get your annuals planted last month, there's still time to add them to your garden. Look for bargains as garden retailers start to clear out their stock. Even if the plants have gotten a little leggy, cut them back during transplanting. Warm weather and proper care will have them blooming in just a few weeks.

Continue to fill in the void spaces left after spring bulbs complete their blooming cycle. Annuals will serve as a living ground cover, shading the soil and reducing weed invasions.

Plant extra annuals in decorative containers, pots, planters, window boxes, and various flea market finds. Let your imagination run wild and create beauty throughout the landscape.

CARE

Develop a watering schedule that meets the needs of the plants. Gardens differ in soil types, sun and wind exposure. To find out the moisture needs of your garden, dig down 2 to 4 inches and check to see if the soil is drying out. Then, give the plants a good soaking with an inch of water. Deep watering encourages a deeper root system and better drought resistance.

To save time and to provide uniform moisture, install a drip irrigation system or wrap leaky hoses around your annuals. They apply water directly to the soil around the plants and reduce overhead watering that may result in leaf diseases.

Check automatic watering systems monthly to make sure they're not clogged. A system that is not working properly will result in stressed or wilted plants.

WATERING

Because most annuals are shallow-rooted, expending energy to bloom rather than developing deep root systems, they will need more constant attention to watering. When rainfall is limited and we experience prolonged dry periods, it is important to maintain uniform soil moisture. Water annuals with drip irrigation systems, soaker hoses wound around the plants, or the old-fashioned frog-eye sprinklers. Water early in the day so the foliage is dry by nighttime.

To conserve water, keep the soil cool, and prevent weeds, spread a 1- to 2-inch layer of mulch around transplants. Shredded cedar, pine needles, and pole peelings are some good organic mulches.

FERTILIZING

If there is no slow-release fertilizer in the soil, you can apply water-soluble fertilizer at intervals recommended on the label.

Most annuals are heavy feeders and utilize lots of nutrients from the soil over the growing season.

Organic-based, granular fertilizer can be applied at monthly intervals. Sprinkle around the plants and water in thoroughly.

Fertilize annuals in containers to keep them growing vigorously and blooming. Frequent watering of container gardens tends to leach out nutrients more rapidly. Apply fertilizer to a moist soil, never to dry potting soil.

 GROOMING

Keep annuals looking fresh and promote more blooms by deadheading faded flowers. Pinch off or snip with scissors the faded blooms of annuals such as **petunia, marigold, annual phlox, verbena,** and others. Also, remove yellowing or dead foliage to reduce the spread of leaf diseases.

Thin seeded annuals if they are becoming overcrowded. This will ensure that plants will get sufficient light and air circulation to grow into healthy and floriferous annuals. Carefully pull up or clip the less vigorous, overcrowded plants.

 PROBLEMS

Pests will arrive in the garden as the weather continues to warm up. Aphids are among the first to attach to the soft and succulent growth of annuals, sapping away their energy and vigor. An easy way to combat aphids is by hosing them off the plants as soon as you spot them. Also, make a homemade soap spray to keep them at bay. See page 283 for more details.

Be on the watch for the beginning stages of powdery mildew disease; a light, white powder will form on the foliage and stems. Make sure plants are getting good air circulation and use the homemade mildew control on page 285 to prevent a severe problem, if needed.

If we experience frequent afternoon rain showers, weeds will pop up in the garden just about daily. Hoe, handpull, or dig weeds as soon as you spot them. They are much easier to control when young with a shallow root system.

NOTES

July
ANNUALS

 PLANNING

Remember to have someone take care of your plants if you go on vacation. Container-grown annuals can be grouped together near the water spigot and placed out of the direct, afternoon sun. Grouping the plants together will help conserve water, and shade will help reduce the need for frequent watering. If there are some containers that need more attention than others, insert colorful sprinkler-marking flags into those pots to bring attention to those plantings. Before you leave, water everything thoroughly. Weed and deadhead any faded or spent flowers.

If you are growing a cut flower garden and want to dry some of those flowers, plan to begin harvesting later in the month, and then continue into the early fall as the various plants begin to mature and produce near perfect blooms. Have materials for drying on hand to use the minute you can pick the fresh blossoms that are blemish-free. Silica gel and a combination of borax and sand are good drying agents.

 PLANTING

You still have time to plant annuals that are container-grown in market packs, the sooner the better to prevent them from getting dry. By now these plants are rootbound, so take time to loosen or tease the matted roots. Plant during a cloudy period or the cool of the evening to minimize transplant shock from the heat, wind, and sun. Water the new transplants in well, then mulch them with compost or shredded cedar.

Early in the month, plant more **sunflower** seeds that will grow into handsome golden and yellow flowers in the autumn. You will find sunflowers in many kinds of colors and of varying heights.

 CARE

If you didn't mulch prior to planting your annual bedding plants, now is the time to do so. Pine needles, shredded pole peelings, shredded cedar, compost, and other organic materials will help to maintain uniform moisture and reduce evaporation of water.

Stake taller annual and biennial flowers including **foxglove, sunflower, larkspur, hollyhock,** and **castor bean.** This will prevent them from blowing over in a high wind. I like to use bamboo stakes that are about a foot taller than the expected height of the plant. Insert the stakes to a depth of 1 foot next to the plants while they are still young transplants. Tie or secure the plants to the stakes with twine or other soft string; loop the tie around the plant stem, then loop the tie around the stake, tying it loosely so there is room for the stem to grow.

Do not disturb the soil in the flower beds during the hot, dry weather. Loosening the soil by cultivation can damage the surface roots and increase water loss from the soil. Inspect the mulch around flowers and replenish as necessary to a level of 2 to 3 inches.

 WATERING

Remember to check the soil **before** you water. Those that are mulched will have to be watered less frequently than plants without mulch. Pull away the mulch and dig down to a depth of 3 to 4 inches to see how moist the soil is. If it is beginning to dry out, it's time to give the plants a good, deep drink.

Use drip irrigation tubes or a soaker hose to water slowly and deeply. This will encourage more drought-enduring plants. If you find the soil moist, avoid over-watering. Leaves will remain wilted and will not perk up in the evening or when temperatures cool down.

FERTILIZING

If you applied a slow-acting fertilizer during the planting process, it is generally sufficient for most plants for six to ten weeks, depending on the product. Check the label to determine if it's time to apply more fertilizer. If foliar plant fertilizer is used, apply it during the cool part of the day, early morning or late evening, to avoid burning the roots.

Avoid the application of high-nitrogen fertilizer. This stimulates plants to produce excess foliage, which can be more susceptible to insects and diseases. Also, too much nitrogen will take away from flower development.

Never fertilize annual flowers that are under stress from drought or extreme heat. This will only add insult to injury.

GROOMING

As the summer heat turns on, some annuals will benefit from thinning and cleanup. Dead-heading the spent flowers and clipping back leggy stems will help promote more vigorous growth and new flower buds. Pinch back stems a few inches. You can do this chore before going on vacation, and the plants will be blooming again with a flush of new growth when you return.

If you desire to minimize reseeding of some annuals in your garden, including **spider flowers (cleome)** and **snapdragons,** pinch or snip off seedpods as they are ripening, **before** they dry, burst, and disperse their seeds. Cutting back the main stem will also encourage more branching.

Pinch the tips of **coleus** every month to keep the plants dense and compact. Since the flowers are insignificant to most of us, pinch them off, too. This will promote more colorful foliage.

PROBLEMS

Watch for spider mites on **marigolds** and **zinnias.** They will cause the foliage to have a dingy, salt-and-pepper appearance. There may be signs of fine webbing weaving throughout the foliage and stems. Mites can be washed off the plants with a strong stream of water; direct the water to both the upper and lower portions of the leaves.

Insecticidal soap sprays or a homemade soap spray (see page 283) and miticides will also keep pests in check. Read and follow label directions.

Pest problems tend to proliferate if we kill beneficial predators by spraying with insecticides. Before resorting to insecticides, try to wash the pests off plant surfaces every few days. Aphids will continue to proliferate on the new, succulent foliage of annuals. Wash them off as described.

NOTES

_____
_____
_____
_____
_____
_____
_____
_____
_____
_____
_____
_____
_____
_____
_____
_____

AUGUST
ANNUALS

 PLANNING

While many of the annuals such as **marigolds, impatiens, verbena, zinnias,** and others are blooming with gusto, some may start to show signs of waning. The summer heat and drought can take a toll on many plants.

If you have spaces that are looking empty or less colorful, plan to buy some of the late summer annuals sold in market packs on sale. They can be quickly added to the garden. It is a good opportunity to get a bargain and still add color.

If you're planning a vacation, visit some of the public gardens where you travel for inspiration. Some regional botanical gardens or arboreta feature plants that thrive and have wonderful color and features.

 PLANTING

This is a hot month to sow seeds or transplant seedlings or annuals. However, if you need to replace the occasional dead or pooped out annual in your container gardens, choose a cloudy, cool day. It is not unusual for an annual to succumb to stress or to be crowded out by other plants. Carefully dig the plant out, and replace with a new addition to keep color appearing through the late summer into fall.

When transplanting small seedlings, water the new plants thoroughly, and mist occasionally with a fine spray of water to keep them cool. This will lessen transplant shock. Young seedlings from self-sowing annuals will sprout here and there in the garden. When they are about 2 to 3 inches tall, thin them to the correct spacing so they can grow more vigorously.

 CARE

Protect the annual and biennial garden from summer's heat and a prolonged drought period. Hopefully, most of our flower beds have been mulched.

As mulches tend to break down with microbial activity, it may be necessary to add more around the exposed areas of the flower beds. It is a good idea to maintain a 2- to 3-inch layer of mulch over bare soil. Mulch will suppress late weed growth and will ultimately enrich the soil with slow-acting nutrients as it decomposes.

The maturing heads of **sunflowers** may need protection from birds and squirrels if you intend to harvest them later. Cover the maturing heads with cheesecloth to prevent birds and other critters from removing the seeds.

 WATERING

During August we can experience extended drought periods and watering is critical to sustain plants and keep them flowering. Flower beds that were not mulched will need even more watering. Dig down into the soil (pull the mulch away as needed) to a depth of 2 to 4 inches and check to see how wet the soil is. If it is becoming dry, it is time to do some deep watering.

Drip irrigation systems will soak the soil deeply and keep moisture from splashing upon the foliage, preventing foliage disease. Otherwise, water with a frog-eye sprinkler that delivers water at a low angle in droplets that will soak down into the soil. Water early in the day or late in the afternoon to allow the water to percolate into the soil and to allow the foliage to dry out before nightfall.

Flowers in containers will dry out faster. Clay and terracotta pots tend to dry out faster if they are placed in full sun. The plants have filled in the container with extensive root systems, leaving less room for soil.

 FERTILIZING

Most annual flowers do not need additional fertilizer if you applied a slow-release form earlier in the season. The only exceptions are flowers planted in containers. Since they are watered more often, nutrients are leached away more rapidly. Use a water-soluble plant fertilizer. I prefer to dilute the mixture to half strength and apply at every other watering. If it has been over six to eight weeks since a slow-release fertilizer was applied, you can apply more to finish off the season. Lightly scratch the fertilizer into the mulch or soil and water in thoroughly.

 GROOMING

Keep flower beds tidy by dead-heading faded flowers, picking off dead leaves and pruning away injured stems. This will help to reduce the spread of diseases.

Do not allow the accumulation of dead or rotted plant debris to sit around in the flower beds, as this will attract slugs and often fosters disease spores.

If you like to collect flower seeds, now is the time to allow some flowers to mature so the seed will ripen. Once the flower heads are dried, take a small paper bag outdoors and place the seed head within the bag. Label the variety and color. Seeds will disperse into the bag and can be collected later and stored for future use.

 PROBLEMS

Powdery mildew is a foliage disease that rears its head at this time of year. It is often prevalent during warm days and cool evenings. **Zinnias, annual phlox,** some **petunias,** and filler plants in containers will show symptoms of a grayish-white residue on the leaves. The best defense is prevention. Increase air circulation so plants are far enough apart to discourage this disease. Pinch or prune plants as needed to achieve this.

When watering the flower garden, water the soil. Try to avoid wetting the foliage, particularly at night.

Powdery mildew is not life threatening to plants, but can weaken them by destroying healthy foliage that is the lifeline of more blooms. It can be treated with the homemade mildew control on page 285.

If you prefer, ignore this foliar disease since many annuals will be pulled up after the first hard frost. You can determine what is best according to the length of your growing season.

Wind, heavy rainstorms, or hailstorms may occur during the month. When possible, you can protect plants with rigid cardboard boxes or netting. Have some handy in the garage or garden shed. Annuals that have been staked will be better protected against high winds.

SEPTEMBER
ANNUALS

PLANNING

Although the gardening season is beginning to wind down, September still has warm days to allow some annuals to finish off in glory. The rich yellow and golden **marigolds** will bloom with gusto until a hard frost. **Petunias** and **geraniums** are still providing plenty of color in the garden.

If you have time and space to overwinter some of your favorite annuals, plan to take some cuttings of **geraniums, verbena, coleus, impatiens, begonias,** and others. Root the tip cuttings in a sterilized potting mixture. They will usually root within four to six weeks and can be potted indoors for winter color.

Plan to condition or move tropical plants growing in containers to an inside porch or patio to protect them from the cold nights. Many filler plants are tropical in nature and cannot withstand the cool nights, so you must decide to either keep them or let them die at the end of the growing season.

As time permits, make notes in your garden notebook or journal. While this year's flower garden and its performance are still fresh in your mind, you can jot down information on which annuals did best, and those that did not grow to your expecta-

tions. This will help you plan next year's annual garden. Maybe there are places that can be improved by adding annuals for long season color or you could use more colorful foliage and annual ornamental grasses to add texture to the garden. There are many seasons to come, and there are opportunities to experiment with a wide variety of plants.

PLANTING

It is getting too late in the season to plant new annuals. However, some will self-sow where they grow and new seedlings will emerge next spring. **Snapdragons** self-sow freely in my garden and will even germinate if the soil remains somewhat warm. Next spring they will continue to grow and flower.

For autumn color and texture in the flower garden, plant **ornamental cabbage** and **kale, violas,** and **pansies.** These are cold hardy and can withstand a light frost.

Containers of flowering annuals may be found on sale at some garden retailers. They are good fillers for the end of the season and will provide color for fall gatherings or outdoor events.

CARE

Monitor the nighttime temperatures during the month, as evenings are getting cooler. When the night temperatures drop to 55 degrees Fahrenheit, it's time to bring in tropical plants that you desire to keep as houseplants. Wash the foliage and stems to remove any aphids and mites that can piggyback indoors. You can spray the foliage and stems with the homemade soap spray, then rinse the plant with water. This will help to dislodge many pests and remove the dust and grime from the foliage.

If you like to overwinter your favorite **geraniums,** it's time to make them ready for the transition to the indoors. Here are some tips:

• Cut back the leggy stems, dig the plants up, and pot them up in a quality potting mixture.

• Add a teaspoon of slow-release granular fertilizer, and mix into the soil. Water the new transplants in well.

• If you don't want to keep the entire **geranium** plant, take stem cuttings from the tips. Insert the cuttings in moistened vermiculite or perlite, and cover with a plastic bag to create a mini-greenhouse effect so the cuttings will root more quickly.

• Place in bright light to encourage healthy stems and foliage.

 ## WATERING

Continue to water the flower garden if rainfall is scarce. With cooler weather and shorter days approaching, you don't need to water as often. Remember to check the soil moisture in the flower bed by digging down with a garden trowel. If the soil is beginning to dry out to a depth of 3 to 4 inches, it's time to water.

Annuals in containers will need more constant attention, as they will dry out faster.

 ## FERTILIZING

There is no need to fertilize annuals in the garden this month. If you have containers you intend to bring in for the winter as houseplants, you can add some slow-release granular fertilizer into the potting mixture. This will provide the plants with nutrients over the next several months.

 ## GROOMING

Clip off broken or diseased leaves and stems from annuals as soon as you spot them. This will reduce the onset of diseases. Pinch off or deadhead old faded flowers to keep the garden looking fresh and tidy. Those annuals that are obviously exhausted and not blooming should be pulled and discarded. Once the annuals are out, spread organic mulch over the bare spots to suppress winter weeds from germinating. Cut back the seedheads of annuals that you do not want to self-sow for next year. When the first frost blackens or kills the tenderest annuals, pull them as soon as possible.

 ## PROBLEMS

Insects and other critters are getting ready for fall and winter. They will seek out nesting sites to spend the cool nights. To reduce pest problems, pull up dead and dying plants promptly and discard them in the trash. If dead or frosted plants are healthy, retire them to the compost pile. They can be shredded or chopped to hasten decomposition.

Deer, rabbits, meadow mice, chipmunks, and other critters can make sneak attacks in the flower garden as they browse about. To repel them, spray the **homemade critter repellent** (see page 284). This will temporarily keep them at bay. Repeat as necessary.

NOTES

OCTOBER
ANNUALS

PLANNING

In the higher elevations, frost may have already ended the season for annuals. See general grooming in September. However, in the lower elevations frost may not yet have arrived. Plan to salvage annuals that you wish to keep as houseplants. These might include **geraniums, impatiens, coleus,** and **begonias.** Take 4- to 6-inch cuttings from the terminal growth and root in moistened vermiculite or perlite.

Annuals planted under the protection of the roof line, near shrubs, stones, or other microclimates will carry on for several more weeks, until a harder frost arrives. Return the frosted, healthy plants to the compost pile. If you have access to a shredder or chipper, grind these into finer materials for faster decomposition.

Note when the first frost arrives. In most regions, it occurs about the same time every year, give or take a week. In the coldest parts of the region, and higher elevations, frost can arrive sooner, so be ready to move container-grown annuals indoors or to protected areas.

PLANTING

Continue to plant **ornamental cabbage** and **kale** as it is available in nurseries. These plants will add color and texture to the flower garden. They can fill in the bare spots and accent the rock garden or terraces. Many that I've planted have tolerated light frosts and will last well into December.

If you have not had time to take cuttings from your favorite annuals, get to the project now before frost. Take these steps:

• Remove any dead or spent flowers, or buds and foliage that are within an inch of the cut ends.

• Insert the cut ends in sterilized potting soil on a bright windowsill. You may dust the ends of the cuttings with a rooting hormone to stimulate faster rooting.

• Cover the container with a clear plastic bag to maintain humidity and enhance root formation on the cuttings.

• When the stems develop tiny root fibers, about an inch long, they are ready to transfer to potting soil. Within a few weeks, tug the plants gently to check if they are rooting in.

Any cuttings you took last month have already developed roots by now. Pot them up in small containers filled with soilless mixtures and some granular slow-release fertilizer. Water the transplants in well. After they adjust to the transplanting, set them where they can get bright light.

CARE

Continue to monitor the flower garden and pull out annuals that have succumbed to frost damage. To encourage copious numbers of free seedlings next spring, disturb the soil as little as possible while removing the dead and dying plants.

Healthy plants can be placed in the compost pile. Cover up the bare spots with a 3- to 4-inch layer of mulch such as compost, shredded leaves, cedar mulch, pine needles or evergreen boughs. This will protect the soil over the winter and suppress winter annual weeds from germinating.

Some garden flowers including **cleome, four o'clocks,** and **love-in-mist** will produce many seedpods or capsules and self-sow into the surrounding soil.

To discourage too many seedlings, rake up the remaining summer mulch and replace it with a fresh layer of chopped wood shavings, pine needles, chopped leaves or compost.

WATERING

When rainfall is scarce, water any annuals and biennials that are still growing strong. In cooler weather they do not require as much frequent irrigation as they did during the hot summer months. Flowers that are mulched will require less watering and the mulch prevents the water from splashing on the foliage. This can greatly reduce foliar diseases.

Keep container-grown annuals watered as the soilless mix begins to dry.

 ## FERTILIZING

No fertilizer is needed at this time, other than a slow-release product incorporated into the potting mixture of container-grown annuals. Check the label to determine the frequency of application. Some may last for several months.

 ## GROOMING

Remember to collect the seeds from any annuals you would like to grow again next year. Cut off the ripening seedheads or capsules prior to throwing the spent flowers into the compost pile or the trash. Store the seeds in brown paper bags in a cool spot, such as the back of the garage

GARDENING WITH AN ALTITUDE TIPS

If you want to extend your garden season into the fall and winter, you can still plant **pansies** in autumn. Pansies will develop strong root systems during the mild fall days when the weather suits them perfectly. They will become well established to survive the winter cold and snow over the fall and winter months. As winter succeeds, and the hardy bulbs start to emerge, the pansies are ready to bloom, providing an undercover to accent the bulbs.

After planting spring-flowering bulbs this autumn, plant **violas** and **pansies** throughout the flower bed for spectacular and colorful displays.

or an old refrigerator. Just as a reminder, flowers and fruits grown from seed can be variable in color and size, particularly those that are hybrid varieties.

Clean up flower beds, and get the soil ready for next year by allowing the chopped leaves from the mulching mower to cover the bare spots. This material will eventually break down and provide organic matter. Mulch the bare soil.

 ## PROBLEMS

Be on the watch for giant aphids as they make their last feeding frenzy on annuals and biennials. To avoid bringing any of these pests indoors, wash down the plants with a forceful spray of water or use the homemade soap spray on page 283. Plan to keep the insect watch going

every few days to keep the pests at bay before they can get out of hand.

When bringing annuals indoors for the winter, insufficient light can be the most limiting factor for their success. Locate the brightest spot possible, such as in an enclosed porch or sunroom, for the plants you desire to keep. You can even construct a lighting structure using fluorescent lights to supplement the low light of fall and winter. A combination of cool white and warm white works well to maintain plants (see page 18 for instructions).

NOVEMBER

ANNUALS

 PLANNING

With the arrival of the first hard frost, the main season for annual flowers is over. Now is the time to plan the garden for future years. If you really enjoyed this year's crop of annuals, you may want to plant more next year and try them in different places. Make notes in your garden journal and notebook to keep track of what needs doing.

If you like picking bouquets of flowers regularly during the garden season, consider planning a cutting garden. This garden plot can be tucked away in an out-of-the-way spot and does not require as much maintenance as other flowers. Old-fashioned **bachelor's-buttons, cosmos, zinnias, asters,** and others are great for cutting. Plant lots of seeds to have a variety of plants to choose from for your cutflower arrangements. Grow plants with interesting foliage, seedpods, or flowers that are good for drying. They can be used later for floral arrangements or crafts.

Plan to gather all the old seed packets that are strewn about and store in a plastic shoebox. Many of the seeds leftover will last another year and can be re-sown. Keep track of seed labels that came with your annuals and keep garden notes. This will help you answer questions about varieties that did best, including colors of the plants and cultural information. These labels will prove invaluable when it comes time to order more seeds in January or February.

 PLANTING

As long as the ground remains unfrozen, you can still plant **pansies** and **violas** for fall and winter color. Experiment with planting them in containers on the patio or windowsill. If they are somewhat protected by an overhang and not exposed to the high winds, these will bloom periodically in the winter to provide some color. Use pine cones and grasses to decorate the containers and help provide some additional winter protection. Don't forget to water the container-planted flowers so they won't dehydrate.

 CARE

Some of the more cold-tolerant annuals such as **ornamental cabbage** and **kale** may have succumbed to a hard frost. It is best to dig these out and send them to the compost pile. Otherwise they will give off a foul odor as they decay.

Mulch any bare soil with compost and lightly work in to allow it to improve the soil structure. Young transplants of **pansies** should be mulched with a few inches of pine needles or shredded cedar for winter protection and to hold in the moisture.

 WATERING

Plants that you decided to overwinter indoors will need to be watered regularly as you turn on the furnace. Check for soil moisture by probing the soil with your finger. If it is becoming dry to the touch, give the plants a thorough watering.

Discard excess water that collects in the drainage saucer to avoid water logging the soil and causing root rot.

 FERTILIZING

Annuals that are overwintered indoors will take some time to acclimate to the indoor conditions. The duration and quality of light is lessened, so expect some yellow and dropping leaves. They need a few weeks to adjust and when new growth is evident, you can apply soluble plant fertilizer. Dilute to half strength so as to avoid building up the salt levels in the soil.

If you added a slow-release granular fertilizer to the soil at transplanting, you don't need to add a soluble plant food. Many overwintering annuals will begin to bloom again in a few weeks if the light conditions are favorable.

GROOMING

Cut back the dying or dead stems of plants overwintering indoors. Also, check for any signs of pests that may have piggybacked in with the plants. Spider mites, aphids, gnats, and soil pests can become a nuisance. Try to control them before they breed. Washing off the foliage and handpicking are safe ways to eliminate many pests. Otherwise, use a homemade soap spray.

PROBLEMS

As heating systems go on in your home, it is a good time for spider mites to proliferate. If you see mottled foliage or fine webbing, wash down the foliage with a soap solution or use an approved miticide. Read and follow label directions when using any kind of pesticide.

GARDENING WITH AN ALTITUDE TIPS
Plant Symptoms

If you were frustrated by a variety of insect and disease problems in your annuals this year, here are some tips to remember to prevent serious problems next growing season:

• Look for signs of sticky sap on the stems and foliage that indicate that aphids are starting to attack the plants. Wash them off the plant with a forceful spray of water or use a homemade soap spray.

• A fine webbing near the main stems and around the leaf stems usually indicates that spider mites are a problem. Wash both the top and underside of the leaves with soapy water. You may need to use a miticide. Read and follow label directions.

• If the leaves are beginning to turn yellow but the veins are remaining a bright green, this indicates a lack of available iron. Fertilize with a chelated iron.

• Leaves that develop a grayish-white coating on their surface indicate powdery mildew. Handpick the worst leaves; treat minor mildew problems with the homemade mildew control.

• When the tender growth of annuals and foliage is twisted and turning yellow or brown, there could be possible herbicide injury. Did some of the herbicide you or a neighbor sprayed on weeds drift to the flower garden?

• Plants that develop lower leaves that turn yellow and begin to drop off indicate something is going on in the root system. Could it be overwatering or the soil not draining properly?

NOTES

_____
_____
_____
_____
_____
_____
_____

DECEMBER
ANNUALS

 PLANNING

In some parts of the lower elevations, the ground remains unfrozen, so you can still enjoy the color from **ornamental cabbage, kale, violas,** and **pansies.** It takes a really hard frost to do them in. Keep dates of the first light and hard frosts to help in planning next season.

Plan to decorate outdoor containers with bunches of dried ornamental grasses, pine cones, and evergreen boughs for winter interest. Catalogs should be arriving, so order early to get the newest plant introductions. Clean up old containers, and store them in the garage or garden shed. Take an inventory of your seed-starting supplies so you'll be ready to order at the start of the new year.

 PLANTING

Lightly tug at the plant cuttings you took earlier in the fall to see if they are rooting. There should be adequate moisture in the rooting medium. Pot up the rooted cuttings into a soilless growing mixture to which you have added slow-release granular fertilizer. If you don't have enough sunlight, suspend fluorescent lights by chains so they hang down close to the foliage. This will develop strong, healthy transplants.

Try sowing **pansy** or **viola** seeds in a sterilized mixture. Scatter the seeds on the surface, and mist the growing medium. Then cover with plastic. Once the seeds germinate, move them to brighter light.

 CARE

Finish cleanup of your annual beds. Chop or shred disease-free plants for the compost pile. Use compost and fallen leaves to improve the garden soil. Spade or rototill the organic amendment into the beds, and leave the soil rough with clods so that winter rains and snow will break them down. The freezing and thawing action is a natural way to make the soil more friable (workable) in spring. Pinch the leggy growth of transplants if the stems are beginning to flop over. This will encourage more branching and a sturdier plant.

 WATERING

Water new indoor seedlings. Allow the growing mixture to dry out slightly between waterings. Check soil moisture of transplants taken from the garden in autumn. If the soil feels dry, add water.

 FERTILIZING

Every six weeks, you can add a slow-release fertilizer to the potting mix for rooted cuttings. Or, you may wish to fertilize with a soluble plant food diluted to half strength. Read and follow label directions. If the plants are growing in a well-lit location, many annuals may start to bloom indoors for welcome winter color.

 GROOMING

As annual plants adjust to growing indoors, they will naturally stretch to get more light. You can pinch back the stems of **coleus, begonia, impatiens,** and **geraniums**. If you don't have a sunny window or greenhouse, place the plants under artificial lights. See plant stand illustration on page 99.

 PROBLEMS

Check for pest infestations weekly. If you detect them, rinse the foliage with tepid water every few days, and follow up with a spray of homemade soap spray or insecticidal soap.

BULBS, CORMS, RHIZOMES & TUBERS

Growing spring-flowering bulbs in Idaho requires simple planning and well-drained soils. Few other garden flowers are so tough—a miracle enclosed in a living capsule. I have chosen a broad definition of the word "bulb" to include plants that form swollen, underground storage roots or stems that allow them to survive through the cold and dry periods of the growing seasons. This includes bulbs, corms, tubers, and rhizomes. Technically, a bulb is made up of the swollen, fleshy bases of leaves. Other storage structures are formed by different parts of the plant; a crocus's corm is a swollen stem base. Some irises have both bulbs and tuberous roots;

others have rhizomes and fleshy storage roots. Dahlias are swollen storage tubers with buds that arise at the tip of the tuber. You can have crocuses peaking through melting snow in February, patches of golden daffodils in March, and radiant tulips and hyacinths in April. These are just a few of the fall-planted bulbs that cast their magic spell in spring.

WHAT TO LOOK FOR

When purchasing bulbs locally, select plump, firm, and blemish-free bulbs. Many varieties have skins like onions that are partially or completely removed. This will not affect their quality

GARDENING WITH AN ALTITUDE TIPS

Bulbs, Corms, Rhizomes and Tubers for Idaho

COMMON NAME	BOTANICAL NAME	HARDINESS
Bearded Iris	*Iris germanica* and hybrids	perennial
Canna	*Canna* x *generalis*	not winter hardy
Crocus	*Crocus* spp. and hybrids	perennial
Daffodil	*Narcissus* spp. and hybrids	perennial
Dahlia	*Dahlia* spp. and hybrids	not winter hardy
Dwarf Iris	*Iris reticulata*	perennial
Gladiolus	*Gladiolus* x *hortulanus*	not winter hardy
Glory-of-the-Snow	*Chionodoxa luciliae*	perennial
Grape Hyacinth	*Muscari armeniacum*	perennial
Lily	*Lilium* spp. and hybrids	perennial
Meadow Saffron	*Colchicum* spp. and hybrids	perennial
Ornamental Onion	*Allium* spp.	perennial
Siberian Squill	*Scilla siberica*	perennial
Snowdrop	*Galanthus nivalis*	perennial
Tulip	*Tulipa* spp. and hybrids	perennial
Windflower	*Anemone blanda*	perennial

as long as the bulb has solid integrity and is free of soft spots. If you find that you cannot plant bulbs within a day or two after making your purchase, store them in a cool (40 to 50 degrees Fahrenheit) and dry location in mesh bags or ventilated containers.

WHEN TO PLANT
To plant your pretty visions of spring, you must start this fall. Spring-flowering bulbs are planted in late September through November. Soil temperatures have begun to cool down, and the embryonic flower inside the bulb requires a cold period to mature for successful spring blooms. Once planted, bulbs must develop a strong, healthy root system before the ground freezes.

WHERE TO PLANT
Spring-flowering bulbs are among the most versatile perennials when planted properly. They can be interplanted with herbaceous perennial flowers, around shrub borders, along pathways, in separate flower beds, and naturalized in lawns. Some of my favorite plantings include crocuses, muscari, daffodils and selected types of tulips in casual drifts around the landscape and along garden pathways. This is a landscape technique termed "naturalizing" since the plants grow and bloom as though placed by Nature's hand.

Most spring-flowering bulbs in our higher elevations perform best with morning sun and afternoon shade. Flowers will last much longer in such a setting, but you must provide protection from drying winds which often scorch flower petals. The early-blooming bulbs, including snowdrops (*Galanthus*) and winter aconite (*Eranthis*), will do beautifully beneath trees and shrubs whose canopy of shade does not unfurl until after the blossoms fade.

WELL-DRAINED SOIL IS THE KEY
All spring-flowering bulbs will grow best in well-drained soils. This is especially important to ensure bulb longevity. If you've ever planted bulbs only to find that they've lasted for just one season, you're not alone. Poorly drained, waterlogged soils may be the culprit.

To prepare the soil, begin by loosening the area with a heavy-duty rototiller or shovel; dig down to a depth of 8 to 10 inches. If your soil is predominantly clay, it is important to mix in a combination of compost or sphagnum peat moss to improve drainage and encourage healthy root development. For the organic gardener: add fortified bonemeal, about a handful per square foot of area; or add an organic bulb fertilizer as recommended on the label. These specialty bulb fertilizers are generally high in phosphorus (the middle number in the formula).

HOW TO PLANT
The bulb planting charts shown in national marketing campaigns that promote fall bulb planting are for well-drained soils, which are not typical of our region. Most bulbs will do best and survive the longest in a sandy loam or clay loam. In heavy, clay-textured soils, plant bulbs 1 to 2 inches more shallow than recommended. Soils with high clay content can be amended with perlite or scoria (crushed volcanic rock) at rate of 25 percent by volume for improved soil texture and proper aeration.

Many gardeners like to dig individual holes for each bulb with a bulb planter, but I've found it much more effective when bulbs are planted in a group or mass plantings. To do this, remove enough soil to accommodate all the bulbs going into a given area. Fertilizer and compost can be easily applied at the bottom of the excavated bed and incorporated a bit deeper where the roots will grow.

After the bulbs are set in place, cover them with approximately half of the amended excavated soil, and lightly scatter additional bulb fertilizer on top. Don't forget to amend the backfill soil with compost (25 to 30 percent by volume) before shoveling it onto the planted bulbs. Then, finish filling in the bulb bed with remaining soil. Finally, water the area thoroughly.

Since we often lack adequate natural precipitation in our region during the fall, it is important to water new bulb beds periodically throughout the season to ensure good root growth. Check the soil with a hand trowel. If it is beginning to dry out, water as necessary before the soil freezes solid. We've found that fall and early winter watering may be necessary every three to four weeks, depending upon the flower bed's exposure.

After the first hard frosts, apply a layer of organic mulch to the bulb bed: 2 to 3 inches of shredded cedar mulch, aspen mulch, dried grass clippings (those not treated with herbicides), or shredded leaves will help to retain moisture, reduce weed growth, and prevent soil heaving.

WHICH END IS UP?

Bulbs should be planted with root end downward and growing end upward. It isn't always easy to tell which is which. Most bulbs, on close inspection, reveal a few root remnants or nubs to help guide you. The growing point is often already formed and apparent. Bulbs such as tulips and hyacinths have a pointed end, which is planted up, and a flattened basal plate, which goes down.

Some of the more difficult bulbs to decide are rhizomes or tubers like *Anemone blanda*, which show very little hints of either growth points or roots. Fortunately, these little bulbs will adjust in most any position, so all you need to do is scatter them.

TENDER BULBS

Bulbs that are not winter-hardy are unable to survive the freezing temperatures. These include dahlias, gladiolus, begonias, cannas, calla lily, and caladiums. Most are planted in the spring after the danger of frost has passed. I like to plant gladiolus corms when the daffodils are blooming because they will not grow through the surface until the danger of frost is over. Stagger planting every two weeks for a continuous bloom over the summer months.

You can get a head start on the flowering season by starting summer-flowering bulbs indoors in pots. Plant them in a commercial potting mixture in containers that have drainage. When the danger of frost has passed, the started plants can be set in the garden. Be sure to have stakes or other plant supports ready. Plant the bulbs, tubers, corms, or rhizomes at the depth indicated on the label.

CARE OF TENDER BULBS FOR WINTER

Tender bulbs must be removed from the garden soon after the first hard frost. Carefully lift the plants, roots and all, with a heavy spading fork. Cut back the tops to the within a couple inches of the crown. Shake off the excess soil and bring the clumps into the garage or patio to dry. After they have dried, separate the clumps, and store them in a cool, dry place over the winter. I like to use Styrofoam coolers that are filled with peat moss. They will help protect the bulbs from frost and retain natural moisture so they won't shrivel.

Check stored bulbs monthly over the winter to make sure they are not rotting or shriveling. If they get too dry, lightly sprinkle them to provide some moisture, but don't overwater.

JANUARY
BULBS, CORMS, RHIZOMES & TUBERS

 PLANNING

For winter color in a short time, plan to plant **paper-white narcissus** bulbs indoors. They are usually available at garden stores now and require no chill period. Just plant them in a pot of moist pebbles, and enjoy the show in a few weeks.

January is good time to select flowering bulbs, corms, rhizomes, and tubers to provide accents in your summer garden. For example, summer-blooming **Gladiolus** are sure to invite hummingbirds to your yard. Study mail-order catalogs to learn more about the various kinds and how they can be used in your landscape.

Summer-flowering bulbs, however, are not hardy except in warmer, protected areas or microclimates. Left in the ground, the bulb, corm, rhizome, or tuber will freeze and turn to mush. They are primarily grown as annuals, planted in the spring when the soil temperature warms up, then dug from the ground for storing or discarding when frost kills back the foliage and stems.

 PLANTING

When the ground is frozen, it's not appropriate to plant bulbs. However, if you have **spring-flowering bulbs** in storage, plant them in pots now rather than leaving them in their bags to dry out. Use a good potting mixture, and water after setting them in their containers. Store them in a cool garage where they can undergo their chilling requirements.

On a day when the soil outdoors is not frozen, work some compost into the area, and plant the spring-blooming bulbs directly outside. Then water in well, and mulch with compost, shredded leaves, or wood shavings.

 CARE

If you received or planted an **amaryllis bulb** for the holiday season, you should cut off the faded bloom and stalk this month. Leave the narrow, straplike foliage. This grows and stores energy for the bulb. Keep in a bright location. Water the potting mixture as you would a houseplant; when the soil begins to feel dry to the touch, give the plant a good drink. Fertilize with a soluble plant fertilizer mixed at half strength at every other watering.

Amaryllis can be moved outdoors after the danger of frost has past. Sink pot and all in the ground in a semi-sunny location or underneath the canopy of a tree. It will continue to grow foliage and store more energy to the bulb. When autumn arrives, and before the first frost, bring the amaryllis indoors, and place in a sunny window. It will bloom again when the time is right.

If you prefer, place your **amaryllis** in the basement, and stop watering to allow it to go dormant. It will need a rest period of three months or so. Then, bring it back to a growing cycle by repotting it in fresh potting mixture and returning to bright light. Keep it watered as needed and the bloom cycle will repeat. The blooms may not be as big as the first time, but it is still worth the effort.

If you planted bulbs in containers for forcing indoors, their chill period has most likely been met. Green shoots will begin to emerge from the potting soil. The bulbs will have developed roots that may be nudging the crowded bulbs up out of the pot or gravel. This is normal and not to be of concern. What you should do:

• Move the potted bulbs first to a warmer area that is about 45 to 50 degrees Fahrenheit for a week, then indoors to warmer quarters. Water the potting mixture as needed.

• Bring the potted bulbs indoors to a bright window (not direct sun) as the buds start to swell. Avoid really warm areas, as this will cause the stems to grow leggy and buds to bloom quickly and fade.

Once **paper-white narcissus** has finished blooming, discard the bulbs since it is almost impossible to force them to bloom again.

WATERING

As the soil dries out, keep the bulbs watered as needed. Do not waterlog the potting mixture as this will cause root rot.

Outdoors, if there is a prolonged period of warm weather without snow or rain, water bulb beds on sunny exposures. Water when the soil is unfrozen, and apply water early in the day so it has time to soak in. Winter watering will sustain the root system and keep the soil cool to delay early emergence.

FERTILIZING

Bulbs already contain all they need to get started, as previously mentioned. Once the potted bulbs have finished blooming indoors and you plant them in the ground come springtime, you can add a slow-release granular to the area.

GROOMING

Deadhead or cut off faded flowers of potted bulbs once they finish blooming. Yellow leaves should also be trimmed away. Droopy leaves indicate insufficient light and may need to be propped up with bamboo stakes.

PROBLEMS

Insect pests may find their way from your houseplants to potted bulbs. Problems to be aware of:

• Aphids can attack the succulent foliage to suck plant juices. Wash them off with a forceful spray of water or use a homemade soap spray.

• Flying gnats can also be a problem, but are easily controlled if you keep the soil surface clean of debris. Allow the soil to dry out between watering, and set up yellow sticky traps. Gnats are not harmful to the plants, just more of a nuisance in the house.

• Overwatering potted bulbs can result in rot that destroys the entire bulb, roots and all. If this should occur, discard the rotting bulbs. Monitor your watering practices to avoid keeping the soil too wet.

FEBRUARY
BULBS, CORMS, RHIZOMES & TUBERS

 PLANNING

This is a fun month in the outdoor garden as we experience some warm sunny days. Plan to get outside to see early color from **snowdrops** and **winter aconite** bulbs. These are a welcome sight to the winter garden tucked among rocks and other parts of the landscape. It is a sign that spring is not too far behind.

If you did not mark the location of your bulb beds, get ready to do so when they start emerging and blooming. This will prove helpful for locating the spots when it comes time to overplant these areas or work the soil this spring. You don't want to dig or rototill areas where hardy bulbs are located.

If you want to plant perennial ground covers in bulb beds, plan on doing so before the bulb foliage is all gone. Ground covers over bulb beds keep the beds tidy, yet allow the bulbs to grow normally and undergo their natural dormancy. Some of my favorites are **sweet woodruff, veronica,** and **woolly thyme.** Consider planting **pansies** as an undercover for bulbs, too. They will provide color when the bulbs' foliage is yellowing and ripening.

Plan to order summer-flowering bulbs from mail-order catalogs early to get the best selection. These will help to fill in some of the empty spots in the flower bed and provide interest to the garden. Your order will be sent in the mail at the appropriate planting times.

 PLANTING

Later in the month when **pansies** and **violas** become available locally, plant them where bulbs are growing. They combine well with **tulips, daffodils,** and **hyacinths.** Cool-weather annuals will add color and interest when interplanted with bulbs and fill in the gaps.

When the **snowdrops, glory-of-the-snow,** and **Siberian squill** have finished blooming and only their green leaves remain, it is a good time to thin them out and transplant them to new areas, if you desire. Lightly lift the clumps and separate the bulbs, then poke them into workable soil, an inch or so deep leaving the foliage intact —that's all there is to it. These are great little gems to use for naturalizing areas in the landscape.

Summer-flowering bulbs can also be planted indoors in containers, if you have space and time. This will give them a head start on the growing season; they can be transplanted outdoors when the danger of frost has past.

 CARE

The early blooming hardy bulbs will be emerging now, and many will be blooming to add color to the winter garden. Those planted in warmer sites, near buildings or heat-retaining walls, may start pushing out of the ground with green shoots. This is normal, as the bulbs are following their internal clock. A light freeze or snowstorm will not harm them. If the bulbs were mulched, this will keep the soil cooler and help to delay early emergence.

During prolonged dry spells in February, you may need to do some "winter watering" of bulb beds to maintain soil moisture and keep the ground cool. Apply water when the ground is not frozen and early in the day so it can soak down. A light watering is all that is required; use the frog-eye sprinkler to complete this chore.

Check the tender summer-flowering bulbs that are stored in the garage or basement. **Dahlias** and **cannas** should be kept cool so they won't sprout. Usually a temperature of 45 to 50 degrees Fahrenheit is ideal. If any of the bulbs are getting mushy or have completely dried out (tubers of dahlias and cannas) discard them.

Gladiolus should be kept dry and cool. I store them in old mesh bags that oranges and grapefruit are sold in. This allows for good air circulation and prevents molds from growing on the corms. In a month or so, you can bring some of these out and pot them up in containers to give them a head start.

 WATERING

Hardy bulbs in the outdoor landscape may need attention to watering if the winter has been dry. Water early in the day when the ground is unfrozen. Mulched bulb beds will require less attention, as the winter mulch will help to retain moisture and keep the soil cool.

 FERTILIZING

It is too early to apply granular fertilizer to bulb beds now. If you will be potting up tender summer-flowering bulbs later in the month, add a slow-acting granular fertilizer to the potting mixture. Follow label directions.

 GROOMING

As the early hardy spring-flowering bulbs have finished blooming, you can pick off the faded flowers, but leave the foliage in place. Leaves are the food-manufacturing organs of the plant and will store energy for the bulbs before they go dormant. Resist the urge to tidy up the garden by cutting back the leaves even though it may look unsightly for a while. Remove the dead and ripened leaves when they have dried up.

 PROBLEMS

As the bulbs begin to emerge from the soil and some early **crocus** are blooming, critters may arrive, too. Sparrows and finches seem to like to feed on crocus by tearing away at the blossoms. You can prevent this by covering vulnerable areas with bird netting.

Squirrels, however, are bolder creatures. They may dig up **tulip** and **crocus** bulbs and find them as tasty morsels early in the season. Bird netting is not strong enough for them. Construct a screen using hardware cloth to lay over threatened bulb beds.

Deer may also arrive to nibble on the foliage and buds of **tulips** and **crocus.** They won't bother **daffodils,** however. Spray the plants with a homemade critter repellent to keep them at bay (see page 284). Repeat after a rain or snowstorm.

NOTES

_____
_____
_____
_____
_____
_____
_____
_____
_____
_____
_____
_____
_____
_____
_____
_____
_____
_____
_____
_____
_____
_____

MARCH
BULBS, CORMS, RHIZOMES & TUBERS

PLANNING

The spring-blooming bulbs are beginning to make their display this month, and can begin early if temperatures climb and the days stay consistently mild. However, plan on fluctuations in weather patterns when a snowstorm rolls in. Have sturdy 5-gallon buckets or wax-lined boxes ready to cover bulbs that have started to bloom. The heavy, wet snow can collapse the stems and smash the flowers. So be prepared, just in case.

Daffodils and **tulips** are among the easiest large-flowering bulbs to grow and come in a plethora of types and varieties. If you made the right choices last fall, you could have blooms from early spring to late spring. Plan for continuing bloom from early March through May by selecting and planting early-, mid-, and late-flowering varieties of your favorite colors and forms.

To check out what's blooming and when, visit public and private gardens. Take notes for your garden journal so you will remember which colors and varieties you want to try. This will help when it's time to place your order later in spring and early summer. Ordering ahead for fall will save you money, and the bulbs will arrive at the proper planting time for your area.

Stock up on compost, support stakes, and bulb fertilizer as needed.

PLANTING

If you want a head start for the tender, summer-flowering bulbs, it's time to pot up **begonias, dahlias, cannas,** and **caladiums** indoors. I use 1-gallon plastic containers with a well-drained potting mixture. Start them in an attached garage where the emerging sprouts will not freeze. Once the sprouts appear, provide light with a light stand to make them grow strong, sturdy stems.

Outdoors, **snowdrops** have completed blooming and the foliage persists. During the next few weeks, you can divide crowded clumps of snowdrops if the ground is workable. Having the leaves intact makes it easy to separate the clumps for new transplants. Here's how:

1. Gently dig masses of **snowdrop** bulbs, and shake away the excess soil.

2. Tease apart the individual bulbs, being careful not to tear the roots or break off the foliage.

3. Discard any bulbs that are damaged or appear diseased.

4. Replant some of the bulbs in their original spot, bury about 3 inches deep and space 3 inches apart.

Pansies, forget-me-nots, violas, and **primroses** are good companion plants for spring-flowering bulbs, and can be planted now. Many cool-tolerant annuals will be available at local garden retailers.

Tulips, daffodils, hyacinths, and **lilies** are often given as gifts during the Easter season. These have been forced to bloom in their pots, but can be salvaged and planted in your garden once they finish blooming and the soil outdoors is workable. When you're ready, snip off the flowers, but leave the foliage so it can grow to produce food energy for the bulb. Grow indoors until the danger of frost has passed and then plant outside in an area where the soil has been enriched with compost. Work a little slow-release fertilizer into the planting holes. These bulbs will readjust to the outdoor schedule and bloom next year in your yard.

CARE

If you like to naturalize bulbs in your warm-season lawn or other parts of the landscape, delay mowing the lawn to allow the foliage to ripen and store energy for the bulbs. *Iris reticulata,* **crocuses,** and **snow crocuses** are wonderful little bulbs to use in naturalizing an area, be it a lawn or open space.

 WATERING

If there has been a prolonged dry spell and the ground is dry, water bulb beds to maintain uniform moisture for healthy strong growth, and to keep the soil cool to help delay premature emergence. Water areas where the ground is unfrozen.

 FERTILIZING

Since bulbs, corms, rhizomes, and tubers are specialized plant structures, they store energy from the previous growing season. They generally do not need fertilizer in the spring until after they have finished blooming. Once the flowers have faded and the leaves continue to grow vigorously, scatter a slow-acting granular fertilizer throughout the bulb bed and lightly cultivate into the soil. Water the fertilizer in thoroughly. This will provide nutrients so the foliage can build up food reserves for the bulbs underground. One application of slow-release fertilize is all that is needed for the spring season.

 GROOMING

To tidy up the bulb garden, pinch off the faded or spent flowers if you desire to keep them from spreading everywhere. This is particularly true of **grape hyacinths** since they can spread throughout the garden bed. If you are naturalizing an area, this is not necessary.

Larger-blooming bulbs, including **tulips, hyacinths,** and **daffodils,** should have their old blooms snipped or pinched off to improve the general appearance of the plants. Allow the leaves to grow. Removing spent flowers that may have been pollinated will also divert energy into the bulb rather than forming seedpods. Do not trim back the foliage while it is still green as this interferes with its job of building food reserves for next year.

 PROBLEMS

During warm and dry winters, it is not unusual to see the shoots of **daffodils, tulips,** and **hyacinths** prematurely emerge from the ground. Often, early emergence is seen on the south or west exposures (on slopes or sides of buildings). A general recommendation is to plant spring-flowering bulbs deeper than common recommendations, especially on hot exposures, as this may tend to delay early emergence. Bulb plantings can be mulched with 2 to 3 inches of compost or shredded wood chips, bark or pine needles. This will keep the soil cooler, an advantage when bulbs are sited on south and west exposures.

If foliage has emerged early, remember the leaves are pretty cold-hardy, but it can be protected with a layer of mulch if frigid temperatures occur. A well-drained, sandy loam soil can be added to about $1^1/_2$ to 2 inches in depth to help protect foliage and add soil depth to the bulb plantings. With added soil depth bulbs should be later to emerge the following season.

APRIL
BULBS, CORMS, RHIZOMES & TUBERS

 PLANNING

Your bulbs really come to life this month. Those garden beds you thought were empty are now brimming with color and style. Take time to enjoy the beauty. Photograph the beds and take a few close-ups. Also, record notes in your garden journal to indicate times of blooming and when the bulbs are in their peak.

Plan to leave the healthy green foliage growing as the bulbs finish up their blooming cycle. Even though you may be tempted to cut it back, the foliage is necessary to store food reserves for next season.

Look for spots in your garden beds where summer-flowering bulbs can be planted to fill in the gaps. Garden retailers are stocking up on packaged summer-flowering bulbs, and the sooner you can purchase them, the better. Left in their bags unattended, bulbs may dry out or rot. You can store them in a cool garage or basement until it is time to plant them.

 PLANTING

Soon it will be time (mid-month) to plant tender bulbs directly outdoors. The soil needs to warm up to 55 to 60 degrees Fahrenheit, and should not be too wet. Be sure the soil has been amended with compost, sphagnum peat moss, or a combination of both. This will improve drainage, retain nutrients, and allow for better root growth.

If you must move established bulbs, now is as good a time as any. Just be careful on how you approach this activity. Follow this method:

1. Carefully dig the clumps out of the ground with a heavy-duty spading fork. Take care not to damage or break the foliage.

2. Gently tap or brush excess soil from the bulbs and carefully separate them, teasing apart the tangled roots at the base of each bulb.

3. If a larger bulb has developed several good-sized baby bulbs with roots, you can divide these from the mother bulb by carefully breaking them apart, or you can plant the entire clump intact. Remember, keep the leaves intact so they can capture sunlight and produce energy for the transplanted bulbs.

4. Check the bulbs for injury from insects or diseases. Discard any that are suspect.

5. Replant some of the bulbs in their former location if there is still adequate sun; space them 4 to 6 inches apart and about 6 inches deep. Water in thoroughly.

6. Plant the remaining divisions elsewhere, or give them away. The smaller bulb divisions generally will not bloom for a year or two, so be patient. This transplanting technique is ideal for naturalizing areas with an overflow of bulbs.

If you haven't already started stored **begonia, dahlia, canna,** and **caladium** bulbs indoors, you still have time. Nudge them out of dormancy by potting them up in fresh potting soil and watering them. It is still a bit too early to set them outdoors. Wait until the danger of frost has passed in your specific area.

If the soil is workable, this is a good time to set out forced bulbs you've been growing in the house. Keep any remaining foliage intact and plant them as you would in the autumn.

Later in the month you can direct plant **gladiolus corms, canna,** and **dahlia** tubers outdoors. Be sure the soil is ready where they are to be planted. Plant at the depth recommended on the label or package. If the soil is still too wet or cold, wait a few more weeks before planting.

 CARE

Check **lily** bulbs, **gladiolus, begonias, caladiums, cannas,** and other tender bulbs when you purchase them. Avoid those that have bruises or show signs of rot. You can divide **dahlia** tubers where they are attached to the main stem. It is critical to keep an "eye" or growing tip with each tuber division. Some dahlia growers will even take stem cuttings from plants started indoors earlier, and plant these up to increase their collection or to give to friends.

Begonias and **gladiolus** that have developed smaller bulbs can be increased by carefully breaking off the bulblets or corms from the original bulb. Since they are small, they will not bloom this year but will increase in size for next season.

 WATERING

Water bulb beds as the soil dries out. If we experience a lack of rain or spring snow, water these flower beds every three to four weeks. Spot watering may be necessary to ensure the bulbs will have good root growth and produce full blooms. If it gets too dry, bulbs may become stunted and bloom poorly.

If you have potted bulbs in containers, allow the potting mixture to dry out between waterings. As soon as it feels dry to the touch, it's time to water the potting mixture. Never keep the mixture soaking wet, as this will cause rot.

 FERTILIZING

Fertilize hardy spring-flowering bulbs to help them grow healthy foliage, but wait until after they finish blooming. Do not overdo the application of fertilizer. I recommend a slow-release granular applied at the base of the bulbs, lightly cultivated into the soil and watered in.

 GROOMING

Continue to cut off or deadhead faded **tulip, daffodil** and **hyacinth** flowers as soon as they finish their bloom cycle. Cut back the stems to where the leaves begin, but **never remove** the foliage. Remember, the leaves are the food factories that build up energy for next year's blooming cycle.

 PROBLEMS

Be ever vigilant for sneak attacks from rabbits, deer, elk, chipmunks, and meadow mice, as they find many bulbs gourmet morsels to feed upon. You can spray the foliage with the critter repellent (see page 284) or put up a temporary screen or wire cages to protect the flowers and foliage.

Watch for the invasion of insect pests, including aphids that prefer to get into the leaf folds of iris. You may need to use a systemic insecticide or wash them off with a forceful spray of water. When using any pesticide, read and follow label directions.

MAY
BULBS, CORMS, RHIZOMES & TUBERS

PLANNING

The danger of frost is past in many areas of the region, but passes later at higher elevations. As the soil dries out, it is time to set out those tender summer bulbs. If you have grown some indoors in pots, harden them off before placing directly outdoors by leaving them out in a semi-sunny spot during the day, and bringing them indoors at night. Within a few weeks they will be ready to plant.

Remember that many of the summer-blooming bulbs including **dahlias, cannas,** and **gladiolus** grow tall and need to be spaced appropriately. Set them towards the back or use as an accent in the center of certain flower beds.

Consider planting hardy **lilies** this spring. They are wonderful plants, not only for background but also for filling in gaps when hardy spring-blooming bulbs are finished.

Take notes on which bulbs did best and when the foliage started to ripen. Consider planting ground covers or other companion plants that will help mask the ripening foliage of bulbs.

If you want a staggering bloom of **gladiolus**, make a note to plant some every two weeks. This will ensure that they will continue to provide color and cut flowers every few weeks. Glads are generally inexpensive, and the corms are easy to plant.

PLANTING

After the frost-free date in your area, it is safe to set out the first of the tender bulbs you've been growing indoors and those that have been in storage. Check the bulbs in storage to make sure they are not mushy or too dried out. Divide the tubers of **dahlias** and separate **cannas** as needed. Remember to make sure a "growing eye" is on each section of a dahlia division.

Be sure that the soil has been prepared where you plant tender bulbs. Set them at the proper depths, and place a stake in the planting hole. Insert the support stake into the ground near the bulb. The stake height should be slightly shorter than the projected height of the plant so the foliage will camouflage it later on. This will prevent you from stabbing the bulb when it has already started to grow. **Dahlias, gladiolus,** some **lilies,** and the narrow leaves of *Crocosmia* will appreciate the support as they grow and are protected from wind damage. Follow the package instructions for planting suggestions. To enjoy a continual bloom of gladiolus, plant corms every two weeks until mid-July.

Finish planting out in the garden those gift bulbs that were forced into bloom. Even the **Easter lily** can be planted in a protected location (morning sun with afternoon shade) and may bloom again in mid- to late summer.

The indoor **amaryllis** bulb can be set in the garden in a shaded spot; sink pot and all in the soil. It will continue to grow its foliage and store up food energy for the next blooming cycle.

CARE

Be sure to maintain uniform moisture in newly planted bulb beds, but do not waterlog the ground. Too much moisture can rot the bulbs before they have a chance to develop roots. Covering the bulb beds with a layer of mulch up to 2 inches deep will help to retain moisture and keep the soil from compacting.

If you didn't stake tall bulbs when planting, do so as they begin to emerge. Insert the stake gently into moist soil so it does not damage the bulb.

WATERING

Keep the soil of newly planted bulb beds uniformly moist. Check the soil moisture by probing into it with your finger or a garden trowel. If it is beginning to dry out to a depth of 2 to 3 inches, it is time to water.

Mulched beds will need less frequent watering than those that are not mulched. Container-grown bulbs will need closer attention to watering because the potting mixture will dry out faster than garden soil. If the weather is particularly hot, dry, and windy, water accordingly to ensure good root growth and healthy foliage.

 ## FERTILIZING

As previously mentioned, bulbs, corms, tubers, and rhizomes come already equipped with food energy to get started. But as the tender summer-blooming bulbs start growing, it is beneficial to provide some supplemental slow-release granular fertilizer for the growing season. I recommend a slow-release granular applied around the base of the plants and lightly cultivated in. Then water the fertilizer in. This will last through the summer

GARDENING WITH AN ALTITUDE TIPS

• Watch for the signs of powdery mildew on plants that have been watered overhead. Make sure the bulbs have good air circulation and try to water early in the morning or early evening so that the foliage goes into the night dry.

• Pinch or cut off diseased leaves and stems and discard in a garbage bag. Do not place them in the compost pile.

• Hand-dig, pull, or hoe weeds while they are still young and you can expose the roots to sunlight and drying conditions. Wait too long, and weeds seem to get harder to dig or pull.

• Mulch bare soil to suppress annual weed seeds from sprouting.

and early autumn. Read and follow label directions.

Container-grown bulbs may need more frequent fertilizer applications because you are watering more often and nutrients are leached away. Use a water-soluble flower fertilizer diluted to half strength, and apply at every other watering.

 ## GROOMING

Finish cleaning up the garden. Spent foliage is easily detached from the plant by gently tugging the ripened leaves at the base. Put this plant debris in the compost pile. Add more compost or mulch in bare spots of the bed to suppress weeds and maintain uniform moisture.

 ## PROBLEMS

It's time for the invasion of early aphids, thrips, and spider mites. You can wash them off the foliage with a forceful stream of water. The homemade soap spray will work to keep these pests at bay, too.

NOTES

_____
_____
_____
_____
_____
_____
_____
_____
_____
_____

JUNE
BULBS, CORMS, RHIZOMES & TUBERS

 PLANNING

As summer approaches, many of the summer-flowering bulbs are forming flower buds and getting ready to put on their show. Consider disbudding some that produce lots of tiny buds, such as **dahlias.** This will make the main flower grow larger.

Keep notes on which plants are performing best and note where they are planted. Knowing where the bulbs are planted will prevent you from digging or cultivating too deeply when you set new plants around the ripened foliage. Consider marking the designated areas with plant stakes to list the variety and color. You can safely plant companion perennials and ground covers in bulb beds to keep the beds looking good year round.

Take photographs of your bulb beds before they are all finished. This will help you plan future beds and know which plants may need replacing. Consider experimenting with different colors and forms.

Catalogs featuring spring-flowering bulbs are already arriving in the mail. Pre-ordering fresh bulbs will save you time, and many mail-order companies offer discounts. The bulbs will not be shipped until later in the fall at the appropriate planting time for your area.

Make sure you have enough mulch for the summer season.

 PLANTING

It's last call for planting summer-flowering bulbs; they need adequate time to root in, grow, and flower. If you don't have outdoor garden space for **dahlias, cannas, begonias,** and **caladiums,** try growing them in large pots. Use a well-drained potting mixture and containers with drainage holes. Plant out another grouping of **gladiolus** corms so there will be glads blooming in succession when the first batch finishes.

Mix slow-release granular fertilizer into the potting mixture prior to planting bulbs in containers. This will save you time. Most slow-acting fertilizers will last for several months.

 CARE

If your bulbs are getting too leggy, it may be a sign of poor light. As landscapes mature shade from trees and large shrubs will change the amount and duration of good light in a specific area. Some of these plants may need more staking or wire support rings around them. Make a note of this so you will know where to plant in following seasons.

 WATERING

Monitor the watering of bulb beds carefully this month. It is important to let them go into dormancy, so don't overwater to the point where the soil becomes waterlogged. It is amazing how bulbs can survive prolonged periods of drought. Their underground storage organs self-protect the hardy spring-flowering bulbs until their cycle starts again in the fall. Most hardy bulbs prefer and do best with drier conditions. Plant companion perennials and annuals with hardy spring-flowering bulbs that are more drought-tolerant, rather than with those that have greater water needs.

Summer-flowering bulbs will need more attention to watering as they are growing vigorously and setting flower buds. Check the soil moisture by probing into the ground 2 to 3 inches; if it is becoming dry, give them a good watering.

FERTILIZING

If you worked in a slow-release granular fertilizer in the spring for summer-flowering bulbs, there is no need to add fertilizer at this time.

Bulbs growing in containers may need supplemental fertilizer since you are watering more frequently. Use water-soluble fertilizer diluted to half strength. Apply every two weeks while the plants are blooming.

When applying liquid fertilizers to container-grown plants, the soil should be moist, not dry. Never apply fertilizer to a dry soil or if the plant is wilted and dry.

GROOMING

Pinch off or cut faded blooms. This will stimulate the plants to produce more buds and blooms. Pick up fallen leaves and flower petals at the base of the plants to discourage slugs and other thugs

---

GARDENING WITH AN ALTITUDE TIPS
Cutting Flowers for Bouquets

1. A special pair of cutting scissors can be purchased that holds the cut-off stem, allowing one-handed operation.

2. To cut thick-stemmed flowers, use sharp shears or a sharp knife to avoid tearing the stem and injuring the plant.

3. Make a slanting cut to expose more surface area for greater water absorption and to keep stems from sealing off when they sit at the bottom of the vase.

4. Immerse the stems immediately in a bucket of tepid water.

5. Allow them to sit for an hour absorbing water before you arrange them.

---

from invading the garden. Remove yellow leaves and broken stems to keep the flower bed looking fresh.

Dahlias and **gladiolus** are in bloom and can be cut for indoor bouquets.

PROBLEMS

Warmer weather signals the season for slugs (snails without shells) and they are fond of the succulent growth of **dahlias, begonias, caladiums,** and other tender bulbs. One method of control is to trap slugs with the homemade slug trap (see page 285.)

You can also discourage them by sprinkling diatomaceous earth (DE) around the base of the plants. The tiny, sharp diatoms will stop slugs in their slithering tracks.

Be on the watch for spider mites making attacks on the foliage of **dahlias.** Stippled foliage and fine webbing are clues that they are present. Wash down the foliage with water or use a homemade soap spray.

Tiny thrips can attack gladiolus and will rasp at the leaves and flower buds. The leaves will take on a grayish-green cast and the buds will not open normally. If they are a major problem, apply a systemic insecticide. Read and follow label directions.

NOTES

_____

_____

_____

_____

_____

_____

_____

_____

JULY
BULBS, CORMS, RHIZOMES & TUBERS

PLANNING

This is the time to enjoy the many colors and forms of summer-blooming bulbs. Take time to watch the hummingbirds as they visit the blooming spikes of **gladiolus.**

If you haven't recorded notes in your garden journal or notebook, take time to do so this month. Sit on the patio or deck and make observations about which bulbs aren't faring well and which ones are healthy and vigorous.

Be prepared for hailstorms that can quickly shred and damage the foliage and buds. Keep cardboard boxes on hand or large 5-gallon buckets to cover the plants.

Plan on cutting some flowers for indoor arrangements, as many summer-flowering bulbs make wonderful cut flowers. **Asiatic lilies, Oriental lilies, gladiolus,** and **dahlias** are excellent cut flowers and add dimension to bouquets, plus they last a long time.

Visit public gardens to see what kinds of bulbs they have planted in their flowerbeds. This may inspire you to try different kinds next year. Take along your garden notebook or journal to record your findings.

The U. S. Netherlands Flower Bulb Information Center (www. bulb.com) recommends bulbs for different garden situations and has a wealth of information on growing and storing bulbs.

PLANTING

This is not the month to plant or transplant bulbs. The heat of summer can take its toll on your investment. Wait until early fall if you need to move hardy bulbs from one area to another.

CARE

Check taller-growing summer-blooming bulbs to make sure their supports or stakes are sturdy. Strong winds can topple the stems and break off flowers. If you need to add more bamboo stakes around plants, do this with care. The soil should be slightly moistened so they will insert into the ground easily. Then tie the stems with a "twist 'em" or twine.

Add more mulch around the base of bulbs if it is decomposing or settling down. I like to use pine needles when they are available, but you can mulch with shredded cedar, dried grass clippings, pole peelings, or compost. Mulches keep the soil from drying out so rapidly in the heat of summer and keep the roots cool. They also discourage the growth of weeds.

WATERING

Keep the bulb garden moist during the heat of summer with regular watering. Apply enough water, about an inch a week, to maintain healthy and vigorous growth. This will also allow the buds to fully develop and open. Check the soil moisture by probing into the ground with a garden trowel and if it is beginning to dry out to a depth of 2 inches or more, give the garden a good drink. Bulbs that are mulched will need less frequent watering.

Bulbs growing in containers will need more attention to watering as they dry out faster. Water thoroughly as needed and allow the excess water to drain out. Pour the excess out of the drainage saucer.

FERTILIZING

Bulbs that were planted with a slow-release granular fertilizer will not need any additional fertilizer at this time. If the plants show signs of nutrient deficiency or a soil test indicates the need for more nutrients, you can apply granular fertilizer at the base of the plants. Lightly cultivate it into the soil and water the fertilizer in.

Soil that is covered by organic mulches will eventually gain nutrients as the materials break down, plus the organic amendments improve the soil's structure.

 GROOMING

Continue to remove or deadhead faded or spent flowers as needed to keep the garden tidy and fresh.

To encourage more branching of **dahlias,** pinch the terminal growth so more lateral branching will occur. This will keep the plants more compact if you wish. If you are growing large decorative dahlias, you don't need to do this. However, pinching out the small cluster of buds, but leaving the center bud, will result in a larger, dinner plate-sized bloom. Experiment to see how you can train and manipulate blooming and growth.

Keep debris from accumulating at the base of the plants to prevent diseases from invading and to discourage pests.

GARDENING WITH AN ALTITUDE TIPS
Controlling Earwigs

European earwigs can be found in almost any garden within the High Plains and Rocky Mountain region. They feed on a variety of plants and are particularly fond of flower blossoms, corn silks, and tender seedlings. Earwigs are primarily nocturnal feeders coming out at night to make their sneak attacks, hiding in the day within flower petals or underneath mulch. Though they look threatening, earwigs do not bite humans with their pinchers. In fact, they have a good side in that they feed on soft-bodied insects such as aphids, tiny caterpillars, and insect eggs.

To control earwigs and eliminate heavy populations without the use of pesticides, loosely roll up several layers of newspaper and moisten them in a bucket of water. Place the moistened newspaper roll in the garden at dusk, and by morning you will have collected a bounty of earwigs. Discard the trap in the garbage and set another if needed.

 PROBLEMS

Earwigs are fond of the blooms of **dahlias.** They can nibble at the petals, thus destroying the symmetry of the bloom. Place earwig traps in the flower bed to capture these little beasties.

Be on the watch for foliar diseases including powdery mildew. It will show up as grayish-white patches on the leaves. Increase air circulation by thinning the plants a bit and avoid watering the garden at night. Water early in the day so the foliage goes into the night dry. If you wish, use homemade mildew control to keep infections at a minimum (see page 285).

Spider mites can be a problem in the heat of summer. If detected early, wash them off the foliage with a strong water spray or use a homemade soap solution.

Keep your summer bulb plants healthy and stress-free by providing proper watering techniques, nutrition, uniform light, and air circulation.

AUGUST
BULBS, CORMS, RHIZOMES & TUBERS

 PLANNING

Summer-flowering bulbs will soon be approaching the end of their season, but there is still time to enjoy some little gems that bloom in the autumn. **Autumn crocus** and *Colchicum* are among my favorites. They have already produced their foliage in the spring and die back in summer. Then in the fall, the flowers poke through to provide a burst of color when you thought the garden was finished.

Plan to renovate some of the older bulb beds that were previously marked. As bulbs grow and multiply, the bed can become overcrowded and run out of energy to produce blooms. As landscapes mature, the shade cast by maturing shade trees may create a site with insufficient sunlight for the bulbs to grow and prosper. Now is a time to do some relocating, if needed. Plan to do this chore as the temperatures cool down and prior to bulb planting time.

 PLANTING

Here's how to divide and conquer bulbs that have become overcrowded or that have lost their vigor.

1. Carefully dig up existing plants and bulbs with a heavy-duty spading fork to lift out the clumps of hardy bulbs without doing a lot of injury to the bulbs. Shake the soil from the bulbs and set them aside in a cool spot. I like to put them in a burlap sack, but you can also use paper bags.

2. Dig the soil deeply or rototill the new planting area and add a generous supply of compost or sphagnum peat moss to improve soil structure and drainage. Remove any stones, old roots, and other plants debris.

3. Now would be a good time to work in slow-release granular fertilizer before replanting the bulbs.

4. Rake the loosened soil to level the area and you will be ready to start planting. Dig holes or planting areas to reset the bulbs and any companion perennials.

5. After planting, set out the frog-eye sprinkler and water the area thoroughly. Mulch to maintain uniform soil moisture and reduce frequency of watering. Mulches will also suppress weed growth.

In some parts of the region, pre-ordered hardy bulbs will be arriving in the mail. It will be time to start planting them, or if you must store them, keep them in a cool location in the basement or garage. **Don't forget about them;** mark your calendar to remind you to plant them before the ground freezes.

You can dig individual planting holes in a random pattern to plant bulbs, or dig an entire bed and plant them in masses for a more bold display. Plant at the depth recommended for each type.

If you have space, **naturalizing** is a way to create an informal display in the same manner as Nature might plant flowers in a woodland or forest setting. This is effective in ground covers or certain lawn areas where you might want to create a meadow effect.

 CARE

As weather turns cooler, summer-blooming bulbs will start to wane a bit. Deadhead the faded flowers and clip or pinch off yellow or brown foliage to keep the garden looking tidy.

If the mulch in bulb beds has began to settle and decompose, top-dress with new mulch to keep the soil cool and moist.

Be prepared for unexpected storms including hail that can shred the foliage and flowers. Have cardboard boxes or netting handy to cover plants prior to a predicted storm.

WATERING

If we experience a period of heat and drought, be sure to water summer-flowering bulbs so they can produce food energy and finish up their blooming cycle. Dig down into the soil and if it is beginning to dry out to a depth of 2 to 3 inches, turn on the sprinkler or drip irrigation system. Try to avoid overhead watering, particularly at night, as this will encourage foliar diseases.

Keep container-grown bulbs watered regularly, as the potting mixture will tend to dry out faster. Don't let the plants wilt.

FERTILIZING

Summer-flowering bulbs will not benefit from fertilizer at this time of the year. They need to complete their flowering cycle.

If you are preparing flower beds for new plantings of hardy bulbs, incorporate · a slow-release granular fertilizer while you add organic matter to the planting areas.

GARDENING WITH AN ALTITUDE TIPS
Creating a Naturalized Planting

1. Buy bagfuls of bulbs that are labeled for naturalizing or bulbs that are not the premium grade type. **Crocus, daffodils, glory-of-the-snow, grape hyacinths,** and others are available at discount prices, so shop around.

2. Scatter the bulbs so they will fall randomly over the areas you want to plant.

3. Dig the planting holes with a portable drill fitted with a bulb auger. Remember to dig the holes at the proper depth for the particular types of bulbs you have selected for naturalizing. This will make the job easier and fun. Get the family involved as this is a fun outdoor activity and everyone will enjoy the results next spring.

4. Cover the holes with soil and gently firm in.

5. Water the area with a sprinkler. During prolonged dry spells in the autumn, water once a month.

GROOMING

Keep on deadheading spent or faded flowers on **dahlias, gladiolus, begonias,** and **lilies.** If needed, cut back the yellowing and browning stems of maturing lilies, but don't pull them out of the soil as this may yank the bulb out of the ground.

Pick some of the flowers that are beginning to open to enjoy in fresh bouquets.

PROBLEMS

Be on the watch for insect pests as they make their last efforts to feed on succulent foliage. Aphids can cluster in masses on the stems. Wash them off with a forceful spray of water or use a homemade soap spray to get rid of them.

Mildew may show up on the foliage since warm days and cool nights favor this disease. Remove severely infected leaves and dispose in the trash. Spraying with the homemade mildew control can prevent severe infections from occurring. Repeat sprays as new leaves emerge.

SEPTEMBER
BULBS, CORMS, RHIZOMES & TUBERS

PLANNING

Check the bulbs carefully when selecting from open bins or even those that are packaged. See the chapter introduction for suggestions on choosing bulbs. Don't forget about the bulbs that arrived earlier in the mail that you may have stored in the basement or garage. Plant them now!

Sketch out a garden plan to mark areas in the landscape where bulb plantings are located. Consider the view from the windows, the height of the bulbs, bloom times and sequence, and colors on the plan. Consider companion perennials to interplant with the bulbs to help camouflage the ripening foliage as the bulbs die back.

Purchase or make garden labels to mark bulb beds and the various kinds planted. This makes it easier to plant new perennials or annuals when the time arrives and prevents injury to the bulbs.

PLANTING

Though spring-flowering bulbs do best in sunshine, that does not mean you cannot plant them near trees and around shrub borders. The leaves on deciduous trees and shrubs usually don't emerge until many spring-flowering bulbs have finished blooming. Avoid the deep shade of tall evergreens, as growing bulbs need to utilize sunshine to manufacture food reserves before going dormant.

Plant **daffodil** bulbs as early as you can get them since they need more time to develop roots before the ground freezes. **Tulips** can be delayed for a few weeks if you don't have enough time to plant all your bulbs this month. They do not need to root right away and seem to be less susceptible to rot if they can be delayed from sitting in warm soil. So let the soil temperature cool down a bit if it's been hot and dry.

Plant fall-flowering bulbs as soon as you can get them. These include **autumn crocus** (*Crocus speciosus* and *C. kotschyanus*), and **meadow saffron** (*Colchicum* spp. and hybrids). You may often find *Colchicum* bulbs blooming in the storage bins at garden stores.

To plant bulbs for maximum effect in your landscape, here are some tips:

1. Dig informal planting beds in the shapes of circles, squares, triangle, or irregular shapes that create the effect you desire. Mass displays are much more appealing than bulbs lined up in rows. Prepare an area as wide and long as the intended bulb bed. Reserve the backfill soil nearby.

2. Work compost, about one-third by volume, into the bottom of the bulb bed and then level the bottom of the bed with the back end of a rake.

3. Plant the bulbs, pointed side up, spaced equidistant, or as you prefer.

4. Sprinkle some slow-release granular fertilizer over the backfill soil and mix it in. If the soil is heavy clay or extremely sandy, this is also a good time to add compost.

5. Refill the designated bulb bed, being careful not to disturb the bulbs.

6. Firm the soil gently over the bulbs, and water in thoroughly.

7. Mulch the area with a few inches of pine needles, wood chips, or shredded cedar mulch.

If you have space in the garage, window well, or cold frame, pot some spring-flowering bulbs in pots. Use a good potting mixture and containers that have drainage holes. Depending on the type of bulbs you're forcing, it will take up to 16 weeks of chilling for root growth and dormancy before they will initiate bloom. **Paper-white narcissus** does not require a cold treatment to bloom.

CARE

When digging or planting new bulbs or perennials, be careful not to dig or injure already-planted hardy bulbs. This is why it is important to mark bulb beds with permanent labels.

If an early frost kills back the tops of summer-flowering bulbs, it is time to make plans to dig them and place them in cool storage. Otherwise, treat them as annuals and discard them on the compost pile as you clean up the garden.

WATERING

During prolonged hot, dry periods, water new hardy bulb plantings as the soil dries out. Fall winds and high temperatures can dry the soil out quickly. Dig down underneath the mulch,

---

> ## GARDENING WITH AN ALTITUDE TIPS
> ### Screen Bulbs from Predators
>
> To protect hardy, spring-flowering bulbs from voles and pocket gophers, cover the newly planted bulbs with a heavy mesh screening that will allow the shoots to grow through. Dig a planting bed or trench about 10 inches deep and spread a $1/2$-inch mesh across the bottom and up the sides of the hole. Plant the bulbs at the proper depth and then finally cover the top with more wire mesh screening.

and check to see how the moisture is holding up. If it is beginning to get dry to a depth of 4 inches or more, it's time to set out a sprinkler to water.

FERTILIZING

Fertilizing should be done at the time of planting hardy bulbs. The easiest way is to sprinkle a slow-release granular fertilizer into the backfill soil and then cover the bulbs with the prepared soil. Never let fertilizer touch directly the bulbs as the salts may damage the bulb and impede root development.

GROOMING

Clean up summer-flowering bulbs by cutting off the ripening foliage with scissors. Deadhead faded flowers. Remove dead, fallen leaves that can harbor diseases and insects.

PROBLEMS

Be on the watch for aphids and spider mites that may still be active in the garden. Evaluate the extent of injury and decide if you need to spray them with a soap solution. Otherwise, a good hosing down with a forceful spray of water will do the trick.

Powdery mildew may show up on the foliage. Again, this late in the season, it is generally not warranted to apply a fungicide to control it since the foliage will soon freeze. Discard diseased plant debris so the spores cannot overwinter in the garden.

OCTOBER
BULBS, CORMS, RHIZOMES & TUBERS

 PLANNING

Bulb-planting season continues while the weather remains mild and the ground gets a chill. Plan to try something new. There are so many kinds of **tulips, daffodils,** and the minor bulbs that can brighten areas of the landscape in spring.

If you are planning on overwintering tender summer-flowering bulbs, locate a spot where the temperatures are about 45 to 55 degrees Fahrenheit. An old root cellar would be ideal, but most of us don't have that option. So pick a spot in the basement, a window well that can be insulated, or an attached garage. An old refrigerator that is still in good working order will do nicely, too.

Visit garden centers and stores that are closing out seasonal garden merchandise. This is good time to stock up on potting soil to force bulbs, bulb fertilizer, tools, and other accessories.

Plan an area to "naturalize" with the minor bulbs such as **crocus, winter aconite,** miniature **narcissus, grape hyacinths,** and **glory-of-the-snow.** You might consider planting a slope with these minor bulbs for a real impact and then interplant with a companion ground cover to conserve water.

 PLANTING

As long as the weather permits and the ground is not frozen, continue to plant spring-blooming bulbs. Plant en masse to create more dramatic effects, or if space is limited, dig a trench at the proper depth for the specific bulb and plant a row along the driveway or sidewalk. Bright colors are always a welcoming beacon.

Mix bulb plantings into perennial flower beds or ground covers. You can plant under trees whose shallow roots will not be disturbed by the shallow planting depth. This is a form of naturalizing an area under the canopy of deciduous shade trees.

The key to successful bulb planting is in good soil preparation at the onset. See the chapter introduction for instructions on preparing soil.

 CARE

Once the frost has killed back the tops of **gladiolus** and **dahlias** and other tender bulbs, it's time to dig them up. They can be stored over the winter in a cool spot. Inspect the bulbs, tubers, or corms for signs of disease or insect damage. Discard any that are suspect. Many will have developed offshoots or new bulblets. I prefer to store the entire clump and separate the new segments in the spring.

Shake the excess soil from the bulbs and store in old wooden crates or Styrofoam coolers that are filled with slightly moistened sphagnum peat moss or sawdust. Place in an area where temperatures are between 45 to 55 degrees Fahrenheit. Check monthly for signs of rot (too moist) or shriveling (too dry).

WATERING

When autumn is dry without significant rain or snow, water newly planted bulb beds to ensure good root development.

FERTILIZING

Remember, when planting new bulb beds avoid scattering a fertilizer layer in the bottom of the planting site. Soluble salts will often burn the root tissues as they emerge. Instead, mix a slow-release fertilizer into the soil when planting.

Sprinkle and lightly cultivate granular fertilizer into established bulb plantings. Water in well.

GROOMING

Finish cleaning up old plant debris that may harbor insects, insect eggs and diseases. Discard in the trash. Never add diseased plant refuse to the compost pile, since it generally will not get hot enough to kill the spores.

GARDENING WITH AN ALTITUDE TIPS
Forcing or Coaxing Bulbs to Bloom Indoors

1. Look for bulbs that are labeled good for forcing; there are certain varieties that undergo this process better than others.

2. Choose containers that are good "bulb pots," wide and shallow, 6 to 8 inches deep. Containers should have drainage holes in the bottom.

3. Put a light layer of potting mixture in the bottom of the pot.

4. Set the bulbs in the planting mixture so their tips are even with the rim of the container. Place them shoulder-to-shoulder since it is okay to crowd them at this time.

5. Water the potting mixture thoroughly.

6. Place the planted bulbs in a cool location (40 to 50 degrees Fahrenheit) for several weeks for the roots to develop.

7. Around Thanksgiving, put the pots where the bulbs will experience mild winter temperatures (35 to 40 degrees Fahrenheit) so they will start their dormancy period. An old cellar, unheated garage, outdoor cold frame, insulated window well, or old refrigerator are some good cooling off places.

8. Watch for signs of sprouting within 12 to 16 weeks, depending on the kinds of bulbs you are forcing.

9. When the green sprouts appear, bring the pots out into a cool room where there is bright light so they will think it is spring.

10. When they are ready to open their flowers, bring them to a spot where everyone can enjoy a spring show even though it's winter!

PROBLEMS

Be on the watch for emerging weedy grasses. Many will germinate in the fall. Handpull or hoe out the clumps before they get a stronghold. Pick off seedheads of any weeds that escaped your attention.

NOTES

_____
_____
_____
_____
_____
_____
_____

NOVEMBER
BULBS, CORMS, RHIZOMES, & TUBERS

 PLANNING

Think about planting bulb kits from the garden store. These make nice holiday gifts with a cheerful touch of color to brighten the recipient's home. **Paperwhite narcissus** and **amaryllis** bulbs are generally available at local retailers now. You can pot them up yourself, or some of the bulbs may already be potted with sprouts beginning to emerge. Choose those that are barely sprouting; this way the recipient will have a longer time to enjoy their growth and development.

Holiday cyclamen (*Cyclamen persicum*) are wonderful holiday gifts. This plant grows from a small corm that produces a mass of foliage with flowers resembling orchids or butterflies, thus the common name **poor man's orchid.** It does best in bright light with cool temperatures.

Cyclamen have a delicate fragrance, green or silver-mottled green, heart-shaped leaves, and come in a wide range of colors from white, pink, red, and lilac to salmon. They will bloom for several weeks in a cool environment.

Plan to check any bulbs, corms, tubers, and rhizomes you put in storage, be it the basement, garage, or root cellar. If the storing medium is getting a bit too dry, give it a light misting.

Do not water too much as this can rot them.

 PLANTING

It's getting late to plant hardy bulbs in most parts of the region, except where the soil is not yet frozen. So if you find some last-minute bargains, purchase them and get them planted right away.

Consider potting up bulbs for forcing into bloom in the winter. Use bulb pans or shallow clay pots that have drainage holes. Use a quality potting mixture that is well drained. See information on "forcing bulbs" in October.

If you discover some bulbs that you forgot to plant last month, you still have time to get them in the ground. **Tulips, daffodils, crocus,** and others are better stored by planting them in the ground rather than leaving them in their packages to dry out. As long as the ground is not frozen solid, find an area to plant them. Break through a lightly frosted soil to get into the ground if necessary. Add compost and plant at the proper depths.

 CARE

Most of the fall-blooming bulbs such as *Colchicum* and **Autumn crocus** have completed their bloom cycle. The faded blossoms will have collapsed to the ground and can remain there, as they will decompose rapidly.

Bulb beds that were planted earlier, but were not mulched, should be mulched after the ground freezes. This winter mulch is not intended to prevent the ground from freezing, but it buffers soil temperatures during the winter to minimize the extremes of our fluctuating temperatures. If bulbs experience alternate freezing and thawing, this will often cause shallow-planted bulbs to heave to the surface. Spread an organic mulch to a depth of 2 to 3 inches over the bulb beds. My favorite is pine needles, but choose from ground bark, shredded cedar or aspen mulch, or chopped leaves.

If the fall has been extremely dry without snow or rain, you may need to do some winter watering.

 WATERING

If you have potted bulbs for forcing, be sure to keep the potting mixture moist, not soggy. This goes for **amaryllis** and **paperwhite narcissus.** Paper-whites in moist gravel just need to have the gravel layer kept moist and they will start sprouting. Once the sprouts emerge, move to brighter light, but in a cool location.

When the soil outdoors is not

frozen, check the soil moisture by digging down with a garden trowel. If rain or snow has been scarce, get out the garden hose and water dry areas, particularly the west and south exposures. Use a frog-eye sprinkler early in the day when temperatures are above freezing to allow the water to soak in.

Check bulbs that were potted for forcing and are in cool storage. Poke your finger in the soil to see if the soil is moist or drying out. Water if it feels dry.

Tender bulbs, corms, rhizomes, and tubers that were dug and stored should be checked monthly. Some may need moisture to keep them from shriveling out; this includes **dahlias, begonias,** and **cannas.** Keeping them in a damp sawdust, sphagnum peat moss, or shredded newspaper in ventilated boxes or bags are some methods for successful storage. Other tender bulbs such as **gladiolus, caladium,** and **tuberose,** do best in drier storage. Place them in netted onion sacks or burlap bags and hang them in the basement or garage. If you kept the bulb packages, check the instructions for storage.

 FERTILIZING

No fertilizer is needed during this month.

GARDENING WITH AN ALTITUDE TIPS
Critter-Resistant Bulbs

Although extremely hungry animals may eat almost anything for survival, some bulbs, like **daffodils** and *Colchicum,* are naturally resistant to attacks from chipmunks, squirrels, voles, pocket gophers, and their kin. Here are other choices to try:

- **Common Hyacinth,** *Hyacinth orientalis*
- **Glory-of-the-Snow,** *Chionodoxa*
- **'Tommy Crocus',** *Crocus tommasinianus*
- **Crown Imperial,** *Fritillaria imperialis*
- **Grape Hyacinth,** *Muscari*
- **Grecian Windflower,** *Anemone blanda*
- **Ornamental Onions,** *Allium*
- **Snowflake,** *Leucojum*
- **Striped Squill,** *Puschkinia*
- **Snow Iris,** *Iris reticulata*
- **True Squills,** *Scilla*
- **Winter Aconite,** *Eranthis hiemalis*

 GROOMING

Finish cutting back the dead **lily** stalks that have already ripened. When they are completely dry, these old stalks are easy to pull right out of the ground.

Tidy up the garden if weeds and other plant debris have blown in. Discard these materials to the trash to prevent the dispersion of seeds.

 PROBLEMS

As you examine the tender bulbs you stored away, be on the watch for rot diseases. If some are getting mushy or show signs of mold, discard them. Keep the storing medium slightly moist, never soggy wet. The temperatures in storage should be between 55 to 65 degrees Fahrenheit. If it's too hot, they will start to sprout prematurely.

If you live in an area where meadow mice, voles, and other critters are a problem, mulch bulb beds only after the ground freezes. This will thwart rodents from trying to set up house for winter in the bulb beds. They will find winter quarters somewhere else, like an open field or in the forest.

DECEMBER
BULBS, CORMS, RHIZOMES, & TUBERS

 PLANNING

Catalogs will start arriving this month touting their spring and summer selections. Study them to see which bulbs will work in your area. It's fun to try hardy new bulbs and even unusual summer-flowering kinds like **tuberose.**

Plan holiday gift shopping at your local garden retailers. Buy **paper-white narcissus**, bulb planters, or gift certificates for spring bulbs.

If the weather has been mild, don't be surprised to find **grape hyacinth** foliage emerging. This is normal and often precedes the flowers by several months. It will easily survive the snow.

Look over your garden journal, and make notes for the New Year. Did your bulb plantings do well, or should you make changes?

If you saved articles about new bulbs, see which ones can be grown in your area, and place your orders.

 PLANTING

Still have bulbs sitting around that you forgot to plant in October? If the ground is not frozen solid, plant them outdoors now.

If you can't plant them outside, pot them up in containers, and store them in a cool garage or basement. At least they won't dry out, and some may bloom in their pots. You can then transfer them to a permanent location.

If you received a gift of an **amaryllis** bulb for the holidays, plant it in a clay pot with a good potting mixture, and begin watering it. Keep it moist, not soggy. It may be ready for bloom on Valentine's Day. Follow the instructions that accompany the bulb for timing it to bloom.

 CARE

Do your monthly check of tender bulbs in storage. If some of the tubers or rhizomes are dry or shriveled, give the storing medium a light misting. Maintain them in cool temperatures, but be sure the temperatures do not drop below 35 degrees Fahrenheit.

 WATERING

Moisten the sawdust, sphagnum peat moss or shredded newspaper that tender bulbs were stored in for the winter season. A simple misting will usually freshen the storing medium.

Bulbs potted for forcing will need some moisture even in cold storage. If the potting mixture feels dry to the touch or if the pot feels lighter, give them a drink. Allow the excess water to drain out, and discard water that accumulates in the drainage saucer.

 FERTILIZING

No fertilizer is needed this month.

 PROBLEMS

Mold may develop on bulbs in storage, due to too much moisture. Be sure there is good ventilation and temperatures remain cool.

NOTES

_____
_____
_____
_____
_____
_____
_____
_____
_____
_____

CHAPTER THREE

LAWNS

Our love affair with lush green carpets of grass is as much a part of Americana as apple pie. The lawn is one of the most integral parts of our landscape, yet it can be the most challenging to maintain. A healthy lawn is more resistant to insect pests, diseases, weeds, drought, and everyday foot traffic. So now is the time to discover new ways to keep your lawn healthy and attractive without consuming all your free time.

Begin with the overall design of the lawn. One of the best ways to reduce maintenance is to minimize lawn size, but don't get rid of the lawn entirely. Lawn grasses serve both aesthetic and practical purposes as a soothing and attractive ground cover and open space for recreation.

Design the lawn so it doesn't encompass trees and shrubs to eliminate the time-consuming task of clipping around trunks and stems. This also prevents a manmade disease called "lawnmower-itis," the nicks and cuts to plants caused by the mower blade and weed trimmers.

When establishing a lawn, be sure to select a grass that is right for your region as well as your landscape and lifestyle. Hybrid bluegrass is often the best choice for a home lawn. Local sod growers produce high quality sod, usually composed of five or more cultivated varieties of bluegrass.

Other cool-season grasses to consider include turf-type tall fescue and perennial ryegrass. Both have advantages and disadvantages. Warm-season grasses that can be planted as lawns include buffalograss and blue grama. Seed germination is best when temperatures are between 70 to 90 degrees with optimum growth occurring between 80 to 95 degrees.

Buffalograss (*Buchloe dactyloides*) is a true sod-forming grass that grows 6 inches tall, can be left unmowed, and can be maintained on 1 to $1^3/4$ inches of water every two to three weeks during the summer. It is a low-maintenance, water-thrifty grass and ground cover. It is green to grayish-green only between May and October, and a handsome straw color at other times of the

GARDENING WITH AN ALTITUDE TIPS
Winter Watering Guidelines

- Water every five to six weeks during a dry winter to ensure the survival of your lawn.
- Water when air temperatures are above freezing and the soil is not frozen.
- Apply water early in the day so it will have time to soak in before possible freezing at night. Heavy ice coatings can mat and suffocate grasses.
- Use a sprinkler that delivers water in a low-arc (such as a frog-eye or twin-eye sprinkler).
- Move the sprinkler as needed to cover all areas of the lawn. Water each area long enough to apply $1/2$ to 1 inch of water. Sprinklers will vary in rate of water delivery, so place empty tuna or cat food cans in the area covered by the sprinklers, and measure the water depth in the cans every 15 to 20 minutes. This will give you a gauge of how much water is being delivered to your lawn.

year. Buffalograss does not tolerate shade or heavy traffic. If overwatered or overfertilized, it will thin, and weeds will invade. It is not recommended for elevations above 6,500 feet. As it grows, it spreads runners and stolons which will require periodic edging along driveways, sidewalks, and shrub and flower beds. Buffalograss can be planted from seed, sod, or plugs. 'Vegetative' cultivars available as sod or plugs include '609', '315', 'Highlight', 'Buffalawn', and 'Prairie'. Other varieties can be planted from seed and include 'Plains', 'Topgun', 'Bison', and 'Sharp's Improved'.

Blue grama (*Bouteloua gracilis*) is a clump-forming grass that grows 10 to 16 inches tall. It is very drought-tolerant and needs little fertilizer or mowing. Left unmowed, it can grow to 15 inches and produce attractive seedheads. Blue grama cannot tolerate high-traffic or shady areas. It does not perform well above 6,500 feet in elevation. In native stands, it grows with buffalograss in short and mid-grass prairies. I recommend combining the two in landscape uses.

Wheatgrasses (*Agropyron* spp.), including crested, western, thickspike, and streambank wheatgrass, are coarse-textured and bunch-type grasses that are adapted to tolerate precipitation as low as 10 inches per year. This makes them well suited for a water-thrifty landscape. During dry spells, wheatgrass goes dormant, but makes a rapid recovery when moisture returns. It is a cool-season bunchgrass recommended for dryland lawns.

Smooth Brome (*Bromus inermis*) is a cold- and drought-tolerant pasture grass with wide leaf blades. It greens up in early spring, needs minimal water, and requires little fertilizer. When maintained as a lawn, it loses some of its density. Smooth brome can be used alone or combined with crested or western wheatgrass for soil erosion control, a water-thrifty lawn, or a mountain lawn. Available cultivars include 'Bromar', 'Lincoln', and 'Manchar'.

MOW WISELY

How you mow a lawn can make a big difference in the health and appearance of grass plants. If grasses are cut too low, a practice commonly called "scalping," this predisposes lawns to bug and weed invasion and more disease problems. Make sure never to cut more than one-third of the grass height. During the heat of summer, allow the grass to grow to about $2^1/2$ or 3 inches in height. Taller grass plants will have a deeper root system and require less water. Longer, thicker leaf blades help to cool the soil and shade out unwanted weeds.

Mulch your grass clippings. This saves time when mowing, and allowing the clippings to lie where they fall will add valuable nutrients to soil. You'll save on fertilizer if you allow clippings to naturally decompose. This also stimulates biological activity in the soil. See section on "Grass cycling."

AERATION AND THATCH

Just like other living organisms, lawn grasses need air to breathe. Earthworms (night crawlers included), while not often considered significant, are actually a lawn's best friends. As they burrow in and out of the soil underfoot, they create tunnels through which air can circulate to promote healthy root growth.

Lawns treated with pesticides and other chemicals will have fewer earthworms and other beneficial organisms, so the soil becomes more compacted, inviting pests and diseases. This increases water usage, and a buildup of thatch will often result.

Thatch is a dense, spongy collection of living and dead grass stems and roots lying between the soil surface and the green grass blades in established lawns. It originates from old stems, stolons (above-ground stems), roots, and rhizomes (below-ground stems) shed by the grass plants as new plants grow. Unlike grass clippings, which generally decay quickly, thatch contains high levels of lignin and decays very slowly, collecting on the soil surface faster than it can decompose. A shallow layer of thatch (less than $1/2$ inch) is okay and actually benefits the lawn. It works as a mulch by retaining moisture and insulating the soil from temperature extremes. It also feeds worms and other beneficial organisms and acts as a natural cushion that enables the lawn to endure wear and tear.

Unfortunately, thatch can become a thick destructive layer, affecting the health, vigor, and appearance of your lawn. Thatch causes such problems when it exceeds $1/2$ inch in thickness. The grass develops roots within the thatch layer where it is unable to obtain adequate moisture and nutrients. Too much thatch provides a habitat for destructive insects and diseases.

To remove or reduce thatch buildup, use a mechanical aerator that removes cores of soil from the ground. Core-aeration should be done in the spring and fall. These cores or plugs are deposited on the lawn and contain microorganisms that help break down the thatch layer. If you prefer, you can rake up the cores and put them in the compost pile. The holes left from aeration will allow air, water and nutrients to reach the growing root system of the lawn.

To prevent thatch problems, use pesticides sparingly for spot-treating specific pest problems. This will minimize the destruction of earthworms and other thatch-decomposers. Fertilize your lawn properly, and be sure to avoid applying excessive amounts of nitrogen.

PROVIDING NUTRIENTS TO YOUR LAWN

In the quest for the greenest lawn in the neighborhood, homeowners generally rely on fast-release chemical lawn foods—only to find that grass plants become more disease-prone and that thatch accumulates faster. Chemical fertilizers will temporarily cause quick growth but will often result in weak and shallow root growth. After prolonged use, the soil's natural humus and nutrient holding capacity is depleted.

Switching to organic and organic-based lawn fertilizers will produce a healthier lawn with long-lasting color. Organic fertilizers are formulated to release nitrogen to the turfgrasses at a slower rate. This "spoon-feeding" avoids the growth surge that occurs when fast-release chemical fertilizers are used. When applied at the proper rates, organic turf fertilizers will provide long-term, acceptable color without stimulating excessive top growth. This also reduces the frequency of mowing.

WEED CONTROL

Let's face it—weeds are one of the main reasons we dislike lawn care. Most of us are easily convinced to use weed killers when weeds rear their heads in our lawns. However, healthy natural maintenance is the secret to a weed-free lawn. If grass plants are growing vigorously and thick, with deep roots, proper watering, and natural nutrients, weeds will stand little chance to compete for space.

Should a weed appear here and there, try pulling it out by hand first or digging it out with an old-fashioned dandelion digger. It's easiest to dig weeds after a good watering or rain. The soil is soft, and you can pull up more of the weed's roots along with the top growth.

If perennial weeds persist, use a herbicide. Spot-treat the weedy areas rather than treating the entire lawn. Be certain to know what kind of herbicide you're using. Read the label and follow the instructions to the letter.

Be sure you understand the selectivity and persistence of the herbicide you choose for lawn weed control. Some products are pre-emergent to control broadleaf weed seeds before they germinate. Once applied and watered in, they kill seeds such as dandelion, spurge, oxalis, clover, and others. Annual grassy weed preventers are used to control crabgrass, foxtail, goosegrass, and barnyard grass.

Post-emergent weed killers are applied to weeds already sprouted and growing in the lawn. Broadleaf weed controls that contain 2,4-D amine are safer than the ester forms and can be applied as a spot-treatment to eliminate dandelions, thistle, bindweed, spurge, and knotweed. Broadleaf herbicides will not harm most cool- and warm-season lawn grasses when applied according to label directions.

It is important to avoid contact or drift of herbicides to sensitive non-target plants including trees, shrubs, perennial flowers and ground covers. Soil types, moisture, temperature, and organic matter content will influence microbial activity and the rate at which most herbicides are broken down.

Weed seeds can remain in the soil and maintain viability for years, awaiting proper conditions for germination. When controlling weeds "the cowboy way" or through mechanical means, try to get them while they're still young. With weed killers, always remember to read the label.

It may take some extra thought and time, and perhaps a little more money, to convert your lawn care to a more natural approach, but the effort is a wise expenditure. You and the environment will benefit. You'll still have a great looking lawn that's healthy, and it will be safe for children, pets and wildlife.

GRASS CYCLING—LET THOSE CLIPPINGS REMAIN ON THE LAWN

Lawn mowing comes around all too regularly, and once you've mowed, there are the grass clippings to get rid of—bagging and dragging the heavy plastic bags of messy, stinky clippings away to the curb for pickup.

What if you could mow without creating and clipping waste? What if the grass clippings could return valuable nutrients back to the lawn and reduce the need for adding fertilizer? These thoughts are no longer dreams of the weekend gardener.

Lawn care specialists have been studying the process of returning grass clippings to the lawn. It is now a valid concept to recycle nutrients from the cut grass blades. Instead of the tedious task of gathering the clippings in a bagger, the mower just spits them back onto the lawn surface.

Necessity has propelled this turfgrass research. Many municipal landfills can no longer accept bags upon bags of grass clippings. Where recycling programs are in place to pick up lawn and garden waste, grass clippings present a heavy and cumbersome part of the pickup process. So reducing this by "grass cycling" makes economic and ecological sense.

The first key to successful grass cycling is to cut the lawn often. That way, smaller pieces of grass are scattered evenly. If your lawn brushes your knees as you mow, it is not a good candidate for grass cycling.

Mow often enough so that you remove about $1/2$ inch of grass blade each time, cutting off about $1/3$ of the total grass blade. This may mean mowing on a more regular schedule, every four to five days during times of rapid grass growth. Just think, if you don't have to deal with a heavy bag of clippings, the mowing process will go much faster. And mow when the lawn is dry; wet grass clippings won't scatter as readily. Keep the mower blades sharp, too! Dull lawn mower blades won't scatter the clippings as well as sharp ones.

Grass clippings contain about 90 percent water, and the small pieces decompose quickly, returning nutrients to the soil. Contrary to many people's beliefs, grass cycling done properly does not contribute to thatch buildup.

Older lawn mowers can be adapted to grass cycling. If you have a rotary mower, you can remove the bag. Some lawn mower dealers offer a special mulching blade to better chop and distribute the clippings. With a reel-type mower, just take off the catcher. If you are thinking about purchasing a new mower in the near future, consider a mulching mower.

Remember, properly done, grass cycling is a win-win situation. The mowing takes less time, waste disposal is reduced, and your lawn will thrive.

WATERING AND FEEDING YOUR LAWN

Watering and fertilizing practices help to maintain a healthy and carefree lawn. Apply slow-release fertilizers that are formulated for our region. Most of the national brands contain no or very little sulfur and iron, essential nutrients for the alkaline soil conditions in our region.

I prefer to apply fertilizer twice a year, first around Labor Day and second around Halloween. These are the most beneficial times to supply your lawn with nutrients for winter survival and early greenup. You can then skip the early spring application, but if you want to apply additional fertilizer, apply one around Easter, another around Memorial Day, and again around July 4th. Do not fertilize during the extreme heat of summer. Water the lawn correctly after fertilizing, as directed on the fertilizer label.

Plan for winter watering as necessary. Cool-season lawn grasses including hybrid Kentucky bluegrasses, turf-type fescue and ryegrass, are prone to winter damage when there is a lack of available moisture. Newly established lawns, whether seeded or sodded, are particularly prone to "winter kill" during dry winter weather. Susceptibility to damage increases with lawns growing on south or west exposures.

JANUARY
LAWNS

 PLANNING

You normally wouldn't be thinking lawns now, but during these quiet times, it's good to evaluate why you have a lawn, how manageable it is, and what kind of grass or mixtures of grass you have in your lawn. If your lawn has become a "pain in the grass," now is the time to think about making changes. Use the questions in the chapter introduction to help decide which turf is best for you.

This is a good time to have your lawn mower blade sharpened during the slow period at local hardware and fix-it shops. Be sure the gasoline is drained from gas-powered engines, the oil has been changed, and the spark plug has been replaced, if needed.

Consider investing in a new lawn mower to replace an older model; maybe you can upgrade to a mulching mower that recycles the grass clippings. If you want to be more ecological, consider a push mower or battery-rechargeable electric mower.

 PLANTING

This is not the time of year to plant lawn seed. You can, however, prepare the soil in areas where new seed or sod needs to be replaced. On warmer, mild days, get outdoors and add compost or well-composted manure to the soil. Snowfall will help settle in the prepared areas and the soil will be ready for planting in March.

 CARE

Some areas of the region are fortunate to have a blanket of protective snow covering the lawns during the winter months; this not only protects the crowns of the grass plants, but also helps to sustain moisture in the soil. There may be one disadvantage in the high country from constant snow accumulations, however: meadow mice and moles. These pests may decide to make runs under the protection of the snow, leaving you to discover serpentine runs throughout the lawn come spring. This can be remedied by core-aeration and fertilizing so the grass plants will fill the areas back in.

Cool-season grasses are vulnerable to drying out from winter sun and winds, even though the top growth is dormant. As long as we can keep the crown and roots alive, the grass will return in the spring. During extended dry periods, and when the ground is not frozen, get out the garden hose and frog-eye sprinkler for winter watering. Apply water when temperatures are above freezing (45 to 50 degrees Fahrenheit), early in the day, so the water can soak into the soil.

During the dry days of winter and during extended periods of warm, winter days, tiny grass mites may start to invade lawns in the shadow of evergreen trees. The south or southwest exposure of large **spruce** and **pine** trees are most susceptible to mite damage. Mites prefer the warm exposures and will suck the plant juices from the crown of the grass plants.

 WATERING

Even though **turfgrasses** are dormant at this time of year, they may need attention to moisture availability in the subsoil. If snow or rain is scarce for over a month, I recommend that you pick a warm, mild day for "winter watering." Hot, windy, dry exposures can dry out quickly, thereby exposing the crown of the grass plants to desiccation. Additionally, the root system will begin to dry out, resulting in the so-called "winter kill. "

Winter watering is accomplished by choosing a mild, winter day when temperatures are above freezing (45 to 50 degrees Fahrenheit) and applying water to areas where the ground in not frozen solid. You **do not** have to turn on your automatic sprinkler system to water, since you had it "winterized" last fall. Bring out the garden hose and a frog-eye sprinkler to spot-water areas that are most vulnerable to drying out. Water each section 10 to 15 minutes, or to the point of runoff, and then move the sprinkler to the next area or zone.

Water early enough in the day to permit the water to percolate into the subsoil so the roots can use it. Remember to disconnect the garden hose, drain, and store in the garage or garden shed. Winter watering can be done every four to five weeks, depending upon weather conditions.

FERTILIZING

There is no point in fertilizing dormant lawns now. If you fertilized in the autumn, a granular, slow-release fertilizer will last for many weeks over the autumn and kick back into gear in the spring.

MOWING

Relax. No mowing this month!

PROBLEMS

Check for grass mites by rubbing the palm of your hand over the exposed grass. If you hand turns a brownish or reddish color, mites are invading that portion of the lawn. Mites can also be detected by examining the leaf blades up close and personal to find the tiny moving dots.

The best control is to "winter water" those areas since this will discourage mites from causing extensive damage. A homemade soap spray will also work to eliminate mites in addition to the application of water. See page 283 for homemade soap spray recipe.

NOTES

_____
_____
_____
_____
_____
_____
_____
_____
_____
_____
_____
_____
_____
_____
_____
_____
_____
_____
_____
_____
_____
_____
_____
_____
_____
_____
_____
_____
_____
_____
_____
_____

FEBRUARY

LAWNS

PLANNING

If you didn't have a chance to get your lawn mower tuned up, now is a good time to do so. Your local lawn-care equipment service center is likely to have more time now than in early spring when everybody else gets the same idea.

For the handy man: sharpen the lawn mower blade, clean the undercarriage, and replace the spark plug. Change the oil and replace the old air filter with a new one. Your mower will be in top running condition when the time comes to use it.

Check your lawn fertilizer spreader. Is it still in good shape or is it rusting out? It may be time to purchase a new one. If your spreader is in good condition, it is helpful to calibrate it ahead of time so you know that you are applying the correct amount of fertilizer come spring.

Most cool-season lawn grasses need one pound of actual nitrogen per 1,000 square feet, per fertilizer application. Measure your lawn to get an accurate number of the pounds of lawn fertilizer you will need. To do this, add a zero to the nitrogen number (first number in the fertilizer analysis). Divide this number into 1,000. The resulting answer will be the number of pounds to apply to 1,000 square feet.

PLANTING

Delay the planting of seed or sod until soil begins to thaw and gradually warm up. Temperatures during the day should stay consistently at 55 to 60 degrees Fahrenheit for the best results with overseeding or installing new sod.

CARE

Take precautions to avoid walking over the lawn if it is frosted or snow-covered. New grass blades are vulnerable to damage from foot traffic, as the ice crystals on the leaf blades tear away membranes when they are crushed. This will leave noticeable footprints in the lawn. Snow-packed areas result in compaction around the growing crowns and may promote snow mold diseases.

Keep de-icing salts off lawn areas, as they will kill spots in the lawn and nearby flower beds and shrub borders. Use non-salt alternatives on sidewalks, driveways, and patios to avoid harmful salt accumulations.

WATERING

Even though the majority of the lawn remains dormant, there may be some areas that are beginning to awaken. The lawn will still need some moisture if rainfall and snow are in short supply. If there has been no rain or snow for more than a month and the ground is not frozen, winter watering is necessary. See January recommendations.

FERTILIZING

It's still too early to apply lawn fertilizer. Wait until the soil begins to warm up. Remember, the fertilizer you applied in autumn still has some residual and will provide nutrients slowly and steadily to help the lawn start off in the spring.

MOWING

Although there's no mowing in February, this is a good time to make sure your mower is in shape and ready to go. Refer to your owner's manual for maintenance intstructions. Check the spark plug and any working belts. If you haven't already drained the fuel tank, do so, and make sure it is clear of debris.

Change the oil. Use care when removing and sharpening the blade. Check for wear, and if necessary, order replacement parts now. Later when the grass is growing, you won't have to wait for parts shipment, and your mower will start easily when you need it.

 PROBLEMS

A disease known as **snow mold** is common in higher elevations where snow cover is prolonged and accumulative. As the snow becomes compacted, this disease may attack **bent grass** or **bluegrass.** After the spring thaw, patches of dead grass may be evident. Symptoms appear as a white or gray fungus or matting, or dead grass that is slightly pink in color.

Snow mold is best prevented rather than cured. In the autumn, prepare vulnerable areas by core-aeration to break through heavy thatch layers; hand rake matted accumulations of dead grass. Avoid the application of high-nitrogen lawn fertilizers in the late season and mow the lawn.

GARDENING WITH AN ALTITUDE TIPS
Lawnmower Maintenance

• Remove and replace the old spark plug.
• Uncover the engine or dust it off with an air compressor, and clean any accumulated gunk and packed grass clippings from the mower deck and engine parts.
• If you didn't drain the gas in the tank after the last mowing in fall, **drain it** now. Leave the tank empty so you can tip the mower on its side to service the mower blade.
• Disconnect the spark plug. Remove the blade for sharpening. Re-install it, or install a new sharp blade.
• Replace the fuel filter; clean or replace the air filter
• Drain last year's oil from the crankcase (in 4-cycle engines) and refill with fresh oil.
• Fill the gas tank with fresh gasoline (oil and gas mix if it is a 2-cycle engine).
• Reconnect the new spark plug.

Mow to a height of 1 1/2 to 2 inches. During the winter, avoid walking on snow-covered lawns and don't pile the snow into huge mountains in the shaded areas. The disease is usually not fatal; lawns will recover with time by good management practices.

NOTES

_____
_____
_____
_____
_____
_____
_____
_____
_____
_____
_____

MARCH
LAWNS

PLANNING

Your lawn is still dormant in the shady areas. In sunny, open areas the lawn may be under drought stress. As weather conditions begin to warm up and spring showers arrive, the lawn will awaken and begin to turn green. If you haven't already given your lawn mower its annual maintenance, now is the time.

PLANTING

As the weather warms up and sod growers begin their harvest, you can begin to install new sod. Just be sure to have the soil prepared at the site of new sod installation. A minimum of 3 cubic yards of organic matter per 1,000 square feet should be added to "fill dirt" to build a good soil for deep and healthy root growth. You can add up to 5 cubic yards of organic matter per 1,000 square feet if your budget allows.

If you plan on seeding your lawn, control weeds prior to seeding by cultivation or spraying the area with a non-selective herbicide such as glyphosate or glufosinate-ammonium. Read and follow label directions.

Once the soil is amended with organic matter, scatter and scratch in some granular starter fertilizer such as 18-46-0. Follow label directions. Smooth the planting area, then seed or sod. Lightly press the seed with the back end of the rake to make sure the seed is in contact with the soil.

Water seeded and sodded lawns daily if spring rains are scarce and infrequent. This is where an automatic sprinkler system is time saving and worth the money. The seedbed must be kept moist to ensure uniform germination.

CARE

When the soil underfoot becomes unfrozen and there is adequate moisture, you can begin to core-aerate the lawn. This will breathe new life into the lawn by allowing water, air, and nutrients to become more available to the grass plants. A good aeration will also break through thatch layers and help microorganisms begin the process of breaking down heavy thatch layers. **Do not power rake lawns that are beginning to green up.**

If your lawn is chronically invaded by annual weeds such as crabgrass, goosegrass, or downy bromegrass, now is the time to plan on applying a pre-emergent herbicide. Wait until the forsythia shrubs begin to bud and bloom as a time line for applying the pre-emergent.

Pre-emergent herbicides kill weed seeds as they begin to germinate. An environmentally friendly pre-emergent is made from corn gluten. I highly recommend this for the bird- and wildlife-friendly landscape. As the corn gluten breaks down, it also adds fertilizer to the lawn. It is very useful to place underneath bird feeders to prevent the germination of wasted bird seed that falls at the base of the bird feeder.

Remember, pre-emergent herbicides do not distinguish between "good" and "bad" seeds. Do not apply to areas where you intend to overseed with lawn grasses or other ground cover plants. It takes several weeks for the pre-emergent to become ineffective. Read and follow the label directions on the herbicide package prior to application. Do not core-aerate the lawn after applying the pre-emergent.

 WATERING

If the spring is dry with extended drought periods, you will need to water your lawn so it can start growing. This is the time to encourage deep root growth while the soil is cool. Water deeply, but infrequently. Usually once a week is adequate. Apply 1 inch of water per week when rainfall or snow is lacking.

Keep new sod and seeded areas moist for a period of 20 days to ensure strong and healthy establishment. Check with your local water provider for updates on water restrictions and apply for a watering permit if you need to for establishing either a new seed or sod lawn.

 FERTILIZING

If you applied an autumn fertilizer in October, it is still too early to fertilize the lawn.

If you have chronic problems with iron chlorosis (lack of available iron in our alkaline soils) in your **turfgrass**, apply fertilizers with chelated iron or a separate form of chelated iron at the manufacturer's recommendations. Iron sources will stain concrete sidewalks, driveways, siding, and other stone surfaces. Sweep it off any of these surfaces **before** watering it in.

 MOWING

In all but the warmest areas of Idaho, **turfgrasses** are still somewhat dormant and do not need mowing for a few more weeks. However, if your lawn or parts that are in warmer exposures are starting to grow, a light mowing is needed before the grass grows to 3 inches or more. This will remove the frayed leaf blades, tidying up the lawn and stimulating new growth.

 PROBLEMS

Be on the watch for the germination of annual weeds that may have been missed by pre-emergent applications. Winter annuals including the mustard family, kochia, and cheatgrass may have already invaded bare spots in your lawn. Deal with them the "Cowboy Way," that is, handpulling or digging when the soil is moist. You can spot-treat weedy areas with an appropriate herbicide; try to avoid routine weed and feed combinations or broad applications of weed killers over the entire lawn.

Dandelions are beautiful and invite honeybees, and I rather like them. They make a mean and tasty Italian salad or dandelion wine. To you, however, dandelions may be just another weed. Resolve to dig them out before they form their characteristic fuzzy seedheads and proliferate like tiny parachutes.

NOTES

_____
_____
_____
_____
_____
_____
_____
_____
_____
_____
_____
_____
_____
_____
_____
_____
_____
_____
_____
_____

APRIL
LAWNS

PLANNING

It's easy to let things slide, and before you know it, the lawn season has snuck up on you. Don't let the grass get too tall; plan to mow before it grows 3 inches or more.

If thin spots need overseeding, you still have time to get this accomplished. Have compost ready to add to bare soil and build a healthy soil foundation for good germination. If you prefer, check with sod growers to see if they have sod available to patch bare spots.

Take time to check your lawn for problems that may arise with the arrival of spring weather. Lawn mites can still be a problem and should be treated to avoid dead spots. In dry, windy exposures, have the hose and frog-eye sprinkler ready to spot-water the dry spots.

Plan to control weeds in warm-season grasses before they start to green up.

PLANTING

Sow new grass seed or install **sod** as it is becoming more available. Cooler weather is ideal for establishing new lawns. If there is weed competition, spray or cultivate the weeds prior to seeding or sodding. You will need to allow one to two weeks for effective weed control prior to seeding or sodding, so plan accordingly. Don't procrastinate.

CARE

You still have time to core-aerate your lawn, both cool- and warm-season grasses. Make sure there is moisture in the soil so the aerator will remove deep plugs.

Continue to monitor weeds that pop up here and there. **Handpick** or **handpull** weeds when they are young before their roots anchor down deeply. It's easiest after a rain or lawn watering when the soil is moist.

For the most difficult and persistent perennial weeds such as field bindweed and Canada thistle, spot-treat with 2,4-D amine (a non-ester form) that won't create fumes to harm other desirable plants. It will not harm lawn grasses. Add a couple of teaspoons of Murphy's Oil Soap to the spray mixture to make the herbicide stick to the foliage.

Spray when temperatures are 60 degrees or above. This will allow the herbicide to move into the plant and get to the root of the problem. You may need to reapply after two to three weeks, depending upon the stubbornness of the weed. Read and follow label directions.

WATERING

If spring rainfall is infrequent or scarce, it is critical to keep newly seeded and sodded lawns watered. Frequent light sprinklings on newly seeded lawns will help them germinate. Sodded lawns need to be soaked good daily for the first two weeks. Following these guidelines will make your lawn develop a vigorous, deep root system that will endure even during short drought periods.

Water the edges of newly installed sod since it tends to dry out quickly. I like to spread a top-dressing of compost along the edges of new sod to help reduce the drying out and wicking effect of the freshly cut sod. In a few weeks the sod should be anchoring and knitting together before the onset of hot weather.

FERTILIZING

If you applied a slow-release lawn fertilizer in October, there is no need to do so yet. You can apply pre-emergent weed controls if warranted for problem annual weeds. Read and follow label directions.

If you want to encourage a more lush and greener lawn earlier in the spring, you can apply fertilizer around Easter. Just remember, you will have to start watering and mowing earlier when growth kicks in.

MOWING

It's lawn-mowing season this month to keep the lawn looking in top shape. Set the mower blade at about 2 inches for the first cut, then raise it to cut at $2^1/_2$ to 3 inches as the weather warms. The length of the grass blades correlates to deeper root growth, and shades the soil to keep weed seeds from germinating.

Mow the lawn when it is dry to obtain a more uniform cut. Dry clippings will fall into the turf rather than mat together in clumps. This also reduces the chances for disease organisms from infecting the grass.

Mow with a sharp mower blade. Dull or nicked blades bruise the grass foliage allowing a larger surface area for fungal diseases to enter the plant. Frayed leaf tips will also dry out faster giving the lawn a yellowish-brown cast.

Don't allow the grass to get so tall that you're mowing a hayfield. I recommend that you mow one-third of the leaf blades at each mowing to maintain a clean, healthy cut. Cutting more than this often stresses the grass plants and leaves a yellowish cast. Spring lawn growth is fast, so expect to mow more frequently than you would in summer. Growth will slow down later in the season as temperatures warm.

PROBLEMS

Check for an accumulation of thatch in your lawn. Lawns that are three to five years old may develop a thatch layer due to certain management practices (over fertilizing, high nitrogen, poor drainage, compacted soils, poor microorganism activity, sloughing off of old leaf blades, etc.). A thin layer of thatch is normal, but as it accumulates it will eventually threaten the lawn by reducing water percolation through the soil. Thatch harbors certain fungal diseases and prevents oxygen from getting to the root system.

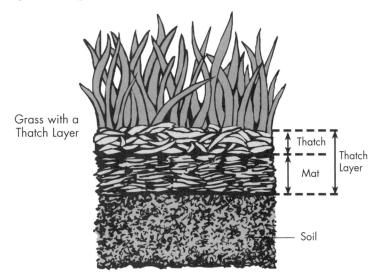

Grass with a Thatch Layer

Thatch

Mat

Thatch Layer

Soil

MAY
LAWNS

PLANNING

If you've just moved into a new home without a lawn, sodding will provide an instant living carpet in the shortest time compared to seeding or planting grass sprigs. This is an excellent time to install sod, so make plans before ordering sod. Sodding, like any other lawn planting, requires planning. Take time to prepare the soil in advance since this is your one chance to have it done properly.

Research to find out what kind of grass will fit your gardening style. You can obtain an updated list of **turfgrass** varieties from your local sod grower. When planting **bluegrass,** select a blend of several varieties to take advantage of the varying degrees of disease- and drought-resistance in each one.

Plan to take a soil sample in advance to test for pH and fertility levels. The soil test will indicate how much fertilizer, if any, needs to be applied before planting. It will also indicate the level of organic matter and make recommendations on adding soil amendments. See the chapter introduction for information regarding preparing the soil before planting.

PLANTING

Before planting or installing sod:

Spread a 2- to 3-inch layer of compost or rotted manure; use a minimum of 3 cubic yards per 1,000 square feet. You can add up to 5 cubic yards if your budget allows and it will form a deeper foundation when mixed with your native soil. This promotes a deeper and more drought-tolerant lawn with fewer disease problems.

Rototill or disc the soil to a depth of 4 to 8 inches and thoroughly mix the organic amendments into the native or existing "fill dirt." You generally don't have to bring in topsoil, but use what you already have.

Right before laying the sod, **broadcast** a starter fertilize such as 18-46-0 and lightly rake in.

Lay the sod in a brickwork pattern, staggering the sod sections to make a nice tight fit. I like to spread a layer of compost around the edges of new sod to prevent it from drying out. Check with your local sod supplier for information leaflets that provide complete instructions on sod installation and care tips.

You still have a window of opportunity to overseed thin or bare spots before the weather turns hot. Keep the seeded areas moist by frequent sprinkling. Light waterings three to four times a day should get the new seed to germinate.

CARE

As the days are advancing toward summer, it is still okay to aerate your lawn if you didn't get it done earlier. Water the lawn the day before you run the aerator over it. The goal is to remove deep cores to break through soil compaction and create channels for water to soak in and nutrients to become more available to the roots.

If you inherited a bad lawn, **top-dress** it with compost **after aeration**. This will allow the organic amendments to filter down into the soil and increase microbial activity and stimulate root growth which will make the lawn grow thicker. A thick, dense turf will discourage weed invasion.

 WATERING

Continue to water sod daily for the first few weeks after installation to ensure healthy rooting. After two weeks, start weaning the turf by watering it every three to four days. It is best to check for soil moisture by probing the turf with a long screwdriver or garden trowel. This will help you gauge your particular watering schedule.

We can't always depend on natural rainfall, so set your automatic sprinkler for cyclic or interval watering. See the chapter introduction for more watering information.

Established lawns that were planted on a good soil foundation can go five to seven days without rain or watering if the soil underfoot was well prepared and not compacted.

 FERTILIZING

If you have not applied a fertilizer since last September (around Labor Day), choose a regional fertilizer with iron and sulfur, and one that has fast-acting (water-soluble) nitrogen for a more rapid greenup and get the grass jump-started. The other components of the fertilizer should have a larger portion of slow-acting nitrogen to maintain uniform, consistent nutrients over many weeks. This allows the lawn to grow the way Nature intended. Read and follow label directions for application rates. Use a good spreader or check your own and calibrate it if needed.

Following a holiday schedule for fertilizing, I typically apply the first spring lawn fertilizer around the end of May or Memorial Day.

 MOWING

Mow your lawn regularly and frequently during the spring as growth is more rapid. Cool-season grasses should be mowed to a height of $2^1/2$ to 3 inches, while warmer-season grasses can be cut shorter. Be sure that the mower blade is sharp for a clean cut that reduces fraying the leaf blades.

 PROBLEMS

Sod webworms may become a problem in lawns. Watch for blackbirds feeding in your lawn. Large flocks may be doing their job of consuming large quantities of sod webworms or army worms. If this is the case, there is no need to apply insecticides, just let Nature take its course.

Thinning lawns may be the result of lawn mites, particularly on the south and west exposures. Pay a little more attention to watering these areas and the grass should recover.

Be on the watch for new ant mounds since it is time for them to swarm and start new colonies. Ants normally nest at the edges of the lawn or around sidewalks, pavement or stones. From there, they venture out into the lawn on pest control, so most are beneficial. If ants become a nuisance, discourage them by digging out their nesting site or pouring boiling water over the nests as they reappear. This will make them move elsewhere.

Weeds will continue to have growth spurts in cooler weather. Stay on top of the situation by pulling them out or spot-treating as needed. Get them before they go to seed.

NOTES

_____
_____
_____
_____
_____
_____
_____

JUNE
LAWNS

 PLANNING

If you normally collect and bag lawn clippings after each mowing, plan to recycle your grass clippings as you mow. If you mow frequently enough, recycled grass clippings can contribute slow-acting fertilizer to the lawn. Grass clippings contain up to 4 percent nitrogen, $1/2$ to 1 percent phosphorus, 2 to 3 percent potassium, and smaller amounts of other essential nutrients. So why waste this valuable fertilizer source?

 PLANTING

Patch bare spots in the lawn caused by wear and tear or by weed invasions. Cut pieces of sod from the edges of the lawn or that which has crept into flower or shrub beds and reinstall to the bare spots. Keep the newly planted sod sections moist daily for a week or more to ensure that they root in. It is helpful to prepare the soil where bare spots appear so that the new sod pieces will be able to root in more quickly during the heat of summer. See May for tips on preparing the soil. If you are not facing water restrictions, you still have time to install sod. Follow the guidelines of your local sod grower.

 CARE

If you have improved the soil, the **turfgrass** will need less maintenance than you might expect during the summer months. A well-developed and deep root system will support nutrients and hold moisture.

Continue to keep your lawn growing thick to prevent the invasion of weeds. In compacted areas where there is more foot traffic, you can spot-aerate with a hand aerator to break through the soil compaction. This will permit water to soak in and introduce air to the ailing root system. Upon completion of aeration, **top-dress** with a fine compost, and water the areas thoroughly to prevent these regions from drying out.

Later in the dog days of summer, cool-season grasses such as **bluegrass** will naturally acclimate to drought conditions by going dormant. The green will diminish, but this does not indicate that your lawn is dead. To help cool-season grasses cope during drought periods, encourage them to grow deep roots with good management practices. Use slow-release fertilizers instead of quick-acting types. Core aerate in the spring and autumn. Water deeply and infrequently. Keep weeds at bay.

 WATERING

If we've been experiencing continued drought years, with lack of winter and spring moisture, it is critical to begin a deep, infrequent watering regimen while the weather is still somewhat cool. This will maintain a deep, healthy, and more drought enduring root system.

Water established lawns in good soil only when it has not rained for a week to 10 days. Then when you do water, water deeply to sustain the roots. Lawns that are growing in poor soil conditions tend to dry out sooner.

Keep new sod watered until it is established. You may need to purchase a watering permit, but consider the investment and value of the lawn. Spot-water the edges of the new sod to prevent it from curling up and drying out.

Have your automatic sprinkler system checked to make sure it is delivering water properly and efficiently. Remember, plants don't waste water, people do.

FERTILIZING

If you used a fast-acting, water-soluble fertilizer in the spring, it may be necessary to repeat another application before June is over. I generally wait until the first part of July (July 4th) to make the second fertilizer application.

Nitrogen needs to be available to grass as it continues to grow with cooler weather. As the temperatures get higher, slow-acting fertilizers are best. These will provide nutrients over a more extended period, four to six weeks, depending upon the product. Read the package label.

Never fertilize a lawn that is already stressed by drought or heat. This will only add insult to injury.

Skip the fast-acting, so-called "miracle fixes." Wait until the weather turns cooler and moisture returns, and then apply a slow-acting fertilizer. Read and follow label directions on the fertilizer product.

MOWING

As the spring growth spurt will begin to stall with the onset of hotter weather, your lawn will generally need less frequent mowing. It will depend on the vigor it developed earlier in the season to sustain hot, dry periods.

You will generally be mowing less often this month, unless natural rainfall is abundant. Recycle grass clippings if possible. If you collect clippings, mix them into the compost pile.

Make sure your lawn mower blade is sharp; have a spare in the garage to change periodically. Keep the mowing height for cool season grasses at $2^1/2$ to 3 inches so the lawn will not brown out in the summer heat.

Alter mowing patterns to minimize soil compaction and wear on the turf. Mow in horizontal rows one week, in vertical rows the next, and in diagonal rows the third week. It will give your lawn a professional look.

PROBLEMS

Be on the watch for white grubs in the lawn. Many will migrate closer to the surface from the deep soil where they spent the winter months. They will begin to feed on the grass roots. Symptoms of grub damage can be detected if you can peel the grass back like a carpet. Tiny C-shaped white grubs can be noticed. A healthy lawn can tolerate a fair number of grubs and the lawn will soon recover because stolons and rhizomes will fill in the damaged areas. However, if grub populations are severe, you may need to treat the lawn with a grub-control insecticide.

For the environmentally friendly lawn care provider: try using a biological grub control that consists of predatory nematodes or milky spore (*Bacillus popilliae*), a bacterium that targets soil-dwelling beetle larvae. These biological controls provide relatively long-term control. Follow directions on the label carefully for application techniques and frequency of use.

NOTES

_____
_____
_____
_____
_____
_____
_____
_____
_____
_____
_____
_____
_____

July
LAWNS

PLANNING

If you are planning a summer getaway, have someone mow you lawn if you'll be away for a week or more. Although the lawn is growing slower now, it will tend to look neglected after seven days and will reveal that no one is home.

It's convenient and time saving if you have an automatic sprinkler system to water your lawn wisely and efficiently. Get bids for installing one later in the season. Modern equipment eliminates the need for trenching, as a sprinkler system can be pulled under the sod and sprinkler heads installed as needed for designated zones.

If you have been plagued by disease and insect problems in your lawn over the years, plan a long-term strategy to combat these problems. Begin to investigate what the underlying causes might be so you can prevent them before they appear. It may be as simple as poor soil conditions, soil compaction, the wrong turf variety for the area, and buried debris underneath the turf. All these cause stress to lawn grasses, making them more susceptible to problems.

Consider having a professional turf expert evaluate your lawn and make suggestions. It will save you time, money, and effort in the future. Keep a lawn care journal or notebook to help you track your lawn care practices and what kinds of materials you are applying.

PLANTING

Heat and drought will be the enemy of many cool-season grasses this month. This is not a good time to seed unless you live in the higher elevations where temperatures are still somewhat cool and there is regular precipitation. Wait till late summer or early fall and seed as soon as the weather begins to cool down.

Buy sod if you need to patch bare spots to prevent weed invasions. Water newly installed sod well and as often as needed to allow the roots to take hold. Spot-watering is usually acceptable, even if you are under water restrictions. If not, consider using gray water to keep the newly sodded areas moist for establishment.

CARE

Continue to mow the lawn every seven to 10 days, or as needed. This is a good time to sharpen your lawn mower blade again or to switch it out with a new one.

Leave the grass clippings on the lawn when you mow (unless you have waited too long and the grass clippings are so abundant that they clump together). Mulching mowers will cut the grass clippings fine enough that they will filter down into the soil and decompose.

To minimize soil compaction during the heat of summer avoid heavy traffic on the lawn. Grass is more likely to be stressed in the heat of summer, so **do not aerate, do not apply fast-release fertilizers, and avoid using weed killers** while the lawn deals with heat and possible drought periods.

WATERING

Water cool-season grasses such as **bluegrass, fescue,** and **ryegrass** every five to seven days if it does not rain. To encourage grass plants to root down deeply and develop drought endurance, **water deeply**, soaking the soil to a depth of 4 inches or more.

Then don't water for three to six days. Compacted or clay soils may require a pause between watering sessions to allow the water to percolate into the soil and to prevent runoff.

Only in sandy soils do you need to water more frequently, but set the sprinkler for shorter durations. Even sandy soils will compact and will benefit from cyclic watering.

Resist the temptation to lightly sprinkle the grass daily just because it feels good to you. This encourages the grass roots to grow shallow and they dry out more quickly.

FERTILIZING

The first part of July (around July 4th) is a good time for the second application of a slow-release lawn fertilizer.

Let the clippings fall where they may when mowing. Over the growing season, their accumulated nitrogen can provide 25 percent of the annual nitrogen needed by the **turfgrass.** The clippings will also break down into organic matter that helps to improve the soil over a long-term basis.

MOWING

Continue to mow often enough to remove one-third of the leaf blade each time. Keep the mower blade set at $2^1/2$ to 3 inches to help grass plants withstand the heat and possible extended drought conditions.

Warm-season grasses including **bentgrass, zoysia**, and **buffalograss** can be maintained at 1 to 2 inches tall.

PROBLEMS

Weeds are opportunistic and will continue to pop up when there are bare spots in the lawn. You can **spot-spray** the tough perennial weeds with a herbicide as needed. Shield nearby desirable plants to avoid herbicide drift. Place a plastic milk jug with the bottom cut out over the offending weed and spray through the top opening. A **homemade vinegar weed spray** (see page 286) will work for spot-treatment and is effective on young weeds.

If you see lots of small moths fluttering around in your lawn, this may indicate the presence of sod webworms. They are laying eggs that will soon hatch into larvae (caterpillars). Birds can be helpful in controlling these pests. If infestations are severe, consult a professional for soil insecticide treatments. Otherwise, a few sod webworms can be tolerated in most vigorously growing lawns.

Watch for the onset of powdery mildew in shady regions of your lawn. Increase air circulation by pruning low-lying branches from trees to allow more light penetration. You can overseed with mildew-resistant turf varieties.

See the homemade remedies section on page 283 for recipes for the baking soda remedy and vinegar weed spray.

NOTES

_____
_____
_____
_____
_____
_____
_____
_____
_____
_____
_____
_____
_____
_____
_____
_____
_____
_____
_____
_____
_____

AUGUST

LAWNS

PLANNING

This is one of my favorite months, as temperatures begin to cool down and the yard is returning to its glory. The entire landscape is maturing with subtle colors, textures, and form.

If we have been experiencing extended drought conditions, it's a good time to learn more about "naturescaping" or "xeriscaping," the latter meaning "dry landscaping." Both these landscape concepts combine water conservation with my Italian grandmother's common-sense gardening techniques. She would recycle the dishwashing water for watering plants if needed and the bathwater to give the garden a drink, and she would build a healthy soil with well-aged manure. See the chapter introduction for more water conservation tips.

Inspect your lawn regularly to identify problem spots. This will help you plan your fall strategy for making repairs or planting a new lawn. The earlier you can identify problems and prepare, the more time the lawn will have to get established before the hard frost in November. Cool-season lawn grasses do best as the weather cools down and will grow vigorous and healthy root systems to survive the winter.

PLANTING

As the end of the month arrives, you can start seeding. It's a good time to overseed lawns thinning due to drought stress or weed invasions. Since weeds are tapering down their activity now, it's an ideal time to seed a lawn or patch bare spots. This is an excellent time to patch areas using sod.

With less weed competition, the grass can get a head start and grow thickly before winter. **Kentucky bluegrass, turf-type fescue,** and **ryegrass** can be seeded starting in mid- to late August. Prepare the soil ahead of time to create a good soil foundation for vigorous, strong, healthy root growth. See the chapter introduction regarding soil preparation.

CARE

If during the heat of summer your cool-season grasses such as **Kentucky bluegrass** have gone dormant, do not fear. It is perfectly natural for cool-season grasses to deal with the heat and water deprivation by turning brown, or shutting down the top growth. Instead of pumping more water to the lawn, allow the lawn to do its natural thing.

Warm-season **turfgrasses** will do just fine, but will require periodic watering to survive and look good. They are genetically equipped to handle the heat and drought better, though their leaf texture may be a bit more rough.

Check for insect pests that may be residing in the soil. Heavy bird activity in the yard may be an indication of larvae of sod webworms or grubs. Let the birds do their thing and consume massive quantities of grubs.

WATERING

Continue to water newly planted or sodded lawns if there is no significant rainfall for 10 days or more. You will note drought stress by a bluish-gray tinge and curled leaf blades throughout the lawn. This means it is time to water. Prolonged drought can kill clump grasses including **turf-type fescue** and **perennial ryegrass**.

Water deeply, but try to extend the waiting period to conserve water and make the turf tougher. The soil underfoot will determine how long grass can go between waterings. In a well-prepared soil, grass plants will have developed deep roots that can capture water deeper in the subsoil, thus being capable of surviving drought. In poor soils, grass roots have no choice but to grow near the surface and will dry out quickly.

FERTILIZING

Delay fertilizing cool-season grasses until the first part of September (around Labor Day). If you are growing warm-season grasses, you can apply one last fertilizer application by mid-August. After that, warm-season grasses will begin to go dormant with the arrival of cool weather and will not benefit from fertilizer.

MOWING

Continue to mow both cool- and warm-season **turfgrasses** as needed. Remember the rule of mowing one-third of the leaf blade at each mowing. Avoid scalping (mowing too short) the lawn as this will stress the grass and cause it to dry out even faster. Leave the grass clippings as previously discussed.

PROBLEMS

Eliminate weeds early in the month if you plan to reseed or sod a new lawn in early September. It will take two to three weeks to get rid of the most stubborn weeds, roots and all. Use a herbicide that contains glyphosate since this targets all weeds, but allows you to plant within a few weeks after application.

One way to sample areas of the lawn for soil insects is to mix 2 to 3 tablespoons of liquid detergent in 1 gallon of warm water. Pour this solution over a 1- to 2-square-foot area. The detergent will irritate soil-inhabiting insects and drive them to the surface. If there are more than five caterpillars per square foot, it may be necessary to treat the lawn with an appropriate soil insecticide. Keep the pets and birds off the lawn if you decide to treat with an insecticide. Read and follow label directions carefully.

NOTES

_____
_____
_____
_____
_____
_____
_____
_____
_____
_____
_____
_____
_____
_____
_____
_____
_____
_____
_____
_____
_____
_____
_____
_____
_____
_____
_____

SEPTEMBER
LAWNS

PLANNING

This is a wonderful month for cool-season grasses as they display their full potential and emerald green color against the beauty of a cobalt blue sky. Cool nights and warm days make it ideal to plan on re-seeding bare spots, plugging in new sod if needed, or starting a new lawn from seed or sod. Plan to have any seeding complete by late September to insure good germination and root establishment before the ground freezes. Adjust planting times according to your specific elevation and growing season.

Before you plant, add your organic amendment (a minimum of 3 cubic yards of organic amendment per 1,000 square feet); rototill or disk to a depth of 4 to 6 inches. This is the time to plan to upgrade or amend lousy soils with a quality organic amendment such as sphagnum peat moss or compost.

If you haven't started a garden journal or notebook, this would be a good time to start one. Keeping a record of your lawn maintenance program, fertilizing schedule, watering frequency, mowing practices, lawn mower servicing, and the type of grass you're growing will provide important information for future lawn care or remind you to make changes when growth is not satisfactory.

PLANTING

This is the best time to seed a new lawn or overseed thin, bare spots in cool-season lawns. It is too late to plant warm-season grasses, unless you intend to do a dormant seeding.

Spot-treat weeds 10 to 14 days ahead of seeding. If the weeds are going to seed, snip off seedheads to prevent their dispersal throughout the yard and garden. Leave the foliage intact so you can spray the leaves with an appropriate herbicide. Read and follow label directions carefully.

Plant a **premium lawn seed** with a hand or mechanical spreader onto the prepared soil.

If you like, cover the seedbed with clean wheat straw or a thin layer of sphagnum peat moss ($1/8$ to $1/4$ -inch). This will help conserve water and hasten germination. See the chapter introduction for more on planting.

Install sod for an instant lawn or to replace bare spots. See the chapter introduction for instructions for sod planting.

CARE

If your lawn experienced heavy foot traffic over the summer, this is a great time to **core-aerate** your lawn prior to the application of lawn fertilizer.

After core-aeration, **top-dress** your lawn with pulverized or fine compost that will filter down into the soil through the holes created from aeration. This will also encourage microbial activity to help decompose thatch.

You may leave the cores left from aeration and they will eventually break down by irrigation and rainfall. If you wish, you can rake up the plugs and recycle to the compost pile. Mowing the cores will dull your lawn mower blade, so remember to sharpen the blade after core-aeration.

WATERING

Water established lawns deeply and infrequently when rainfall is scarce. I usually water the lawn once a week during the fall months. This will encourage strong root and rhizome growth of cool-season grasses such as **Kentucky bluegrass.** Test for soil moisture by probing the soil with a heavy-duty screwdriver or garden trowel. When the soil is moist to a depth of 4 inches, you don't need to water. If the soil is beginning to dry out, give the lawn a deep watering.

Keep newly seeded areas continuously moist to insure healthy establishment. As sprouts grow into seedlings, water deeply, but less often, to encourage the roots to grow downward for drought endurance.

FERTILIZING

For your cool-season grasses, apply a complete lawn fertilizer that contains iron and sulfur the first of the month (around Labor Day). This will be the first of the autumn lawn fertilizer applications. It is helpful to core-aerate the lawn prior to putting down the fertilizer. **Water** the lawn after the fertilizer is applied.

MOWING

Continue to mow cool-season grasses at $2^1/2$ to 3 inches. Be sure the blade is sharp.

When you mow the lawn in autumn, use a mulching mower that will finely cut the grass blades. The finely cut leaf fragments will filter down between the grass blades to decompose and enrich the soil. You are, in effect, mulching the grass plants,

just as you would other landscape plants to conserve water and keep the soil cool. If you collect clippings, put them in the compost pile. Be sure the clippings are not contaminated with weed seeds or pesticide residues.

PROBLEMS

Powdery mildew can continue to be a problem in shady areas of your lawn. You can overseed those spots with grass varieties that are mildew-resistant. This will reduce the problem in future years. Treat powdery mildew with the homemade remedy on page 285 if you desire.

Broadleaf and grassy weeds continue to grow until a hard frost. Take advantage of the warm days to spot-treat with an appropriate herbicide. Read and follow label directions. Controlling weeds in the autumn gives you a head start on next season. By all means take time to pick the seedheads off maturing weeds, put them in a big plastic bag and dispose. Don't let weed seeds disperse everywhere this fall.

White grubs may continue to damage lawns in the early fall. You will notice dead patches appearing throughout the lawn

or at the edges of sidewalks or driveways. Flocks of black birds feeding on the lawn generally indicate that soil insects are present. Even skunks will find grubs a food source and will dig holes in the lawn seeking these delectable morsels. As long as the soil temperatures remain in the 65-to 75-degree range, you can treat grub problems. Grubs begin to migrate deeper in the soil below the frost line to overwinter. A long-term biological approach to managing grubs and larvae in the soil is with milky disease, a naturally occurring bacterium (*Bacillus popilliae*). It will infect many types of beetle grubs including white grubs.

NOTES

_____
_____
_____
_____
_____
_____
_____
_____
_____
_____
_____

OCTOBER

LAWNS

PLANNING

In October, established cool-season lawns are taking advantage of the cooler weather to store energy from the leaf blades to the root system. Cool-season grasses including **Kentucky bluegrass, turf-type fescue,** and **perennial ryegrass** perform at their best in autumn. Soil temperatures are ideal for vigorous root growth, and rhizome root systems are making the lawn grow thicker. If you seeded or sodded a lawn in September, plan to maintain uniform moisture to ensure the grass plants are deeply rooted before the ground freezes.

PLANTING

It is getting too late to plant new grass seed. You can try dormant seeding, but remember that birds, other critters, and the wind may be factors that will affect successful germination. Dormant-seeded lawns in areas without snow cover are exposed to winter winds, strong sunlight, and drought.

Soil conditions are ideal for sodding. Sod a new lawn, or patch up bare spots with pieces of new sod to fill in the thin areas. Remember to prepare the soil prior to laying down new sod. A good soil foundation is the key to a healthy and drought enduring lawn.

CARE

Keep new grass seedlings thriving by regular watering. This is the time the plants need to establish a vigorous, strong root system to survive the winter.

Rake or blow excessive amounts of fallen leaves from newly seeded lawns so the grass plants receive proper light, water, and air movement. **Don't apply lime** to the lawn if your soil is alkaline. This can aggravate the soil and make nutrients less available. If you are not certain what the pH of your subsoil is, have the soil tested first.

Older lawns will benefit from top-dressing with organic matter to condition the soil. Core-aerate the lawn prior to applying the topdressing.

WATERING

When there is a lack of fall rainfall, continue to water lawns every seven to 10 days, or as determined by moisture in the soil. Newly seeded or sodded lawns need particular attention to proper watering until the ground freezes solid.

FERTILIZING

Apply your second application of fall fertilizer in late October (around Halloween). This fertilization is very important while the grass is still green and growing roots. This application will last throughout the fall and provide slow-release nutrients so that you will not have to apply an early application in the spring. If weather permits, a third application can be made around Thanksgiving.

MOWING

In warmer areas, lawn mowing will continue until the grass begins to go dormant. Do not scalp, or mow the lawn too short. Lawn grasses that are cut too short are more subject to wind desiccation and the soil will dry out more rapidly. Keep the mowing height at $2^1/2$ to 3-inches to encourage good root growth.

Toward the end of leaf-fall, when the layers of leaves become thinner, mow the lawn and leaves with a mulching mower. This will chop the leaves into finer fragments that will fall between the grass blades and mulch the soil for the winter.

PROBLEMS

Keep watching for white grubs.

NOVEMBER

LAWNS

PLANNING

If you have worked on improving your lawn by spring and fall aeration, the grass plants will start to fill in and grow a stronger root system, establishing a more drought-enduring lawn.

- Evaluate the size of your lawn and its function in your landscape. You can reduce lawn maintenance by reducing the size of your yard. Consider removing grass from sloped areas and creating a rock garden.
- Identify areas where lawn grasses perform poorly. Heavily shaded areas are not the best sites for thick turf. Consider replacing grass under trees with groundcovers or mulch.

Ideas to reduce lawn care are:
- Widen the areas around shrub borders or around perennial flower beds.

If you've always wanted a deck, gazebo, or patio; plan on building one to replace turf areas.
- Construct a dog run so the dogs have their own space.
- If you have children or grandchildren, create a play area with a swing set or playhouse.
- If your budget allows, install a swimming pool?
- Widen walkways or pathways to eliminate large turf areas.
- Place a ring of organic mulch under trees to avoid thinning **turf grasses** and prevent mower damage to the bark.

- Create a water garden or water feature in your landscape. Re-circulating water is a common-sense way to conserve water. You only need to add water occasionally to keep the water garden functional.

PLANTING

It is too late to seed new lawns or overseed dead patches.

CARE

If the soil remains unfrozen and you have established a good soil foundation, you can still install sod. As long as sod growers are cutting and delivering sod, you can lay it until the ground freezes solid.

WATERING

If there is little or no rainfall or snow, water newly seeded or sodded lawns. The grass plants need to develop a deep root system before the ground freezes. If you reside in the high country, you can usually depend on the snow cover during the winter months to protect the grass, and you will not have to worry about "winter watering."

FERTILIZING

There is no need to fertilize now. You should have applied the two fall feedings already; one around Labor Day and the second around Halloween. If weather permits, a third application can be made at Thanksgiving.

 MOWING

Continue to mow the lawn if needed. Even though grass growth is slower, a light mowing will keep the turf looking neat and healthy. Alternate your mowing patterns to reduce soil compaction. Mow in horizontal rows one week, in vertical rows the next and then diagonally.

PROBLEMS

Field bindweed, Canada thistle, and dandelions are just a few perennial weeds that persist. Spot-treat with an appropriate herbicide. Read and follow label directions.

The homemade **"Weed Buster"** that contains vinegar is an environmentally safe topical weed killer. See page 286 for information. Otherwise, hand-pulling or digging will help reduce the weeds.

DECEMBER
LAWNS

 PLANNING

In many years, a properly maintained cool-season lawn will still be green in December. If there hasn't been any snow yet, plan on winter watering. As long as the ground remains unfrozen, the subsoil needs moisture to sustain the grasses' root system.

If you have had problems with warm-season weedy grasses such as **crabgrass** and **bermudagrass** invading your lawn, these warm-loving grasses will be visible as drying out brown patches. Plan to dig them out, removing as much of the root system as possible. You can also note these areas and plan to control them next spring. Perennial bermudagrass can be sprayed with a nonselective herbicide when it begins to leaf out next year.

 PLANTING

Did you know that you can lay sod in limited areas where the ground is not frozen? I installed a lawn in mid-December and it rooted in very nicely and cut down on dust and mud throughout the winter season.

Remember, you can install sod as long as sod growers are harvesting it and your soil has been prepared prior to laying it down (see the chapter introduction for more information).

Keep new sod watered during open dry periods to keep the pruned roots alive. They will start to grow and anchor down when soil temperatures begin to warm up a bit. Sod is an amazing grouping of living plants with great resiliency.

 CARE

Dormant lawn grasses need minimal care in the winter. Remember to provide moisture on the open, warm days when there has been little or no snowfall and the ground is not frozen.

 WATERING

Water established lawns and particularly newly seeded or sodded lawns during extended dry periods of winter. Winter watering should be done when temperatures are above freezing and the soil is unfrozen. Water early in the day with a frog-eye sprinkler so the water can percolate down to the subsoil where the roots can utilize it.

 FERTILIZING

Relax this month. No need to fertilize.

 **MOWING**

No more mowing this year!

 PROBLEMS

Look for annual weeds that are dead now and pick off any seedheads before they get a chance to disperse. Place the seedheads in a large plastic bag and dispose. I recommend that you do the same if perennial weeds have produced visible seedheads.

De-icing salts to melt snow and ice accumulations on the sidewalk and driveway are harmful to most lawn grasses. The runoff from sodium-based de-icing products or the spray from city snow removal plows may end up on your nearby lawn. When this dissolves and enters the soil, it is harmful to the grass roots, causing the plant cells to die.

Flood turf areas that you know have been contaminated with salt de-icers. This will leach out the harmful sodium and percolate it down into the soil below the actively growing roots. Use non-salt de-icing products to melt snow and ice. Consider kitty litter, coarse sand, or wood ashes on your sidewalks and driveways.

CHAPTER FOUR

PERENNIALS

If you pine for flowers with attributes of permanence in your garden, plant perennials—the plants that return year after year. The word perennial comes from Latin, meaning "enduring" or "perpetual"—a plant that will survive for several growing seasons. Although the top portion of many herbaceous perennials will die back in winter, their roots remain alive, and the plants will awaken when conditions are suitable for growth (unless your perennial acts like a "perannual" and refuses to survive cold winters and fluctuating climatic conditions).

Perennials offer gardeners tremendous variety in color, height, bloom time, shape, size, flower form and foliage color. Don't be intimidated by the vast numbers of varieties. Start with tried-and-true plants to build your gardening confidence. Later you can branch out into some of the more exotic offerings.

Perennials tend to have fairly short blooming times, so if you want a garden that flowers from spring through fall, choose plants that will succeed each other in blooming times.

Signs of life all over the perennial garden will awaken your spirits as little green shoots and buds emerge in spring. Some perennials remain evergreen all year round. Some, like the

GARDENING WITH AN ALTITUDE TIPS
Perennials for Idaho

- Artemisia, *Artemisia* spp. and hybrids
- Aster, *Aster* spp. and hybrids
- Blanket Flower, *Gaillardia* x *grandiflora*
- Blazing Star, *Liatris spicata*
- Bleeding Heart, *Dicentra spectabilis*
- Blue False Indigo, *Baptisia australis*
- Butterfly Weed, *Asclepias tuberosa*
- Chiming Bells, *Mertensia ciliata*
- Coneflower, *Rudbeckia* spp.
- Coral Bells, *Heuchera* spp. and hybrids
- Coreopsis, *Coreopsis* spp.
- Daylily, *Hemerocallis* hybrids
- Evening Primrose, *Oenothera macrocarpa*
- Gentian, *Gentiana* spp.
- Goldenrod, *Solidago* spp. and hybrids
- Hardy Chrysanthemum, *Chrysanthemum* x *grandiflorum*
- Hardy Geranium, *Geranium* spp.
- Hosta, *Hosta* spp. and hybrids
- Hyssop, *Agastache* spp.
- Japanese Anemone, *Anemone* x *hybrida*
- Joe-Pye Weed, *Eupatorium purpureum*
- Lamb's Ears, *Stachys byzantina*
- Lenten Rose, *Helleborus orientalis*
- Lupine, *Lupinus* spp. and hybrids
- Oriental Poppy, *Papaver orientale*
- Penstemon, *Penstemon* spp. and hybrids
- Peony, *Paeonia lactiflora* and hybrids
- Perennial Flax, *Linum perenne*
- Perennial Salvia, *Salvia* x *superba*
- Purple Coneflower, *Echinacea purpurea*
- Rocky Mountain Columbine, *Aquilegia caerulea* and hybrids
- Russian Sage *Perovskia atriplicifolia*
- Sedum 'Autumn Joy' *Sedum* 'Autumn Joy'
- Shasta Daisy *Leucanthemum* x *superbum*
- Siberian Iris *Iris sibirica*
- Sneezeweed *Helenium autumnale*
- Sweet William *Dianthus barbatus*
- Veronica *Veronica spicata*

hellebores, will brave the cold days of winter with a show of unique blooms.

Part of the pleasure of gardening with perennials comes from orchestrating a garden for all-season color and interest and planning seasonal flower and foliage combinations. Attractive leaves will develop the charm and texture of a well-planned perennial garden and become the unifying ribbon that ties the garden together.

Perennials are a hardy bunch and will grow in a wide range of conditions. It's a good thing that perennials are so adaptive, because we have such diverse conditions. We are blessed with quality sunshine and low humidity in our region, so we can grow perennials without the high incidence of plant diseases that often plagues more humid parts of the United States. Perennials are generally long-lived and adapt to our various soil types, and they have few insect pests and diseases when planted in the right location and if properly maintained. The secret to growing perennials successfully is having the right soil for the right plant. Soil preparation is especially important since perennials are meant to remain in one location for years. They may outlive the gardener who plants them! Before planting, get to know a little about the plant, and amend the soil as needed.

When choosing perennials for your landscape, consider what they will look like even when they're not blooming. Many bloom for only a few weeks, but their foliage can be an important element in the garden all season long. Hostas, for example, are grown more for their leaves than for their flowers. Additionally, you are not limited to growing perennials in sunny borders, since there are many perennials that will thrive in partial to full shade. With so many new and interesting plants coming into our region all the time, it's tempting to want to grow one of each. Certain qualities can help you determine which ones will be hardy and reliable in your garden. If you're looking for plants that require the least amount of maintenance, be sure to choose varieties that don't require staking, or site the plants so that other plants will help support them.

Perennial plants are more expensive than annuals, which means that choosing perennials is a financial as well as an aesthetic decision. Since they are expected to be around for a long time, making good choices from the onset of planting makes good sense and cents.

Perennial growers and evaluators apply good standards to determine a plant's superiority, but they cannot take into account the special circumstances that exist in your specific landscape or area. A perennial should be selected for its cold-hardiness in the horticultural zone where you garden. The zone numbers reflect cold-hardiness, but most plants also have a varying heat-hardiness.

GARDENING WITH AN ALTITUDE TIPS

How Many Plants Do You Need?

The following chart will help you determine the number of plants per square foot for a given spacing:

Spacing (inches)	Spacing Multiplier (plants per square ft.)
12	1.00
15	0.64
18	0.44
24	0.25
36	0.11

If you have a bed that measures 48 sq. ft. (8 feet long by 6 feet wide) and you want to plant perennials 15 inches apart, use this equation to find out the number of plants needed for the bed:

Area of the bed x Spacing Multiplier = Total number of plants
(Example: 48 sq. ft. x 0.64 = 31 plants)

Plants that can grow at higher elevations may not be able to handle the summer heat at lower elevations.

Take time to observe plants that have performed exceptionally well for you in the past or in area gardens, those that come back year after year regardless of heat, drought, and soil conditions. Other factors, including disease- and pest-resistance, ease of propagation, multiseason interest, deer-resistance, and low water demand, will be part of the criteria that make specific perennials the most valued for your specific area.

Become familiar with the soil types in your landscape. There are probably places where the soil is less than ideal, such as that close to the house where the contractor piled in "contractor dirt" that contains a variety of debris. Other areas may be too sandy or rocky to grow anything. Take this into account and improve the soil in these areas, or better yet, consider growing perennials in raised beds. This way you can control the soil conditions to fit the specific perennials.

It is easier to adapt the plant to the soil, rather than vice versa. Aim to place the right plant in the right site—that's an important secret to successful gardening in Idaho.

CONSTRUCTING A NEW PERENNIAL BED

Use a sod cutter to remove grass, roots and all. Roll up the sod and remove it. You may grind it up for the compost pile. Dig down into the exposed soil at least 10 to 12 inches, deeper if possible, to create a good soil foundation. Add several inches of compost or sphagnum peat moss to the overturned soil to help clay and sandy soils hold air, improve drainage, retain moisture, and make nutrients more available. Sprinkle starter fertilizer such as 18-46-0 over the newly dug area. Follow the recommendations on the package label. Rototill or plow the organic amendment and fertilizer into the loose soil.

Break up any large, hard clods, and remove debris including stones, roots, and construction waste. Rake the prepared soil smooth and level. Cover the area with a mulch of shredded bark, pine needles, or compost to await the planting season.

CHECK PERENNIALS BEFORE BUYING

Wilted foliage indicates a root problem—probably improperly watered or stressed. Yellow, limp leaves and stems may indicate poor light conditions when growing or insufficient fertilizer. Blotches on the leaves or whitish-gray coating on the foliage indicates possible fungal diseases. Blackened leaf margins is usually a sign of frost damage. The plants can outgrow this, however. Brownish-tan or tiny specks on the leaf undersides may confirm a problem with spider mites or other insect pests. Thin, lanky stems means the plants were grown with insufficient light.

Lots of old flowers on an undersized plant generally means the plant is aged or overfertilized. Roots emerging from the container's drainage holes mean the plant is rootbound and needs transplanting soon. Weeds growing in the container are a sign of a poor growing mixture or lack of care.

KEEPING PERENNIAL BEDS COLORFUL

Choose perennials that bloom in midsummer, late summer, and early fall. Look for the plants that have colorful or variegated foliage. To fill in the empty gaps, plant annuals among perennials for early color. Pansies and violas are good companions for early-blooming bulbs. Choose perennials that are noted for long bloom periods. Check local gardens to see what is blooming. Deadhead faded flowers and stems to promote repeat blooms.

JANUARY
PERENNIALS

PLANNING

Wouldn't it be nice to have a perennial garden that provides color throughout the seasons? Now is the time to plan such a garden. You can even have "winter roses" (**hellebores**) in February. If you have kept a garden notebook or journal, get it out during the dreary, cold days, and evaluate last season's garden. You may have made notes on which plants need to go and other plants you would like to add.

If you've never drawn a perennial garden blueprint, it's not that hard. Just sketch it out on a blank sheet of paper, note the plants you already have, and play around with the plan to revitalize the perennial bed. Consider height, spread, time of bloom, and color combinations that suit your gardening style.

As garden catalogs arrive this month, browse through them to discover new perennials that may have potential in your area. Though the wonderful photographs may not be realistic for how the plants will fare in your garden, information about their cultural requirements will help you determine if you want to try them. Plan to get orders in as early as possible, especially if you want new or unusual perennials. Note the zone hardiness

before making definite plans to order. Some can be very costly, but they must have proven to be hardy in our region.

PLANTING

While it remains too early to plant perennials outdoors, it is not too early to start some from seed. If you have a space and good light, maybe a cold frame, perennials can be started early to assure their germination and give them a head start on the season. Sow those varieties that need 12 to 14 weeks indoors before they can be transplanted outside.

Thoroughly clean any pots or flats for starting seedlings. Unwashed flats or pots can harbor pests and diseases. Sterilize the containers in a 10 percent solution of liquid bleach (one part bleach to 10 parts water). Rinse after 30 minutes or so.

Unlike annuals, most perennials are fussy about their cultural requirements for germination. Follow the label directions carefully to provide proper growing conditions and temperature requirements. Unless you have the time or want to start a new hobby, let the professional growers do the complicated propagation.

Select perennials that will come true from seed. Some perennials are hybrids, so if you have collected seed, you often end up with offspring that will resemble one of their grandparents rather than the hybrid plant. Buy fresh seed of specific varieties you wish to grow and try in your garden.

CARE

Periodically check the outdoor soil conditions in your perennial garden. It's that time of year when temperature fluctuations can cause some perennials to suffer from frost heave. Press soil around heaved plants, and cut off broken or damaged stems. If mulch has blown away from around the base of your perennials, top or renew mulch in those areas. Winter mulching is meant to keep the soil cool and prevent frost heave. If you have leftover evergreen boughs from the holidays, use them to mulch beds. This can provide additional protection to plants with shallow roots.

Inspect for plant damage from rodents in your perennial bed. Walk on pathways where possible.

Avoid excessive de-icing salts on pathways, driveways, and sidewalks. As the salts accumulate in the soil around perennials, they cause harm and kill the roots. Instead, use an inexpensive fertilizer such as ammonium sulfate or wood ashes to de-ice if you must.

 WATERING

If the weather has been unseasonably dry for an extended period, check the soil moisture around your perennials. Pay particular attention to south and southwestern exposures, or those areas that are subject to continual wind. Water on a warm day when temperatures are above freezing. Apply water early in the day so it can percolate down to the root system. Disconnect and drain the garden hose, and return to storage for future "winter watering" as needed.

 FERTILIZING

No fertilizing this month.

 GROOMING

If some of your perennials are beginning to lose their winter interest, it's okay to cut back the dried and broken stems from fall-blooming perennials including **asters, hardy chrysanthemums,** and **goldenrod.** Leave the ornamental grasses stand-

---

GARDENING WITH AN ALTITUDE TIPS
Perennials You Can Start from Seed

There are many perennial flowers that can be started from seed collected in your garden. Here are just a few suggestions:
- **Summer Pastels Yarrow,** *Achillea millefolium* 'Summer Pastels'
- **Shasta Daisies,** *Chrysanthemum x superbum* 'Alaska' and 'Snow Lady'
- **Blue Bouquet Speedwell,** *Veronica spicata* 'Blue Bouquet'
- **Baby Gold Goldenrod,** *Solidago Canadensis* 'Baby Gold'
- *Coreopsis grandiflora* 'Early Sunrise', 'Sunray', and 'Sunburst'
- **Gay Butterflies Butterfly Weed,** *Asclepias x* 'Gay Butterflies'
- **Cardinal Flower,** *Lobelia cardinalis* 'Queen Victoria'

If you plant perennials from seed, here are some tips for success:
- Use a sterilized, soilless potting mixture or seed-starting mix.
- Cover the planted containers or flats with a pane of plexiglass or plastic to maintain humidity around the shallow-sown seeds.
- Don't forget to label the containers with the names of the plants sown.
- Provide the proper temperature regime for the specific variety of perennial.
- Heating cables can be used to provide warm beneath the potting mixture, unless cool temperatures are specified.

---

ing as long as possible. The grass seedheads continue to provide structure and form for winter garden interest.

 PROBLEMS

Be ever vigilant for activity from deer, elk, rabbits, meadow mice, and other critters that may visit your garden. As their food sources may become scarce they will make early morning or evening visits to your garden. Any foliage that remains somewhat green may be vulnerable to nibbling. You can spray the stems and foliage with hot pepper spray (see page 284 for homemade recipe). This will help to temporarily repel critters that like to graze.

FEBRUARY
PERENNIALS

 PLANNING

One of the primary reasons to plant perennials is that they will generally return year after year, that is if the crown and root system survive the winter. Select plants suited for your area.

Most local garden retailers and nurseries will routinely stock perennial plants that are best suited to the local climate, soil, and temperature regimes. Talk to fellow gardeners to find out what grows best for them. They can help provide invaluable advice on which plants have performed well in their gardens over the years. If you decide to order from catalogs, do your research ahead of time. Be sure the plants you want are cold hardy for your part of the region. Otherwise, plan to protect the 'marginally hardy' perennials by mulching or planting in a microclimate.

 PLANTING

You can still plant perennials from seed indoors. If you don't have a space with enough natural light, such as a sun porch or greenhouse, try growing them under artificial lights. Fluorescent lights work well and can be suspended from the ceiling with adjustable cables or chains. This will allow you to keep the light source within inches of the seedlings as they germinate. Lack of light will make plants weak.

Be sure to read the directions on seed packets and follow the guidelines for growing perennials indoors. I like to sow seeds directly into a cold frame and let Nature take its course. The plants seem to be more acclimatized and will transplant with less shock.

As seedlings begin to grow, lower the fluorescent lights to within an inch or two of the sprouts. Provide 14 to 16 hours of daily artificial light if you don't have any natural sunlight.

Do not allow the seedlings to dry out, but on the other hand, don't waterlog the growing mixture. Too much moisture can result in diseases which will kill the seedlings.

 CARE

As the weather permits, it's a good idea to take a walk around the landscape to check out the perennials. Where frost has heaved the soil, make sure the crowns and roots have not been exposed to the drying winds. Replant or reset, if needed, any plants that have been disturbed. If the ground is frozen, pile mulch or evergreen boughs over the plants temporarily. Replace mulch that may have blown off the beds exposing crowns and roots to drying winter winds.

To prevent early perennials from emerging prematurely on extended warm, sunny periods, maintain a layer of mulch over the plants. Winter mulch holds in some of the chill and helps to delay early growth until there is less risk of damage from late freezes and extreme temperature fluctuations.

 WATERING

If your perennial beds have been properly mulched, they are less likely to dry out, but prolonged periods of dry weather can damage crowns and roots. Though dormant, perennials do need moisture.

Dig down to a depth of 4 to 6 inches when the ground is not frozen, and check subsoil moisture. If it is beginning to dry out, get out the garden hose and frog-eye sprinkler for winter watering. Do not overwater native plants and rock garden perennials as this can rot the crowns.

For seedlings growing indoors on the cold frame, remove the plastic covering and let them gradually acclimate to less moisture. When the soil is dry to the touch, either water from the bottom or sprinkle lightly with a mister to avoid damaging the tender seedlings.

Do not overwater as this will often result in damping-off diseases.

FERTILIZING

As the perennial seedlings develop their first set of true leaves (not just the initial small leaves), you can lightly fertilize them. Soilless growing mixtures do not contain much in the way of nutrients, so use a water-soluble plant fertilizer such as 10-15-10. I prefer to apply it at half the strength recommended on the label to avoid burning the tender seedlings.

It is too early to fertilize outside perennials, but you can stock up on slow-release, organic-based fertilizer and other supplies if you find them on sale.

GROOMING

It is always tempting to get outdoors and clean up the perennial garden. Resist the urge, however, as the natural growth and dried stubs help to catch and hold snow cover. This provides needed moisture and a winter mulch.

Pick up dead stems and other debris that may have blown into the perennial bed. Check for signs of the early emerging bulbs like **snow crocus** and *iris reticulata*. Avoid walking on the soil if it is wet, as this will compact the ground and impede the movement of air and water to the roots.

PROBLEMS

Weeds are always opportunistic and will pop up unexpectedly in perennial beds. Be on the watch for the first signs of downy brome or cheat grass. If it appears, handpull or dig it out when the soil is moist. You can also suppress the growth of winter annual weeds by applying a shallow layer of mulch over open areas.

Damping-off diseases can be a problem on seedlings you've started indoors. Cutting back the frequency of watering can control it. Increase the amount of light and provide better air circulation around crowded seedlings. Sometimes it helps to thin seedlings and transplant those you wish to save.

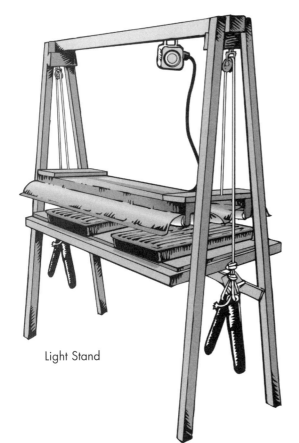

Light Stand

MARCH
PERENNIALS

PLANNING

The **"winter roses," hellebore** or **Lenten rose,** are beginning to bloom. Plan to get outdoors and take in the beauty of your perennial beds. Clean up and oil garden trowels that were not taken care of last fall. Sharpen pruners, or have this done professionally. It is so much easier to prune and clean perennials with sharp tools.

Take advantage of early garden sales for stakes, wire cages, and other support for taller perennials like **delphiniums** or floppy ones like **peonies.**

Stock up on compost, slow-acting fertilizer, and horticultural oil for tackling chores as the weather permits.

Plan to expand or reduce the size of a perennial bed, depending upon your wants and maintenance routine. Consider a raised island bed to reduce the size of the lawn area. Sketch a plan of your proposed garden in a notebook to determine how many plants you will need.

PLANTING

March can be tricky here in Idaho. It can be snowy, cold, dry, windy, or a mixture of all of the above. If it's too muddy to plant, wait until the soil begins to dry out. Never work wet soil, as this will destroy the soil's structure and leave you with lots of hard clay clods. Sandy soils will benefit from the addition of organic matter to retain moisture and make nutrients more available. Test your soil **before digging in** by grabbing a handful of soil and squeezing it. If it crumbles in your hand, it's workable. If water drips when you squeeze or it remains in a sodden ball, wait a week or so before digging.

Perennial seedlings started indoors may need transplanting. If the roots are growing through the drainage holes or the mixture dries out rapidly, it's time to move them. Gently remove the seedlings by tugging on the top set of leaves, not the tender stems. Transplant into a container half full of soilless growing medium, with slow-release fertilizer added. Set each seedling into the new growing mixture at the same level it was growing. Fill in around the seedling with more medium, and lightly press down the growing mixture. Remember, do not plant too

deep. Water and return the transplants to good light.

CARE

Perennials that are established in the garden can cope with Nature's vagaries of spring weather. They have a built-in time clock that will let them know when to awaken. Perennials planted on south or hot exposures may be fooled into growing too soon. Protect them with additional mulch or a light watering to keep the soil cool.

It is inevitable that some perennials will emerge early and start to bloom. If a hard cold snap is predicted, pick some flowers to enjoy indoors.

Late frosts are the norm, but established perennials can usually cope. When a heavy, wet snow is on its way, have 5-gallon buckets or boxes handy to cover the foliage of plants that have already emerged and those that are subject to damage from the weight of snow.

Some perennials you ordered may start arriving via the mail. If the soil is workable and not too wet, go ahead and plant them to their designated homes. Bare-root perennials will transplant easily and root in nicely while conditions are cool.

If conditions are too soggy or cold, store bare-root plants in a cool, dark place so they will stay dormant until actual planting time. Keep the roots slightly moist.

 WATERING

Check the garden soil before watering the perennial bed. March snow and rains can often provide adequate moisture. If, however, we are experiencing a prolonged dry spell, get out the garden hose for spot-watering. Use a frog-eye sprinkler to water dry areas for 10 to 15 minutes. Avoid overwatering native plants and rock garden plants that do best with sharp drainage and thrive on just the natural precipitation.

Keep new perennial seedlings watered as needed, but allow the soilless mix to dry out slightly to harden up the plants. Move the transplants outdoors during the day in a semi-shady spot to help them acclimate if they were started indoors. Bring back inside at night to prevent freezing.

 FERTILIZING

As the soil begins to dry out and perennials start to show signs of growth, you can apply a slow-acting granular fertilizer throughout the perennial bed. A slow-release formula will provide a more consistent, uniform supply of nutrients than a fast-release formula. Some will last for several months. Read and follow label directions.

Lightly fertilize perennial seedlings (use at half-strength) every few weeks. It won't be long they can be transplanted to the garden directly.

 GROOMING

This is the time to begin garden cleanup. Cut back dried grasses, stems and flower heads to tidy up the garden and make way for the new perennial shoots.

 PROBLEMS

Be on the watch for aphids and flea beetles. Check under organic mulches for slugs and their eggs. If you find them, handpick or set traps. See slug remedy on page 285.

Continue to monitor emerging weeds. Pull them by hand or spot-treat with an appropriate herbicide. Read and follow label directions.

NOTES

_____
_____
_____
_____
_____
_____
_____
_____
_____
_____
_____
_____
_____
_____
_____
_____
_____
_____
_____
_____
_____
_____
_____
_____
_____

APRIL
PERENNIALS

 PLANNING

Plan on keeping a watchful eye as your perennials begin to send out their new growth. Some perennials are in such a hurry to grow that they become top-heavy before you know it. Plan what supports you'll need to prevent them from bending or toppling over. I like to use the old-fashioned tomato cages to support the **bleeding heart, catmint**, **peonies, delphinium,** and some of the taller-growing **asters.**

If you plan support before plants get too large, the support structures are easier to install and will soon be hidden by the foliage. You can purchase specially designed peony cages, plastic or bamboo stakes, metal perennial stakes, or, my favorite, tomato cages.

Position stakes so the plants will eventually hide the supports. When securing the stems to the support apparatus, tie with soft twine or plastic in a figure eight to avoid binding the stems.

You may also consider pinching the taller growing perennials to train them to grow more compactly. Pinch or cut back the top growth at least eight weeks before flowering to keep their height within bounds.

 PLANTING

If you haven't already hardened-off the indoor perennial seedlings, get to it. Gradually expose them to outdoor conditions by moving them to a cold frame or unheated porch for at least a week before planting in the garden.

Plant bare-root perennials as soon as they arrive in the mail or when you purchase them locally. It is best to get them in the ground before major growth resumes. This will encourage a strong, healthy root system to support the plant.

When planting ornamental grasses, here's a simple Green Thumb rule for spacing:

Place plants as far apart as their eventual height. For example, grasses that can grow to a height of 3 feet can be planted 3 feet apart from center to center.

 CARE

Mulch newly planted perennials, and renew mulch around established plants as needed.

Pinch or prune back perennials you desire to keep at a specific height. You can pinch back the new growth until the later part of June for fall-bloom-ing perennials to make them grow more compact.

 WATERING

April showers may be sufficient to keep emerging perennials in good shape, but as this may not be the norm, it's often necessary to water the plants as the soil becomes dry. Test the soil with a garden trowel around the root system. When needed, **water deeply** and infrequently to encourage more drought-enduring plants. Newly transplanted perennials will require a bit more attention for the first few weeks to become well established.

 FERTILIZING

If your garden soil is not very fertile with humus or other organic matter, sprinkle slow-acting granular fertilizer around newly emerging and established plants. Avoid the use of quick-release nitrogen, as this will make the plants grow spindly and topple over.

 GROOMING

Pinching is a technique that removes $1/2$- to 1-inch of each growing shoot, up to 2 inches of shoot tips if desired. When you pinch perennials, they will produce more, but smaller flowers than plants that are left untouched.

Pinching is also used to stagger the blooming times of plants, particularly hardy garden **chrysanthemums**. It prevents them from growing too tall and straggly. Experiment pinching different perennials. I like to pinch back **asters, Joe-Pye weed, turtlehead, spike speedwell, 'Autumn Joy' sedum,** and others. You may like the results you can create.

If the young perennials you started indoors are growing too tall, pinch them back, too. Snip or pinch to a node above the second set of leaves. This will stimulate them to develop into more compact plants.

 PROBLEMS

Be on the watch for the hatch of insects. As the weather warms up, overwintering adults will emerge to feed on the new, tender growth of perennials. Insect eggs will hatch as daytime temperatures remain consistently warm. Check for aphids and slugs.

Leaf miners may show up on the foliage of **columbines**. They will leave a serpentine tunnel

GARDENING WITH AN ALTITUDE TIPS
Planting Container-grown Perennials

• Hold your hand over the top of the pot with the plant stems between your fingers. Tip the pot upside down and gently tap the plant (rootball and all) into your hand.

• If the roots have begun to circle the rootball, loosen them with your fingers to encourage growth into the surrounding soil.

• A paring knife can be used to make three shallow cuts into the mass of roots of tightly rootbound perennials. Make shallow slices along the length of the rootball.

• Dig the planting hole two times as wide and the same depth as the rootball.

• Set the plant in the hole so the crown is at or slightly above ground level.

• Cover and firm the soil lightly around the plant.

• Water thoroughly to settle the soil around the roots. Check for moisture every other day, and water as the soil becomes dry to a depth of 4 inches.

• Mulch with a 2- to 3-inch layer of shredded wood shavings, compost, or pine needles to conserve water and suppress weed growth. Do not pile mulch over the crown, as this may invite rodents to nest or feed there.

between the upper and lower leaf surfaces. There can be several generations of larvae and adults. Control of leaf miner is simple: Crush the tiny caterpillars inside the leaf before the foliage becomes too disfigured or by cutting off the infested leaf.

Diseases, including Botrytis blight, may attack **peonies,** causing the buds to mummify, turn black, and not open up. This disease can also attack the crown, stalks, leaves and leaf petioles. Remove and dispose of infected plant parts as soon as you spot symptoms. Early in

the season when temperatures are still low, you can apply sulfur dust as a fungicide treatment. Read and follow label directions.

Continue to pull or dig weeds before they go to seed.

MAY
PERENNIALS

PLANNING

May is the major planting month throughout most parts of the region. Plan on visiting local garden retailers to see the newest varieties and to get the freshest crop. Start with smaller young plants rather than the bigger gallon-sized plants. Smaller plants are not only more economical, but they start out better.

Be patient: Unlike annual flowers, perennials are slower to establish and bloom. It may not be until their second year that they really show off their color and display. If you are impatient, try a few of the larger potted plants to get more immediate results. Choose healthy, vigorous-growing perennial plants, and pass up those that are stunted and yellow.

PLANTING

No matter how healthy a new plant is, unless it is sited properly and planted in soil with good drainage, it will not thrive or perform to expectations. Check plant labels for the proper sun or shade exposure, cold-hardiness rating, and cultural requirements. See *My Rocky Mountain Gardner's Guide* for more complete information on plant selections.

Keep newly purchased plants moist, not soggy, until planting time. Then dig the planting hole two times wider than and as deep as the plant's container. Slip the plant from its pot and set it in the planting hole. Make sure it is at the same depth or slightly higher than ground level. Fill in with prepared backfill soil, firm around the rootball, and water in thoroughly.

Some perennials can be planted in containers and combined with annuals to provide color during the summer. Use a good, soilless growing mixture and add a slow-release granular fertilizer at planting time. There are no guarantees that perennials will survive the winter in containers unless special precautions are taken.

CARE

As established perennials grow and expand, many will send out stem or root runners to form new plants nearby. Some develop into larger clumps as their crowns enlarge and send up more stems. Either way, perennials reach a point when they become too large or woody for their space in a garden bed.

When they begin to crowd out other plants or to die out in the center, it's time to divide and conquer. Divide perennials before or shortly after they bloom; just avoid digging and dividing in the heat of midsummer.

• Simply take a heavy-duty spading fork and lift the clump. For ease in digging and handling, divide perennials when emerging shoots are only a few inches tall.

• Dig under the root system and soil to lift the entire plant out of the ground. Choose a cool, cloudy day when possible.

• Use a sharp knife, garden fork, or sharp flat spade to cut through tough clumps of roots to make rooted divisions.

• Discard the oldest, woody dead centers of older plants.

• Transplant one of the viable rooted divisions into the former planting site, and plant the other divisions elsewhere or share with fellow gardeners.

• Mulch newly planted perennials with a 2- to 3-inch layer of compost, shredded wood chips, or pine needles.

Monitor growth of perennials that may benefit from support, particularly if you live in a windy area. **Delphiniums** and **foxgloves** in my garden are in constant need of support from bamboo stakes or tomato cages. Insert the supports 12 to 14 inches into the soil and place them slightly shorter than the plant's maximum height. They soon will be camouflaged by the foliage, but will protect the plants from wind damage.

Young perennials you started indoors should now be acclimated to the outdoors and can be situated in the garden.

 WATERING

Check perennials weekly for moisture requirements. If the weather has been dry and windy, more frequent watering will be necessary for newly planted perennials. Use mulch to help conserve water, plus suppress weed growth.

Since everyone's soil is different, check the subsoil around your perennials every four to five days. If it is beginning to dry out at that level, give the plants a deep drink of water. Mulched plantings will not have to be watered as frequently.

Some perennials will go dormant after blooming later this month. This is normal for **bleeding heart, Oriental poppies, bluebells,** and other early season bloomers. These are truly the water-thrifty plants to include in your garden where water is of concern. As these plants go dor-

mant for the summer, they surely will return next year. Just don't overwater areas where they are planted.

 FERTILIZING

If you fertilized your perennial garden earlier with a slow-release granular product last month, they do not need any additional fertilizer at this time. Check the fertilizer label for the number of weeks or months the fertilizer will last. Do not overfertilize perennials since this will make them grow lanky and produce fewer blooms.

 GROOMING

As some of your early spring-flowering perennials have finished blooming, deadhead or remove the faded flowers. This will not only improve their appearance, but many perennials will develop new flowering buds. I like to use a hedge trimmer to clip off the faded small flowers from low-growing perennials such as **candytuft, pinks,** and **creeping phlox.** Use a regular hand pruner for larger, faded flowers and woody stems.

 PROBLEMS

If you see ants crawling all over the buds of **peonies,** don't be alarmed. This is a normal occurrence since the ants are seeking and feeding on the sweet nectar secreted by the peony buds. They actually farm the sweet substance and bring it back to the nest for young ants.

Aphids are now in full force on **iris** buds. They will cause the flowers to become distorted or to not open at all. Until their natural predators arrive (lady bird beetles), you can control aphids by pinching off infested plant parts and discarding them in the trash. Homemade soap sprays and insecticidal soaps may prove helpful, too.

NOTES

_____

_____

_____

_____

_____

_____

_____

_____

_____

JUNE
PERENNIALS

 PLANNING

If you haven't started a garden journal, now is the time. Record dates of perennial bloom, how long the flowers last, special cultural requirements, pest and disease problems, and other features. A perennial garden has a relatively short bloom period, though the plants will display foliage for much of the growing season. This is one reason to choose varieties that have attractive foliage to add interest and texture to the garden. By keeping a record of your plant selections, you can determine if you have the right mix of spring-blooming, summer-blooming, and fall-blooming perennials for an all-season display.

 PLANTING

Before the weather turns hot, continue to plant perennials that were grown in containers. Reduce transplant shock by planting on a cool, cloudy day. Perennials that are left in their pots will languish, dry out, and become rootbound.

Also, divide and transplant larger perennials that are outgrowing their space. You can easily divide older perennials by taking root cuttings or dividing the older clump. Try to do this

early in the month to avoid the stress from summer's heat. Otherwise, wait until fall when the temperatures turn cooler.

 CARE

If you haven't added mulch around your perennials, do so before the plants get so full that it becomes a difficult chore. A layer 2 to 3 inches of compost, shredded wood shavings, or pine needles will work nicely. Do not place plastic under the mulch, as this will impede the movement of air and water to the root system. In fact, plastic mulches tend to encourage shallow root growth. If you decide to use artificial mulch, choose a landscape fabric that will allow water, air, and nutrients to get to the roots. However, even fabrics can interfere with the natural propagation process of most perennials.

Support perennials that develop taller stems or large clumps. Waiting too late makes it difficult to set in cages or stakes, and you generally end up breaking stems and flower buds. Train the stems to grow upright early in the season instead of waiting until they begin to flop.

 WATERING

Keep established perennials deeply watered with about an inch of water weekly. Those in sandy soils will need more attention because the soil drains so quickly. Apply organic mulches to help retain moisture and reduce the need for frequent watering. If you mixed a balance of organic matter into the soil at planting time, this will provide better moisture holding capacity, plus support nutrients that the roots can assimilate.

Since everyone's soil is a bit different, check soil moisture to determine your watering schedule. Use a garden trowel to dig down to a depth of 4 inches or more. If the soil is beginning to dry out, give the perennials a deep soaking. During periods of prolonged drought, check soil moisture often, and use mulch to help reduce evaporation and prevent runoff.

 FERTILIZING

If you added a slow-release granular at planting time, this fertilizer will continue to offer nutrients as the plants need them. Check the package label to see how long the fertilizer will last.

Perennials growing in containers will benefit from the application of a soluble plant fertilizer since you are watering the soil mix more often and nutrients will leach out. Follow label directions for dilution rates and frequency of application. Dilute the fertilizer to half strength and apply at every other watering to prevent buildup of soluble salts in the soil.

GROOMING

Continue to pinch back the stretching stems of hardy **chrysanthemums** by half to encourage more branching and a more compact plant. This will also result in more flowers in late summer and fall. Pinching will delay the development of buds, so you can follow this technique every few weeks until the end of the month if you want flowers in late August and September. If you decide not to pinch back **mums,** they will bloom earlier in the season, and this may be your preference.

To train or guide the growth of other perennials, cut back newly growing stems by one-third to half after they have grown a foot tall. This will delay flowering but will control the height and spread of the plants. Try this on **beebalm, asters, golden-**

rod, and **artemisias.** Experiment with other perennials, too. Plants are resilient and can be trained to fit just about any space.

Prune off the stems of **daylilies** whose blooms have faded. This will promote development of new flowering stems and buds in reblooming varieties. It also improves the appearance of the daylily bed.

PROBLEMS

Warmer weather means slugs and other thugs are on the move. Slugs are snails without shells, and they love to invade the garden at dusk and during the night to feed on succulent foliage and stems. Look for the signs of slimy, shiny trails. They are known to hide under mulches or stones, so check these periodically for slugs and their eggs. If you find them, collect them and dispose in the trash or sprinkle them with wood ashes.

Tiny spider mites may be hard to detect. Check for mottling and a salt-and-pepper appearance on the leaves. If fine webbing is noted between the stems or on the underside of the foliage, it is likely that mites are making a run. Hose down the foliage, top and bottom, to discourage them.

If flower buds fail to open,

you may have thrips. They feed by rasping the plant tissues and sucking out plant juices. Thrips can be controlled with insecticidal soaps early in the season or systemic insecticides when infestations are severe. Read and follow label directions for application rates and methods.

Continue to dig or handpull weeds while they are still young, and don't let them go to seed.

NOTES

_____
_____
_____
_____
_____
_____
_____
_____
_____
_____
_____
_____
_____
_____
_____
_____
_____
_____
_____
_____
_____

JULY
PERENNIALS

PLANNING

As the dog days of summer approach, you may find that prolonged heat will cause a pause in perennial flowering. This is Nature's way of acclimating the plants for survival. Your perennials continue to thrive through summer with adequate moisture and a bit of maintenance. Plan to add more mulch to conserve moisture where mulch has settled or blown away.

Make notes in your garden journal about which plants are responding best at this time of year. You might want to choose perennials to fill in the gaps for future years. If needed, plan to plant some annuals to add color to the bare spots.

Choose plants that have colorful foliage or variegated leaves to provide interest and texture. This will bridge the gap between peak flowering times of other perennials. Look for plants with silver, white, yellow, or variegated leaves to add to the color mix even when flowers are insignificant. For recommendations, refer to *My Rocky Mountain Gardener's Guide* for companion plants to use with perennials.

Plan on placing ornamental grasses in the perennial garden. They not only add height, but their texture and form will also provide a focal point. Grasses also add sound as the summer breezes wisp the foliage.

PLANTING

As the summer heat advances, it is not advisable to plant or transplant perennials, unless absolutely necessary. Although you can buy and transplant perennials in July, to avoid transplant stress follow these guidelines:

• Plant on a cloudy day or in the late evening. Watch the weather forecast for predications of a cool down to plan your transplanting.

• Shade newly transplanted perennials for a few days if they are in a sunny exposure and subject to high winds.

• Delay planting until the heat breaks and temperatures are lower.

• Cut back the foliage by one-third to one-half to minimize moisture loss through transpiration.

• Water and mulch new plantings to assure sufficient soil moisture during establishment of the root system.

CARE

Check perennials for signs of heat stress: wilting leaves, flower buds that "blast" (fail to open), and scorch on the leaf margins. These could indicate lack of available subsoil moisture. Check the soil moisture every few days to prevent severe stress to the plants.

Organic mulches around plants will begin to break down with summer heat and moisture, so replenish it around plants as needed. Spread a fresh layer of compost or pine needles to maintain a 2-inch layer around the root zone. Pull any weeds that may have popped up through the mulch.

Stake or support plants before they grow so wide or tall that their stems flop. It only takes a minute or less for a summer hail storm or heavy rain to flatten the stately flowers of **phlox, bee-balm, delphinium, columbines,** and others. In some cases, be ready with cardboard boxes or 5-gallon plastic buckets to protect plants when hail is predicted. The extra effort will protect the flowers and reduce tearing of the foliage. Damaged plants are more susceptible to disease infection.

 WATERING

If the summer has prolonged periods of drought, it is important to check the watering needs of both established and newly transplanted perennials. Dig down around the root zone to a depth of 4 inches or more. If the soil is beginning to dry out, it's time to give the perennials a deep watering.

Perennials that are mulched are better able to withstand short periods of drought than those that are not mulched and are exposed to sun and wind. Shade perennials should be checked periodically, too. Even though shade cools the soil, tree and shrub roots compete for soil moisture and can stress the plants. Check the soil by probing an inch or two down and under the mulch layer. If the soil is dry, apply water.

 FERTILIZING

All that organic mulch and compost you place around perennials will eventually decompose and add slow-release nutrients to the plants. The humus will also encourage beneficial organisms such as earthworms to till the soil naturally and release nutrients.

Slow-release fertilizers are much more available in soils enriched with organic matter.

If it's been more than six weeks since you added a slow-release fertilizer to the soil, late summer blooming perennials will benefit from another dose of granular fertilizer. Some slow-acting fertilizers can last for the entire growing season, so read the label to determine if you need to apply more.

 GROOMING

Continue to cut off any broken, insect-infested, or diseased stems and foliage.

Deadhead spent blooms to encourage new buds for future flowers. Some perennials that need deadheading include **daylilies, perennial salvia, phlox, coneflowers, rudbeckia, beebalm, coreopsis, Stokes' aster,** and **yarrow.**

Make the last pinch of hardy garden **chrysanthemums** by July 4th to ensure flowers in late summer or early fall.

 PROBLEMS

Check perennials daily for invasions of insect pests. Aphids, whiteflies, caterpillars, and spider mites continue to be on the prowl in summer. Most can be controlled by washing them off the stems and foliage with a forceful spray of water. Homemade soap sprays, insecticidal soap, and miticides can also be used to keep their numbers in check. Read and follow label directions when applying any insecticide or miticide.

Leaf diseases may be showing up on perennials growing in the shade or those that are too crowded. Watch for the signs of powdery mildew: a grayish-white coating on the leaves is a classic symptom of mildew. Use the homemade mildew control (page 285) to suppress a severe infection or cut off diseased leaves and discard in the trash.

Continue to pull, dig, or spot-treat weeds as they appear. Don't let them grow so fast that they produce seeds. With proper spacing of perennials, there should be minimal weed invasions since the soil will be shaded naturally to inhibit weeds from germinating.

AUGUST

PERENNIALS

PLANNING

August is a good time to evaluate your perennial garden and make more notes on what did best and what didn't do so well. You can plan to make improvements in the garden in early fall. Many garden retailers will be putting their plants on sale and you can acquire some good bargains for autumn planting.

Perhaps it's time to dig out older plants for replacement this fall.

Note the perennials that really shined in your garden despite drought conditions. Which ones took the least amount of attention? Make these notations in your notebook or journal.

If you have space and want your perennials to naturalize, plan on letting some of them go to seed. **Rudbeckias, coneflowers, hellebores, Shasta daisies, monarda, asters** and others will self-sow their seeds.

While some gardeners welcome self-sowing of perennials, others do not want to deal with all the tiny seedlings next season. The choice is yours. Young seedlings can be dug up and transplanted to more desirable locations or share them with garden friends.

Another benefit for leaving some seedheads is to create a wildlife-friendly garden. Visiting birds such as finches love the seeds of **coneflowers** and **black-eyed Susans.**

Plan to visit public and private gardens to see what perennials are showing their stuff. Make notes in your garden journal so you can act on them next growing season, if not this autumn.

PLANTING

This is a good month to propagate or start new perennials from soft-wood cuttings. This can be done at almost any time during the active growing season.

- Cut stem sections that have become somewhat mature; cut 6 to 8 inches back from the tip just above a node at the point where the leaves emerge. Select stems that are tipped with healthy foliage, or pinch off any flowers.
- Remove the lowest leaves so that an inch of so of the stem is bare. Dip or dust the cut end with a rooting powder (rooting hormone).
- Insert a pencil or dibble into a pot filled with moistened vermiculite or a sterilized growing medium to make a hole for the stem cutting.
- Then, stick the treated end of the cutting into the moistened rooting medium.

- Water in well and cover the container with a clear plastic bag to maintain humidity around the cutting.
- Place the containers in light, but not direct sun. Make sure the rooting medium does not dry out. The emergence of small leaves is a good sign that roots are establishing on the cutting.
- Remove the plastic cover and increase sunlight gradually. Water in with a soluble plant fertilizer diluted to half strength.
- Transplant into larger containers if desired and place in the cold frame for overwintering, or plant directly into a prepared perennial bed. Shelter the young plants from harsh winds.
- Mulch with a few inches of compost or other organic material. Water as needed when the soil begins to dry out.

CARE

Continue to water new transplants as the soil begins to dry out. Cut off diseased or insect-infested stems or foliage. If you haven't already staked late-season perennials, do so before they are subject to toppling over. Inspect the mulch layer around perennials. If wind and natural decay have reduced its thickness to an inch or less, apply more mulch to raise the level to 2 to 3 inches. Leave only about a $^1/_2$-inch thick layer around the base of the crowns. This will discourage rodents from setting up home and will also prevent rot diseases.

WATERING

Established perennials can survive without supplemental water for a week to 10 days if they are properly mulched and watered deeply. During periods of little or no rainfall, be sure to water new plants when they need it, and not by the calendar or a water provider's calendar. Check the subsoil moisture by digging down a few inches and inspecting underneath the mulch. If the soil is beginning to dry out, it's time to apply a deep watering.

FERTILIZING

You do not need to apply fertilizer after mid-August. Except for those perennials that bloom in the fall, most plants are already preparing to enter dormancy.

Unless you have six weeks or more before the first frost arrives in your area, any new growth stimulated by late fertilizer applications is likely to be killed by the frost.

GROOMING

As the summer wanes, the perennial garden may begin to look a little shabby. Regular deadheading and cutting back spent flower and dried foliage will tidy up the garden. Thin out crowded perennials to improve air circulation and reduce the incidence of leaf diseases.

PROBLEMS

Continue to be on the watch for pests in the perennial garden. Plants that are infested with mites will have pale, faded, or stippled leaves. Remove these tiny pests with a strong stream of water from the garden hose. You can also apply a homemade soap spray if their numbers are high and damage is significant. Hosing down, too, can control aphids. Let the natural predators like lady bird beetles visit your garden to feast on aphids.

Fungal diseases can start to show up with warm days and cool nights. Powdery mildew can be controlled with better air circulation, the homemade remedy on page 285 or appropriate fungicides. Read and follow label directions.

Weeds should be controlled before they go to seed. Handpull or dig as needed. Dispose in the trash; never put seedheads in the compost pile, as they are likely to survive to invade the garden another day.

NOTES

_____
_____
_____
_____
_____
_____
_____
_____
_____
_____
_____
_____
_____
_____
_____
_____
_____
_____
_____
_____
_____
_____
_____
_____
_____
_____

SEPTEMBER
PERENNIALS

PLANNING

Labor Day weekend traditionally marks the end of summer, even though there are several weeks left before fall officially arrives. This can be a glorious time in the perennial garden. The lower temperatures tend to intensify the colors in the garden and crisp the foliage. The changing angle of the sun casts a different light and creates warm hues throughout the landscape.

Many of the earlier blooming perennials have set seedheads or pods that accent the garden. **Black-eyed Susans, datura, turtlehead, tall sedums, asters**, and others will sport interesting textures amidst the foliage. You can either deadhead these or leave them for fall and winter interest. Remember, some will self-sow seeds as well.

Continue to add to your garden journal. Make notes on what's blooming this month as the garden season winds down. If you notice large gaps in the blooming sequence, times when nothing is flowering or the foliage is boring, think about acquiring plants that will add blooms during these times. Check with local nurseries or visit public gardens to see what they use to fill in the gaps.

Refer to *My Rocky Mountain Gardener's Guide* for suggestions on perennials that bloom at various times to extend the flowering season.

PLANTING

Late summer and early autumn are good times to plant perennials, either the ones you started from stem cuttings, or plants that are available locally. Just be careful about purchasing plants in containers. They may not look great at this time of year because they, too, are getting ready for the winter. Some may have already become rootbound and need immediate transplanting. But if the plants are on sale it's a good buy, so just get them in the ground as soon as possible.

Plant them as early as you can so they can establish a vigorous, hardy root system before the ground freezes. They do not have to produce foliage and flowers this time of year, so the plants put their energy into expanding their root systems.

Take special care if plants have roots that are matted and wrapped around themselves from being confined in the containers for such a long time. Tease apart the roots, or gently pry them loose so that they can expand and grow into your native soil.

Divide clumps of perennials that have grown too large for their space. Wait to divide spring bloomers until after they bloom next spring.

CARE

Keep the perennial beds tidy and weed-free by regular dead-heading and digging or pulling out weeds that have snuck into the garden before they go to seed. If plants in certain parts of the landscape have not performed well, there could be a problem with the soil. Look for symptoms of yellowing foliage, stunted growth, and lack of vigor. These could also be signs of pest invasion, too. Consider having a soil test performed to determine if there is a lack of available nutrients.

WATERING

Monitor watering of newly set perennials so they can establish a healthy root system. New transplants need the most attention before the soil freezes. If the plants are well mulched, they will need moisture less frequently. Dig down several inches underneath the mulch to see the depth of subsoil moisture. When the soil begins to dry out, it's time to water.

Cooler weather generally means less watering. During a prolonged drought and hotter than usual month, however, the rules may change. This is why it is important to check the soil regularly to develop a proper watering schedule for your particular soil conditions.

FERTILIZING

Fertilizing is not necessary this late in the season. Allow the perennials to initialize their dormancy cycle so they are well equipped to tolerate the winter weather.

GROOMING

When the birds have had their fill of seedheads from **coneflowers** and **black-eyed Susan**s, you can cut back the old stems to the ground. To maintain a tidy garden, continue to prune out dead and dying stems and foliage. Deadhead spent flowers to keep perennials and their foliage appealing.

PROBLEMS

If slugs are a problem in shady exposures of the garden, set out baited traps. My favorite is to mix 1 teaspoon raw sugar and

---

GARDENING WITH AN ALTITUDE TIPS
Drying Flowers from the Perennial Garden

• Pick only the best flowers at different stages of development; include some colored buds, too.
• Harvest flowers late in the morning when plants are dry, but not wilted from the heat and sun
• Tie six to eight stems in bunches about 2 inches from the stem ends. Use a rubber band to fasten them together.
• Hang upside down in a warm, dry place with adequate air circulation. The attic, garden shed, or garage is just fine for drying.
• Your plants should be thoroughly dry when the stems snap easily. This can take up to three to four weeks.
• Store in a cool, dry, dark location to keep the flowers from fading.

$1/4$ teaspoon yeast into 1 cup of warm water. Put this liquid brew into shallow containers, such as empty tuna cans. Bury the containers in the ground to their rims. The slugs crawl in, but won't crawl back out. Repeat as needed.

Continue to wash aphids and spider mites off plants that are infested. It's getting late enough in the season that knocking these pests off the foliage and stems will soon do them in. Remove infected leaves that have mildew or rust and dispose of them in the garbage. Do not add diseased plant debris to the compost pile.

Don't turn your back on weeds. Summer annuals including goosegrass and crabgrass are going to seed now. Get rid of them before they disperse their

seeds everywhere you don't want them.

NOTES

_____
_____
_____
_____
_____
_____
_____
_____
_____
_____
_____
_____
_____
_____
_____

OCTOBER

PERENNIALS

PLANNING

Perennials are beginning to slow down this month with the onset of lower temperatures. If frost has not yet arrived in your area, there are some lingering plants that are still blooming including **asters, mums,** and **hibiscus.**

Plan to expand a perennial bed or reduce the size of one that is getting out of hand.

Refer to your garden journal to find out what plants you want to add or replace.

Take time to prepare the soil before planting a new perennial bed. The key to success is in a well-drained soil that is enriched with humus.

Do you need to replace or repair a pathway? With pleasant weather conditions, now is a good time.

Clean and sharpen garden shovels and trowels. Get them ready for storage by wiping the metal parts with light motor oil. Add comments to your garden journal or notebook while things are still fresh in your mind.

PLANTING

You can continue to plant perennials practically anytime the ground is not frozen. It is much better to plant them than to store them in their cramped containers over the winter. The earlier you plant, the better head start the plants will have to establish roots before the ground freezes.

If you have a slope and want to design and install a stone wall, this would be a good time. It's fun to plant and watch plants grow and develop among native rocks. Stack the lower layer of rocks on a solid foundation of sand and make it level. Then work your way upwards with more rocks to the desired height. For a major project, consult a stonemason to help you design and construct a sturdy wall.

CARE

Herbaceous perennials will soon die back with the arrival of Jack Frost, although their roots still grow underground. Clean up dried, dead leaves and dried stems that have flopped over. Some of the more rigid stems can be left upright for fall and winter interest. They can be removed later next spring.

Avoid adding mulch to the perennials until the ground freezes. Mulching too heavily in the fall is an invitation for rodents to nest at the crown of our perennials.

Some perennials will keep green foliage over the winter. **Hellebores** provide attractive semievergreen leaves year-round if it is not a drought year.

Biennials are plants that require two growing seasons to complete their life cycle. They will remain green late into the fall and send up their flower spikes next year. If this is the first autumn for biennials, mulch them well for the winter. If this is the second fall, the plants will die by the hard frost, and you can pull them out. However, watch for new seedlings they may have self-sown in areas where they were cleaned out.

WATERING

Water any new transplants as long as the ground remains unfrozen. When there is little or no persistent snow cover, soil moisture is essential to maintain the root system. Make sure that biennials are getting adequate moisture as well.

If you desire, this is a good time to install a drip irrigation system into the perennial garden. Once the tops have died back to the ground, it is easy to lay out a drip system, placing lengths of drip hose through the beds and among the perennial plants. Attach the drip hose to a feeder line that links them to a faucet or sprinkler zone. Then spread winter mulch over the system. Next year, you can water by deep soaking, allowing the water to drip slowly into the soil at the root zone of plants. This greatly reduces diseases due to wet foliage from constant overhead sprinkling.

FERTILIZING

No fertilizers are needed, but now that the leaves are shedding from deciduous trees, it's an excellent time to construct a compost pile. Leaves are a valuable source of organic matter as they break down. Plan to rent a shredder or chopper to grind up the coarser, waxy leaves. This will speed up their decomposition.

Dig new beds, add organic matter, and let them set for the winter. Rains and snow will moisten the beds and they will be ready to plant next spring.

GROOMING

The first hard-killing frost is a signal to clean up the blackened foliage and stems. Cut back soggy, water-soaked stems and dried, broken plant debris. Leaves that were infected with powdery mildew should be raked up and collected, then discarded to the trash. Pull or cut back weeds. Be sure to get all the seedheads to reduce seed dispersal.

Leave ornamental grasses in their full-grown glory. Their mature seedheads and bleached stems provide form and structure in the landscape both fall and into winter.

Clean up old pots, twigs fallen from trees, and other wind-blown debris. Pull out garden supports and stakes, and put them back in storage. Bring in decorative containers that are subject to freeze damage. This includes statuary, birdbaths, and garden decorations that are not constructed to withstand freezing and thawing.

Mow leaves with a mulching mower as they lie on the lawn, and then bag them up with grass clippings for use as mulch. You can also put them into the compost pile.

PROBLEMS

Rodents will be looking to construct new winter homes; don't let them find homes in your perennial garden. Meadow mice, voles, chipmunks, and others like to build nests in a deep, fluffy mulch, so delay the spreading of mulch until the ground freezes. By then, the rodents will have found alternative nesting sites.

Fallen leaves that mat together will prevent moisture and air from getting into the soil. Lightly rake leaves or chop them up to reduce matting. Use a shredder to grind them into smaller pieces, then cover the soil with them.

NOTES

_____
_____
_____
_____
_____
_____
_____
_____
_____
_____
_____
_____
_____

NOVEMBER
PERENNIALS

PLANNING

It is possible with the right planning to have a winter perennial garden. The ornamental grasses you planted in the spring will become the highlights of your fall and winter garden. Their mature seedheads add height and form to the landscape, and the rustling of the bleached leaves adds a relaxing sound.

Though few perennials bloom in winter, with the exception of *Erica carnea* (**hardy evergreen heath**) and *Helleborus* (**Lenten rose**), they will periodically produce flowering stems. Our native *Arctostaphylos nevadensis* is one of the few broadleaf evergreens that will accent the winter landscape.

With some careful planning and a judicious selection of plants, you can create a perennial bed that provides winter interest when there is little or no snow cover. Choose a site that is visible from a window so you can enjoy the tapestry of plants when you are shut in by the cold weather. A winter garden might include:

• Colorful evergreen foliage of **hellebores, hardy ferns, hardy evergreen heath,** and **kinnikinick.**

• The semievergreen foliage of **mahonia, barrenwort** and **heuchera** will have foliage that transforms into purplish to red hues. This will last for several weeks when weather conditions are mild to moderate.

• Interesting dried stems of **coneflowers, dwarf astilbe, black-eyed Susans,** and others provide various textures in the garden.

• The silver foliage that persists on **lamb's ears** and **artemisias** is always a welcome sight.

• Dried **yarrow** stems and seedheads add architectural lines, as do tall **sedums** and other perennials.

PLANTING

Outdoor planting is past in most parts of the region. If you purchased perennials too late to plant, you can **heel** the plants into a trench, pots and all. Cover with protective winter mulch until you're ready to plant in the spring. If you're lucky enough to have a cold frame, many perennials will winter there and survive the rigors of temperature fluctuations.

If you feel the urge to plant, try planting perennial seeds. Certain perennials require a lengthy period to germinate, and some need a cool, moist period

to break dormancy before they will grow. After the frost arrives, conditions are favorable for planting seeds in pots filled with a moistened growing medium.

• Lightly cover the seeds with growing medium. Cover the pots with plastic to keep their moisture from escaping into the air.

• Set the containers outdoors in a cold frame or protected location where they can experience winter conditions, but will not be damaged by high winds or rodents.

• Temperatures should be around 40 degrees F. Leave the sown seed there for six to eight weeks.

• Check containers for sprouting seeds as the winter wanes and temperatures rise. Different perennials respond to slightly different conditions. Experiment and try to grow some native plants.

• When sprouts do emerge, remove the plastic, and move the pots into brighter light conditions. You can begin to lightly water them or let snow or rain do it for you.

• Make sure the seedlings experience the same outdoor temperatures that established perennials are experiencing.

• As the perennial seedlings develop in late winter to early spring, scatter a slow-release organic fertilizer into the soil.

• They are ready to plant in late spring, or early fall if they have grown large enough to set in the garden safely.

CARE

Now that the ground has frozen, you can spread winter mulch up to 4 inches deep on the soil over the root zone of perennials. I like to use pine needles, but shredded wood chips, chopped leaves, pole peelings, and shredded cedar will work nicely, too. Applying the mulch after the soil is cold or frozen serves several purposes:

• It protects the soil from compaction by heavy rains or snow.

• It will insulate the soil by buffering temperature extremes of the freezing and thawing cycles that often heave soil and plant crowns out of the ground.

• Mulch helps to retain moisture.

• Winter mulch keeps the soil cool in early spring to delay premature emergence of perennials.

• A good mulch will suppress weeds early in the season by inhibiting light to the seeds.

WATERING

Late autumn and early winter dry spells are not unusual. There may be little or no snow cover in the Plains, Foothills, or even some parts of the High Country. A prolonged dry winter can be disastrous to some perennials. When this should happen, bring the garden hose and frog-eye sprinkler out from storage. Water early in the day as long as the ground remains unfrozen. Once water starts to run off, move the sprinkler to another area. Disconnect the hose, drain, and return to storage. Pay particular attention to newly planted, transplanted, and divided perennials.

FERTILIZING

No fertilizing this month.

GROOMING

Garden cleanup is generally finished by this time of year, but if you didn't get some chores done, you still have time. Except for those perennials that will provide winter interest, cut back all dried, dead stems, leaving short stubs of stems to mark plant locations. This will also serve to catch snow and provide winter moisture when it arrives.

PROBLEMS

Drying winter winds and temperature fluctuations can be harmful to a newly planted perennial garden. Until the plants have become established for a few years, be sure to provide protective winter mulch. Leave 4- to 6-inch lengths of stems on perennials when cutting them back during garden cleanup. This will trap and hold compost or chopped leaf mulch so it is less prone to wind erosion. Construct a low windscreen made from landscape fabric or burlap; fasten it to stakes at the front of the wind-blown beds to block the wind.

NOTES

_____
_____
_____
_____
_____
_____
_____
_____
_____
_____
_____
_____
_____

DECEMBER
PERENNIALS

 ### PLANNING

Cold and snow will soon be arriving at lower elevations, and it is already striking the High Country. The perennial garden is in its dormant mode now. Just like trees and shrubs, perennials will benefit from a winter watering every five weeks or so, as long as the ground remains unfrozen.

As the garden catalogs arrive, check your garden notebook, and plan what perennials you'll add next year. Also, make a list of holiday gift ideas for gardening friends. Winter is also a good time to enroll in gardening and landscaping classes at your local library or botanic garden. You can gain more knowledge and experience from local gardeners to become more successful in your perennial gardening endeavors.

 ### PLANTING

As long as the ground remains unfrozen, work some compost into soil around your perennials to improve the soil structure and drainage. Winter is a good time to add organic amendments, as the alternate freezing and thawing will break down organics and mellow the soil for spring planting.

 ### CARE

Finish up any lagging chores and necessary grooming of ripened perennials. Mulch all perennials that are exposed to winter wind and fluctuations in temperatures to prevent frost heaves. Collect and store perennial plant stakes and supports.

 ### WATERING

Until there is a major freeze and winter sets in, keep in mind that perennials may need supplemental irrigation during prolonged dry periods. Check the soil moisture underneath the mulch with a garden trowel or hand cultivator. As long as the ground remains unfrozen, apply the water early in the day when temperatures remain above freezing so it can soak in. Winter watering need only be done every four to five weeks during dry spells. Make notes in your journal or notebook to document the dry years and the general weather conditions, which vary from year to year.

Remember that some rock garden perennials may not appreciate too much water. They will do best in soils that are gritty and well drained. Native perennials are more adapted to local weather vagaries.

 ### FERTILIZING

No need to fertilize.

 ### GROOMING

The taller-growing perennials that have attractive seedpods can be left to add winter interest. As long as they remain erect and provide structure and texture to the garden, don't prune them back quite yet. A heavy snow can flatten these dried stems, so they will have to be cut back eventually. Once the seedheads have been depleted by the birds and other wildlife and lose their winter interest, cut them back to tidy up the perennial bed.

 ### PROBLEMS

If wind continues to blow mulch off exposed garden beds, consider anchoring it down with chicken wire. Use landscape pins to hold the wire down over the mulch.

Alternative mulches may prove helpful. I like to use pine needles because they knit together nicely and are less likely to blow away.

ROSES

There are more than 10,000 varieties of roses available, with more to come. This can make it overwhelming to make the right choice for your landscape. Whether you plan to add a few roses to your landscape or to create a new rose garden, take time to select the right kind of roses to suit your gardening style and level of expertise. Unless you're willing to commit to a regular pest control program, choose durable, easy-care roses. Among my favorites are species roses and old-fashioned shrub roses.

Roses play a lovely, visual role in the landscape. The secret to success with roses is to know their cultural requirements.

Almost all roses are sun worshippers. Most modern varieties do just fine in direct sun, especially miniatures, ground cover, shrubs, and species roses. A maximum of six hours brings out their best. The hybrid tea roses, grandiflora, floribunda, and climbing roses, however, will appreciate some afternoon shade during periods of extended drought conditions. Under afternoon shade, the moisture in the soil lingers longer, which means less frequent watering. It also helps to group or mass roses together. This creates a more stunning effect in the landscape.

SOIL CONSIDERATIONS

Roses do best in fairly rich soil and open space with good air circulation. Space roses a minimum of 3 feet away from competing plants. Improve the soil to aid in moisture absorption, retention, and drainage before planting a rose garden. Many soils throughout the region are clay. When compacted, they absorb moisture slowly, but they are slow to dry out. Amend the soil with compost, aged manure, sphagnum peat moss, or a combination of these organic amendments at the rate of one part amendment to two parts of your native soil. It is important to mix the organic amendments well throughout the soil. This will speed up the absorption rate, aid in fertility, increase air circulation, and promote timely drainage to deter oxygen starvation and root rot.

GARDENING WITH AN ALTITUDE TIPS
Miniature Roses Indoors

Miniature roses can ornament your indoor spaces as flowering houseplants, if you have space to accommodate them. They do best with lots of bright light to avoid loss of vigor that invites spider mites and diseases. Locate them in a sunny south or west exposure, or supplement low-light areas with fluorescent light fixtures. Rig the lights 3 to 4 inches above the rose foliage. Use a timer to ensure 12 to 14 hours of light a day.

Insufficient humidity can be a problem when we run heating systems. Install a humidifier, or place a cool mist vaporizer around your plants. You can construct a pebble tray by using a waterproof saucer filled with moist gravel. As the moisture evaporates, it creates humidity around the canopy of the plant.

DESIGNING A ROSE GARDEN

Choose a site that receives at least six hours of full sun daily in the summer. Remember that the sun's angle shifts in the autumn and winter, so it will light a slightly different portion of your landscape.

Designate a measured area by outlining with a hose or twine, or that iron bed frame. Remove existing turf or other plants to ready the soil for planting.

Dig or rototill the ground to a depth of 18 inches or more. Clay, sandy, or rocky soils will benefit from the addition of a quality organic amendment. If you have a very difficult, hard clay or granite-based soil, build up the soil to create a raised garden a couple feet above original ground level to facilitate drainage and provide a foundation for healthy root growth.

Add at least one-third by volume of compost or well-aged manure to the rose garden to improve the soil's ability to drain well, yet retain moisture and nutrients. Remove large rocks and other debris; rake the soil smooth and level.

Cover the rose bed or prepared areas with a 2-inch layer of pine needles or chopped leaves to help retain moisture in the soil. It will mellow and be ready to plant come springtime.

Draw a plan on paper to create a rose garden with varieties you would like to grow. This plan will help you determine how many rose bushes will be needed to fill the space and what types would look best in a specific area. Then you will be ready to place an order in January or shop locally in early spring.

Wait until March or April to plant.

PLANTING BARE-ROOT ROSES

Remove the plants from their wrappers. Trim and remove damaged or broken roots. Place the rose's naked roots in a bucket of water; soak for up to eight hours before planting to hydrate the roots.

Dig a saucer-shaped hole that is as deep as the rose bush's root system, but dig the hole 2 to 3 feet wide.

Replace one-third of the native soil with compost or sphagnum peat moss. This will improve drainage and add porosity to the planting area. Reserve this to fill the hole later. Mix a handful of slow-release, granular fertilizer into the bottom of the hole.

To plant, first make a cone of prepared soil in the bottom of the hole. Set the rose bush over the cone so the bare roots splay down along the sides. The bud or graft union should be about 1 inch below ground level when the plant is in its final position.

For non-grafted roses including old-fashioned shrub and species roses, adjust the crown so that it is just level with the ground.

Backfill halfway with soil, firm it gently around the roots, and add a bucket of water. After the soil has settled, add the remaining soil and soak again.

Hill more soil or compost over the crown and base of the stubby canes until temperatures moderate and leaf buds begin to swell.

TRANSPLANTING CONTAINER-GROWN ROSES

Before moving container-grown roses outdoors, let them acclimate by placing them outside during the day, then moving them indoors at night if temperatures are freezing.

Dig the planting hole as deep as the container, but two times as wide. Prepare the native soil with organic matter as directed above.

Carefully remove the rose bush from its container and set it at the same depth in the planting hole. For grafted roses, it may be necessary to dig the planting hole deeper to be sure the graft union is covered. This will protect the graft union from extreme winter temperatures.

Backfill with prepared soil and water in well.

GARDENING WITH AN ALTITUDE TIPS

Remedy for Mildew

An effective homemade remedy for powdery mildew uses baking soda as the main ingredient. At the first sign of the disease or as a preventative, you can apply this homemade remedy: Mix 1 tablespoon of baking soda to a gallon of water, add a squirt of lemon-scented liquid dish-washing soap. (Avoid detergents that may contain additives phytotoxic to plant foliage.) Mix thoroughly. Pour into a spray bottle. Apply to the uninfected foliage and stems. This spray can be applied every three to five days. Repeat after a heavy rain or overhead irrigation. This is especially effective where shady conditions favor mildew. It will help to prevent a severe outbreak of the disease.

WATERING YOUR ROSES

Adequate soil moisture is essential to the vitality of roses. We can seldom rely on natural rainfall to be adequate. A Green Thumb rule is to apply 1 inch of water per week, but the actual frequency of watering will depend on your soil type and climate, as well as the age of the rose plant.

It is best to water slowly until the soil is soaked 12 to 18 inches deep. Inexpensive watering devices include a soaker hose, bubbler attachment, or an old-fashioned frog-eye sprinkler. These devices will distribute water low to the ground for more uniform coverage. Drip-irrigation systems are also very effective and make the watering process a breeze.

FERTILIZING YOUR ROSES

Though there's less agreement about fertilizing roses than any other aspect of their care, experts generally recommend applying a complete analysis in the spring after pruning, then another when flower buds develop, and again every four weeks through mid-August. Roses growing in fast-draining or sandy soils benefit from more frequent applications at half the manufacturer's recommended dilution or rate.

Never fertilize rose bushes that are under stress conditions, whatever the cause of the stress. Soluble salts that cannot be utilized add insult to injury and may further damage the plant. Deep watering and occasional misting in the morning will help them through extended hot and dry periods.

MULCHING AND SUPPORTING YOUR ROSES

Organic mulch around the base of roses provides a summer relief. A layer of shredded cedar mulch not only adds a pleasant aroma to the landscape but also keeps down weeds, keeps the soil uniformly moist, and eventually adds nutrients.

Add an organic mulch as the weather begins to warm up and before the weeds emerge. Mulch can be applied anytime during the growing season if you first remove weeds and lightly cultivate the soil. Spread 2 to 4 inches of mulch over the rose bed, leaving some space open around the base of each rose bush. Replace the mulch as it deteriorates over time.

Coarse compost, shredded leaves, dried grass clippings (from lawns not treated with herbicides), and shredded bark mulches are some good choices. The coarser the mulch, the longer it takes to break down during the growing season. Be

GARDENING WITH AN ALTITUDE TIPS
Roses for Idaho

HYBRID TEA ROSES

Cultivar Name	Color
Brigadoon	pink blend
Dainty Bess	light pink
Duet	medium pink
Garden Party	white, near white and white blend
Legend	medium red
Midas Touch	deep yellow
Miss All American Beauty	deep pink
Olympiad	medium red
Peace	yellow blend
Pristine	white, near white and white blend
Sheer Bliss	white, near white and white blend
Touch of Class	orange pink and orange pink blend
Tribute	deep pink
White Masterpiece	white, near white and white blend
Fragrant Roses	
Dolly Parton (HT)	orange red and orange red blend
Double Delight (HT)	red blend
Fragrant Cloud (HT)	orange red and orange red blend
Hansa (Hrg)	medium red
Lagerfeld (GR)	mauve/mauve blend
Mister Lincoln (HT)	dark red
Perfume Delight (HT)	medium pink
Pink Parfait (GR)	pink blend
The Prince (Shrub)	dark red

POLYANTHAS

Cultivar Name	Color
China Doll	medium pink
Dick Koster	deep pink
Margo Koster	orange/orange blend
Mothersday	dark red
The Fairy	light pink

GRANDIFLORAS

Cultivar Name	Color
Gold Medal	medium yellow
Love	red blend
Olé	orange red and red blend
orange	
Queen Elizabeth	medium pink
Sonia	pink blend
Tournament of Roses	medium pink

FLORIBUNDAS

Cultivar Name	Color
Europeana	dark red
Eyepaint	red blend
French Lace	white, near white and white blend
Gene Boerner	medium pink
Iceberg	white, near white and white blend
Nearly Wild	medium pink
Purple Tiger	mauve/mauve blend
Showbiz	medium red
Simplicity	medium pink
Singin' in the Rain	apricot/apricot blend
Sunsprite	deep yellow

SHRUB ROSES

Cultivar Name	Color
All That Jazz	orange pink and orange pink blend
Ballerina	medium pink
Bonica	medium pink
Carefree Delight	pink blend
Golden Wings	light yellow
John Cabot	medium red
Linda Campbell	medium red
Morden Centennial	medium pink
Oranges "n" Lemons	orange/orange blend
William Baffin	deep pink

GARDENING WITH AN ALTITUDE TIPS

Roses for Idaho (continued)

CLIMBING ROSES

Cultivar Name	Color
America	orange pink and orange pink blend
Blaze	medium red
Golden Showers	medium yellow
Jeanne Lajoie (Cl Min)	medium pink
Joseph's Coat	red blend
New Dawn	light pink

MINIATURE ROSES

Cultivar Name	Color
Acey Deucy	medium red
Crazy Dottie	orange/orange blend
Cupcake	medium pink
Dee Bennett	orange/orange blend
Light of Broadway	red blend
Millie Walters	orange pink and orange pink blend
Minnie Pearl	pink blend
Party Girl	yellow blend
Rainbow's End	yellow blend
Simplex	white, near white and white blend
Snow Bride	white, near white and white blend
Starina	orange red and orange red blend
Valerie Jeanne	deep pink

sure to keep the mulch from touching the rose canes or crown. Placing it too close will invite rodents to nest and nibble at the canes; also, a moist, warm environment favors some diseases and insect pests.

As the canes of climbing and rambling roses grow, fasten them to their support trellis or arbor. Roses are not able to cling or twine on their own. Use green jute twine or commercial plant ties. Loop them around the canes, then around the support structure and fasten. Do not tie them tightly; leave a bit of flex in the ties.

WEEDS IN THE ROSE GARDEN

Handpull or hoe out weed seedlings that pop up throughout the rose garden. Remember, a properly mulched garden will have fewer weeds. Grasses are the most difficult to control, especially when they are growing close to the crown. Hand-dig or pull when the soil is moist. Spot-treatments to the grassy weed's foliage with a herbicide that contains glyphosate can also eradicate weeds. Do not get any on the rose foliage or canes. You may also apply a pre-emergent herbicide labeled for ornamental plants to prevent annual weed invasions. **Read and follow label directions for application methods and frequency.**

PRUNING TECHNIQUE

Climbers bloom on short, 6- to 12-inch laterals on 1- to 2-year-old canes. Keep all the canes except the oldest (dark brown and scaly). Prune off the dead ends to just above a healthy, outward-facing bud. If the long canes have come loose from their trellis or a fence, carefully reattach them as needed.

Just before spring budbreak, prune the short laterals to 3 to 6 inches or three to four buds for the most prolific bloom. Ramblers flower on 1-year-old wood, so prune out all the canes that are two years or older. Remove them at ground level with a pruning lopper or pruning saw.

JANUARY
ROSES

PLANNING

Roses can be planted as garden focal points or integrated into other facets of your landscape. Take time to consider placement of roses carefully. Assess your site. Do you need a colorful hedge to screen an unsightly view? Will you uses roses as a border or fill, or will you add a formal rose garden?

Browse garden catalogs, and study the new introductions. Ask local rose gardeners about the most reliable roses for your area. A great resource is the "Handbook for Selecting Roses," a booklet published annually by the American Rose Society (American Rose Society, P.O. Box 30,000, Shreveport, LA 71130-0030; www.ars.org). It covers everything from old garden to modern roses.

All-America Roses Selections, Inc. (AARS) in a nonprofit research organization founded in 1938 for the purpose of evaluating and identifying roses that have outstanding vigor and adaptability. Roses are grown in test gardens throughout the U.S. by commercial rose producers, then scored on characteristics including vigor, growth habit, hardiness, disease resistance, and flower production.

PLANTING

Although it's still too early to plant, this is a good time to make sure you have the space in your landscape, plus the time to tend roses. Order plants early to ensure that they arrive at the proper planting time for your area.

CARE

Outdoors, check your rose bushes for broken or damage stems or canes from wind or the weight of snow. It may be necessary to do some periodic cleanup as the weather permits. Determine whether protective mulches are still in place. If the weather has been dry and windy, you may need to replace protective mulch that has been blown away by the wind.

WATERING

Inspect outdoor roses for soil moisture. On warm, sunny days and during dry periods without snow, it may be necessary to "winter water" your roses. Pick a warm day when temperatures are above 50 degrees and the ground is not frozen, and give your roses a deep drink of water. Bring the garden hose or frog-eye sprinkler out of storage, and soak the root zone for 15 to 20 minutes. Water early in the day, and allow the water to soak in before freezing temperatures at nightfall. During extended periods of drought, wind, and warm temperatures, water the soil monthly to maintain moisture to the roots. Don't forget to drain the hose and return it to storage when finished.

Indoor **miniature roses** should be watered carefully. Avoid overwatering because this often results in root rot or stress to the plant. A stressed plant is more prone to insect and disease invasion.

Water thoroughly to saturate the soil, but discard excess water in the drainage saucer after an hour or so. Allow the soil to dry out slightly between waterings to allow the root zone to receive oxygen. Simply poke a finger into the potting mixture to check; when it begins to feel dry to the touch an inch down, it's time to water again.

Because of our low humidity indoors, place potted roses on waterproof pebble trays. Simply fill a shallow plastic saucer with 1 to 2 inches of gravel. Keep the gravel layer moist so it can consistently promote humidity around the **miniature rose plants.** Maintain moisture in pebble trays by keeping the gravel damp, but not so full that the bottom of the container sits in a pool of water. Grouping plants together also creates more humidity

FERTILIZING

Roses growing and blooming indoors will need an occasional application of fertilizer. I prefer to mix time-released fertilizer into the soil at planting so it can sustain the plants for several months.

Otherwise, you can use a water-soluble rose fertilizer. Apply to a moist, never dry, potting mixture. Follow label directions for dilution rates and frequency of application.

If plants are not vigorously blooming, use fertilizer diluted to half strength.

Miniature roses that are not blooming can be repotted into fresh potting soil, if needed. Check the roots and carefully root prune potbound plants. Move into a container one size larger than the old pot. After replanting, water in thoroughly.

GROOMING

Miniature roses need to be kept tidy during their stay indoors. Pinch or prune off spent blooms. This not only improves appearance, but will encourage more flower buds to form. Remove yellow leaves from the plant to prevent the onset of pests and diseases. Fallen leaves on the potting soil should be picked up and disposed of to keep fungus gnats from becoming a problem.

Outdoors, check roses for damaged canes from wind or heavy snow loads. If needed, prune off damaged canes by making a clean, smooth pruning cut.

PROBLEMS

Forced-air heat in our homes decreases humidity and can cause indoor roses to become more susceptible to spider mite invasion. Be on the watch for fine webbing developing among the stems and leaves. Foliage may become stippled and have a "salt and pepper" look. The safest way to keep mites at bay is to wash the foliage in a solution of lemon-scented dishwashing soap and tepid water every few weeks or as needed. Use 1 teaspoon of soap per gallon of water. Rinse foliage under the kitchen faucet after applying this homemade remedy. More severe pest invasions may require the use of insecticidal soap or a systemic insecticide applied to the soil. Read and follow label directions.

If you're growing **miniature roses** indoors for winter color, keep a close eye on them for signs of fungus gnats, spider mites, and powdery mildew disease. A white powdery coating on the young stems and foliage is often a sign of powdery mildew. Increase air circulation around the plants and remove infected plant portions. If fungus gnats become a problem, place yellow sticky traps around the plants to capture these nuisance pests. Allow the potting mixture to dry out slightly between waterings to discourage larvae in the soil.

NOTES

_____
_____
_____
_____
_____
_____
_____
_____
_____
_____
_____
_____
_____
_____
_____

FEBRUARY

ROSES

 PLANNING

Valentine's Day is just around the corner, and who doesn't like to receive roses during this winter month? A bouquet of long-stemmed roses is a classic gift of love at Valentine's Day, but a long-lived rose bush will continue to keep on giving.

Catalogs may be arriving in the mail this month. Before ordering, it's always best to sketch out a plan to make sure you have the proper location and space for your desires. Now is a good time to learn about the various roses and how they might fit into your garden style.

Order bare-root roses so they will arrive at the appropriate planting time for your area. Most mail-order companies are good about sending the plants at the proper planting time for your locality. Many will allow you to make your request for shipment to ensure they do not arrive too late in the spring.

 **PLANTING**

It's still too early to plant roses outside, but if you have **miniature** potted **roses** indoors, they may need to be repotted. Check the root system by carefully slipping the soil ball out of the pot. If the roots are growing towards the inside of the container or coming out through the drainage hole, it's time to move the plant up to the next pot size. Use a quality potting mixture that has good drainage when repotting **miniature roses.** They are fussy about moisture and don't tolerate being waterlogged.

 CARE

Check the mulch placed around the base of your roses to make sure there is still adequate amounts for good insulation from temperature fluctuations. **Hybrid tea roses** are typically more susceptible to winter injury because they are grafted. The graft union is the swollen knob, located at the base of the rose bush. If it is not protected from winter temperature fluctuations, the top portion of the rose will die and growth will come from the rootstock. This wild stock grows vigorously and produces smaller blooms than the grafted variety, or none at all.

My favorite roses are the hardy **old-fashioned shrub roses** that are typically on their own roots. They are not as susceptible to "winterkill" as their crowns and roots survive to regrow new shoots the following season.

If you did not apply a horticultural oil in the autumn, pick a warm day and apply to the bare canes of roses that have a history of insect or disease problems. Dormant oils kill pests by smothering overwintering insect eggs and fungal spores. This reduces the incidence of problems during the growing season. Read and follow label directions on the product label when using any pesticides in your rose garden. Heavy horticultural oils should only be applied when the roses are leafless and dormant. Light, or superior oils, can be applied at any time of the year.

 **WATERING**

Water the rose garden if you experience clear, dry weather conditions for extended periods. Giving the rose garden a good drink on a warm, sunny day when temperatures are above freezing will insure their survival. This only needs to be done every five to six weeks during dry spells and as long as the ground remains unfrozen.

Indoors, **miniature roses** should be watered regularly to compensate for the lack of humidity and the drying conditions of forced-air heat. Poke you finger into the potting soil to the depth of your second knuckle; when the soil begins to feel dry to the touch, give the plant a thorough watering such that water runs out the drainage hole. Discard excess water from the drainage saucer after an hour or so.

FERTILIZING

Outdoor roses do not need any fertilizer now, but this is a good time to apply a layer of compost over the root zone of your roses to improve the soil conditions and fill in low spots. It doesn't matter if the ground is frozen, as snow and rain will moisten the compost and allow it to work into the soil as the spring thaws start up.

Miniatures indoors will benefit from a light fertilization of liquid plant food with an analysis of 10-20-10 or something similar. Follow label directions.

GROOMING

Periodically check indoor roses for insect pests and powdery mildew disease. Remove and discard portions of the plant that may harbor these problems. Leaves that have fallen around the base of the plant should be picked up and disposed of. Not doing so will encourage little

black fungus gnats that soon become a nuisance in your home.

Prune excess gangly twig growth from vigorously growing indoor roses to encourage better air circulation, which reduces the incidence of diseases.

PROBLEMS

Be on the watch for critters that nibble at the rose canes during the winter. Deer, elk, and rabbits are notorious for chewing on landscape plants when there is a lack of natural winter feed. To protect valued roses, surround them with wire cages tall enough so the deer cannot reach down inside. You can also spray the exposed canes with my homemade critter-repellent. See page 284 for the recipe. Remember, if the snow is unusually deep, critters will be able to reach higher on the plant than usual.

If you live in an area where mice, voles, and pocket gophers are a concern, check the mulch around the base of the roses periodically. They can be nesting in the mulch and will feed on the bark and damage or kill the stems. If you find the nesting site, pull away the mulch and destroy the nest. Reapply the mulch as needed to continue winter protection. Surround the mulch with

a wire cage to discourage pests from nesting. To prevent critter damage in the future, delay winter mulching until after the ground freezes so that such rodents will seek other places to build a home. If necessary, spray the homemade critter-repellent on the canes, repeating applications after heavy snowfalls.

NOTES

_____
_____
_____
_____
_____
_____
_____
_____
_____
_____
_____
_____
_____
_____
_____
_____
_____
_____
_____
_____
_____
_____
_____
_____

MARCH
ROSES

 PLANNING

Spring is approaching, and the snow is beginning to melt. As the days get longer and temperatures rise, rose bushes begin to awaken in the garden. You'll see signs of buds swelling and little sprouts starting to develop at the base of the plants. Don't get in a hurry to prune too early. Pruning will stimulate new growth more rapidly, but there is still a chance of late spring frosts that will damage tender new growth. I prefer to prune later in the month and trust the wisdom of Nature to guide the plants.

Pull back mulch a bit to check the condition of the canes. If they are still green and firm, they have survived the rigors of winter. Rose bushes that have no signs of green or those that have turned brown or black all the way down to the graft union are most likely damaged. Plan to order or buy replacements as needed.

If you haven't ordered roses through the mail yet, you'd better jump to ensure that your order is processed and you can still get specific varieties. Some garden stores only stock roses early in the season, so call ahead.

 PLANTING

Now is a good time to transplant roses that need relocation in your landscape. Prepare the new site in advance to make the job easier. You can begin transplanting established plants as soon as you see the new buds swelling. Don't wait until the rose bush leafs out; there will be more transplant shock.

This is an excellent time to plant bare-root roses. Be careful about working the soil; don't work it if it is too wet, as this can destroy the soil structure and leave it lumpy. Allow the soil to dry out slightly so that it is crumbly when you grab a handful.

Dormant, bare-root plants will adapt quite well and suffer less transplant shock than you might expect. Plus, bare-root plants are less expensive than container-pampered plants.

 CARE

As your rose bushes begin to grow, you can start to remove the winter mulch. If you leave the plants covered in extended warm weather, the new shoots will be etiolated (white and weak) and may die back if exposed too late. Nature's signal for removal of mulch is when the **forsythia** shrubs are flowering.

If you have overwintered **tree roses** in trenches, carefully dig them out and reset them in their upright position. **Climbing roses** should be inspected for winterkill, and damaged stems pruned back to healthy, green wood. Tie up climbers to their supports.

Spread a 2-inch layer of mulch over the root zone of roses to keep the soil from baking and to discourage annual weed growth. Mulches also help conserve moisture.

 WATERING

If the weather has been windy and dry, water the rose garden deeply to charge the subsoil. Keep newly planted roses watered weekly to ensure they get off to a good start. Allow the soil to dry out slightly between waterings to encourage healthy root growth. Properly mulched roses will manage longer between waterings and rains than unmulched plants.

FERTILIZING

With established roses, now is a good time to apply a slow-release fertilizer around the root zone. Lightly cultivate the fertilizer into the ground and water in well. Follow label directions for application rates. Fertilizer can be sprinkled over organic mulches and scratched into the mulch. Rain, snow, or your watering will move the nutrients into the soil and to the roots.

GROOMING

As Nature signals the expansion of new growth and winter protection has been removed, it's time to prune. Prune roses to maintain their health and shape the plants to fit their designated areas. How much you prune depends on the type of rose shrub and your method of growing and training.

Make sure pruning loppers, hand pruners, and pruning saws are sharp and ready. Remove all dead and damaged canes on all types of roses. Roses that have signs of winterkill should have stems pruned back to healthy live wood that is solid; cut as low as needed.

Disinfect pruning tools between cuts by spraying the blades with rubbing alcohol or household disinfectant. Pick up and discard fallen debris that may harbor insects, eggs, or fungal disease spores.

Hybrid tea, floribunda, and **grandiflora roses** do best with a hard pruning. Keep the center of the shrub open to sunlight. Select three or more healthy young canes spaced openly to form a vase shape. Cut them back 7 to 9 inches tall. Cut off all other canes at the base with pruning loppers. Make the cut ends approximately $1/4$ inch above an outward-facing leaf bud; angle the cut so the water will drain away quickly.

Landscape roses benefit from rejuvenation and renewal pruning. Remove about one-third of the older canes and weaker branches. Reduce the height of the remaining canes by one-third their length.

Polyanthas and **miniature roses** need basic grooming. Prune back stems to 3 to 6 inches. Cut off twiggy growth and open up the center of the plant to allow more light to the plant and promote more flowering.

Ground cover and **hedge roses** can be sheared. Prune the canes to about 6 inches.

PROBLEMS

Now is the time for early prevention measures in your rose garden. Proper pruning assures removal of dead, diseased, and insect ridden wood. It also establishes better air circulation to prevent leaf diseases. Good sanitation techniques of removing debris will eliminate disease spores and overwintering insect pests.

Choose disease-resistant rose varieties to reduce the use of pesticides in your garden. Prepare the soil to encourage healthy and vigorous growth.

NOTES

_____
_____
_____
_____
_____
_____
_____
_____
_____
_____
_____
_____
_____
_____
_____

APRIL
ROSES

PLANNING

Although we can expect more cold and spring snows, Spring has arrived! Consult your garden notebook to refresh your memory about roses. Do certain kinds do better than others? Should some be transplanted or replaced? Begin now to visit public gardens to see firsthand what kind of roses are growing and performing best in your area.

Make changes in your rose garden early in the season. Replace roses that are not doing well or tend to be more susceptible to disease problems. Select hardy rose varieties that are more disease-resistant.

Have you ever tried integrating roses into other parts of your landscape? Their colors and forms blend well with many perennials and can be used as a backdrop. Many **hybrid tea, miniature, floribunda,** and **tree roses** are adapted to grow in large containers on the patio or deck. Plant fragrant roses where you entertain or sit to relax so the fragrance can be enjoyed.

PLANTING

Container-grown roses are readily available this month and are easy to transplant. Just be careful not to break the rootball during the transplanting. Many garden retailers force roses into early bloom so you can experience the fragrance and see the colors of the various types. Though this is not my favorite way to plant roses, it provides instant gratification.

Plant container-grown roses any time the ground is not frozen. If you purchase them ahead of time, keep the soil in the container uniformly moist until planting time. Dig the planting hole as deep and twice as wide as the container in which the rose is growing. Add compost or sphagnum peat moss to the soil removed from the hole at the rate of one-third by volume. This helps to improve drainage and adds porosity to the soil for healthy root development. Reserve this prepared soil to fill the hole later.

Carefully slide the rootball out of the container, taking care not to break the rootball or damage healthy roots. Prune or slowly untangle any roots that are matted together or circling the inside of the container. Set the rootball

into the planting hole. The top of the rootball should be level with the ground.

If this is a grafted rose, set the plant an inch deeper to allow for added winter protection. Look for a knob at the base of the plant; plant the rose a bit deeper so this knob will be covered with an inch of soil when you fill the hole with prepared soil you dug out. Mix in a handful of granular, slow-release fertilizer formulated for blooming shrubs or roses.

Water the entire root zone thoroughly. To help maintain moisture and reduce weed invasion, spread a layer of organic mulch around the base of each rose bush. This will aid the establishment of the plant as well.

CARE

By the middle of the month, it is probably safe to remove mulch from rose bushes, but if a hard frost is predicted, throw garden blankets or burlap sacks over tender plants for the night hours.

Replace old mulch with fresh mulching material. Add just enough to provide a 2-to 3-inch layer around the root zone. Do not allow the mulch to touch the rose crowns or stems as this can encourage rodent damage and reduce air circulation.

Organic mulches will help discourage annual weeds and help control leaf diseases by reducing the splashing of fungal spores resting in the soil onto the above ground foliage. Mulch reduces water loss from runoff and evaporation, and helps to insulate the roots from summer's heat and winter's cold.

Begin to train **climbing roses** as their canes start to expand and branch out. Climbers produce the most blooms on canes that grow horizontally within a 45-degree angle of the ground. Train along fence rows and retaining walls for a spectacular display.

 ## WATERING

Keep newly planted roses watered deeply once a week or as the soil begins to dry out. Check the soil every few days to determine a schedule that works best for your soil conditions and the rose's exposure to sun and wind. Roses that are mulched will require less frequent watering. Unmulched soil will need to be checked by digging down with a small garden trowel for dryness every three to five days. When watering roses, avoid excess watering of the foliage, particularly at night.

 ## FERTILIZING

If you have not already applied a granular, slow-release fertilizer to your roses, do so now. Follow the instructions of the fertilizer label for application rates and frequency. Later, when the warm weather arrives and plants have been flowering for a time, you can apply a quick boost from a faster-acting water-soluble rose tonic. See page 284 for details. This is optional.

 ## GROOMING

If you have not done your final pruning yet, now is the time to prune **climbers** and **ramblers** to remove any winter-damaged, dead, or broken canes. A pruning rule of thumb from a horticultural colleague: "Prune when the **daffodils** are in bloom." Start just as the leaf buds are beginning to enlarge, but it is better to prune later than too early.

 ## PROBLEMS

Be on the watch for early aphid infestations on the new, tender growth or succulent rose buds. Masses of pear-shaped, soft-bodied insects will be visible. If there are just a few aphids, carefully rub them off, being careful not to damage the tender shoots. If aphids heavily infest a single shoot, pinch off the shoot and discard in the trash. You can also try to hose off with a forceful stream of water. Do this every few days in the morning hours. More serious aphid infestations can be controlled with a homemade soap spray (see page 283) or insecticidal soap. Apply to the aphids directly.

Weed your rose garden diligently. Keep the garden clean by removing yellow or fallen foliage. Regularly monitor the garden for insect pests and encourage beneficial bugs including ladybugs and lacewings.

NOTES

MAY
ROSES

PLANNING

Buds are just waiting to burst into bloom. Some rose varieties are already blooming, including *Rosa foetida bicolor* with its brilliant orange-red flowers. Plan more new additions to your garden. Many garden retailers stock both old and new varieties of roses including the **Canadian explorer series** and **David Austin English roses**. Search out disease-resistant varieties. I am particularly fond of **old-fashioned shrub roses** that grow on their own rootstock and don't require special pampering.

While you're shopping for new roses, consider rose-gardening accessories such as durable pruning tools or a handsome, sturdy trellis to show off your favorite **climbing roses. Miniature roses** in terracotta or lightweight planters are especially attractive on a patio or deck.

Container-grown roses in full bloom make wonderful Mother's Day gifts. One of my mother's favorites is the floribunda 'Europeana'. It has mildly fragrant, deep red blossoms borne in five to seven flowers per cluster. **Floribundas** are durable and display repeat flowering all summer.

PLANTING

May is it an excellent time to continue planting container-grown rose bushes. Follow planting guidelines in the March and April section for planting.

Bare-root roses may need special attention since it is getting a bit late. If your receive mail-order bushes late, take precautions to 'sweat' the canes that are stubborn about sending out new growth. You can do this by placing a large, 5-gallon bucket over the entire rose plant. Place a large stone or several bricks on the top of the inverted bucket to keep it in place. Within a week or so, buds should start to emerge; this indicates the roots have taken hold and you've saved your investment.

Roses are very compatible with flowering perennials and will add special interest in the garden. Use your imagination. **Climbing roses** should be sited at least 1 foot from the side of the house or a retaining wall to allow for proper air circulation and maintenance.

CARE

If you haven't mulched your roses, now is a good time to augment existing mulch that may have settled or blown away before summer's heat. Support **climbing** and **rambling roses** with a trellis, arbor or stakes, tying loosely with jute twine or plant ties. If you've acclimating your indoor **miniature roses** to the outdoors, late in the month is a good time to site them outdoors for the season. Do not place them in the sun immediately, as it will scorch their foliage.

WATERING

Keep an eye on the watering of newly planted roses; do not overwater. Allow the soil to dry out slightly between waterings. This will allow for the healthiest and strongest root development. Roses need lots of water, especially as the weather warms.

Water roses weekly, and if we experience prolonged drought periods, be sure to water the rose garden deeply every five to seven days, depending upon water restrictions in your area. Water the soil and root zone, not the leaves. Apply early in the morning to reduce the incidence of leaf diseases. If you must water in the evening, do it early so that any damp leaves will dry before night.

FERTILIZING

Check your garden journal or notebook to see if it's time to apply more slow-release fertilizer over the root zone. I prefer to use one that will last six months. Some have a shorter longevity and will need reapplication. Refer to the manufacturer's recommendations and follow label instructions.

Roses bloom best with a consistent source of readily available nutrients. It is common in our region to experience iron chlorosis—the lack of iron because of our calcareous soil conditions. If you have this problem, use a granular fertilizer that contains both iron and sulfur.

Some roses, such as **hybrid teas, grandifloras, floribundas,** and **climbers** are heavy eaters if you want more prolific flowering. If you have time, apply a foliar fertilizer spray or my homemade rose tonic (see page 284) once a month through mid-August as a supplement to the slow-release granular incorporated earlier in the season.

GROOMING

Now that the rose foliage is expanded, basic maintenance is all that is required. If stems are beginning to emerge from below the graft or knob at the crown, remove them closely at the point of origin. These wild shoots will look different than the main plant, with vigorous growth and seven or more leaflets.

Continue to remove and dispose of fallen leaves and plant debris, as this material often will harbor insect pests and diseases. If necessary, trim back rose canes that are encroaching on the sidewalk or pathway. Use your good judgment and common sense to trim back growth.

Pick a bouquet of roses to enjoy indoors. After all, they are to be appreciated inside as well as in the garden. Make rose potpourri for your dresser drawers and for gifts.

PROBLEMS

Be on the watch for foliar diseases, including leaf spot and powdery mildew. You can prevent these by removing leaves or stems showing early signs of infection. Early applications of my homemade powdery mildew control made from baking soda and vegetable oil can prevent a severe outbreak, and it is people and wildlife-friendly.

If certain roses in your garden develop droopy and deformed buds, this is often a sign of rose midge infestation. This will dra-matically reduce blooms. Deadhead and dispose of infested buds and spent flowers. You may need to spray the buds and tip growth with a systemic insecticide labeled for roses. Read and follow label directions.

If rose buds or flowers are pierced with tiny holes, and you see bent necks supporting the buds, this a telltale sign of the rose curculio. This attractive maroon to orange-brown snout beetle wreaks havoc in the rose garden with its piercing snout. Remove infested buds, then handpick these tiny critters and drop them into a pail of soapy water. Insecticides can be used also. Read and follow label directions.

NOTES

_____
_____
_____
_____
_____
_____
_____
_____
_____
_____
_____
_____
_____

JUNE
ROSES

PLANNING

Roses are at their peak this month unless "the white combine" or hail hits your garden. Many of the one-time bloomers will be finishing up depending upon your elevation. **Hybrid tea roses** are beginning to peak by midmonth. The first flushes of bloom are the freshest and most abundant. It is a good time to keep notes on varieties that you like for fragrance, color, and form. You may want to rogue out those that are not performing to your standards.

Rose bushes that are integrated with perennials and other shrubs will manage pretty well on their own. Plan to spend some time deadheading spent flowers and checking for pest problems on a weekly basis. Growing disease resistant varieties will save you time and energy.

Hybrid tea roses will require more of your time if you want them to produce an abundance of flowers. When several roses are planted in relatively close proximity, the incidence of disease and insect pests increases. Monitor these situations daily to prevent severe problems later.

Enjoy your rose garden during peak blooming. Pick fresh bouquets to display indoors. And remember to keep notes in your garden journal. List some of the following:

- Blooming times of each variety
- Size and condition of the blooms
- Size of the plant
- Disease problems
- Insect pests
- Bushes that should be removed and replaced

PLANTING

By this time, the majority of your planting and transplanting should be complete, well before the major blooming period. It's too late for planting **bare-root plants.**

You can still remove and replace roses that are not performing up to your standards. Garden retailers should still have good selections of container-grown plants available. Rose bushes are already in full foliage and are blooming in their containers. They will transplant fairly well over the next few weeks as long as the weather is not too hot or dry. These can be planted up to early fall following planting guidelines from March and April.

Pick a cloudy day to plant whenever possible, or shade the new plants with a large cardboard box for a few days to allow them to acclimate in hot weather.

CARE

Keep the rose garden tidy while the plants are in their prime. Add fresh mulch as needed, and edge the beds if grass is beginning to invade. Pull or dig weeds as soon as you spot them. Continue to check **climbers** and **ramblers** to make sure they are securely fastened to their supports. New growth continues throughout the early season. Guide the growth on their supports to encourage more blooming laterals.

Remember that growing **hybrid tea roses** takes a bit more effort if you want healthy plants and abundant flowering. Deadhead spent flowers daily, remove yellow or diseased leaves, and apply preventative sprays to reduce pest invasions and disease infections.

WATERING

Properly mulched roses will get along fine with usual spring weather and can endure much better when summer's heat arrives. Even so, give established roses a deep drink at least once a week to maintain their vigor and promote repeat flowering.

FERTILIZING

Sprinkle a slow-release granular fertilizer over the root zone of newly planted container-grown roses so they get an extra boost after transplanting. Lightly scratch into the soil surface and water in well.

Roses that repeat blooming over the summer will benefit from another application of granular fertilizer as early March applications are becoming depleted by now. Most slow-release products last eight to 10 weeks.

Hybrid tea roses and other repeat bloomers appreciate a monthly fertilizer application to give them an extra boost for continued flowering. Use either fast-acting, water-soluble products or the homemade rose tonic on page 284. Read and follow label directions for dilution rates and amount to apply.

GROOMING

Cut and enjoy your **hybrid tea roses** for colorful bouquets. Clip off spent flowers to encourage more blooms. Prune stems back

---

GARDENING WITH AN ALTITUDE TIPS
Prolong the Life of Cut Roses

Cut roses early or at dusk when the air cools. Cut blooms in the late bud stage, just showing colored petals. Use sharp hand pruners to make a clean cut, cutting the selected stem at a 45-degree angle back to where a five-leaflet outward-facing leaf bud joins it. Immerse the stems immediately in a bucket of warm water. Place the cut roses in a cool, shaded place, and allow them a few hours to absorb water. Re-cut the stem ends, and create a bouquet. Use the homemade flower preservative (see page 288) to prolong the life of the blooms.

---

to just above a point where a second five-leaflet faces outward on the stem. This will stimulate the production of new buds and helps control the shape of the bush.

Some **landscape roses** such as **Meidiland®, Carefree,** and **Polyantha** do not require frequent deadheading of spent blooms to maintain flower production. However, if you have time, pruning does improve the plant's appearance and helps to keep the bushes more compact and shapely.

PROBLEMS

Continue to monitor roses for infestations of aphids, spider mites and thrips. Mites are favored by hot, dry weather and can be discouraged by hosing down the underside of the foliage every other day or two.

Insecticidal soap sprays will also help control many rose pests.

Thrips are very small, slender brownish-yellow insects that hide inside the buds and blooms. They cause damage by rasping the flower petals. They can be a problem on white and light colored varieties. Deadhead and dispose of spent blooms to reduce invasions. Insecticidal soap, Neem oil, pyrethrum-based insecticides, or systemic insecticide can be applied to the buds and blooms. Read and follow label directions.

If caterpillars attack the foliage, apply a product with Bt (*Bacillus thurengiensis*) to the infested foliage following label directions. Caterpillars will soon become sick and die.

Rose slugs can be controlled by sprinkling wood ashes on them; they soon become crispy critters. Neem oil can also be used for control measures.

JULY
ROSES

PLANNING

As early blooming roses wane, the continuous blooming types show off their color. Summer heat can burn the petals of light-colored varieties. Monitor your watering schedule to reduce stress and prevent severe spider mite infestations. Plan to check the rose garden daily to assess its needs.

While the garden is in full show, take notes on highlights and disappointments. Note off-color foliage or rose mosaic virus. Mosaic causes streaked or mottled leaves and stunted growth. Remove severely infected plants. If certain varieties have been on the decline or plagued by chronic problems, dig them out and throw them away. Then plan to try newer varieties.

PLANTING

If roses must be planted during the heat of summer, take time to cover the re-planted bush with a large cardboard box to provide some protection from heat and wind for three to four days. Mist the plant a couple of times daily to cool the environment. When the foliage is no longer wilting, the covering can be removed.

Avoid the urge to feed newly transplanted roses with fast-acting fertilizers that can overstimulate top growth and add more soluble salts to the root zone. The newly transplanted rose does not yet have a sufficient root system to support excess top growth.

Consider adding **miniature roses** in decorative containers. Miniature roses perform well outdoors in the summer and can be transferred indoors for the winter season.

CARE

Roses can tolerate summer's heat, but they suffer in prolonged periods of extreme heat and drought. When temperatures reach and stay above 90 degrees Fahrenheit, foliage and flowers will wilt and may scorch. The root system can't keep up with the rapid loss of moisture from the top growth. Daily misting can help cool the environment, but don't do this in the evening.

Spread new or refresh old mulch over the soil beneath your rose bushes to maintain uniform soil moisture and reduce weed invasions. If weeds do sprout up, they are easier to pull out from an airy mulch.

Landscape, shrub, species, and **old-fashioned roses** are generally much hardier than many classical **hybrid tea roses.** Most are on their own rootstock, have a freer growth habit, are more adapted to a wide range of soils and can handle varied climatic situations and elevations.

WATERING

Without sufficient water during the heat of summer, roses will become stunted, blooms are smaller, and flowering may cease. Monitor the soil by checking it to see how fast it dries out. Use a garden trowel and dig down a few inches; as the soil begins to dry out, it's time to apply water. Apply an inch or more of water weekly or at the first signs of wilting. Use an organic mulch to help maintain soil moisture and conserve during water restrictions.

Monitor soil moisture of container-growing roses by digging down or inserting a long screwdriver into the pot a few inches. If the soil is beginning to dry out, water pots thoroughly until water comes out the drainage hole. Discard excess drainage water after an hour or so.

FERTILIZING

It's best not to fertilize roses in the extreme heat or during extended drought periods. If you applied a slow-release fertilizer earlier in the season, it should sustain the plants until later in the month. However, you may have to fertilize roses that are susceptible to iron deficiency; yellowing foliage and lack of vigor are indicators. Use a granular or wettable powder form of chelated iron.

Wait for weather to cool before applying the homemade rose tonic (see page 284) in late July. Apply to the soil, not to the foliage.

GROOMING

One of the most useful tools for routine summer pruning is a sharp pocket knife. To protect your thumb from cuts and index finger from thorns, use two short pieces of old garden hose. Slice them down them the middle so that you can slip your thumb and index finger over them. When you make a pruning cut, you simply hold the stems between the thumb and finger of one hand and make the cut.

If you want bigger blooms, disbud the sideshoots from larger-blooming varieties to encourage larger flowers. Routinely check bushes for damaged or broken canes and faded flowers. Remove them to keep the garden clean and reduce disease problems. Pick up dead and fallen leaves and other debris on the ground to prevent splashing of soilborne fungus disease spores onto the lower leaves of the rose bushes.

Prune spring and early flowering rose varieties, including early blooming **climbers**, **shrub roses,** some **rambling roses**, and **perpetual hybrids** shortly after they have flowered. This will help to shape the plants and give them ample time to set buds on new wood for next growing season.

PROBLEMS

Monitor the rose garden every few days for summer insect pests. Leaf cutter bees leave very noticeable damage by cutting out very precise ovals and circles from the leaves. These pollinators are beneficial and use the leaf sections for nesting. No controls are warranted. If you desire to stop leaf cutter bee damage, net your prized plants.

Rose midge larvae will cause deformed buds and dead stem tips. They can quickly infest and devastate the rose garden if left uncontrolled. Prune off and destroy infested buds and stem tips. Treat the soil with a proper insecticide, and spray buds and new growth with a systemic insecticide. Read and follow label directions.

Spider mites wreak havoc in the summer rose garden. Stippled leaves, dusty-looking foliage, webbing, and premature leaf drop are indicators. Keep the plants adequately watered, and routinely spray the underside of the leaves with forceful water pressure. You can place a frog-eye sprinkler under the plants and turn it on occasionally to thwart mites. If necessary, use the homemade soap spray or a proper miticide. Read and follow label directions.

NOTES

_____
_____
_____
_____
_____
_____
_____

AUGUST
ROSES

PLANNING

As midsummer heat approaches, rose bushes start to harden off for the season. Although roses usually take this month in stride, they will benefit from regular attention. Monitor soil moisture by probing down a few inches with a garden trowel, and determine a watering schedule. Also, think about planning an automatic drip irrigation system for the future. Gather information to find out which kind would suit your needs.

Take note of roses throughout your region as you travel. You many discover some to add to your landscape next year. Typically, the informal **landscape roses** catch my eye. They produce colorful, simple flowers and some, like *Rosa glauca,* the red-leaf rose, not only have handsome foliage but produce drooping, orange-red rose hips that persist into winter. A good ground cover rose is *Rosa nitida* that has stunning reddish-orange fall foliage and is loaded with small, bright rose hips for winter interest.

When you go on vacation, regular watering will be a concern if we're experiencing a drought period. Make plans to have a friend or neighbor check the garden and water as needed. This is where that drip irrigation system would come in handy.

PLANTING

Later in the month and through mid-October as the heat subsides, you can plant container-grown roses that are usually on sale at garden retailers. Since they've been sitting at the store in a container all summer, it's best to get them planted right away so they can acclimate before the soil freezes.

Follow the guidelines on planting container-grown roses in the April Planting section. Untangle or lightly prune off matted roots and circling roots caused by the confinement of the pot. This will help them transplant more successfully.

Prepare the soil by adding compost to your native soil; use one-third compost to two-thirds native soil. Throw a handful of high-phosphorus granular fertilizer into the bottom of the planting hole and lightly mix. If you like, prune off flower buds so the plant can divert its energy on establishing new roots to withstand the fall and winter.

CARE

Continue to maintain a 2- to 3-inch layer of clean organic mulch over the soil in the rose garden. Pick up fallen leaves to prevent the incidence of leaf diseases. Among my favorite mulches are old pine needles; if they are available in your landscape or neighborhood, use them as they hold together nicely and provide a natural look.

Some rose varieties are grown for their handsome rose hips as the flowers fade on the stem. By midmonth, stop deadheading spent flowers, and allow the rose hips to form. This practice, combined with shorter daylight hours, will signal the plant to slow its growth and prepare for fall and winter. Later in the season the rose hips will provide winter interest and a nutritious food source for birds and other visiting wildlife.

Check your **climbing** and **rambling roses** to make sure that new growth is securely fastened to their supports. Winds that accompany late summer storms can loosen the canes, resulting in breakage and a ragged look.

 WATERING

Continue to water weekly, especially if rainfall is sparse. Usually an inch of water a week is sufficient.

 FERTILIZING

One last application of the homemade rose tonic (see page 284) can be made the first week of the month, but it's wise to finish up any fertilizing by midmonth. Again, we want the roses to harden up before winter, and feeding them too late in the season will encourage softer, more frost-sensitive stems. It is important for roses to spend this time storing energy in their root system to prepare for fall and winter.

 GROOMING

Continue to remove any dead, diseased, and dying branches from your roses as needed. Dispose of any debris in the trash, as composting methods usually do not get hot enough to kill disease spores and weed seeds. Carefully inspect for any signs of pests or disease problems. Rust, a leaf disease that causes orange-red pustules on the underside of the leaves, may start to show up on certain varieties. Prune out infected canes and pick up fallen leaves.

Prune out suckers that may have sprouted up from below the graft union of **hybrid tea roses.** This sucker growth has a different look from the original rose variety—faster-growing, heavier leafed foliage. It generally produces no flowers or very tiny blooms.

Growth from the rootstock is unsightly.

 PROBLEMS

Powdery mildew, rust, and blackspot, are a few foliar diseases that may show up this month. Be on the watch for these problems and take appropriate action. Use a preventative such as the homemade powdery mildew control on page 285. If diseases are a major concern, have them properly identified before using a fungicide. Read and follow label directions when applying any pesticide in your garden.

A virus disease known as rose mosaic will occasionally show up in the rose garden. Infections are systemic, working their way throughout the plant. Plant growth may be stunted, and foliage will develop a splotchy pattern of light green or yellow. There is no cure for plant viruses, so you may want to remove infected plants or stems. But since there is no adverse effect on actual flowering, you may choose to leave the bush alone and ignore the virus if it doesn't seem to be moving through the entire plant.

Spider mites and aphids may still be a problem on rose foliage this month. These pests will target plants that are stressed or weak. Consider their appearance as an alert, and try to discover why the bush is struggling. It may be in an improper location; if so, you can make plans to move it next spring. Prevention, early detection, and proper treatment are your best defenses.

NOTES

_____
_____
_____
_____
_____
_____
_____
_____
_____
_____
_____
_____

SEPTEMBER
ROSES

 PLANNING

While the media promotes Labor Day as the beginning of fall, summer conditions continue for several more weeks, and good weather stays with us in most parts of the region. Nights are cooler, but days are still warm. Take time to enjoy rose bushes in bloom. You may find that the plants will respond with more intense blooms with the break from the heat.

If this is your first season with roses, you have gained valuable experience. You may have discovered that some roses are easier to grow than others. The keys to success are proper siting and care. Roses do best if you meet these following requirements:

• Site in at least six hours of full sunlight; they seem to prefer more sun in the morning and some shade in the afternoon to cool them down.

• Provide good air circulation

• Have excellent soil drainage

• Water with at least 1 inch of water weekly

• Allow at least 18 inches of distance from walls and fences

• Use an organic mulch to conserve water and maintain uniform moisture

• Monitor for insect pests and diseases

Now is the time to check clearance sales for rose plants and garden accessories. You will find container-grown rose bushes, trellises, arbors, benches, gazing balls, decorative containers, pruning tools, and much more all marked down.

 PLANTING

Even though it's fall, you can still plant container-grown roses if you get it done soon. This will allow for proper root development before the ground freezes. Follow the planting guidelines in April Planting. You can add a handful of granular phosphate fertilizer (0-20-0) into the bottom of the planting hole but not a complete fertilizer. Water newly planted roses thoroughly, and continue as the long as the weather remains dry and the soil is unfrozen.

Roses growing in containers need to be heeled into the ground or planted so they will successfully overwinter. To heel them in: dig a hole that is wider than the container and about an inch deeper. Set the entire bush, pot and all, into the hole, and line the sides with shredded wood mulch or compost. Keep the soil in the container watered at least monthly during extended dry periods.

Miniature roses can be planted outdoors as suggested above, or you can repot them in fresh potting soil and bring them indoors for the winter. Provide bright light and relatively cool temperatures indoors.

CARE

Avoid the urge to prune back roses in September, as it can stimulate new growth that won't have time to harden off for winter. Remember, rose bushes need to utilize as much foliage as possible to produce the stored energy that helps them survive the winter.

Continue to deadhead **hybrid tea roses,** and there may still be time for late buds to open. Discard fallen leaves and other debris that may be harboring insects, their eggs, or plant diseases.

Top-dressing the soil around your roses with compost or composted manure is not essential, but it is a good way to keep the soil conditioned. As the material works its way into the ground, it helps improve soil structure and will provide some slow-release nutrients for the bushes come springtime. You can combine this task with season-end cleanup.

Delay piling mulch up over the crowns and lower stems of roses for winter protection. It's still too early. Wait until the plants have become more dormant and there is frost in the ground.

Prepare **miniature roses** you want to continue to grow indoors:

• Wash their leaves and stems with soapy water, then rinse with clear water. Repot into fresh potting mixture if the plants have become rootbound. Lightly prune the roots to remove any circling around the container.

• Spray the foliage with Neem oil to eliminate any residual aphids or spider mites, including the egg stages.

• Reverse-acclimate the plants to prepare them for their indoor environment. Reduced light will cause some leaf drop. Have them spend a few hours at a time indoors in bright light (south or west exposure); more every few days for a few weeks. Eventually, your miniature rose can remain overnight when outdoor night temperatures approach 45 to 50 degrees Fahrenheit.

 WATERING

If natural precipitation is limited, continue to water roses in both the garden and containers. Water deeply once every seven to 10 days, depending upon weather conditions and how fast the soil dries out. Monitor soil moisture with a soil probe, or dig down with a garden trowel. Proper watering during this season will help the roses get ready for winter conditions as they gradually harden off their canes. Keep them healthy, and they will continue to reward you for years to come.

 FERTILIZING

Outdoor roses do not need supplemental fertilizer applications at this time, but top-dressing with compost or aged manure can condition the soil. Indoor **miniature roses** can be fertilized with a soluble plant food once a month to keep them healthy and growing vigorously. As they acclimate to the indoors, new flower buds will develop.

 GROOMING

Continue to deadhead spent blooms and to pick up fallen leaves. Remove damaged or broken canes as soon as you discover them. Delay structural pruning until spring. The more healthy canes that remain, the better the chances of winter survival.

 PROBLEMS

If your roses continue to show signs of leaf diseases such as mildew or blackspot, cut away infected portions, and discard in the trash. Preventative sprays of baking soda and horticultural oil can also be helpful. See John's Homemade Remedies on page 283. Soon the leaves will drop and you can clean them up to remove disease spores.

If weeds have popped up, handpull or dig them out so they won't get a chance to go to seed. It's much easier to pull weeds when the soil is moist after a rain or routine watering. If summer's mulch has decomposed or thinned out, refresh with new mulch to keep weeds at bay.

NOTES

_____
_____
_____
_____
_____
_____
_____
_____
_____
_____
_____
_____

OCTOBER
ROSES

PLANNING

October is one of my favorite times of the year. Cool nights, crisp mornings, and comfortable days make it an ideal time to enjoy your landscape. Take time to travel throughout your area. There are so many beautiful sights, sounds, and aromas to be discovered in our region.

Visit public and neighborhood gardens to see what roses are growing and how they are sited in the landscape. It has been tradition to plant roses in beds where they show off their stunning blooms. In their own beds, they are easy to prune, water, fertilize, and maintain. One of my favorite ways to accentuate a rose bed is to plant **hybrid tea, grandiflora,** or **floribunda roses** in an actual antique iron bed frame. When sited in full sun, the roses will grow and bloom to create a colorful tapestry.

October is a good time to design a rose garden, either a separate bed or a section in your landscape, to accommodate roses of your liking. Be picky about the location to provide optimum growing conditions.

PLANTING

Although it's pushing the envelope to plant roses now, you can gamble and plant container-grown roses that you find on sale. Dig the planting hole two to three times as wide as the container, and prepare the soil with compost or sphagnum peat moss. See March and April Planting guidelines.

Rose bushes planted this late will need special attention during fall and winter months. During extended dry periods without natural rainfall or snow, provide water on a warm day to sustain the root system. Water when temperatures are 50 degrees Fahrenheit and water early in the day to allow the moisture to soak. I recommend a frog-eye sprinkler placed over the root zone for 15 to 30 minutes.

CARE

It still can be too early to apply winter mulch to protect grafted roses, except at higher elevations. Wait until there is frost in the ground. Winter mulch is meant to keep the bush dormant, not to pamper it with a warm collar that can stimulate growth. Winter mulches also prevent the alternating thawing and freezing that causes plants to heave out of the ground and become more vulnerable to winter damage.

Rose trees are difficult to overwinter in some parts of our region. **Tree roses** have two graft unions and are therefore doubly vulnerable to weather fluctuations and temperature extremes. To protect them over the winter, pot the plant up in a large container, and store in an unheated garage where temperatures are between 35 to 50 degrees Fahrenheit. Another, more time-consuming method is to dig a long trench (the height of the rose tree) 2 feet deep. Then, lay the entire rose tree horizontally in the trench. For rose trees planted directly in the ground, loosen the earth around the crown and roots so it is easier to tip the tree into the trench.

A light frost in early October is not a problem with roses. Damage is generally limited to some blackened foliage and browned flower petals. If you want to extend their blooming period and you have advance warning of a hard frost, throw an old bedspread or sleeping bag over the tops at night; then remove the covering in midmorning.

 WATERING

Continue to monitor soil moisture in your landscape. It is especially important to water newly planted roses to ensure good root development. If there is little or no natural precipitation, bring out the hose and frog-eye sprinkler, and do some fall watering every three to four weeks. Don't forget to disconnect and drain the hose by nightfall and put it back into storage. Mulched rose gardens have the advantage of not drying out so quickly and can go longer between waterings than they did in summer.

If a routine of watering is becoming a chore, now is a good time to plan and install a drip irrigation system where rose bushes are planted. Once the drip system is snaked throughout the rose garden, cover it with organic mulch. It will be ready to go come springtime.

Drip hoses are an alternative to place throughout the rose bed where they will sweat moisture along their length to irrigate the roses. You will have to time your waterings to soak deeply into the ground and charge the subsoil. Drip systems are a time-saver, help to conserve water, and keep water from wetting the foliage at night.

 FERTILIZING

You don't need to fertilize your outdoor roses. It's even best to delay fertilizing any recently planted roses until next spring. A 2-inch layer of compost spread around the root zone of newly planted roses is all that's needed. Fertilize **miniature roses** indoors once a month as new growth appears. Use a water-soluble fertilizer, and apply to an already moistened soil.

 GROOMING

No major pruning is needed now. Extremely long stems or canes that are subject to wind damage can be secured to supports or lightly pruned at the top to prevent them from whipping in the winds. Keep deadheading faded blooms. Cut about midway down the stem, leaving half the leaves to store energy. Clean up fallen leaves that may mat together and impede moisture and air movement to the root system. Put fallen leaves to use by shredding and adding to a compost pile.

 PROBLEMS

Deer, elk, and rabbits may nibble on rose stems and any remaining foliage if their food sources are scarce. Given alternatives, critters generally avoid plants with thorns, but if there is not much else available, they will feed on rose bushes. If necessary, spray with the homemade repellent (see page 284), or construct a cage around your valued rose specimens.

Meadow mice, voles, and pocket gophers are often inclined to nest in mulch placed too close to shrubs. Wait until a hard frost to spread your winter mulch. Here's where procrastination pays off, as rodents will have set up winter headquarters somewhere else.

NOTES

_____
_____
_____
_____
_____
_____
_____
_____
_____
_____

NOVEMBER
ROSES

PLANNING

The holiday season is fast approaching and gardening becomes less a priority. Take time to review your growing experiences with roses this season. Make comments in your garden notebook or journal. They will help you in assessing your rose garden and will serve as reminders on what roses may need transplanting or replacing. Which varieties performed the best? Were some more disease-prone than others? Was the location right for a designated variety or is it outgrowing its spot? Maybe you would like to automate watering by installing a drip irrigation system next year.

Get on the mailing list for rose specialty catalogs. They serve as a great resource for new and unusual rose varieties, rose gardening accessories, and other unique items that are not available locally.

PLANTING

Planting and transplanting should not be done during this month, unless you are willing to gamble. Shorter days, cold temperatures, and frost in the ground are not conducive for successful root development. If the weather remains relatively warm, you can experiment and plant some of those bargain rose bushes.

Be sure to amend the soil from the planting hole as recommended in the March and April Planting sections. Water new rose bushes thoroughly. In this situation, apply an organic mulch over the root area to keep the soil from freezing so the root system can acclimate before a prolonged cold spell.

Miniature roses are available at garden shops and can be transplanted into decorative containers for gifts or as a future blooming indoor plant. Locate them in bright light and a cool location. If you have forced-air heat, place a cool mist humidifier near them.

CARE

One of the best management practices to prevent disease problems is routine sanitation in the garden. Continue to clean up fallen leaves that accumulate around the bushes. Disease spores, insect pests, and their eggs can overwinter in plant debris. If you have a compost pile, recycle non-diseased leaves and other plant debris, but discard disease-infected foliage

and seed-producing weeds. Remember, it takes a hot compost pile to destroy the harmful fungus spores and weed seeds.

Roses in containers are more difficult to overwinter than plants in the ground. Their roots are above ground and exposed to temperature extremes and drying out. If you must retain them, store the plant, pot and all, in a cold frame. If you have space in your yard, heel them into the ground by digging a hole deep enough to hold the container. Set the pot an inch or two deeper than ground level, and apply a protective mulch around the area.

Don't forget to water these potted roses during prolonged dry periods. This may need to be done every three to four weeks, depending upon local weather conditions. Water early in the day when temperatures are above freezing and the soil is not frozen to allow the moisture to soak down.

Once all the leaves have fallen from deciduous trees and the arrival of hard frost occurs, it's time to **winterize** roses, especially grafted varieties. They should be dormant by now.

Landscape roses are typically rugged and need only minimal winter protection. Water them deeply if precipitation has been scarce, and mulch around the root zone with compost or shredded wood chips, chopped leaves, or something similar.

Hybrid tea roses and other grafted types need more care and attention. You may cut back any extremely tall canes that will whip around in the winter wind. Canes should be no shorter than 2 feet. Pile up soil, compost, or other mulching material (pine needles, pole peelings, shredded wood chips, or chopped leaves) over the crown, graft union, and lower parts of the canes. Be sure that the knobby graft region is covered with mulch.

Climbing roses benefit from winter protection if winter temperatures dip below zero for extended periods. Unfasten the canes from their supports and gather them together in a horizontal bundle on the ground. If you desire, dig a shallow trench in which to lay the canes. Cover the crown and canes with a loose soil, finished compost, shredded wood chips, or pine needles. If it is too difficult to remove the canes, make sure they are tied up securely on their supports. Mound soil or mulch as high up as possible on the bush. You can also construct a cage that encircles the climber and fill with organic mulch.

 WATERING

If it's been an Indian summer and conditions are dry, water all roses in your landscape before the ground freezes hard. Check your soil moisture by inserting a long screwdriver or soil probe into the ground. Bring out the garden hose and frog-eye sprinkler, and pick a warm sunny day when temperatures are above freezing. Water early in the day to permit the water to soak in, then drain the hose before storing it away.

 FERTILIZING

If your indoor **miniature roses** did not have a slow-release fertilizer added to the potting mixture, fertilize with a soluble plant food once monthly. Read and follow label directions.

 GROOMING

From now until spring, avoid the urge to prune your roses except to remove storm-injured canes from dormant rose bushes. Canes should remain 18 to 24 inches long because a certain amount of winter damage will occur at the stem tips. Extra length protects strong, healthy wood lower on the plant.

 PROBLEMS

Watch for spider mites and aphids on indoor **miniature roses.** They tend to proliferate in warm, dry conditions indoors. To catch infestations early, routinely check for signs of pale or dull leaves and fine webs streaming throughout the plant. Wash plants under the faucet every week or so to prevent mites from becoming a problem. If you do get an infestation of spider mites or aphids, control them with the homemade soap spray (see page 283) or **Neem** oil. Read and follow label directions.

If the leaves develop scorched tips due to lack of humidity, place a cool mist vaporizer near your **miniature rose** plants. This will also reduce the incidence of spider mites.

NOTES

_____
_____
_____
_____
_____
_____
_____
_____
_____
_____

DECEMBER
ROSES

PLANNING

As the year draws to an end, it's a good time to reflect on all the blessings we experienced in our rose garden this season. Continue to make notes in your garden notebook or journal as friendly reminders on what needs doing next year. If you have taken photos of your roses and garden, be sure to label them before you forget.

PLANTING

If the ground is not yet frozen in your area, it is still possible to plant roses with proper preparation. However, I generally do not recommend planting this late.

CARE

If you haven't already provided winter protection, hill up soil, mulch (pine needles, shredded wood chips, pole peelings, chopped leaves) over the crown, graft, and lower canes of **hybrid tea** and other grafted rose varieties. The grafted region, or bud union, should be planted below ground level in most parts of our region. Winter mulch should be piled 4 to 6 inches deep around the rose bush. This will insulate the ground to prevent the alternate freezing and thawing that damages the roots over the winter.

WATERING

Monitor soil moisture as needed. During prolonged dry, windy periods, get out the garden hose for winter watering. Water when temperatures are above freezing, early in the day, and when the soil is unfrozen. This will allow the moisture to soak in to where it is needed. Be sure to disconnect, drain, and store the hose away by nightfall.

Water **miniature roses** indoors as soon as the soil begins to feel dry to the touch. Avoid keeping the potting mixture too soggy—roses don't like wet feet. Provide good drainage by discarding excess water in the bottom saucer after an hour or so. This will prevent fungus gnats, too.

FERTILIZING

If you did not apply a granular, slow-release fertilizer to the potting mixture of indoor **miniature roses,** you can feed your roses a water-soluble fertilizer. Or, if you prefer, sprinkle some granular plant food on the surface of the potting mixture, and lightly scratch it in. Read and follow product labels for frequency of application.

GROOMING

No more pruning this year. Relax.

PROBLEMS

Wind and drought can be the nemesis of all roses. Add to that, periods of warm winter weather that trick the plants into premature growth, followed by temperatures plummeting below freezing. In some years, roses must endure extensive winterkill. Be sure that climbers are securely tied to their supports if left upright. If the canes of **shrub roses** are becoming battered by frequent winds, tie extra twine around the plants to steady them.

Indoor **miniature roses** can become stressed from lack of sufficient light and humidity. Check them often. If necessary, increase artificial light, and consider placing them on a pebble tray to add humidity.

SHRUBS

Shrubs unify disparate elements in a landscape, including ground covers, lawns, perennials, buildings, and trees. Shrubs can soften hardscape features, define areas, screen utilities, delineate property lines, buffer noisy streets, anchor flower beds and borders, bear attractive flowers and fruit, and provide winter interest.

Before planting shrubs, draw a plan of your landscape to indicate areas for public viewing, privacy, and utility. Use shrubs to hide utility poles, air conditioning boxes, compost piles, or alleys.

Shrubs should emphasize a house's entrance, with plants lowest at the entrance and tallest beyond the house corners. Select mixed shapes, textures, and colors of the right size to suit your space. Diversity will also help to attract birds and butterflies to your yard. Check *My Rocky Mountain Gardener's Guide* for recommendations.

The secret to growing shrubs begins with proper planting. Follow these steps when planting (see instructions below). It is important to keep newly planted shrubs watered the first year. About 1 inch of water per week is adequate; overwatering can waterlog the roots, especially in clay soils. Mulching will help to maintain uniform moisture, conserve water, and suppress weed growth.

PRUNING TECHNIQUE
Pruning at the right time is essential for enhancing flowering, fruiting and healthy growth. Shrubs pruned at the wrong time will fail to bloom. If improperly pruned, shrubs may lose stems and succumb to pests and diseases. Prune spring-flowering shrubs immediately after the blooms begin to fade. This will allow the shrubs to form new buds for the next flowering season. Prune ornamental fruit trees after the fruits set, and selectively prune older or crisscrossing branches and stems. Prune all other shrubs in late winter or early spring when you can see the shrub's structure unobstructed by the foliage.

For continuous renewal pruning, remove one-third of the oldest stems all the way to the ground. Doing this yearly stimulates new stems from the bottom of the shrub. It will keep the shrub full and shapely and results in a canopy that is never more than three years old. Following renewal pruning, head back overly long stems. Make your cut at a shorter side shoot that is growing in the same direction. This will reduce the size of the shrub without destroying the natural growth habit.

Rejuvenation pruning will restore old shrubs and hedges that are bare at the bottom with all the foliage at the top. Cut these shrubs all the way down to within a few inches from the ground. They will grow back full to the bottom. Prune hedges wider at the bottom than at the top to allow light to reach lower stems and branches.

FALL AND WINTER WATERING
Lack of available soil moisture can take its toll on shrubs during a prolonged fall or winter dry spell. Water shrubs when temperatures are above freezing and the ground remains unfrozen. This may need to be done every four to five weeks, depending upon your local weather conditions. After winter watering, don't forget to disconnect the hose, drain, and store it away for later use.

GARDENING WITH AN ALTITUDE TIPS

Shrubs for Idaho

DECIDUOUS SHRUBS

- American Plum, *Prunus americana*
- Apache Plume, *Fallugia paradoxa*
- Barberry, *Berberis* spp.
- Beauty Bush, *Kolkwitzia amabilis*
- Blue Mist Spirea, *Caryopteris incana*
- Burning Bush, *Euonymus alatus*
- Butterfly Bush, *Buddleia davidii*
- Common Ninebark, *Physocarpus opulifolius*
- Cotoneaster, *Cotoneaster* spp.
- Currant, *Ribes* spp.
- Daphne, *Daphne* spp.
- Dwarf Arctic Willow, *Salix purpurea*
- Firethorn, *Pyracantha coccinea*
- Forsythia, *Forsythia* x *intermedia*
- Glossy Buckthorn, *Rhamnus frangula*
- Honeysuckle, *Lonicera* spp.
- Hydrangea, *Hydrangea* spp.
- Leadplant, *Amorpha canescens*
- Lilac, *Syringa* spp.
- Mockorange, *Philadelphus* spp.
- Mountain Mahogany, *Cercocarpus montanus*

- Oregon Grape, *Mahonia aquifolium*
- Potentilla, *Potentilla fruticosa*
- Red-twig Dogwood, *Cornus sericea*
- Rock Spirea, *Holodiscus dumosus*
- Rose-of-Sharon, *Hibiscus syriacus*
- Saucer Magnolia, *Magnolia* x *soulangiana*
- Scotch Broom, *Cytisus scoparius*
- Sea Buckthorn, *Hippophae rhamnoides*
- Siberian Pea Shrub, *Caragana arborescens*
- Silver Buffaloberry, *Shepherdia argentea*
- Snowberry, *Symphoricarpos albus*
- Spirea, *Spirea* spp. and hybrids
- Sumac, *Rhus* spp.
- Viburnum, *Viburnum* spp.
- Witchhazel, *Hamamelis vernalis*

EVERGREEN SHRUBS

- Arborvitae, *Thuja occidentalis*
- Chinese Juniper, *Juniperus chinensis* cultivars
- Dwarf Mugo Pine, *Pinus mugo var. pumilio*
- Rocky Mountain Juniper, *Juniperus scopulorum*
- Yew, *Taxus* x *media*

EVERGREENS FOR SMALL SPACES

Remember that small spruce tree that was so darling? Now it has grown so huge, it's ready to take over the house and driveway. This is a typical scenario in landscaping with evergreen trees.

With today's limited landscape space, the traditional native blue spruce or Ponderosa pine will eventually dominate the yard, limit activities, and create potential hazards. An alternative is to select dwarf conifers. Many of these smaller-growing specimens are noted for unusual growth habits or interesting foliage colors, such as weeping spruce, variegated juniper, and prostrate pine.

These evergreens can be grouped for an attractive border or screening effect. Just keep in mind that as the plants grow, branches will intertwine and compete. Pruning and maintenance will help to keep the plants at desired heights and spread, but it is best to preserve the natural shape and form as much as possible.

As you make selections for your landscape, check climate zone rating and hardiness in your area. Also consider plant exposure to sunlight, daily temperature fluctuations, drought endurance, winter sun exposure, and the roller-coaster effect of late winter and early spring weather.

SOILS FOR SMALL CONIFERS

Soils play a critical role in the success of growing small conifers. Our typical clay soils have poor drainage and can limit root growth. Knowing your soil and amending it accordingly can be the difference between success and failure. Soils become so mixed up when houses are built that the end result is "contractor dirt," unfit for any self-respecting plant to thrive. Additionally, the soil in the front yard can be different from the back yard.

Before planting a shrub, loosen the soil thoroughly in all directions for several feet. This aeration will help promote vigorous root growth. If the soil is a heavy clay, add 25 to 30 percent by volume of a quality compost, well-aged manure, or sphagnum peat moss, and work into the planting site at least 10 to 12 inches deep.

WATERING

Like large shade trees, small trees are dependent on adequate soil moisture for survival, especially during the fall and winter. Dig down into the soil at least 10 inches, and feel for soil moisture around the root zone. This is the best way to determine watering intervals. Water if the soil feels dry.

To effectively deep soak the root zone, water shrubs with sprinklers or soaker hoses placed at the drip line, the outermost perimeter of the shrub's crown. Watering should even extend beyond this drip line area since shrub roots grow farther outward. The key to effective watering is to allow the water to percolate deeply into the subsoil and spread laterally to cover the root zone.

OTHER POINTS TO CONSIDER

Dwarf evergreens take time to propagate and are generally slow-growing, so plants at the local garden store may be relatively expensive. Most selections do best in full sun with good air circulation or partial shade. Read plant descriptions carefully. Most dwarf evergreens need winter protection from the wind and severe desiccation. Use organic mulches to conserve soil moisture. Once dwarf conifers are established, they are considered low-maintenance.

Before purchasing a dwarf conifer, find out its mature size. If a specific species grows to 75 feet

and the dwarf selection grows only to 30 feet, is it still suited for your landscape situation? Following are some selected dwarf conifers that do well:

Abies balsamea 'Nana'—This is a dwarf Balsam fir (15 to 18 inches tall) with deep-green, glossy needles. Needles are short and flattened. Needs some shade and good moisture.

• *Abies concolor* 'Compacta'—A very compact, pyramidal form white fir (4 feet by 2 feet). Noted for its blue-green needles. Does best in well-drained soils and full sun.

• *Picea pungens* 'Globosa'—A dwarf blue spruce with densely branched globe shape (3 feet tall and wider). Bright blue needles that hold color throughout the year.

• *Picea pungens glauca* 'Pendula'—A weeping form of Colorado blue spruce with variable height. Does best in full sun.

• *Picea glauca* 'Conica'—A dwarf Alberta spruce with cone shape 4 to 6 feet tall, 2 to 3 feet wide and holding dense bright-green needles. A slow grower that requires winter shade and wind protection or "winter burn" will result.

• *Pinus sylvestris* 'Fastigiata'—A columnar Scotch pine that grows 3 to 4 feet wide and 20 feet tall. Makes a nice addition to narrow landscape settings. Noted for its twisted 2-inch-long, bluish-green needles.

• *Pinus strobus* 'Nana'—A dwarf Eastern white pine with branched pyramidal habit that is 3 to 7 feet high and 6 to 10 feet wide. Slivery, blue-green needles make this an interesting rock garden evergreen.

• *Juniperus communis* 'Compressa'—An upright juniper with compact, narrow, conical shape (3 to 4 feet by 6 to 8 inches). Slow-growing with bluish-green needles; prefers partial shade.

If you like to invite birds and other wildlife into your landscape, choose shrubs that produce shelter and food for various types of wildlife. Visit a wild bird specialty store to learn more about planting a bird-friendly garden. Shrubs for birds include cotoneaster, snowberry, and honeysuckle.

PLANTING BARE-ROOT SHRUBS

• Dig the planting hole wide enough to accommodate the bare roots when they are spread out. Dig only as deep as the length of the roots; measure from the healthy root tips to the crown of the shrub, or the knob where its roots join its stems. It is more important to have a planting hole that is wider than extra deep.

• Take about one-third of the soil from the hole and build a cone of firmly packed soil centered in the bottom of the otherwise empty hole. Amend the rest of the loose soil with compost; use one-third compost to two-thirds of your native soil.

• Set the shrub in the planting hole so its crown rests on top of the mounded soil and the roots splay down along the sides. Check that the shrub crown is level with, or just slightly above, the ground level.

• Fill the planting hole with prepared backfill soil, intermittently gently firming it around the bare roots. Packing it down too hard will damage the fragile root system.

• Water the newly planted shrub thoroughly to eliminate any air pockets in the hole. Check the shrub depth again to make sure it has not sunk below ground level; if it has, gently pull to raise the crown to the proper depth.

• Spread a 2- to 3-inch layer of organic mulch over the root zone of the shrub. Do not pile the mulch up against the stems of the shrub.

PLANTING BALLED-AND-BURLAPPED SHRUBS

• Loosely tie tall shrub stems together so the rootball is visible and easier to handle. Keep the rootball moist prior to planting. This will keep the soil and roots intact during transport.

• Dig a wide, saucer-shaped hole with sloping sides. Prepare the hole two to three times wider as the rootball and only as deep as the rootball is high.

• Set the shrub's rootball on firm soil, oriented as desired. Make sure that it is not sitting any lower than the surrounding ground level. In clay soils, set the rootball an inch higher than ground level.

• Cut or carefully remove the nylon twine holding the rootball and burlap. Then unwind as much of the burlap away as possible since it is very slow to decompose in alkaline soils. If there is a wire basket, use a bolt cutter to remove the top half of the basket to allow for root growth and prevent girdling of roots. Gently brush off the top of the rootball until the root flare at the base of the shrub is exposed and level with the ground.

• Backfill the hole with prepared soil (one-third compost to two-thirds removed soil); gently firm the soil around and over the rootball. Then fashion a rim of soil beyond the edge of the rootball with the remaining soil to create a water-holding reservoir.

• Water the shrub within this soil dike so it soaks down 8 inches or more. Do not fertilize for the first season.

• Spread a 2- to 3-inch layer of organic mulch over and slightly beyond the planting area to maintain moisture and prevent weed invasion.

PLANTING CONTAINER-GROWN SHRUBS

• Dig the planting hole with sloping sides two to three times wider than the shrub's container. The hole should be only as deep as the container.

• Carefully remove the shrub from the container; gently tease the rootball to remove excess potting mixture from around the roots. If the rootball has become potbound, lightly score or cut the tangled roots to encourage them to grow outward.

• Set the rootball into the planting hole, position as desired, and level with or slightly above the ground level. Check to make sure the root flare at the base of the stems is not too deep, but level with the surrounding soil.

• Mix the soil removed from the hole with one-third compost by volume and use as backfill. Fill in around and over the rootball. This soil mixture will allow for a better transition for the roots to grow into the harsh reality of your native soil. Roots need to grow and explore beyond the growing medium in which they were started.

• Gently firm the soil around the rootball; you can use extra soil to form a water basin around the shrub. Water in thoroughly. Then spread a 2- to 3-inch layer of organic mulch over the planting area and beyond, up to the root flare. Water as the soil begins to dry out. Check soil moisture with a garden trowel or soil probe.

FORCING SHRUB BRANCHES TO BLOOM

• Prune the branches on a warm day when temperatures are above freezing. Be somewhat selective so you won't disfigure the natural growth form of the shrub.

• Cut the branches 6 to 12 inches long.

• Bring the cut branches indoors, and make a second cut on a slant just above the original cut before placing in water. Then, make several 1-inch-long slits in the end of each cut stem to expose more surface area for water to soak up.

• Place the cut ends in a bucket or vase of water into which a flower preservative has been added; see homemade flower cocktail on page 288. Place the container in a cool, dark spot where temperatures are 45 to 50 degrees.

• When the buds start to expand and show color, move them to bright light, but keep them out of the direct sun. Lower temperatures will prolong the life of forced blooms if you plan on using them in floral arrangements.

• Some, like pussy willow, will root in the water and can be carefully transplanted outdoors later in the spring. Have fun.

LAYERING SHRUB BRANCHES

Simple layering, a process of bending branches over and covering the tips with soil, is commonly used to start black and purple raspberries and grapes. Before layering, be sure to work some compost into the soil. Begin the process by wounding the branch with a slanting cut about 2 inches long on the upper side of the branch, about 12 inches from the tip. Dust this wound with a rooting hormone. Then, pin the branch down between the trunk and the cut with a peg or wire wicket, or weight down with a stone.

After the branch is fastened to the soil, bend the tip upright. As you do this, gently twist the branch as if you were turning a screwdriver one-half turn. This will open the cut.

Next, place a second pin or peg over the branch directly at the point of the cut. Cover the prepared branch with several inches of soil, and mound the soil around the upturned stem so the wound is 4 inches underground. Pack the soil firmly.

Mulch the soil with compost or leaf mold. Water frequently; keeping the covering soil moist. When the layer has formed roots the following spring, cut the rooted branch free from the parent plant. Leave it in place for a few weeks, then you can transplant it to a new location.

PROTECTING SHRUBS WITH WINTER SNOW SHEDS

If you grow evergreen shrubs close to the house and they are vulnerable to a heavy snow load sliding off the roof construct temporary snow sheds to protect them from damage.

Make the sheds out of plywood sheets attached to sloping two-by-four frames, and set them over the vulnerable shrubs in autumn. Any snow that slides down from the roof will land on the snow sheds and slide to the ground. Make the slope of the sheds steep enough that the snow won't stick to their roofs. Some snow can be quite heavy, so make the sheds strong enough to withstand the weight and the impact.

JANUARY
SHRUBS

 PLANNING

Now that the holiday season is over, take time to relax and enjoy your winter landscape. Look out of your windows to see which shrubs are in view. Do they have eye-catching features including persistent berries, interesting bark, evergreen foliage, or colorful stems that add form and structure to the winter landscape? Or are most of your shrubs planted too near to the house, to be viewed and appreciated only by the passerby on the street?

Check your garden notebook to see which shrubs were infested with pests or plagued by diseases. It may be time to make plans to replace the undesirable ones.

Examine nursery and garden catalogs arriving in the mail. As you pore over photographs of attractive shrubs, learn about their adaptability and hardiness to our region. Before you buy new shrubs, draw a sketch or design to help you in spacing and selecting the right kinds of shrubs for a particular site. If you don't feel comfortable doing this, consult a landscape designer, contractor, or certified landscape architect.

 PLANTING

This is not the time to plant shrubs, even if the soil is not frozen. Temperature fluctuations, prolonged periods of drought, wind, and other variables can make it a challenge for plants to transplant. The one exception would be the living **Christmas tree** if you chose one in December. Rather than trying to maintain and grow it indoors, it is much better to plant or heel it outdoors. For a week or so, acclimate the plant in an unheated garage before moving directly outdoors. For planting instructions, see page 153.

 CARE

You may need to protect newly planted shrubs from winterburn

Snow Shed

by shading them with burlap screens or snow fencing on their south, southwest, or south sides. Temperamental evergreens like **Alberta spruce** may also require similar sun and wind protection to prevent the foliage from turning brown and getting scorched.

Ice and snow can bend and break weak-wooded shrubs. Gently brush wet, heavy snow off the shrubs as it falls, before it weighs down the branches. Use a broom to lift the stems upward, NOT DOWNWARD, to allow the snow to slide off the branches. A light accumulation of snow is not harmful and will actually insulate the plant, so don't get carried away about brushing off the snow. In some areas, snow protects the lower parts or stems that will produce blooms in the spring.

Protect shrubs planted near the street from salt sprays. Salts accumulate in the soil and will stunt or kill shrubs. Set up burlap screens or other barriers to pro-
vulnerable shrubs.

GARDENING WITH AN ALTITUDE TIPS
Planting a Living Holiday Evergreen Shrub or Tree

Pick a warm day to dig the hole well before the ground freezes. I like to do this sometime in late October or November. Choose a proper location to accommodate the shrub's growing habit and maturing size. Dig a large saucer-shaped hole two to three times wider than the shrub or tree's rootball. Dig the hole only as deep as the container in which the plant is growing, or the same depth as the rootball.

Set the shrub in the planting hole, remove the container or as much of the burlap that surrounds the rootball. Cut away the top half or more of the wire basket if there is one holding the rootball together. Be careful not to break the rootball during this process. If you live in a windy area, stake the plant before backfilling to avoid damaging the rootball. Once the plant is situated in the hole, fill around the rootball with prepared soil.

Gently firm the soil around and over the rootball and water in thoroughly. Do not add any fertilizer at this time; wait until spring.

If you desire, spray the bark and foliage with an antidesiccant liquid to help retard the loss of moisture from the plant, particularly during drying winds.

Spread a 3-inch mulch over the root zone to maintain soil moisture. Don't forget to water the new plant addition during extended dry periods of winter. This may need to be done monthly if snow or rain fall is scarce.

 WATERING

Check underneath the mulch around your shrubs to see if the soil is moist. If it is not, winter watering is in order. Choose a warm day when temperatures are above freezing. Set out a frog-eye sprinkler at the drip line of the shrub, and let it run for 15 to 30 minutes. Do this early in the day to allow the water to soak in. Don't forget to disconnect and drain the garden hose after winter watering; otherwise, you may end up with a very expensive plumbing repair.

 GROOMING

Limit pruning to removal of injured or broken branches or stems. Make clean cuts where the branch joins a larger branch or the main stem. Take care not to cut into the main branch or trunk, as this will cause further dieback. You don't need to apply any wound dressing to pruning cuts. They will close over on their own.

 PROBLEMS

Be on the watch for rabbit, deer, field mice, and other critters nibbling at stems or upper branches. It may be time to apply more homemade repellent (see page 284).

Construct protective wire cages around plants that are most vulnerable to deer and elk. Cages should be tall enough to deter deer that stand on deep snow cover. If permitted in your area, an electric fence will keep them at bay, too.

FEBRUARY
SHRUBS

PLANNING

The cold days of winter are a good time to evaluate the positioning of shrubs in your landscape. A shrub in the wrong place can hit the sides of the house, grow over a pathway, or obstruct your view from a window. If the plant is healthy, make plans to move it yourself, or hire a professional landscaper to do it for you in early spring. Get the new site ready on the warmer days of the month.

How would you like some early spring color indoors during the winter? Though I don't recommend pruning at this time, a little bit can be planned so you can force flowers inside. Spring-flowering shrubs whose flower buds were formed on last year's wood can be coaxed into early bloom indoors once their dormancy requirements have been met. While this varies between species, at least eight weeks of temperatures below 40 degrees Fahrenheit is generally sufficient for most blooming shrubs. See branch forcing instructions on page 151.

PLANTING

Even though the soil may be beginning to thaw, don't jump the gun to plant new shrubs or transplant existing ones quite yet. A good timeline for planting is when the garden stores begin to bring out their nursery stock of shrubs. Transplant shrubs in your yard when their buds are just beginning to swell, but before total leaf expansion.

Dig out and dispose of problem shrubs that are diseased, dying, or otherwise too old to rejuvenate. Then, later in the month you can transplant existing shrubs that are positioned incorrectly to new locations in the landscape.

If you placed an order via the mail, bare-root shrubs may be arriving in your area. If the ground is still frozen when they arrive, store bare-root stock in a cool place and keep the root system moist until planting time. An unheated garage or cool basement will work for temporary storage.

CARE

Routinely check any structures or snow fence you set up to protect your shrubs to makes sure they are still functional. Until the chances of snow and severe weather are over, they can still be useful.

For weak-wooded shrubs, carefully remove snow from the branches, particularly if it is a heavy, wet snow. Use upward strokes from beneath, not from the top. Start knocking snow from the lower branches first so that snow from the top ones will not overburden, and possibly break, the lower branches. Use an old broom, and gently bump it upward from underneath to dislodge and scatter the snow. To finish up, redo the lower branches to clear the snow that had fallen from above.

Do not disturb stems or branches that are iced over because they are likely to break. When the ice melts, they will resume their former posture. Check the shrubs after every storm, and take action to prop up those that need it, and prune out severely damaged branches.

WATERING

Water shrubs whose soil is not frozen solid if there has been little or no appreciable snow or rainfall for a month or more. Water early in the day to allow the water to soak down to the roots. Well-mulched shrubs usually survive better than those left unmulched since the mulch helps to retain moisture and prevent the soil from heaving.

GROOMING

You can commence late-winter pruning of shrubs now, but remember that pruning spring-flowering shrubs will remove their flower buds and reduce flowering. Wait to prune spring bloomers until after they finish blooming. Minor renewal pruning can preserve most of this year's flowers though, so prune gently.

It's time to renew shrubs that produce colorful winter bark such as the **red-twig** and **yellow-twig** dogwoods. Cut out at least one-third to one-half of the oldest canes to the ground with a pruning lopper. Older stems tend to lose color after a few years and can become infested with scale and canker diseases. Any overly long or scraggly branches can be headed back to shorter branches that are growing in the same direction.

To get an early spring feeling indoors, selectively prune some budded branches from spring-flowering shrubs. See details on forcing branches in the Planning section. The closer to their natural blooming time you cut the stems, the more quickly they will bloom indoors.

Severe heading back renews overgrown shrubs.

Heading back the tips of the shoots encourages branching below the cuts to maintain a desired height and width.

Thin out one-third of the oldest branches from multistemmed shrubs.

Prune **currants, raspberries,** and **gooseberries** starting in mid- to late month. Remove all the weak, spindly canes, and winterkilled wood. Every year, remove all but half a dozen of the older branches to the ground. This will help these fruits to produce new vigorous growth. Begin to prune **grapes** late in the month or wait until March.

PROBLEMS

Continue to be on the watch for damage by deer, elk, rabbits and other critters. They will nibble on tender branch tips and the succulent stems of young shrubs. The only dependable deterrent is a deer-proof fence. Check with your local Division of Wildlife for more information on deer-proofing your landscape.

If you are relying on spray repellents, it's a good idea to repeat applications every few weeks as they breakdown in sunlight and are washed away after snow or rainfall.

MARCH
SHRUBS

 PLANNING

Now is the time to get serious about purchasing new shrubs for your landscape. Make a sketch or a detailed plan so you choose the proper shrub for the proper site. If the location receives full sun, partial shade, or shade, select plants accordingly so they will perform in that area. Check soil conditions to make sure the area is well drained, or make plans to improve that area prior to planting. Once you have an accurate list of shrubs that will fit into your landscape, you are ready to place an order with the nursery or garden store.

By now, some of the mail-order stock may be arriving at your door. If the soil is ready, it's time to plant. If your area is not ready to plant, store bare-root plants in a cool spot and keep their roots moist up to planting time.

 PLANTING

Try to avoid working the soil if it is too wet. Doing so will leave it with lots of clods and poor structure. As the soil begins to dry out enough to work, you can begin planting. Check by taking a handful of soil and squeezing it into a ball. If the soil ball easily crumbles, it is ready for planting. If it stays sticky, it is still too wet.

Plant bare-root stock while it is still dormant; it will suffer less transplant shock than if you wait until the buds leaf out. Keep bare-root nursery stock in a cool location and the wrapping moist until you plant them outdoors. For planting instructions, see page 150.

 CARE

You can gradually begin to rake out old leaves and other debris that has collected in your shrub bed during the winter. Collect fallen leaves and put them in your compost pile or shred and work them into the vegetable garden. Take care not to disturb any emerging perennials or spring-flowering bulbs. Gradually remove winter protection from shrubs by mid- to late-month. Keep a watch for any damage to the shrubs from the winter, such as broken branches or critter-feeding injury.

Neglected shrubs can be renovated now. Those showing lots of overgrown, tangled, or dead wood can be pruned back hard. As long as the shrub is otherwise healthy, it will respond to rejuvenation pruning. One method to renew an older shrub is to gradually prune out dead and old wood over several seasons. In situations when a **deciduous shrub** is a total mess, the best

way to renew it is to cut it back to the ground. This may seem radical, but it will eventually stimulate vigorous new growth, giving the shrub a whole new lease on life.

Rejuvenation pruning can be done before spring growth expands, either before leaf or bud break. With **evergreens,** prune before the new, soft needles form. On old, tired **deciduous shrubs,** systematically cut back every stem at 4 to 6 inches from the ground. Use sharp loppers or pruners; in some cases, a chain saw will be needed to remove thick, large canes.

As young replacement growth begins to appear, you can clip or pinch off some of the weaker canes to encourage the development of fewer, but stronger remaining ones. These will make up the basic structure of the shrub.

Shrubs that are growing in their natural form and are well balanced can be pruned to thin out crowded or crisscrossing stems. As the stems grow 6 inches, pinch out the terminal bud to promote more branching, if desired. New branches will emerge just below the pinch.

 WATERING

Water newly planted shrubs as soon as the soil begins to dry out. Established shrubs need a deep watering every few weeks. To avoid waterlogging the soil around your shrubs, always check soil moisture with a soil probe, or dig down several inches with a garden trowel.

 FERTILIZING

When signs of new growth appear, it's time to apply a slow-release granular fertilizer over the root zone. I recommend a complete 5-10-5 to give them a boost in spring. Lightly scratch the granules into the soil with a rake, and water well. Use the amount recommended on the package label. Over-fertilizing can increase soluble salts in the soil and damage the roots.

Evergreens can be fertilized as soon as you see the new soft growth emerging. Use a higher nitrogen fertilizer such as 10-10-10. If you prefer, you can apply a timed-release fertilizer that will last for several months. Follow directions on the package label.

 GROOMING

Prune early spring-flowering shrubs like **forsythia** and **quince** when they finish blooming. Avoid pruning other shrubs that bloom later, as this will remove the flower buds. Shrubs that are overgrown or neglected can be renewed by pruning out one-third of the oldest canes to the ground. This will not severely reduce the bloom this season, but will encourage new, healthy, vigorous growth. Head these plants back when flowering is finished. Cut back another third next year. Cut back the final third the year after that. In this way you have renewed an old shrub with new, vigorous, and more flowering stems.

Finish pruning your small fruits including **raspberries, blackberries,** and **elderberries** before the buds swell. Remove the weakest canes, and oldest wood, leaving 6 to 8 canes per plant. You can head back the remaining canes of **red raspberries** to 3 to 4 feet tall. On **black raspberries** and **blackberries,** cut back lateral branches on remaining stems to 10 to 15 inches long. If desired, after pruning **bramble fruits,** tie them to supports for easier maintenance.

If you grow everbearing **raspberries** for a late summer or fall crop, you can get out the lawn mower or pruning lopers, and cut the canes to the ground. The new canes produced this spring will bear an abundance of fruit without any further pruning. Remove damaged canes and dead wood from **currants** and **gooseberries.**

 PROBLEMS

Be on the watch for overwintering insects including aphids and scale. You can control them effectively now by applying a dormant oil spray before bud break. Lighter oils can be applied even during leaf emergence. Read and follow label directions for application rates and timing. Do not use oils on bluish-green **evergreens,** as it will remove the waxy coating that produces the coloration.

Weeds will begin to pop up this month. Handpull or dig them out as soon as you spot them. Spread more mulch, if needed, especially to bare soil to discourage germination of annual weed seeds.

NOTES

_____
_____
_____
_____
_____
_____
_____
_____
_____
_____
_____
_____
_____

APRIL

SHRUBS

 PLANNING

Now is the time to have a camera ready to shoot pictures of spring-blooming shrubs. Take photos at the different stages of blooming to keep track of the succession of bloom and foliage over the season. Pictures are helpful when evaluating plants in your landscape.

Even though there may be some winter encores, spring has arrived. It is planting time, but before you purchase, be sure of your shrub choices. Will they suit the location and not outgrow the area? Consider the exposure; is it full sun, partial sun, or shady? Check soil drainage and amend as needed prior to planting.

Watch for the flowering cycle of conifers including **pines, spruces,** and **junipers.** On a windy day you can see the air fill with yellow pollen as it blows from the male flowers that look like tiny cones. Later in the season, you may see the true cones on pines and spruces that develop from the female flowers.

 PLANTING

This is the best time to finish up planting bare-root shrubs before they fully expand their buds into leaves. Shrubs are available as container-grown and balled-and-burlapped. Getting them in the ground early will allow them to develop a strong root system before the onset of hot weather. They will have become well established before winter arrives and better equipped to survive.

 CARE

Learn more about the care and maintenance of your shrubs and any special requirements. Look them up in *My Rocky Mountain Gardener's Guide.*

Mulch shrubs to maintain uniform moisture and conserve water. A 2-to 3-inch layer of mulch over bare soil under and around shrubs will hold in soil moisture, eventually enrich the soil, and discourage weeds. Do not put the mulch in direct contact with the basal stems of shrubs though. It can create a problem with rodents nesting and nibbling on the tender bark. Keep the mulch 4 to 6 inches away from the crown to promote better air circulation and reduce disease problems.

 WATERING

Newly planted shrubs will need to be watered weekly if there is insufficient rain. Set a slowly running hose or frog-eye sprinkler beneath the shrub at the root zone and let it run until the ground is saturated or the water-holding reservoir is filled. In soils that are clay, water 10 to 15 minutes, let it soak in; then resume watering for another 15 minutes and let that soak in.

If your budget and time allow, install a soaker hose or drip irrigation to save time and assure a good, deep watering. Be careful not to overwater shrubs during their establishment. More shrubs are killed by too much water than by not enough. Established shrubs need, on average, about an inch of water a week either from rainfall or from you. More watering is needed in hot weather, less when it is cool. Check the soil with a soil probe or dig down with a garden trowel.

Mulched shrubs may go longer between waterings. Dig underneath the mulch to check soil moisture. This will help you in determining a schedule for watering in your soil conditions.

 FERTILIZING

Newly planted shrubs need one growing season to promote strong roots outward into the planting hole and beyond. They do not need to be fertilized the first year. For a boost, however, you can apply a slow-release 5-10-5 granular fertilizer over the root zone. Do not use a high-nitrogen product. Lightly scratch it into the soil and water in well. Reapply mulch as needed. Established shrubs can be fertilized with a complete 10-10-10 or similar fertilizer; use one pound per 100 square feet of shrub bed. For individual shrubs in the landscape, apply a cup or two spread evenly over the root zone and lightly scratch in. Water in well.

Don't forget to fertilize small fruits at this time, too. Use a slow-release 5-10-5. Read and follow label directions on the product package.

GROOMING

Prune early flowering shrubs after they finish blooming if you need to shape them or gradually renew an older shrub that is losing vigor. Remove dead or damaged stems and branches. Use sharp pruning tools.

Renew older shrubs by cutting out one-third of the oldest stems to the ground each spring. This will help them grow new, vigorous shoots. Cut the taller remaining branches to shorten them if desired. Prune to an outside bud that is growing in the same direction as the longer stem to maintain the natural growth pattern.

Prune hedges to shape them to your liking. The best way to reduce storm damage to hedges is to prune the shrubs to a narrower top and wider bottom. This will allow for better shedding of snow and will reduce stem breakage. It is better to thin out weak stems and older wood than to just shear away the tops.

If you did not prune the stems of **butterfly bush** in late fall, now is the time to remove any winterkill or cut the shrub back to within 4 to 6 inches of ground level. This will allow for healthy, vigorous growth that will bloom this summer.

PROBLEMS

Be on the watch for aphids on the new tender growth. Some caterpillars may be showing up now, too. If you observe ants running up and down the stems, it usually is a sign of an aphid infestation, as ants like to farm aphids for the sweet honeydew they produce.

Use a homemade soap spray (see page 283) to thwart these pests early in the season.

If pest problems are severe, you may have to use an insecticide labeled for that shrub. Read and follow label directions.

Weeds pop up like wildfire after April showers. Pull or hoe them out promptly before they go to seed. Tough perennial weeds can be spot-sprayed with a nonselective weed control. Read and follow label directions. This will ensure that you not only kill the tops, but the roots, too.

Rejuvenation

MAY

SHRUBS

 PLANNING

May is the month that spring really arrives in the landscape. Some of the most spectacular shrubs are in bloom now including **lilac, spireas, viburnums, daphnes,** and **mockorange**. Their fragrances permeate the air, especially in the evening. Open the windows and let it in! The days begin to get warmer, and soon cool ones will be outnumbered. Shrubs are growing vigorously, sending out new foliage, and extending their stem length. Later spring-flowering shrubs are developing their flower buds. Evergreens are extending their soft, paler needles or scales at the tips of the branches that signal they are growing vigorously, too.

As shrubs bloom in your landscape, make notes in your garden notebook or journal. Record the date you make observations for future reference. Note botanical names whenever possible, so if you need to replace a shrub in the middle of a hedge, you can match the variety. Watching how shrubs grow and develop will guide you in the correct timing for treating insect pests and diseases.

This is also a good month to visit public and private gardens to see shrubs that may have potential in your landscape. Keep a record of those you want to try. Note the height and spread of the shrub so you can determine if it will work in your space. Check with local nurseries for the availability of shrubs you'd like. Some may need to be ordered via mail or the Internet. Note hardiness of the shrubs you wish to grow. You may have to create microclimates to successfully grown certain species.

 PLANTING

Container-grown shrubs can be planted from now until early fall. Local garden stores are aware of the impact of shrubs in bloom and will usually have excellent displays to choose from. If you see varieties of shrubs you particularly like, now is the time to add them to your landscape. Planting container-grown shrubs differs from planting bare-root or balled-and-burlapped shrubs. See instructions on page 150.

 CARE

Routinely check the condition of your shrubs. Gently bend stems or branches that appear dead. If they are still flexible rather than dry and brittle, the stem may still be alive. Do the fingernail test by scraping a bit of the bark off the stem; if there is still green tissue beneath the bark, the stem is still alive. Lightly prune back the stem about halfway, and see if it will regenerate new growth.

If you didn't get around to pruning spring-flowering shrubs by now, do so before the end of the month. They will soon start to develop next year's flower buds, and pruning too late will remove next season's blooms. Add fresh mulch as needed around and over the root zone as the mulch layer thins to less than a few inches.

 WATERING

Continue to water shrubs when rainfall is scarce or during prolonged dry periods. If shrubs are mulched properly, they can go longer between waterings. Dig down through the mulch to check subsoil moisture to determine your watering schedule.

Newly planted shrubs and those in containers will need more frequent watering to ensure healthy growth. An inch of water per week will usually suffice. Do not forget to use mulches, even with shrubs planted in large containers. This helps maintain uniform moisture while conserving water, too.

FERTILIZING

Any fertilizer should have been applied by now, but if you forgot, you still have time to apply a complete fertilizer such as 5-10-5 or 10-10-10 around the root zone. Lightly scratch it in and water in thoroughly.

For shrubs that are potted in containers and because they are watered more frequently, use a diluted soluble fertilizer labeled for shrubs or perennial flowers. Apply every two weeks when you water these shrubs. Read and follow label directions. Do not use more than recommended. I prefer to dilute soluble plant foods by half the recommended rate to avoid salt accumulations.

GROOMING

Deadhead or remove the spent flowers from blooming shrubs unless you want them to produce fruit for the birds. Avoid shearing off the tops or tips of shrubs. This destroys their natural growth habit and causes denser interior growth that is subject to spider mites.

Continue to prune spring-flowering shrubs as they finish up blooming. Shrubs perform best when annual pruning removes one-third of the oldest canes to the ground. This makes the shrub produce fresh, new stems for future blooms. Head back overly long or straggly stems to side shoots growing in the same direction.

PROBLEMS

Be on the watch for insect pests; as the days stay consistently warm, insect eggs will hatch. Control early invasions with an insecticidal soap spray or make your own homemade soap spray (see page 283).

Lilac borers and other boring insects will make sneak attacks now. Be ready to prevent them. Place pheromone traps in your landscape to detect their presence. This will allow you to apply control measures at the proper time.

If your **junipers** have a white frothy substance on their branches that resembles spit, it is being invaded by spittle bugs. Hose them off with a forceful spray of water.

NOTES

_____
_____
_____
_____
_____
_____
_____
_____
_____
_____
_____
_____
_____
_____
_____
_____
_____
_____
_____
_____
_____
_____
_____
_____
_____
_____
_____
_____
_____
_____
_____
_____

JUNE
SHRUBS

PLANNING

This is a month of transitions. Spring-flowering shrubs are finishing up bloom, while summer-flowering types are setting bud. The sweet fragrance of **mockorange** will soon fill the air. Summer is just around the corner and temperatures are rising. Plan to be on watch for the pests of summer. Routinely monitoring your garden, at least every few days will help you prevent severe problems.

Properly sited and maintained, shrubs play an integral part in the landscape—defining borders, providing a cooling screen from summer's sun, reducing noise from the street, and providing an attractive backdrop to the flower garden. Take pictures of your shrubs to keep track on how they function in your landscape.

If you don't have shrubs that will bloom later in the season, you still have plenty of time to plant some. Garden stores have container-grown shrubs that will bloom from mid- to late-summer through early fall. One of my favorites is **butterfly bush** (*Buddleia* sp) which is a magnet for summer's butterflies and hummingbirds. Don't forget to include shrubs that produce attractive autumn berries to feed the wild birds that visit your landscape.

Plan to evaluate how shrubs are performing. Corrective pruning may be needed to improve shape and flowering. Some may need replacement because they are just not working for the area.

PLANTING

You can still plant container-grown shrubs, the earlier in the month, the better. Summer's heat can take its toll on newly transplanted shrubs unless you give them extra attention to help them get established. Daily misting of the foliage, covering the shrub with a large cardboard box for a few days to allow it to acclimate, mulching, and watching your watering carefully, are some things to help ensure late planted shrubs will make it successfully.

It is too late to move established shrubs from one part of the landscape to another; put this project off till next spring. Some shrubs can be propagated now by **layering** the flexible stems (see page 151). If a branch of shrub is wounded and the wound covered with a rooting medium—loose soil or sphagnum peat moss—the branch usually will strike roots while it is still attached to the parent shrub. It can then be severed from the parent plant and transplanted as a new shrub. Layering is best done in late spring or early summer; rooting is most vigorous in cooler temperatures.

CARE

With the heat of summer arriving, it is important to monitor moisture in the soil to prevent stress to the shrubs. A stressed plant is more vulnerable to insect pests and diseases. Spread mulch around shrubs to retain moisture in the soil and prevent weeds.

You can safely move potted indoor shrubs including **citrus, fig, bougainvillea, Norfolk Island pine, hibiscus** and others outdoors to a covered porch or deck. Gradually acclimate them to the outside by bringing them indoors at night if it is still cool. Do not set them in direct sunlight, or the leaves will become scorched. After a week of this, they can stay outdoors until early fall. To maintain uniform moisture and reduce frequency of watering, spread a layer of organic mulch over the soil in the container. Always check the potting mixture before watering to avoid waterlogging the rootball.

WATERING

Check the soil underneath the mulch of newly planted and established shrubs every 3 to 4 days. Give them a good, deep drink of water if it is dry. Use a soaker hose or frog-eye sprinkler and irrigate slowly to allow the water to soak in deeply. If you have large planters or containers that are out in the garden, don't forget to water them every few days or as the soil begins to dry out.

Just because a shrub's foliage is wilting does not mean the plant needs water. Excessive heat, poor drainage, or root stress may cause wilting. Wait to see what happens later in the day when temperatures fall to check if the leaves remain wilted. If they regain their turgidity, it was the ambient heat. Always check the soil before watering.

FERTILIZING

Once the shrubs have completed their flowering cycle and produced seasonal growth, there is little need for additional fertilizer. Fast-release fertilizer can stimulate excessive stem growth, which stresses the plant during drought periods, may attract pests such as aphids, and may interfere with winter dormancy.

GROOMING

Limit pruning to removing broken, storm-damaged, or diseased branches from now until autumn. Do not shear new growth on shrubs, as this will only induce fast-growing water sprouts or a "witches broom." These succulent shoots are more susceptible to winter injury and desiccation.

Remove spent or dead blooms from flowering shrubs unless they are types that typically produce fruit. This will help to tidy the plant. Don't delay this process, as late pruning will remove flower buds that are developing for next year.

PROBLEMS

Insect pest activity may be expected now. As soon as you notice aphids, caterpillars, sawflies, spider mites, and others, handpick or squish those you can reach. Wash off others with a strong stream of water from the hose. Do not assume that every bug you see is a pest; there are many beneficial insects visiting the garden now. Look for lady bugs, lacewings, and praying mantises that are there to feed on the bad bugs.

Chlorosis may appear on certain shrubs; you will notice the foliage becoming pale or yellowing between darker green veins. This is usually an indication of iron deficiency. Although our region generally has iron in the soil, it is not readily available in a form that the plant can utilize. It helps to acidify the soil by adding powdered sulfur on the area over the root zone and watering it in. If the foliage does not green up in a few weeks, it is best to apply a chelated iron to the soil or leaves. Select an iron additive in the form of a wettable powder (WP on the label). Read and follow label directions.

NOTES

_____
_____
_____
_____
_____
_____
_____
_____
_____
_____

JULY
SHRUBS

PLANNING

July is the month of heat and possible drought conditions. It is also a time to enjoy the shrubs in your landscape. Though the spring-flowering shrubs are finished by now, summer-flowering shrubs will continue to put on a show.

If you are planning a summer vacation, make arrangements to have a friend of neighbor check your landscape while you're gone. This is especially important if we should experience a prolonged period of heat and drought. An automatic sprinkler system and drip irrigation will help, but is still a good idea to have someone check up on things to make sure everything is working correctly. Leave instructions on what to do if something should go wrong.

Shrubs provide framework and background for other plants, including flowers, ground covers, and lawns. They create a transition from the lawn to the home and other structures. Shrubs can be utilized to create privacy from a nearby neighbor, enclose a patio or deck, or provide a barrier to traffic—but are not as expensive or intimidating as walls and fences. Plan to use them more in your landscape if you don't already. A well-planned and well-designed landscape with a mix of shrubs, trees, vines, flowers, and ground covers will enhance your property.

PLANTING

This is not a good time to plant shrubs, unless there is a period of cool, overcast days. You may find shrubs on sale, but proceed with care. Newly planted shrubs can suffer from heat and drought conditions; you will have to give them extra attention to ensure their survival.

If planting new shrubs at this time, follow the same guidelines for planting container-grown shrubs in the May Planting section.

Periodically mist the foliage on hot days to cool down the plants and help them acclimate as they send out new roots after transplanting. I have often found it helpful to shade new transplants with a large cardboard box or burlap for a few weeks after they are set out in the landscape. This will protect them from intense sun, heat, and wind that may put them under stress.

CARE

Discourage birds from eating the berries of **raspberries** and other small fruits by draping bird netting over these shrubs.

Check the organic mulch spread over the root zone of shrubs. It may be settling or need replenishment. As summer's heat and frequent watering accelerates decomposition of mulch, the layers begin to get thinner and gradually help enrich the soil—a good thing. To work at its best, organic mulches need to be 2 to 3 inches thick. This will help to hold in moisture and discourage the invasion of annual weeds. Avoid piling it higher than 3 inches, however, as too thick a mulch can deprive roots of oxygen, impede drainage, and invite rodents. **Note:** Never apply mulch directly against the stems or canes of shrubs. It can result in crown rot and possible rodent damage. The stems need proper air circulation.

Be careful when using weed-trimmers around your shrubs. The fast-moving nylon string can girdle the stems, which allows entry points for diseases and certain insect pests. Though it is more tedious, get down on your hands and knees and pull weeds that are growing close to the stems. It's a good way to get in touch with Mother Earth as well!

WATERING

Make sure your shrubs are getting adequate water during the

hot, dry periods of summer. If we should be experiencing a period of drought, water shrubs deeply at least once a week or as often as your water provider will allow. This will reduce severe stress and dieback.

Give shrubs a deep drink by using a soaker hose around the root zone or placing a frog-eye sprinkler in the vicinity of the root area. Allow the water to run slowly until you notice it beginning to run off. Leaky hoses or pipes that sweat water through their pores can be strung throughout a shrub border so all of them can be watered at one time. Organic mulches will help to conserve the water you apply during the hot summer period. Use them judiciously.

GROOMING

Limit pruning to removing dead, diseased, storm-injured, or insect-ridden branches and stems. Do not shear shrubs unless you prefer this look. Shearing too late in summer results in dieback, scorch to the lower foliage, and browning of **evergreens.** It is best done in the cooler weather of spring.

You can cut out the old fruiting canes of **bramble fruits** such as **raspberries** and **blackberries** as soon as the fruit is harvested. The older canes will not bear much fruit again. This will promote better air circulation, reduce leaf diseases, and discourage stem borers. Pinch back the tips of small fruits to reduce their overall height, if desired.

PROBLEMS

Continue your garden watch for summer insect pests and late-summer diseases. Keep pests at bay by periodic handpicking and washing them off with a forceful stream of water from the garden hose.

Large caterpillars may be discovered nibbling on the foliage. The larvae of the cecropia and hawk moths can grow to colossal size if left undisturbed. Use the handpicking method of control or spray heavily infested plants with Bt (*Bacillus thuringiensis*) — a microbial insecticide. Caterpillars that ingest the Bt will soon become lethargic, sicken, and die. It is very safe, people- and wildlife-friendly. Read and follow label directions.

Encourage beneficial insects to your landscape to keep the bad bugs under control. You can purchase lady bugs and praying mantises at some local garden stores or via mail order. Birds are also helpful in eating bugs that invade the landscape, more of a reason to avoid using toxic insecticides in your yard.

NOTES

_____
_____
_____
_____
_____
_____
_____
_____
_____
_____
_____
_____
_____
_____
_____
_____
_____
_____
_____
_____
_____
_____
_____
_____
_____
_____

AUGUST

SHRUBS

PLANNING

If you are planning a summer vacation now, established shrubs should do fine as long as you give them a deep watering before you leave and have them properly mulched. During an extended period of heat and drought, make arrangements with someone to check your landscape if you're gone for several weeks.

An automatic sprinkler system and drip irrigation would be most valuable at this time. In the long run it can save you money, water, and time. Drip systems are not that difficult to install, but if you don't feel comfortable doing it yourself, consult a sprinkler contractor. Get several bids before you make a decision.

Shrubs are excellent plants to attract birds to your landscape. They not only provide some shelter, but many produce edible fruit for the late summer and into the autumn and winter months. If you don't have shrubs that invite wildlife, now is a good time to plan to add some. Find out what kinds of birds visit your area and make a list of shrubs that will attract them. Look over your landscape, and see what areas would benefit from new shrubs, and mark these spots with stakes. Next spring you can plant the shrubs for a permanent addition.

PLANTING

Early August is not a good time to plant shrubs, particularly if there are high soil temperatures. This will only inhibit root growth and stress new plants. If you desire to plant, plan to spend extra time attending to their basic needs for establishment. Follow the guidelines for planting container-grown shrubs on page 150.

As temperatures begin to fall later in the month, or during extended periods of rain and cooler days, you can transplant container-grown shrubs to their permanent locations. Remember to dig the planting hole 2 to 3 times wider to encourage strong root development, which allows them to become acclimated by winter.

As Labor Day approaches, many garden stores will promote sales for their overstock of shrubs. It is a good time to take advantage of the bargains and make new additions to your landscape. Purchase healthy, disease-free shrubs. Avoid stressed plants that will just sulk and be slow to start off.

CARE

Shrubs require minimal care this month. Just be sure to provide ample water during extended periods of drought and heat. Newly planted shrubs will benefit from some temporary shading if they show signs of scorch on hot exposures of the south or west. You can construct a lean-to onto which burlap or shade cloth can be stapled. Also, misting the foliage will help reduce severe stress to newly planted shrubs.

Make sure shrubs receive adequate air circulation to minimize the incidence of powdery mildew disease on the foliage. This may require selective pruning of the older stems that are crowded in the center of the shrub.

Blackberries and **raspberries** are producing a good crop by now. Harvest them daily before the birds beat you to them. You can also cover vulnerable fruit with bird netting. Support the netting with stakes taller than the canes to prevent birds from perching on the netting and sneaking out exposed fruit.

Pay attention to those shrubs recently planted in the heat of summer. They still have a limited root system and will require proper watering to get established. Mist their foliage as needed to cool them down and spread mulch around the root zone if you didn't earlier.

 WATERING

Be sure to monitor soil moisture around newly planted shrubs, particularly during hot periods. Dig down several inches; if the soil is becoming dry to the touch, it's time to water deeply. Proper mulch around shrubs will also retain soil moisture and help keep the soil from baking.

Established shrubs should be just fine with a deep watering every seven to 10 days, depending upon weather and soil conditions. Mulch over the root zone will reduce the frequency of watering, plus discourage weeds from invading.

 FERTILIZING

Do not fertilize shrubs now. This is the time shrubs are acclimating for their winter rest period. The stems and branches will need to harden off so they won't be susceptible to frost injury. New growth that is induced now will usually not have adequate time to harden off. Don't think that fertilizing a stressed shrub will save it. Applying soluble salts to a stressed root system will only add insult to injury. Wait to fertilize in the early spring as the growth begins to expand.

 GROOMING

Keep weeds from invading the shrub border now. They are in seed-making mode now and this will just add to the weed population next season. Dig, handpull or hoe weeds as soon as you spot them. Dispose of weeds that have started seedheads, as they continue to ripen and disperse if left in the garden. Do not compost weeds with seeds.

 PROBLEMS

Some insect activity will continue this month. Be on the watch for pest infestations. Aphids, spider mites, and eriophyid mites may be a problem. Keeping the shrub stress-free can prevent a severe problem. Hosing down infested plants will help, as will the application of insecticidal soap sprays. Do not apply insecticides during the heat of the day; apply very early in the day or toward evening as temperatures fall

Powdery mildew disease is common by now on **lilac, dogwood, honeysuckle** and other shrubs that experience shade or poor air movement. You will notice a whitish-gray coating on the leaves and new growth. While it looks ugly, it is generally not fatal to the plant. In a few weeks the foliage will be dropping anyway. If you are concerned about mildew and want some kind of control measure, try my homemade remedy on page 285.

Remember, good air circulation goes a long way to control many leaf diseases.

Spider mites can be a problem on **evergreen** shrubs that are stressed by heat and drought. Look for signs of sickly, yellowish foliage and a thin webbing among the branches and needles. Use a strong stream of water from the garden hose to wash them off and discourage a repeat attack. Repeat this every few days for a couple of weeks. Light horticultural oils can also be used against mites. Use as directed on the product label. Avoid insecticides that kill the beneficial bugs that are predators of mites.

NOTES

_____

_____

_____

_____

_____

_____

_____

SEPTEMBER

SHRUBS

PLANNING

Though it is not officially fall on Labor Day weekend, it marks the end of the summer for many. Most schools are back in session, and the days are getting shorter with the approach of fall. Shrubs have already started to respond to the change; many, like sumac, are transforming from green to scarlet.

The cooler weather is a welcome change from summer's heat. It also signals that it's time to get things done before the ground freezes solid. There will be opportunities to plant new shrubs offered for sale at local garden retailers. Check plants out carefully before purchasing; the healthiest specimens are the best candidates for fall transplanting.

Plan to take time to enjoy this slower time of year. Jot down notes of how your shrubs change color with the season; accentuate the positive as well as noting the not so desirable attributes. It will help you in changing your landscape when spring arrives next year.

If you have space in your yard, consider starting a compost pile. It is an excellent way to recycle garden waste into "black gold," compost for organic-deficient soils.

• Find an area in your landscape that is out of plain sight and receives at least half a day of sun. This is the spot where you will be depositing lawn and garden waste.

• Collect herbicide-free grass clippings, prunings, weeds without seeds, disease-free annuals, and fallen leaves. Throw them into a pit or a heap. Do not add meat, bones, or pet waste to a compost pile.

• Rent a shredder/chipper to chop coarse organic materials into smaller pieces so they will decompose more rapidly. You can chip small branches and twigs into wood waste that will break down into an earthy compost.

• If you have a lot of garden waste, consider enclosing the compost with fencing, wood pallets, cinder blocks, or use a commercial compost bin.

• Spread yard waste into 4-inch to 6-inch layers; add an inch of soil between layers to introduce microbes that will aid in the digestion of the organic materials. Keep the compost lightly moist to speed up the decomposition.

• Next spring to early summer, you can begin to harvest the finishing compost at the bottom of the pile or pit. This organic amendment will crumble in your hands and have an earthy smell.

PLANTING

Early fall is an acceptable planting season. Waiting too late in the season can jeopardize the plant's ability to transplant successfully. For most parts of the region, get fall planting completed by mid-October or sooner. I recommend planting **evergreen shrubs** in the spring instead of the fall.

The shrubs you purchase now are not in bloom; hopefully the tag-along labels are still in place. You need this information to ascertain light and soil requirement, height and spread, flower color, and any special requirements. To plant container-grown stock, review the guidelines on page 150.

This is not a good time to relocate your established shrubs to new locations in your landscape; wait until spring. In the interim, insert a sharp shovel into the soil around the root zone to prune roots. This will stimulate more fibrous root growth, which makes the shrub easier to move next year.

CARE

Continue to care for newly planted shrubs by watering once deeply as soon as the soil begins to dry out. This is especially important during periods when rainfall is scarce. Replace mulch over the root zone if it is beginning to diminish. Mulches help to maintain uniform moisture in the soil and discourage weeds. Established shrubs will need attention, too. Water at least once a month to allow them to properly harden off before fall frost arrives.

Tender shrubs such as **citrus, fig, Norfolk pine, bougainvillea** and others that have been spending the summer outdoors will need to come indoors before frost. Now is the time to check whether they need repotting; if so, increase the size of the container an inch or two and make sure the container has drainage. Use a good potting mixture to which you can add slow-release granular fertilizer. Set the plant at the same depth in the new container that it was in its previous pot. Lightly firm the potting mixture to fill in spaces, and water in well.

Check plants for any signs of insect pests. Wash their foliage with water or use the homemade soap spray on page 283. Rinse the leaves, allow to dry and then bring indoors. If you have a serious pest problem, you may spray the foliage and stems with a light horticultural oil. This will suffocate most pests and their eggs. Read and follow label directions on the product package.

 WATERING

When natural precipitation is lacking and during prolonged periods of drought, water shrubs if the soil is becoming dry. Check underneath the mulch to determine if the soil is drying out.

 FERTILIZING

Delay fertilizing newly planted and established shrubs until next spring.

 GROOMING

Limit pruning to insect-infested stems, storm-damaged branches, and dead wood. Use sharp pruning equipment to make clean cuts.

 PROBLEMS

Insect problems should be slowing down by now. If there are late outbreaks of aphids, hose them down with a forceful stream of water from the hose. Homemade soap spray can be used, too. Frost will soon arrive and wipe out a good majority of the wimpy bugs.

Mildew continues to show itself on shrub foliage. It is primarily unsightly and does not need to be sprayed. Leaves will soon be shedding; plan to clean up and discard diseased leaves that drop to the base of the shrub. This will help reduce the spread of this disease next season.

Continue to pull or dig weeds; don't let them go to seed. Prevention of weed seed dispersal will cut back a bad invasion next year.

Protect new shrubs from possible damage from wildlife and rodents. Have repellents ready to use; build wire cages to erect around vulnerable shrubs. These will reduce severe gnawing damage from deer and elk. You can make homemade collars to protect stems from the ravages of rabbits, mice, and voles. Do not place mulches right around the base of stems as this often encourages rodent nesting.

OCTOBER

SHRUBS

 PLANNING

Cooler weather and bright sunny days make October in Idaho a real pleasure. This is when we appreciate the last colors of autumn. Some shrubs not only show colorful fall foliage but also yield berries to feed the birds in winter.

 PLANTING

Plant **evergreen shrubs** no later than mid-October to help ensure their survival before the soil freezes hard. You can safely plant shrubs till midmonth, but waiting too late can jeopardize root growth if the soil freezes suddenly. Mulch around newly planted shrubs to keep the ground from freezing. This will give extra time for root growth, and it helps retain more uniform moisture. To plant container-grown shrubs, follow the guidelines on page 150.

 CARE

As the leaves fall, collect and discard those that are infected with diseases such as mildew. Other leaves can be collected and put in the compost pile. Add more mulch over the root zone of shrubs if needed, but do not place the mulch against the stems. To do so may invite gnawing critters to nest for winter.

 WATERING

Deeply water all shrubs before the ground freezes solid. Shrubs suffer severe desiccation during the winter season. Though the damage is not apparent until next spring, roots are actually killed during prolonged periods of winter drought. **Evergreen shrubs** continue to lose moisture through their foliage in all seasons, and drying winds exacerbate the problem.

 FERTILIZING

No fertilizer is needed this month.

 GROOMING

Limit pruning to removal of diseased, damaged, dead, or broken branches and stems. Trim back overgrown branches if they are prone to whip in winter winds. Reduce their height by one-third or to that of the rest of the branches. Selectively prune berry-laden branches for autumn decorating. **Hollies, viburnums,** and **pyracantha** make attractive displays in outside containers.

 PROBLEMS

Most insect problems will cease with the arrival of cooler nights. A hard freeze is on its way if it hasn't already occurred once in your area. Diseases can be reduced by raking and collecting leaves that can carry over the fungus spores. Do not add diseased leaves or plant parts to the compost pile. Continue to hand-pull or dig invading weeds before they make seeds.

Bundle upright **evergreens** and other weak-wooded shrubs that are prone to spread apart under snow loads. Use binder twine, and start at the bottom, pulling the twine upward. The twine should be removed in late spring when the danger of heavy snows has past. Do not cover shrubs with plastic cones or plastic. They will be cooked on sunny days even if temperatures are cold at night.

NOTES

_____
_____
_____
_____
_____
_____
_____
_____
_____

NOVEMBER

SHRUBS

 ### PLANNING

November is a slow month in the garden. Interesting bark such as that of **burning bush, winged euonymus, red-twig** and **yellow-twig dogwood** will make a nice contrast in the landscape. Plan to set out bird feeders as berries and other natural food sources become scarce. Don't forget to include a birdbath or other source of water for birds, too.

Some shrubs in your landscape lend themselves to holiday decorating. Pick a warm day, string your lights, and test them so you can replace burnt-out bulbs. Be sure they are low-wattage and UL approved for outdoor use.

 ### PLANTING

If you didn't get container-grown shrubs planted, you'd better heel them in a trench before a hard frost visits your area. If stored above ground, freezes will damage their root system. Dig a trench deep enough to place the containers within and fill in the spaces with compost or other organic mulch until they can be planted in spring.

 ### CARE

Delay spreading winter mulch over the root zone of newly planted shrubs. It is best to wait until there is frost on the ground. Layer organic mulch 3 to 4 inches deep, but do not allow the mulch to rest against the bark of stems.

Protect shrubs from winter sun and wind by placing shelters around vulnerable plants. Use burlap, commercial shade cloth, or snow fencing. When the ground freezes, mulch new shrubs planted this fall. **Bramble fruits** can be mulched as well. Use compost, shredded bark, or other organic materials.

 ### WATERING

Check soil moisture monthly and water heeled in shrubs as needed. Water early in the day when temperatures are 45 degrees Fahrenheit or above. **Evergreens** are the most susceptible to winter desiccation, so give them a good, deep drink before the ground freezes solid.

 ### FERTILIZING

Dormant shrubs will not benefit from the application of fertilizers now. Wait till spring.

 ### GROOMING

Limit pruning to removal of dead and broken branches. If pruning to collect berries or short **evergreen** boughs for decorations, do so selectively to preserve the natural shape of the shrub. This is a good time to sharpen, clean, and oil pruners. If you don't know how, take them to a professional garden shop that offers this service.

 ### PROBLEMS

Deer, elk, rabbits, and porcupines may make visits to your landscape and nibble on shrubs. Protect valuable plants by applying a repellent spray, or hang out bars of perfumed soap or mesh bags of human hair. Placing wire cages or fencing around individual shrubs is the most reliable way to thwart deer and elk. Use hardware cloth to make collars to protect vulnerable stems from rabbits and mice.

DECEMBER

SHRUBS

 PLANNING

December is a month to relax and reflect on the garden season. Browse nursery catalogs, and learn about shrubs that interest you. Check out climatic zones, and select the hardiest species for your area. Bring your garden notebook up to date, and decide on your gardening New Year's resolutions. If you haven't installed your outdoor holiday lights yet, do so now. Turn them on, and enjoy the festive addition to your garden.

 PLANTING

If you decided to have a living **holiday tree,** keep it indoors for 5 to 7 days, no longer. Otherwise it will break out of dormancy which makes it difficult to plant directly outside after the holidays. Allow the potted tree to acclimate in an unheated garage or porch for a week or so before you plant it outdoors. Choose a day when temperatures are above freezing to plant. Water in thoroughly after planting and spread a layer of organic mulch over the root zone. See the chapter introduction for planting instructions.

 CARE

Construct windbreaks around sensitive **evergreen** and **deciduous shrubs** that are predisposed to winter damage or winterkill. Safeguard them from sunscald, wind, snow, critters, and desiccation. Protective snow sheds can be temporarily set over foundation plantings that are vulnerable when snow slides off the roof.

Some **evergreen shrubs** tend to flop over or break off in heavy snowfall. They will benefit from tying. Loosely gather the branches against the stems, and loop some binder twine around the entire bundle. Start at the bottom, and wrap twine upward.

 WATERING

There is always a chance that December will be a dry month. Check soil moisture underneath the mulch if three to four weeks pass without appreciable rain or snowfall. During periods of prolonged drought, pick a warm day and water shrubs. As long as the soil is unfrozen and you water early in the day, moisture will soak down so the roots will benefit.

 GROOMING

You can selectively prune a few branches from **evergreen shrubs** to use in holiday decorations. Try to maintain the natural form and beauty of the shrub. If you grow **holly,** prune some of the branches with red berries to decorate those empty outdoor containers. Mix in a few sprigs of **juniper** or **pine,** and those outdoor pots won't be so drab looking.

 PROBLEMS

This is the season that critters visit the yard to nibble on the tips and bark of shrubs. Every once in a while check for signs of rabbits, field mice, and voles feeding at the base of shrubs. You may need to pull away mulch if it touches the base of the stems. Deer and elk hoofprints in the snow or mud and gnawed bark on shrub stems will clue you in that these four-legged creatures are visiting your garden. You may need to put up deer fencing or other barriers. Repellents are only temporary.

TREES

Planted in the proper location, a tree will live for generations, silently cleaning the air while providing shade, beauty, and shelter for wildlife. Trees are a living link between the past and the future. The most important consideration in growing trees successfully in Idaho is choosing the right type of tree for your specific site and needs. Are you looking for an evergreen for year-round greenery? Maybe a tree that has an ever-changing seasonal display? A tree just for shade? Or do you want a tree that will grow fast for privacy? After a long chilly winter, who doesn't look forward to the beauty of a flowering plum, redbud, hawthorn, or crabapple?

Trees are functional all year. They sharpen our awareness of the changing seasons, from the first green buds in spring through the cool and lush summer foliage. Deciduous trees give us shade in summer, cooling our living environment by blocking out the hot sun. Later, the brilliant autumn yellows and golds of native aspen trees inspire visitors and residents alike to take a drive to the High Country. As winter arrives, deciduous trees can be dramatic and sculptural as their graceful branches ornament the otherwise stark landscape. Bare of their leaves in winter, they allow sunlight and warmth to reach us when we need it most.

GARDENING WITH AN ALTITUDE TIPS
Trees for Idaho

EVERGREENS
- Arborvitae, *Thuja occidentalis*
- Austrian Pine, *Pinus nigra*
- Bristlecone Pine, *Pinus aristata*
- Colorado Spruce, *Picea pungens*
- Concolor Fir, *Abies concolor*
- Douglas Fir, *Pseudotsuga menziesii*
- Limber Pine, *Pinus flexilis*
- Pinyon Pine, *Pinus cembroides edulis*
- Rocky Mountain Juniper, *Juniperus scopulorum*

DECIDUOUS TREES
- Amur Maple, *Acer ginnala*
- Cottonwood, *Populus deltoides*
- Flowering Crabapple, *Malus* spp.
- Goldenrain Tree, *Koelreuteria paniculata*
- Green Ash, *Fraxinus pennsylvanica*
- Hawthorn, *Crataegus* spp.
- Hedge Maple, *Acer campestre*
- Kentucky Coffee Tree, *Gymnocladus dioicus*
- Linden, *Tilia* spp.
- Mayday Tree, *Prunus padus*
- Norway Maple, *Acer platanoides*
- Oaks, *Quercus* spp.
- Ohio Buckeye, *Aesculus glabra*
- Ornamental Pear, *Pyrus calleryana*
- Quaking Aspen, *Populus tremuloides*
- River Birch, *Betula nigra*
- Serviceberry, *Amelanchier alnifolia*
- Thornless Honeylocust, *Gleditsia tricanthos* var. *inermis*
- Weeping Willow, *Salix* spp.
- Western Catalpa, *Catalpa speciosa*
- Western Hackberry, *Celtis occidentalis*
- White Ash, *Fraxinus americana*

GARDENING WITH AN ALTITUDE TIPS
Recycled Holiday Trees

You don't have to banish your traditional holiday tree to a landfill at the end of the holiday season. Only you can help your tree continue to "give" throughout the year. Fresh-cut holiday trees are biodegradable, so you can make mulch from the branches and trunk with a shredder/chipper. Branches can also be cut and used for winter protection of perennial flowers and ground covers; remove the branches in the spring.

Holiday trees make great outdoor bird feeders, too. Place fruit and seed garlands on the tree to attract birds. The branches will provide shelter for the birds over the winter.

Spruce and pine needles can be used to make fresh, aromatic potpourri.

Furthermore, trees add value to our property. At selling time, a mature, healthy tree may add as much as $1,000 to the purchase price of residential property, and trees certainly add curb appeal.

Trees make excellent living gifts for special family events. Give a tree to commemorate the birth of a new baby, a death, an anniversary, or holiday. You can even make the tree planting a part of a family reunion.

PLANTING BARE-ROOT TREES

Bare-root trees are grown in a nursery field, harvested when dormant (early spring or late fall), and made available to gardeners. Once dug, these trees should be planted as soon as possible so their roots don't dry out, and preferably before the leaves emerge in spring.

Here are some timely steps for planting bare root trees:

1. Dig the planting hole two to three times wider than the root system. This will allow you to spread the roots out completely when they are set into the hole. Don't break or bend the roots to make them fit. You wouldn't want to be bent out of shape, would you?

2. Form a cone of soil in the bottom of the planting hole, and lightly tamp down the top. This helps to prevent the tree from settling down too deeply. It is best to keep the tree planted at the same depth it was originally grown in the nursery.

3. Set the root system on top of the cone of soil. Drape the roots evenly over the top. The topmost root should be positioned so it's just under the soil surface. You can use a shovel or broom handle to help gauge the correct planting depth. Lay the handle across the hole, and position the tree accordingly.

4. Gently work the soil in among the bare roots with your hands. Backfill the hole halfway with soil, and water in. Add the remaining soil after the water has soaked in, and water again. If the tree has settled too deeply, grasp the trunk and gently lift the tree to raise it to the proper planting depth.

5. Apply an organic mulch of compost or shredded wood chips around the root zone to help maintain uniform moisture. This will also reduce the need for frequent watering.

PLANTING BALLED-AND-BURLAPPED TREES

Specimen trees are often sold balled-and-burlapped, meaning their rootballs are wrapped and secured with a wire basket and twine. To plant ball-and-burlapped trees:

1. Dig the planting hole two to three times wider than the rootball and as deep as it is high. Keep the rootball moist prior to the actual planting time.

2. Set the tree in the empty planting hole, and position it as you desire. Use the handle of the shovel to check that the root flare at the base of the trunk is situated at or about an inch higher than ground level. Take care not to injure the tender bark on the trunk or break the rootball.

3. Cut away as much of the burlap wrapping as you can reach. Remove at least the top one-third to one-half of the wire basket **after** the tree is situated in the planting hole. Use a bolt cutter to cut through the stiff wire, and carefully pull it away. This will allow the upper portion of the rootball to develop healthy roots.

4. Remove any nylon twine around the trunk, as this material will not decompose and can girdle roots and the trunk years later.

5. Fill the hole with backfill soil that has been amended with one-third compost or sphagnum peat moss. Do not over-amend the soil, as this can cause an accumulation of salts around the root zone. Firm the soil snugly around the rootball to eliminate air pockets.

6. With the remaining backfill soil, fashion a rim beyond the rootball's edge to create a water-holding reservoir.

7. Spread a 2- to 3-inch layer of organic mulch such as compost, shredded wood chips, or pine needles extending slightly beyond the planting area.

8. Water the planting area thoroughly so that the soil is moist down to at least 8 to 10 inches. If your soil is clay, water for a while, and then stop. Resume watering in about one half-hour, and allow the water to percolate deeply.

9. Do not fertilize the tree for the first year.

PLANTING CONTAINER-GROWN TREES

When selecting container-grown trees, look for signs of healthy new growth. As you plant, check the root system. If roots have grown into a mass, encircling the rootball, they should be teased or even cut at planting to encourage lateral growth. The nice thing about container-grown trees is they can be planted most anytime of the year, but spring is ideal, as soon as the ground can be worked. Those so-called "plantable" containers **are not**. Take the tree out of its container when planting. Carefully remove the plastic or fiber pot.

Here are some of my tips for successfully planting container-grown trees:

1. Dig the planting hole with sloping sides, making it two to three times wider and just as deep as the tree's container.

2. Carefully remove the tree from its container, and gently knock or brush off excess potting medium from around the rootball and on top of the rootball. If the rootball is rootbound (roots are growing to the inside of the container in a mass or circling the inside of the pot), special precautions should be taken to prepare the root system. With rootbound container-grown trees, score the rootball in three equally spaced areas along the rootball. This will encourage the roots to grow outward into the planting hole and prevent the roots from continually growing in a tangled mess. If the roots are loose, you can carefully tease them out so they will fit into the planting hole.

3. Set the rootball into the planting hole, position or orient the branches as your desire, and level with or slightly above the surrounding ground level. Make sure that the root flare at the base of the trunk is visible at the top of the rootball **now and after** the tree is planted.

4. Amend the backfill soil with a quality soil amendment such as sphagnum peat moss or compost. Add one-third organic amendment to your native soil to become your backfill mix. This soil mixture will provide the proper transition for the roots that have been growing in the container mix to the actual soil in your landscape as they will grow outward.

5. Gently firm the soil over the rootball, using the excess soil mixture to make a ridge or dike beyond the filled hole to create a water-holding reservoir.

6. Spread a 2- to 3-inch layer of organic mulch over the planting area up to, but not on top of, the root flare. Water the tree in thoroughly. Repeat watering at least once a week. To determine if watering is needed more frequently, dig down around the root zone with a garden trowel to a depth of 6 inches; if the subsoil is beginning to dry out, give the tree another watering by filling the reservoir with water and allow it to soak in.

SOIL CONSIDERATIONS

As with all plants, the secret to growing trees successfully is to start with good soil. Few trees will thrive in heavy, compacted, or poorly drained soils or clay. The lack of available oxygen to the roots will surely result in stunted growth or early death. Nor will trees survive drought in sandy or rocky soils that have no ability to retain moisture. Trees produce vigorous, healthy growth if they are planted in soil that is well-drained, loosened as deeply as possible, and amended with organic matter. There is one caveat, however: don't over-amend the soil with too much "stuff." If too much amendment is added to the planting hole, the tree's roots may decide to remain within the hole, growing in circles, and never exploring the surrounding soil. This causes a "bathtub" effect. Remember, roots will grow into soil that contains oxygen, so the best recommendation after years of research is to dig the planting hole much wider than deep. Also, loosen the soil around the planting hole thoroughly.

MULCH AND WATER

After planting, spread a 2- to 3-inch layer of organic mulch over the root zone, but not up against the trunk. Piling mulch over the base of the tree trunk can keep the bark soft and wet (conditions which favor diseases), and it may also encourage rodents to gnaw. Mulching does help to reduce weed growth, keep the soil cooler, and conserve moisture. Water deeply and thoroughly to moisten the rootball and the surrounding soil. This encourages new roots to grow into a wider area. Watering the first year is critical because young, transplanted trees need ample moisture to become established. Build a soil dike about 3 inch high around the root zone as a reservoir to hold water. This allows it to soak down to the roots. Apply 1 to 2 inches of water to the root zone on

GARDENING WITH AN ALTITUDE TIPS
Living Holiday Trees

If you have space to plant a living holiday tree in your yard, consider a balled-and-burlapped evergreen tree. Living evergreens come with roots intact, ready for planting after the holiday lights and ornaments have been removed. A live tree tends to dry out and break out of dormancy after a week in the warmth of your home, so display it indoors no more than five days. Keep the tree in a cool location for a week or two so it can acclimate, then plant the tree outside when temperatures are above freezing.

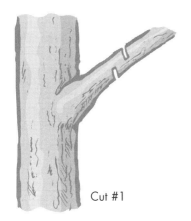

Cut #1

Cut #2

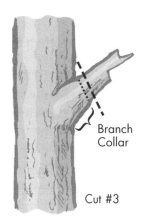

Branch Collar

Cut #3

Limb Removal

a weekly basis, but do not overwater. A good way to determine if the tree needs water is to dig down around the root zone a depth of 4 to 6 inches and feel the soil. If it is still moist, wait a few days.

As trees grow and mature, watering needs will vary by species. It is important to deeply saturate the soil around the drip line (the area on the ground beneath a tree's outermost branches). For larger, maturing trees, the area beyond the drip line should be watered, too. The most effective way to provide water is to place a frog-eye sprinkler at the outer edge of the drip line. Move the sprinkler around this zone every 10 to 15 minutes to allow for overlap and complete coverage of the root zone or until water runs off.

Lack of available subsoil moisture can take its toll on trees during the fall and winter season. When there is little or no rain or snow, it is critical to winter water trees when temperatures are above freezing and as long as the ground remains unfrozen. This may need to be done every four to five weeks, depending upon weather conditions. After winter watering, don't forget to drain and store your hoses.

THREE-CUT METHOD FOR REMOVING DEAD OR DAMAGED LIMBS

• Make the first cut upward about a foot from the trunk and one-third of the way through the bottom limb.

• Make the second cut downward from the top of the branch a couple of inches away from the first cut, farther away from the trunk. As the branch falls, the undercut causes the limb to break away cleanly.

• Finish by removing the stub by making the last cut outside of the branch collar (a swollen area at the base of the branch). The collar region is the boundary between the trunk and the branch that acts as a natural barrier to decay-causing organisms. Don't leave a stub. Stubs usually die and are entry points for insects and diseases.

JANUARY
TREES

PLANNING

This is a month to take time to relax and enjoy your winter landscape and your favorite trees. Look out your windows to see which trees are in view. **Deciduous trees** are showing off their attractive bark, architectural trunk and branch structure now. Enjoy! One of my favorite trees is the **Pinyon pine** (*Pinus edulis*). To me it represents strength and durability. Its evergreen foliage softens the landscape year-round and offers shelter to winter birds.

If you are keeping a garden journal or notebook, check it now to see if pests plagued any trees last season. It may be time to plan to replace certain trees that have become problems. You can have them removed and replaced when spring arrives.

Order bare-root fruit trees and ornamentals if you want to get a good bargain early in the season. Mail-order catalogs offer many bare-root trees, and your local nurseries may stock some. Check around to see what's available in your area. But before you shop, do your homework. Be familiar with the growing conditions required for the trees you want. In addition to full sun and well-drained soils, **fruit trees** will need regular pruning, watering, and pest con-

trol if you want to reap a bountiful, blemish-free crop.

PLANTING

This is not the best time to plant new trees, even though some may be showing up at garden retailers.

If you set up a living **holiday tree,** make plans to plant it outdoors when temperatures are above freezing during the day. Hopefully you chose a proper site, dug the planting hole in November, and covered it for safety. Use the unfrozen backfill soil to plant the **evergreen.** Then water in thoroughly, and apply 2 to 3 inches of mulch over the root zone.

CARE

Trees planted last fall should be checked for signs of wind damage or winter desiccation. If they were staked for wind protection, make sure the rubber or nylon straps are secured to the lowest point on the trunk to give the tree a little room to move back and forth. This encourages the development of a stronger, thicker trunk.

If the tree stakes have started to heave out of the ground due to frost, hammer them back down. Make a note in your garden notebook or journal to remove the tree straps in the spring after growth has started.

WATERING

During dry winter spells, when temperatures are above freezing and the ground is unfrozen, water fall-planted trees including **evergreens** and **deciduous** types. Established trees may need supplemental water as well. Use a frog-eye sprinkler; set over the root zone, and water each area for 10 to 15 minutes. Allow the water to soak in before nightfall.

Trees planted on south and west exposures, and those subject to drying winter winds, are more susceptible to winter desiccation. The subsoil needs to be charged with adequate moisture that will be available to the trees even during the winter months. "Winterkill" does not become apparent until the summer, although root damage occurs in the dry winter months.

FERTILIZING

This is not the time to fertilize trees. Wait until at least bud-break (as the buds begin to expand in the spring).

GROOMING

If you're planning on pruning your trees in winter, have a purpose in mind so you will maintain the tree's natural growth habit and health. If you are uncomfortable doing the pruning yourself, have a certified and experienced arborist examine your trees. An arborist can make an assessment of needs and provide a bid for services.

Pruning is both an art and a science. Studying trees and appreciating their natural growth patterns will develop your skill. January is a good time to see the framework of **deciduous trees.** Since they are without leaves, you can determine which branches need removing and mark them with a bright orange or red spray paint.

When temperatures outdoors are comfortable, thin out any dying, dead, or pest-infested twigs and branches by cutting them where they join the limb or trunk. Thinning opens up the center of deciduous trees to more sunlight and reduces the number of water sprouts that may grow along the branches. Proper thinning will not dramatically change the tree's natural appearance or growth habit, or give it the "just-pruned" look.

Never "top" or head back the limbs of maturing trees. You are likely to weaken their structure by causing the growth of numerous fast-growing water sprouts. The remaining stubs will be exposed to attacks from insects and disease.

January is a good time to remove a branch if it is rubbing or crossing another. Wounds that create entryways for invading insects and diseases will develop on rubbing branches.

Remove branches that form narrow, V-shaped angles to the trunk. These are weak points that may split with the weight of snow and ice. Branches that form at an angle of less than 45 degrees from the trunk or point of attachment (10 and 2 o'clock) are best removed. Also prune out upright side limbs or suckers that tend to grow taller than the main trunk.

You don't need to apply tree paints or wound dressing to the cut ends. There is no scientific evidence that dressing wounds prevents decay. Paint can actually retain moisture and encourage disease organisms to enter the wound. If you start pruning after the coldest part of winter has passed, this will allow the tree wounds to heal and will reduce dehydration of the cut ends.

PROBLEMS

Check trees for any signs of past pest damage, especially borers. You should be able to detect tiny entry or exit holes if borers were a problem. Control them later in the year when they become active.

NOTES

_____
_____
_____
_____
_____
_____
_____
_____
_____
_____
_____
_____
_____
_____
_____
_____
_____
_____
_____
_____

FEBRUARY
TREES

PLANNING

You still have some time to order bare-root trees, but don't delay. Bare-root stock needs to be planted early before it leafs out.

Now is the time to get outdoors on warm sunny days, walk around your trees, and give them a good inspection. You may discover some interesting features and appreciate their winter structure.

Look for any nibbling on the bark of the lower trunk from rabbits or other critters, including meadow mice, voles, or pocket gophers. They are particularly fond of the young tender bark. Many critters will set up residence in heavy mulch, leaves, or persistent snow around the base of trees. Take time to pull back mulches to check for visible damage.

You may need to place protective collars around the trunk to thwart rabbits, deer, elk, meadow mice, and voles. Even with these protectors, rabbits can still damage the bark if they can stand on the snow and reach above the protective collar, so plan accordingly.

Of course, the taller critters can reach beyond the protective collar to nibble branches and tender twigs. Wire fencing may be needed to exclude deer, elk, and roaming livestock.

Ice and snow can damage trees. Following a storm, check whether any damage has occurred, and prune accordingly. Make a list of tasks to improve the shape and form of your trees.

If you're thinking about planting a home orchard, now is the time to make a plan. Locate the orchard in a sunny spot with a gentle slope. This will reduce frost damage in spring. If you haven't already ordered **fruit trees,** do so soon. Pick varieties that are hardy in your area. Check with local nurseries or gardeners who have experience growing fruit in our region.

Fruit trees can be obtained as standard, semidwarf, and dwarf, depending on the growing space you have. The rootstock on which the trees are grafted will determine whether the trees are dwarf. Keep in mind that standards take longer to mature and produce fruit.

Grafted trees can sometimes have their own problems, including suckering from the rootstock. You will have to prune the suckers off each summer as they appear. Many of the heirloom fruit trees are grafted onto hardier rootstock, which allows them to be grown in a wider variety of soils.

If you're thinking about growing a fruit tree from seed, think again. These generally will not come "true" from seed. There will be much variability in the resulting progeny, and you may be disappointed when the plant finally produces fruit, if it ever does.

Where trees can be obtained on their own roots, they are to be preferred. They will acclimate and establish much stronger. Determine your needs, and grow fruits that you and your family will enjoy. Oh, by the way, birds will eventually share your crop, too! Plan to have some bird netting around when the cherries start blooming.

PLANTING

This is not the preferred time to plant trees.

CARE

Heavy, wet snow and ice accumulation can damage **evergreens** that have multiple leaders or trunks. Remove the weight of snow carefully. Snow-laden branches can snap if you move them too vigorously, so gently lift the snow off with an upward sweep of a broom or rake (never downward).

When removing snow from walks and driveways, avoid piling it up around the base of tree trunks. It can create a haven for critters to set up residence. Meadow mice or voles can girdle trees very quickly. Instead, shovel the snow around the trees' drip lines (the area where the outermost branches extend) to provide moisture to the root zone.

The limbs of valuable and ornamental trees can be protected from snow and ice breakage with flexible supports. You can use old bicycle tire inner tubes; loop the rubber tubes around weak branches and the trunk to provide extra support, yet allow some flexibility. You can also create horizontal supports by securing bungee cords throughout the framework of the tree and attaching their ends to posts oriented on the outside of the tree. At the end of winter,

examine your trees and prune out any broken or dead limbs.

WATERING

Be sure to get outdoors on those sunny warm days, and check whether your trees need winter watering. This goes for both **evergreens** and **deciduous trees.** Just because they are dormant on top doesn't mean they don't need water in the root zone.

When temperatures are above freezing and the ground is not frozen solid, set out a frog-eye sprinkler, and water around the root zone. Place the sprinkler at the drip line, and water for 10 to 15 minutes. Then move as needed to cover the entire root area. Water early in the day so the water can percolate into the soil. The roots are not able to take up moisture when the soil is frozen. Afterward, disconnect the garden hose, and store it back in the garage or garden shed.

FERTILIZING

It's still too early to fertilize trees in our region.

GROOMING

You can continue to prune when the coldest days are past and before new growth begins. February is a good time to study the structure and form of your trees to determine which branches need removal. To safely remove large, heavy branches or limbs, follow the three-cut method to prevent the branch from tearing or stripping the bark farther down the trunk as it falls (see page 177).

Wait to prune **evergreens** until new growth begins to emerge. This will allow for better shaping and a stronger branch structure to develop. With **pines,** the best time to prune is when the new growth is just beginning to expand or "candle."

PROBLEMS

Check for signs of insect damage or possible overwintering eggs on the branches or limbs. If necessary, you can apply a horticultural oil spray when temperatures are above freezing. Read and follow label directions.

MARCH
TREES

 PLANNING

Now is the time to make plans for bare-root trees. These are available through mail-order catalogs and local nurseries. They are harvested from the growing fields, bundled, and stored in cool storage. The majority of my fruit trees can be planted bare-root in early spring with great success. The root system adapts to the soil conditions very favorably and has strong growth early in the cool season. If you haven't tried bare-root trees, give them a try, but be sure to plant them before they leaf out. Dormant stock suffers less transplant shock and will get off to a quick start.

Some **ornamental** and **fruit trees** require special training and pruning, which varies by type, age, and variety of tree. The objective is to develop a strong framework on fruit-bearing limbs and shoots. Let's face it, to get a good crop of fruit requires time spent pruning and training your trees. If you don't, you will be left with an untrained, often unruly tree with entangled masses of suckers or shoots that will produce little or no fruit. This creates a perfect environment for pests and diseases.

 PLANTING

Bare-root, **deciduous trees** are best planted while they are still dormant, about a month before the last freeze in your area. Plant them as soon as possible after they arrive in the mail or after buying bare root stock locally. Unwrap the root system and soak in a bucket of water at least six hours before planting. If there are any broken or damaged roots, prune them back cleanly to behind the break. For more instructions on planting bare-root trees, see page 174.

 CARE

Newly planted trees that are exposed to high winds may need to be staked to keep them from blowing over. The wire from the stakes should be attached to nylon tree straps to protect the bark of the tree. Make sure that the supports are secured at the lowest point on the trunk to allow movement back and forth. This will encourage a strong, thick trunk. Remove the supports after one growing season.

 WATERING

During mild spells, when there is little or no precipitation, water trees. Pay particular attention to fall-planted trees and **evergreens.** They are most vulnerable to desiccation during dry, windy conditions.

Use a frog-eye sprinkler to spot-water trees that are planted in open exposures. Apply water early in the day to allow the water to soak down to the root system.

Mulch newly planted trees with a 2- to 3-inch layer of compost or other organic material to help retain moisture and prevent excessive weed growth at the root zone.

 FERTILIZING

Don't be in a rush to fertilize your trees. Trees growing in lawn areas generally receive adequate nutrients from the application of lawn fertilizers. (Don't use weed and feed combinations around the root zone of trees as this will eventually cause damage.)

The best time to fertilize trees is at the start of budbreak, when new growth begins to emerge in the spring. Use a complete fertilizer analysis such as 20-10-10.

Follow the label directions for the amount of fertilizer to apply for the type and size of tree you are about to fertilize. Aerate around the root zone and scatter the granules over the area. Water the area to move the fertilizer down to where the roots can assimilate it.

GROOMING

Remove broken or dead branches. Trees that tend to "bleed" or excrete sap profusely such as **maple, elm, aspen,** and **birch,** should not be pruned now. Although bleeding is unsightly, it is not harmful. To **minimize** bleeding, prune these trees after the leaves have expanded and green up in the summer and the shoot stops growing. Some arborists recommend fall pruning to reduce bleeding, but this practice must be weighed against the possibility of making the trees more susceptible to winter injury. Use your best judgment when making this decision for your particular climate conditions.

Thin out suckers or upright growth on trees. Some trees like the **Bradford pear** will produce a lot of upright branches that grow closely together on the trunk. Weak branch growth makes the tree more vulnerable to snow, ice, and wind breakage.

To keep evergreens such as **pines** and **spruces** from growing out of bounds, you can trim the new growth or "candles" back each year. Timing is critical; do this pruning when the new needles are about one-half inch long. Pruning the candles at this time will allow the new shoot buds to develop below the cuts. These will sprout next year.

Pines, spruces, firs and most **junipers** should not be pruned back to older, bare branches. Any needleless branch will eventually die and this will result in a hole or gap in the evergreen.

PROBLEMS

Inspect trees for signs of insect damage or overwintering eggs that are getting ready to hatch. If you detect a problem, you still have time to apply a horticultural oil to suffocate insect eggs and some of the overwintering stages of pests. Oils will help to reduce the onset of disease spores, too. Read and follow label directions when using oil sprays.

Do not apply oil sprays to **blue spruce** or other evergreens that have the bluish bloom on their needles. Oil will dissolve the bloom and thereby turn the evergreen a sickly green.

NOTES

APRIL

TREES

 PLANNING

This is the month when many states celebrate **Arbor Day**. You can take part in this celebration by planting a new tree in your landscape. If you don't have space, think about donating a tree to a park or other community center where many can benefit from a tree's beauty and function.

Learn more about trees for the area in *My Rocky Mountain Gardener's Guide*. This will help you become more familiar with various tree selections that are best suited to our unique climate and soil conditions. Visit parks and preserves to see native trees in their natural environments. Take notes on what grows well in your particular area. Take photographs of the trees and show them to knowledgeable plant experts to help you identify them, or use a good field guide with color photos and line drawings.

When you find your favorites, avoid the urge to dig up native plants from their native habitat. It is illegal to dig up plants from the wild, except on your own private land. There are ethical, legal, and scientific consequences to the practice of pirating wild plants. It is best to purchase from local nurseries that special-ize in native plants or to order them from mail-order sources.

When choosing a tree for your landscape, consider its ultimate size. A small spruce may be cute planted near the house when it is only 3 feet tall, but this tree will grow and spread to encroach on the house and surrounding sidewalks or driveway.

 PLANTING

It's a good time to plant container-grown trees and also larger trees that are balled-and-burlapped. Pay careful attention to the watering during their establishment phase. Most of us are likely to overwater a newly planted tree, and this will often lead to its demise.

 CARE

Now that it's mowing time for cool-season grasses, take precautions to avoid bumping into tree trunks with the lawn mower or weed trimmer. A manmade disease called "lawnmower-itis," caused by skinning the bark with lawn machines, will give diseases and insects entry into the tree. Any wound on the trunk can be quickly colonized by fungus diseases or infested by borers. A ring of mulch or a living ground cover around the root zone will protect the trunk.

Stake newly planted trees only if they are vulnerable to windstorms or other harsh weather conditions. Remove any staking from trees planted last spring. Check others to see if the supports and ties are getting too tight for the growing tree. Left unchecked, nylon and rubber straps can girdle the bark.

 WATERING

April showers are usually not adequate to keep your trees deeply watered. Dig down around the root zone and check the subsoil moisture. If it is beginning to dry out to a depth of 4 inches, it's time to give the roots a good soaking with a frog-eye sprinkler. With cooler weather, I generally recommend that you deep water every two to three weeks during the spring to maintain subsoil moisture for spring growing conditions. Let the weather guide you, and check the soil moisture before watering.

 FERTILIZING

By now most trees have begun to bud out, and it's time to apply a slow-release granular fertilizer. Core-aerate around the root zone to create channels for the fertilizer to work its way down to the roots. Select a complete fertilizer such as 10-10-10 with iron and sulfur. An amount to provide 1 to 2 pounds of actual nitrogen per 1,000 square feet once a year meets the nutrient needs for most trees. Fertilizer applications are not to be used as a rescue effort for stressed, injured, or declining trees. Do not use combination weed and feed products over the root zone of trees. Fertilize **fruit trees** at the rate of one-half pound of slow release granular 12-12-12 or something similar per tree. Water thoroughly after applying fertilizer to help it percolate down to the root zone.

GROOMING

Remove vertical suckers that grow within the framework of fruit trees and various ornamental trees including **Bradford pear, hawthorn, aspen,** and **crabapple.** When pruning out diseased branches from crabapples, disinfect your pruning tools after each cut by spraying them with a disinfectant, or wipe them off with 70 percent rubbing alcohol. Do not use bleach, as it will rust metal parts.

Most **evergreens** have a natural symmetrical growth habit, so pruning for shape is generally not needed. Brittle branches that were broken in storms should be removed, however. Cut away jagged edges where the break occurred as soon as you notice damage. A smooth cut near the branch collar will "heal" best.

PROBLEMS

Aphids will soon appear at the tips of the branches where the growth is succulent. You can eliminate severe infestations by spraying them off with a forceful stream of water from the garden hose every few days. If there are major infestations, you may decide to use a homemade soap spray (see page 283) or a commercial insecticidal soap. Read and follow label directions.

To avoid killing our beneficial and pollinating bee population, **delay** spraying **fruit trees** until after blooming has ended. Then choose something that is environmentally friendly, or use insect traps to keep pests at a minimum. The apple worm trap is very effective for the codling moth. If you detect tent caterpillar nests at the tips of the branches, cut them off, place in a plastic bag, and dispose of these pests in the trash.

As weeds begin to invade the orchard or poke up through the mulch, pull them out when the soil is moist. Use a clean organic mulch such as compost, shredded wood chips, or pine needles to keep weeds from growing around the root zone of trees. For more persistent weeds like bindweed and thistle, you may spot-treat with a non-selective herbicide that contains glyphosate. Read and follow label directions. Wrap newspaper around the trunk's base before you spray to prevent herbicide from contacting the bark.

NOTES

_____
_____
_____
_____
_____
_____
_____
_____
_____
_____
_____
_____
_____
_____
_____
_____
_____
_____
_____

MAY
TREES

PLANNING

Record your observations in your garden journal. Note trees that are blooming, display interesting characteristics, or have pest problems. You will be able to use this information when you add new trees to your own landscape. For example, if an **aspen** tree is being plagued by diseases and insects, you might find it helpful to replace it with a **hawthorn** or **serviceberry.**

Keep a list of the trees in your landscape. By knowing their scientific names, you can ask for the same species or cultivar next season if you like—or avoid it if it did not perform to your specifications.

It's a good idea to photograph your trees to note their progress over the years and note any special care they required. This may include pruning frequency, bracing, cabling, or spraying. This documentation will prove helpful for insurance purposes if trees are damaged by storms or vandalism.

PLANTING

Most trees are grown and sold in containers. Container-grown trees are easy to handle and can be planted at almost any time of year, except when the ground is frozen solid. Exercise caution if planting during extreme heat or drought. Be sure to have the planting site ready prior to planting (see chapter introduction).

Evergreens, including **pine, spruce,** and **fir,** transplant best in spring and early summer when they are actively growing. This allows them to establish a healthy and vigorous root system before the onset of autumn. Plant in well-drained, humus-enriched soil that is slightly acidic to neutral. Add sphagnum peat moss to help acidify the soil. Mulch with compost or pine needles after transplanting.

CARE

As mulch begins to decompose and diminish, weeds may start growing. **Renew** the mulch layer to 2 to 3 inches to prevent weed invasions and to help retain uniform moisture. Spread the mulch up to, but not over, the root flare at the base of the trunk. Surrounding the root zone with a ring of weed-suppressing mulch will also prevent lawn mower and weed trimmer damage to the trunk.

Successful pollination of **fruit trees** in the home orchard may laden the branches with excessive fruits. Over the next six weeks, thin out the small crowded **apples, pears, peaches,** and **plums** so the fruits are approximately 4 to 6 inches apart. This allows for better air circulation, reduces insect pests, and will promote larger, more colorful fruits.

WATERING

Keep a regular watering schedule for newly planted trees. Research has shown that the establishment time for trees takes up to 12 months per inch of trunk caliper (the trunk diameter measured 6 to 8 inches above the ground). Check the soil moisture to a depth of six inches with a garden trowel to determine if it's time to give them a good drink. Avoid overwatering, as this will starve the new roots of oxygen and waterlog the soil. This scenario usually results in the death of the tree.

FERTILIZING

Look for signs in the foliage and growing tips to determine if your trees are "hungry" for nutrients. As previously mentioned, trees grown in lawn areas generally receive adequate nutrients from lawn fertilizer applications. Visual symptoms that trees need additional nutrients include stunted growth, leaves that are smaller-than-normal, poor leaf color, early leaf drop, and thinning foliage. These symptoms may also be caused by other factors, including poor soil drainage, insects, diseases, or environmental conditions. If you are uncertain, consult with a reputable arborist or horticulturist in your area.

If fertilizer is recommended and you desire to encourage more growth, apply it this month. Fertilize with a slow-release, complete fertilizer such as 20-10-10. Read and follow label directions. Water in thoroughly after application.

GROOMING

Remove dead or diseased wood as you discover it in your trees at any time of the season. If you are coping with a disease called **fireblight**, be sure to disinfect your pruning tools with alcohol or a spray disinfectant. These materials are less corrosive than the traditional mixture of water and household bleach. This can help to prevent the spread of the disease to other branches. Dispose of diseased branches so they will not remain to carry the bacteria.

Cut off **suckers** that originate at the base of the trunk or those that are appearing in the yard. These will often harbor woolly aphids and other insects that will later spread to the upper portions of the tree.

PROBLEMS

Insect invasions can start to show up on trees this month. Be on the watch for aphids, soft-bodied pests found clustered at the ends of the new tender growth. They feed by sucking the plant sap with their piercing mouth parts. This causes the foliage and new tips to curl and become malformed. Luckily there are many predators that feed on aphids, including birds, ladybird beetles, lacewings, and syrphus fly larvae.

The ash sawfly may appear later in the month and wreak havoc on the new foliage. They feed by puncturing tiny shot-holes in the leaves. On a quiet day, you may hear the chewing if you're standing underneath the tree. The older larvae feed on the leaves more extensively, leaving only the main leaf veins. Sawflies are wimpy pests and are easily controlled with insecticidal soap sprays or a homemade soap spray (see page 283).

Evergreens may be attacked by a variety of pests including the Cooley spruce gall adelgid which causes the tips of **spruce** to develop cone-like galls. This will kill the terminal growth, but does not harm the overall tree itself. During June, the full-grown adelgids leave their gall home-steads and migrate to **fir** trees. On the **Douglas fir**, spruce adelgids are noticeable as the "woolly aphids" that suck sap from the needles. Symptoms develop into yellowing and twisting needles.

To control spruce adeligs and woolly aphids, allow natural predators to keep them in check; if infestations become severe enough to cause considerable damage, use a systemic insecticide labeled for evergreens. Read and follow label directions exactly.

NOTES

_____
_____
_____
_____
_____
_____
_____
_____
_____
_____

JUNE
TREES

 PLANNING

This is the month to enjoy the beauty and shade provided by your valuable trees and to visit private and public gardens to see which trees are blooming. These visits will inspire and educate you about what grows successfully in your area. Take a camera and notebook so you can keep a record of **deciduous** and **evergreen** trees that are of particular interest. You may want to add one or more to your landscape next year.

 PLANTING

So many trees are available as container-grown stock, but the planting time is limited by extremely hot weather or drought. If you plant in June, take special precautions to ensure success. Newly planted trees will need regular watering for the first six to 12 months. Unless you are willing to put in the time and commitment, wait until early fall when the odds of successful transplanting are more favorable. Refer to planting container-grown trees on page 175.

 CARE

Use either a ring of mulch or stakes around tree trunk bases to protect bark from "lawn-mower-itis." Do whatever is necessary to avoid damaging the tender bark.

You still have time to remove the support stakes from trees planted last year. The root system has had adequate time to grow and can generally support the tree by now. Trees need to have some natural movement to grow a strong and healthy trunk.

Avoid parking vehicles within several feet of the outer edge of a tree's canopy or "drip line." Though your teenager may want to plant his rig in the shade, the resulting soil compaction is ultimately harmful to the health of the tree's root system.

If any of your trees have suffered major wounds or branch damage from storms, consult an arborist. Get several bids before deciding on which tree expert to hire. Make sure that the company is licensed and bonded before you allow them to do any major tree pruning or repairs.

 WATERING

During the heat of the summer months, trees perform best on 2 inches of water per week. This can be critical to their survival during extended drought periods. Water slowly and deeply by using a frog-eye sprinkler, or if feasible, install soaker hoses or drip irrigation underneath the mulch of your smaller, medium or newly transplanted trees. Use organic mulches under trees to reduce moisture evaporation and prevent runoff of excess water from sprinkling or a hard rain. I find it helpful to core-aerate over tree root zones so water will percolate through compacted soils and reach the roots.

 FERTILIZING

I recommend that you limit tree fertilizing to spring. Only when you have an expert diagnosis of a nutrient-related problem should you apply a fertilizer this month. For example, if your trees have iron chlorosis (yellowing leaves with green veins), it would be necessary to fertilize. However, do not fertilize when trees are stressed by heat, drought, pests, or disease problems.

Granular slow-release fertilizers release nutrients consistently and gradually over the growing season as soil temperatures and moisture are adequate to help trees utilize the nutrients. Fertilizing in the spring will sustain older trees in your landscape, and the younger ones should do just fine, too. Also, remember that when you apply lawn fertilizer, trees growing in and around lawn areas will benefit.

GROOMING

Prune out dead or damaged branches immediately. Summer storms can leave wounds that are vulnerable to insect and disease entry. Consult with an arborist to remove large branches damaged by storms. Verify that the company is licensed and bonded.

If some branches are still bare, don't assume they are entirely dead and prune them off. To determine whether a branch is still alive, bend some of the twigs or branches to see if they are flexible. You can also do the "finger nail" test: scrape the bark with your fingernail to see if there is moist, green cambium beneath the bark. It may take a little extra time for some branches to leaf out if the tree is under stress. Brittle, brown twigs are dead and should be pruned back to where the wood shows signs of life.

PROBLEMS

Just because some trees such as **cottonwood, aspen,** and **crabapples** drop leaves, twigs, bark, and fruit early in the summer, this doesn't mean that they are in trouble. Some trees are inherently prone to do this as they mature. Many older trees will routinely slough off strips or patches of bark, and **evergreens** will shed older needles or scaled leaves (**junipers**) to make way for fresh growth.

Be on the lookout for more aphids feeding on tender growth. Hose down with a forceful spray of water or use a soap spray. Larger trees may need attention from a professional arborist.

As temperatures begin to rise, spider mites will soon be on the scene. These minute pests will cause the foliage to turn a sickly yellow or brown. Look on the underside of the leaves to detect them. Fine webbing may be noticeable between leaves and twigs. If you have a severe infestation, use an appropriate miticide, or consult with a arborist trained in treating for insect and mite problems.

Be on the watch for powdery mildew, a disease that looks like someone sprinkled flour on the leaves. It is usually caused from poor air circulation, and some trees are more susceptible than others. Tip-prune the heavily diseased areas, and dispose of the prunings.

Baking soda and horticultural oil can be used as a preventative on smaller trees (see remedy on page 285).

Employing bacterial warfare can safely control caterpillars that feed on the foliage. Use Bt (*Bacillus thuringiensis*) as soon as you see young larvae begin to feed on the leaves.

NOTES

_____
_____
_____
_____
_____
_____
_____
_____
_____
_____
_____
_____
_____
_____

JULY
TREES

 PLANNING

Properly placed shade trees make the landscape a wonderful retreat on hot summer days. Even my dog enjoys the cooling shade during the "dog days of summer." Birds, butterflies, and squirrels find trees a nice retreat, so look upward to observe the happenings around you. So many things are going on in the landscape now.

To my Italian grandmother, water conservation was just common sense. Good landscaping techniques of choosing water-wise plants, soil preparation, mulching, and deep watering all combine to help conserve water throughout the yard and garden. It's now been termed **"xeriscaping"** even though this implies a "desert-like landscape," or dry landscaping. Following are the seven basic principles of "xeriscaping," or as I like to call it, "naturescpaing" (following the wisdom of nature for a more realistic landscape for our region). Observe what grows natively in your area and plan accordingly.

Principle 1: Careful planning and design. Divide the landscape into "hydrozones" (areas within the design that receive low, moderate, or high amounts of water use).

Principle 2: Reduce lawn areas to more functional spaces and try growing more native grasses if they meet your lawn requirements.

Principle 3: Prepare the soil well by using organic materials such as compost or sphagnum peat moss to help improve the soil's structure. Organic matter is the best way to improve air and water movement so the soil drains water properly. It also helps the soil to retain moisture and nutrients.

Principle 4: Make appropriate plant selections and group plants together that have similar water needs. Because xeriscapes and naturescapes have low, medium, and high water use "hydrozones," you can grow a wide selection of trees. These include **junipers, pines, spruces, firs, arborvitae,** and other trees that can survive extended periods of drought after they have become properly established.

Principle 5: Use drip and micro-sprinkler systems to create efficient watering methods that will help to conserve water.

Principle 6: Mulch, mulch, mulch. Blanket the soil around the root zone of trees with an organic mulch to conserve and maintain uniform moisture to the roots. Mulches will also reduce weed invasions and enhance plant growth.

Principle 7: Follow proper landscape maintenance procedures. Water, fertilize, and prune—the common-sense way to produce healthy and water wise plants.

Incorporating these seven principles into a landscape can help to reduce water consumption by 30 percent or more. It reduces maintenance costs and increases the survival rate of trees during drought periods. Droughts won't last forever.

PLANTING

Summer planting can be tricky, but follow the guidelines in the chapter introduction. Keep the rootball and surrounding soil uniformly moist, not waterlogged, until the trees become somewhat established.

To minimize summer transplant shock, plant when there are several days of overcast, relatively cool weather in the forecast. You can also construct a shade cloth awning to shield the young tree from the hot afternoon sun.

Shadecloth is available at many local hardware stores or nurseries. Water generously, but do not drown the rootball. The roots still need oxygen to grow and function. Dig down to determine the soil moisture's needs. Mulch the soil to keep it cool and retain moisture.

CARE

Some fruit trees like **cherries** and **apricots** may be about to produce fruit. Check daily, and harvest the ripening fruit. It is best not to allow overripened fruit to fall to the ground and rot. This invites bees, wasps, and other critters into your home orchard.

WATERING

When rain showers are scarce, check soil moisture under the mulch around newly transplanted trees at least weekly. If the soil is beginning to dry out to a depth of 6 inches or more, it's time to give the tree a good, deep drink. Mulch will effectively cool the soil and deter runoff of valuable moisture when the rain does come.

FERTILIZING

It is getting too late to fertilize trees in July. They will soon be making a transition for fall dormancy, and there is no benefit of applying fertilizer to stimulate late succulent growth.

GROOMING

Continue to cut away water sprouts and suckers that originate around the base of the trunk or in adjacent lawn areas. Except for removing broken or diseased branches, delay major pruning until the trees are dormant to avoid stimulating yet more new growth that will be vulnerable to frost or storm damage.

PROBLEMS

Blister beetles and others may arrive in hoards to attack tree foliage. These pests can cause considerable damage by stripping the leaves from branches. Control these pests by hosing them down or knocking them into a jar of soapy water.

Caterpillars of certain butterflies and moths may feed on some of the foliage of specific trees, but it is often not necessary to control them since damage is nominal. If infestations are severe, apply Bt (*Bacillus thuringiensis*). If you have a butterfly-friendly landscape, it is perfectly acceptable to allow these caterpillars to feed so you can enjoy the metamorphosis of various winged beauties in your landscape.

Weeds may pop up in and around the root zone of newly planted trees. Follow the "cowboy way" of handpulling or digging them out while the weeds are still young. Otherwise, spot-treat with glyphosate based herbicides; do not get any herbicide on the bark. Suppress weed growth by renewing the layer of mulch around the root zone.

NOTES

———————————————
———————————————
———————————————
———————————————
———————————————
———————————————
———————————————

AUGUST
TREES

PLANNING

Now is the time to start planning for autumn planting. Keep in mind the naturescape or xeriscape principle: choose appropriate trees that are adapted to your area. Select plants thoughtfully, and plant them in an environment that is closely matched to each tree's native habitat. Some trees are quite adaptable and will perform well in a variety of situations. If you need to replace aging and diseased **aspen** trees, consider **river birch** that are well suited to low, moist areas but can also grow in well-drained soils on higher ground.

Plan to replace trees that did not survive transplanting or that suffered injury from storms, drought, poor pruning, or compacted soils. As the fall sales arrive, take advantage of early fall planting.

Perhaps it's time to retrofit your landscape. Think about how trees would contribute diversity and functionality. How would they affect both the outdoor and indoor climate of your home? Would the tree shade afternoon sun in summer, but still allow solar radiation in winter? Do you need to create a windbreak to block the wind?

If you are thinking about cutting down an old, maturing tree to make room for construction or reduce shade, think twice. Healthy, mature trees add value to the property. If it is necessary to remove the tree, consult with local arborists and nurseries that may have tree spades large enough to relocate the tree. Professional tree spades can dig up large trees and a good portion of the rootball, then transport them to a new site.

Plan to transplant new trees in late August through late September. Get the planting area prepared in advance to save time when the tree arrives. Gather mulch for use after transplanting.

Research tree species that interest you to determine their requirements for light, soil, and moisture. Get to know their growth habits, mature sizes, and shapes. This way, you can make sure you have the appropriate site on your property for a tree's mature height and spread.

PLANTING

Delay the purchase of balled-and-burlapped trees for several more weeks, until the weather is cool. As temperatures cool down, growers will dig and wrap new trees to sell. These are much better than those heeled in during the heat of summer with their rootballs exposed to the heat and drying conditions.

Container-grown trees can be planted now. This will allow them adequate time to get established before the ground freezes. See planting container-grown trees on page 175. Pay attention to regular watering during the first few weeks after planting. Check soil moisture with a garden trowel to a depth of 6 inches or more, and if it is beginning to dry out, apply water to the water-holding reservoir.

CARE

To lengthen the life of your trees, try as much as possible to duplicate their native conditions. In the wild, trees grow in communities and their soil is not compacted. Organic matter is continually being replaced by decomposing leaves and twigs on the forest floor. They generally do not have to compete with lawn grasses for water and nutrients. Trying to reproduce similar conditions will reduce stress to your trees and increase their life spans.

Start harvesting early **apples, pears,** and **peaches** from your home orchard as soon as they ripen. Keep them off the ground to avoid rotten fruit that invites yellow jackets, earwigs, and diseases.

 WATERING

If it has been a droughty summer and you are under water restrictions, then implement a triage system for watering your valuable trees.

 FERTILIZING

Trees do not require fertilizing at this time of year. If anything, apply an organic mulch or compost around the root zone to renew decaying mulch applied in the spring.

 GROOMING

Prune only to maintain shape or for topiary or espalier training of trees. Remove broken branches as needed, and watch for diseased branches. Prune out water sprouts and suckers anytime they emerge. Suckers that arise from the base of the trunk should be removed at the point of origin below the knobby place where a tree may have been grafted to a specific rootstock.

 PROBLEMS

Spider mites are very active during hot, dry weather, especially on **evergreens** and many **ornamental trees.** Symptoms of mite invasions include salt-and-pepper or bronze-colored foliage. You may often see a network of tiny webs forming a highway for mites to travel from one branch to another. Tap a suspect branch over a white sheet of paper, and look for moving specks.

Natural mite predators can control mite populations. A strong spray of water from the garden hose applied to the undersides of the leaves will dislodge many adult mites throughout the growing season. Insecticidal soap sprays, homemade soap spray, (see page 283), or a miticide can help. Read and follow label directions when using miticides or insecticides.

Powdery mildew diseases can be most prevalent now with cooler night temperatures. Prevention is the best defense. Grow powdery mildew-resistant varieties whenever you have a choice. Prune the tree for better air circulation and sunlight penetration. Also, reduce the use of high-nitrogen fertilizers to avoid late season, succulent growth that is more susceptible to mildew.

Cercospora leaf spot is a common disease on **aspens** and **poplars.** It causes brown lesions on the leaves, and foliage will eventually turn yellow or brown and shed from the trees. Maintain good air circulation in the trees by proper pruning practices.

NOTES

_____
_____
_____
_____
_____
_____
_____
_____
_____
_____
_____
_____
_____
_____
_____
_____
_____
_____
_____
_____
_____

September

TREES

PLANNING

This autumn, plan to recycle your fallen leaves for mulch or add them to the compost pile. Leaves are a great source of free organic mulch for use under trees or in shrub borders. If you do not have a compost pile, use the leaves to start one.

Choose a hidden spot as a collection area for organic materials from flower beds, pruning, and leaf fall. If you have excessive grass clippings, you can recycle them, too. Even if you don't do anything more than pile the organic materials in layers and let it decompose, you will end up with a useable compost next year. Eventually you may want to neaten the compost pile by enclosing it in a fenced area or between wooden pallets or cinder blocks. You can speed up the decomposition of organic yard waste by following these tips:

• Shred and chop materials into smaller pieces. Use a lawn mower or commercial shredder to finely cut the leaves and twigs.

• Turn the compost pile frequently, as soon as the interior of the pile heats up to 150 degrees Fahrenheit.

• Add special composting worms called "red wigglers."

In colder areas of the region, you might expect a first fall frost toward the middle or end of the month. It's time to clean up, repair, and refill bird feeders.

Shop for new tools, if needed. A new, durable rake will help with leaf cleanup. Invest in a compost thermometer, a chipper/shredder, hardware cloth to protect tree trunks, and more quality birdseed.

PLANTING

Labor Day is a traditional time to plant new trees to replace ones that have died or if you just need more trees. Container-grown trees are still readily available and can often be purchased at sale prices. Follow the tree planting guidelines on page 175.

CARE

Delay refreshing the mulch around trees until after the ground freezes to keep rodents for setting up house. Make them choose other areas for their cozy winter nests. Thin or remove ground cover plantings to within a foot of the tree's trunk. Protect trunks of young trees by encasing them in hardware cloth to keep critters from nibbling the tender bark over the fall and winter.

WATERING

Continue to water newly planted trees as needed. Check the soil moisture by probing into the root zone to a depth of 4 to 6 inches. If the soil is becoming dry, give the tree a good watering to maintain subsoil moisture before the ground freezes. Water established trees during prolonged periods of drought. Use a frog-eye sprinkler or soaker hose to water deeply and keep the subsoil charged with adequate moisture. This is generally needed every five to six weeks, depending upon weather conditions.

FERTILIZING

Trees at least seven to 10 years old and those that are growing perfectly well do not need fertilizer every year. Their root systems have been exploring lawn areas and beyond. They receive adequate nutrients from lawn fertilizers and even fertilizer applied to shrubs and flower beds. Decomposing organic mulch will help to improve the soil over the tree's roots and will eventually provide some slow-acting nutrition as the tree needs it.

GROOMING

Delay most pruning until late winter or early spring when the trees are leafless. You can prune out dead, dying, or diseased branches at any time. Use sharp and clean pruning tools to make clean cuts.

PROBLEMS

Prepare now to protect trees from deer, elk, and rodents that like to feed on the bark. Protect trees from deer and elk with fencing enclosing the trunk. Keep the fencing 2 feet away from the trunk by using stakes to create an encasement around the trunk. Smaller animals such as rabbits and voles can be deterred by installing hardware cloth or plastic guards around the trunks of young shade and fruit trees. To discourage voles and meadow mice, pull the mulch away from the trunk about a foot.

GARDENING WITH AN ALTITUDE TIPS
Dealing with Water Restrictions

Water trees first since they are the most expensive, most permanent, most difficult to replace and contribute more to the value of your property. Water newly planted trees on a regular basis so they can properly establish; then water older trees. Use a frog-eye sprinkler or soaker hose to water deeply and less frequently. Water recently planted shrubs and established shrubs as needed. Check the soil moisture by probing down with a garden trowel to a depth of 4 inches or more. Water perennial flowers, then annuals, which are less expensive and easier to replace, if need be.

Water lawns last. Thoroughly water the soil to the depth of the lawn's root system. Don't water again until it becomes dry at that depth. Deeper, infrequent watering promotes a deeper, more drought-enduring root system. To avoid runoff and wasting water, practice "cycling" or "interval watering." Rather than applying the water all at one time, water an area to the point of runoff (15 to 20 minutes), then shut off the water to allow it to soak down for 30 minutes or more. Repeat the watering cycle in the same area to allow for deeper water percolation into clay soils. This technique is helpful for watering sloped areas where water naturally runs downhill.

Hardware cloth cylinders can be constructed to keep rabbits and voles from chewing the bark. Use a shovel to cut the ground around the tree just enough to insert the wire cylinder. The bottom edge of the cylinder should be at least 6 inches below the ground level. To avoid future injury to the trunk, move the hardware cloth cylinder farther away from the trunk after one or two years. Be careful not to injure the feeder roots in the process.

NOTES

_____
_____
_____
_____
_____
_____
_____
_____
_____
_____

OCTOBER

TREES

PLANNING

Many ornamental trees will brighten the autumn skies with an assortment of colors ranging from golden yellow, fiery reds, oranges, and yellows. This coloration occurs naturally as days grow shorter and the pigments become unmasked. Yellow xanthophylls, orange carotenoids, and red anthocyanins are present in the foliage. The anthocyanins are manufactured by the conversion of sugars in the autumn; the other pigments have been there all along, but are not visible until the masking green chlorophyll breaks down in the fall.

Take photographs of the trees in their autumn glory, and decide which colors you would like in your landscape. This will help you plan your tree plantings next spring.

It's not too early to plan how you will overwinter small trees in their pots. You can choose one of three ways, and some early preparation is necessary. So this is a good time to decide, based on your landscape, which method will work best for you:

1. Place the tree in a cold frame or unheated garage or garden shed if the ground is frozen solid.

2. Bury the tree, pot and all in the ground, and mulch with compost or shredded wood chips.

3. Partially bury the tree in a sheltered place in the yard with shredded wood chips and compost piled generously over the pot.

Whichever method you choose, you'll need to water periodically, every three to four weeks if the winter is dry.

PLANTING

You still have the opportunity to plant new **deciduous trees** provided you get it accomplished by midmonth. Waiting too late is a gamble and may result in transplant shock and tree losses. Trees that are planted earlier in the fall will have a better chance of getting acclimated before the ground freezes solid. Remember to make the planting hole two to three times wider than the rootball to allow for strong and healthy root establishment. Dig the hole only as deep as the rootball.

Purchase high quality trees with strong, uninjured trunks or branches. Not all trees on sale are a bargain but may be "a pain in the ash." Branches should be well spaced to avoid costly training by pruning practices.

CARE

This is the time of year when many **evergreens** shed their older needles. If you see this happening with needle shed occurring from the inside of the tree towards the outside, it is a natural phenomenon. Do not try to fix this by giving the tree more water and please do not add fertilizer; this will only add insult to injury.

WATERING

Water your **evergreens** deeply as the soil dries out. This should be done before the ground freezes. **Pines, spruces,** and **firs** continue to lose water by transpiration during the fall and winter, but when the ground is frozen they cannot replenish the water if it isn't already there.

In fall and early winter, don't forget to water newly planted trees during extended dry spells to help maintain moisture to their roots. Water on an "as needed" basis by testing the soil around the root zone.

To test for soil moisture: Using a garden trowel, dig a small hole in the loosened backfill soil. Squeeze a handful of soil from the top and another from the bottom of the hole. If water drips between your fingers or the soil feels sticky, it is too wet. If the soil crumbles and falls from your hands as you open your fingers, you will need to add water. If the soil samples stay together in your hand as you open your fingers, the moisture level in the backfill is just right. Take time to check the rootball to find out if your trees need watering.

FERTILIZING

No fertilizer is needed at this time of season.

GROOMING

While you can still identify them easily, continue to prune out dead and diseased branches and twigs from your trees.

PROBLEMS

Diseased leaves that have fallen at the base of trees should be collected and disposed of. They will harbor disease spores that can infect new foliage next spring. Do not place diseased debris in the compost pile, as compost temperatures rarely get high enough to kill the pathogens.

To protect trees against deer damage, there are several deterrents you can try. One of my favorites is a homemade remedy that really works (see page 284). It will need to be reapplied after a heavy rainfall or as the sunlight breaks it down. Some gardeners report success by hanging strong-scented soap bars or mesh bags filled with human hair on the outer branches with no more than 3 feet between them. Remember, deer soon become accustomed to any object, so alternating items will confuse them and keep them away longer.

The most reliable way to keep deer away from prized trees is fencing. Excluding deer from the landscape is a sure way to ensure your trees' health and beauty. Both woven wire fences and multistrand electric fencing will do the job of deterring deer.

Some perennial weeds do well in cool weather. Field bindweed, Canada thistle, and others will continue to grow and go to seed. Take advantage of the mild weather to deal with these stubborn perennial weeds. **Spot-spray** them with a non-selective herbicide that contains glyphosate. Read and follow label directions. Shield the trunk of trees or lower branches with newspaper or a canvas tarp.

NOTES

_____
_____
_____
_____
_____
_____
_____
_____
_____
_____
_____
_____
_____
_____
_____
_____
_____
_____
_____
_____
_____
_____
_____
_____
_____

NOVEMBER

TREES

PLANNING

Trees add winter interest with their form and structure. When planning your landscape or retrofitting to make it new, take advantage of a tree's winter characteristics. The bark, branches, and architectural forms give both **deciduous** and **evergreen trees** character. Look for the exfoliating or peeling bark in trees such as **birch** and **sycamore.** Located in the proper sites, these trees may add attractive interest to your landscape.

Season's end is a good time to update your tree records. Note major pruning, problems, and observations for trees in your landscape. Jot down the flowering dates or fruiting times as well. This information and a brief summary of the weather conditions over the season may prove helpful in the future when planting more trees of a similar species.

If you are ecologically minded and plan to display a living **holiday tree** in your home, now is the time to decide which kind you want. The tree will be planted outdoors in the landscape to grow and prosper for many years to come, so plan ahead so you'll be ready when **evergreens** go on sale at reputable area nurseries. **Pine, spruce, fir,** and **juniper** are

well adapted for a living holiday tree, so examine your landscape, and choose which would work best. But remember, living holiday trees must be treated properly to ensure survival.

It is important to dig the planting hole now, before the ground freezes solid. Cover the backfill soil so it won't be subject to freezing. You can amend the soil with sphagnum peat moss or compost at the rate of one-third compost to two-thirds soil. **Cover the hole with wooden planks or a sheet of plywood.** This safety measure will prevent accidents.

To be successful with a living **evergreen tree,** you should plan to schedule your purchase so you can limit the days you keep the tree indoors. Too long indoors will make the tree break out of its dormancy, so you'll have more difficulty keeping it healthy. A period of five to seven days is considered safest to prevent the tree from breaking dormancy. Plan to move the tree back outside to an unheated garage or porch for a week or so before you actually plant it in the landscape. This will help acclimate the tree before it is set outside permanently. If the outside temperature is below zero, you'll have to wait until it's above freezing to plant the tree outside.

So decide now where and how you will store the tree. You'll also need loose mulch to hold in moisture after you water the tree and to provide winter protection for the roots, so this is a good time to stock up.

PLANTING

You can still plant trees if the soil remains unfrozen, but it is becoming more risky this month. If you should acquire a tree, it is better to plant it than to try to store it over the winter.

CARE

Protect multistemmed **evergreens** by tying up the branches with sisal twine, working the twine up from the bottom of the **evergreen** in a spiral fashion. This will prevent heavy winds and snow from splitting the leaders apart and resulting limb breakage. Remember to remove the twine in late spring.

Check guy or support wires around newly planted trees to be sure the hose sections still shield the wires to prevent girdling the bark. Add additional renewal mulch after the ground freezes. This will help to reduce frost heave at the root zone.

 WATERING

If fall rains or snows are inadequate to keep newly planted trees watered, get out the garden hose and frog-eye sprinkler to do some fall watering. Sending the tree into winter with plenty of moisture reduces the potential for winterkill next year.

Evergreens continue to lose moisture from their foliage all fall and winter, but once the ground is frozen, they will be unable to take up enough water to replace it. Providing a deep watering before the ground freezes will reduce the potential for damaged evergreen needles.

 FERTILIZING

Do not fertilize at this time of year under any circumstances.

 GROOMING

Do not be in a hurry to prune just because you're bored and have a need to get out there and cut away. The only pruning to do now until year's end is the removal of broken or diseased branches. Any time the protective bark covering is broken open, there is the potential for desiccation. Remove dead, damaged, or diseased branches with a smooth cut through healthy tissue just beyond the branch collar. This will remove a source of further infection and help the tree begin to close or "heal" the wound.

 PROBLEMS

If within reach, remove all mummified fruit from your **fruit trees,** and rake up and dispose of any on the ground. Good sanitation practices reduce the reinfestation of insects and disease organisms the following growing season.

If you didn't protect trees from animal damage, you still have time during the mild weather. Wrap trunks in hardware cloth to keep critters from nibbling the tender bark.

NOTES

_____
_____
_____
_____
_____
_____
_____
_____
_____
_____
_____
_____
_____
_____
_____
_____
_____
_____
_____
_____
_____
_____
_____
_____
_____
_____

DECEMBER

TREES

 PLANNING

To ensure that a living **holiday tree** will survive, display it inside for no more than five days. See the planting instructions in November. You'll also find tips for recycling holiday trees on page 174. Browse mail-order catalogs, and order bare-root trees for early spring planting (see page 174).

 PLANTING

Except for your living holiday tree, this is not the time to plant trees.

 CARE

Once you plant your holiday tree, check often for adequate soil moisture.

 WATERING

During extended dry periods, check soil moisture for all your trees by probing the soil around the root zone. If the soil is dry to a depth of 4 to 6 inches, water early in the day when temperatures are above freezing. Be sure to drain, disconnect and store your hose after use.

GARDENING WITH AN ALTITUDE TIPS
A Holiday Tree Preservative That Really Works!

Keep a fresh-cut holiday tree green and supple with this economical homemade preservative. Most ingredients can be found in your kitchen and laundry room. Use a tree stand that will hold a couple quarts of water. Saw a few inches from the tree's base (butt end) to open up the water-drinking tubes that may be clogged with resin. This will allow the tree trunk to "drink." Ingredients: 1 gallon hot water, 1 cup light corn syrup (such as Karo®), and 1 to 2 tablespoons liquid chlorinated bleach (Clorox®).

Mix these ingredients together, being careful not to spill the bleach. Allow the mixture to cool to tepid, and pour into the tree stand bowl. Check the tree stand daily, and add more preservative so it always covers the butt end. Stir the solution each time before adding to the tree stand bowl. **Caution**: Store unused preservative in a plastic gallon container that is labeled as tree preservative. Keep out of the reach of small children and pets.

 FERTILIZING

Trees do not need fertilizing at this time.

 GROOMING

Limit pruning to collecting boughs and cones for holiday decorations. Place the cut ends in tepid water immediately, and keep them in water until it is time to make decorations. Spray **evergreen** decorations with an anti-desiccant to preserve moisture in the needles and stems. It is better to purchase evergreen boughs from a nursery than to extensively prune your own evergreens.

 PROBLEMS

Strong winter winds can threaten young and newly transplanted trees in some exposures. Either stake them or construct wind barriers of burlap to block the worst of the wind's force; don't use plastic.

Watch for critters that like to munch on the tender bark of trees. Wire cages may be necessary to protect the trunks of trees if deer and rabbits are of concern. Try the homemade deer repellent on page 284 that will help to deter critters. Respray after a wet snow or every few weeks as the materials will break down when exposed to sunlight and moisture.

CHAPTER EIGHT

VEGETABLES

For the gardener who has the desire, time, and space, there is nothing like growing and harvesting homegrown vegetables. Growing vegetables can be rewarding for the beginner and the seasoned gardener alike. Whether you garden to unwind from stress or to enjoy more nutritious and flavorful produce, your own vegetable garden provides a sense of accomplishment and pride.

Even if you live in an apartment or have limited garden space, you can grow vegetables successfully in containers. Make use of your deck, balcony, patio, or an unused corner of the yard for your "mini-vegetable garden." When planning, take time to observe the amount and duration of sunlight, wind, slope, soil, and drainage on your selected site.

Your vegetable garden can include both annual and perennial vegetables. Some of us like to grow herbs to add special flavors to salads and meals. Have you ever grown heirloom vegetables? These are prized for their flavor and tenderness, even though they may not have the disease-resistance of the newer hybrids. Heirlooms can be saved from seed year after year for generations. Visit with local gardeners to find out which favorite heirloom vegetables they grow.

A plan sketched out on paper will help determine the kind of vegetables your family likes best and how many plants you'll need. Make your plan early so you can determine which cool-season plants can be planted early and which warm-season crops can be started indoors.

If you have been growing a vegetable garden for several years, plan to rotate crops from one area to another. This age-old technique is a good cultural practice that helps to reduce disease and insect pest invasions.

Use the many vegetable seed catalogs to help you choose which varieties you and your family would like to grow and eat. Review your garden notebook or journal from last year to find out which plants did well. It's easy to get excited when the catalogs arrive, but reference notes from previous years can help us make wise choices.

AMENDING SOIL, THE KEY TO SUCCESSFUL GARDENING

If the soil supports a healthy crop of weeds, then you have good ground for a vegetable garden. If even weeds won't grow in the proposed area, you may have a serious problem with soil contamination and may need a complete soil test. Check with your local state university, or consult with a private soil testing laboratory.

Soil improvement is a continuing process of utmost importance. Take a lesson from successful farmers; pick up a handful of soil, and feel the earth. You will find it contains three basic things: soil particles, air, and water. The percentage of these ingredients will vary in different soils. Ideally, a productive soil will contain about one-half particles, one-quarter air and one-quarter water. This ratio should be what you strive for when adding anything to the soil.

Clay soils have low air space and are known for poor drainage. Poor plant growth results when roots are deprived of oxygen. Clay soils benefit from organic amendments including compost and sphagnum peat moss. You can add amendments by handspading, rototilling or plowing. Incorporate materials to a depth of 8 to 12 inches. Try to get a uniform mixing of the soil and organic matter. Avoid pockets of organic matter scattered through the garden.

Adding organic matter should be an annual process in a new garden. As organic material breaks down and releases nutrients for plant use, it will need replenishing. Within five years, your soil will start to develop a loamy texture and yield more productive crops.

If you inherit an especially bad soil (heavy clay or extremely sandy), incorporate as much as 4 cubic yards of organic material into a 1,000 - square-foot area. Spread the compost, well-rotted manure or sphagnum peat moss over the area so it is about $1^1/2$ inches thick, and till it in.

Adding too much soil amendments at one time will result in poor plant growth due to soluble salt buildup. If barnyard manure is used, be sure it is at least six months old, preferably a year or more.

Does fertilizer need to be added? As with organic amendments, fertilizer can be overdone, too. High-nitrogen fertilizers are the biggest offenders. Nitrogen encourages nice, green leafy growth—which may detract from bean, pea, tomato, pepper or root crop development.

If you follow a regular soil improvement program using quality compost and other organic materials, no other fertilizer should be needed except for specialty crops. If in doubt, get the soil tested. For general purposes, the application of a 5-10-5 or 6-10-4, slow-release granular fertilizer can be side-dressed around vegetables during the early growing season.

SELECTING THE RIGHT VEGETABLES
Once the soil is ready to go, what do we plant? Simply put, plant what you and your family like to eat. But don't expect all vegetables or all varieties to thrive under your growing conditions. Growing seasons vary in our region.

Select vegetable varieties that are suited to your growing area; take into account microclimates as well. Make vegetable gardening fun by trying new things each year. Seed companies introduce new varieties, from space-saving vegetables to colossal vitamin-rich species with improved flavor. Keep records of the varieties you grow, and after a few years, you will know what does best in your garden.

CARING FOR THE VEGETABLE PLOT
If you intend to use a mechanical rototiller to keep weeds down and reduce soil compaction, plant your garden rows at least 2 to 3 feet apart. Orienting the rows north and south will maximize the amount of sun they receive because tall crops will not shade the shorter ones. If you orient rows east to west, locate taller plants to the north to keep them from shading shorter ones.

Check the labels and seed packets for plant names so you can remember what you planted; then next year, you can decide if you should plant the same ones or try different varieties. Keep track of the planting date, weather conditions, insect pests and their arrival, diseases, and harvest dates.

Watering the vegetable gardening is a simple concept: water, watch, weed and wait. Avoid the urge to overwater because this will deprive young plants of oxygen. Check soil moisture by digging down to the depth of root growth and feel the soil. If it feels dry, water thoroughly, and allow the soil to dry out before watering again. Remember, frequent light waterings will benefit the weeds more than the vegetables.

Mulch the vegetable garden to maintain uniform moisture and suppress weed growth. Use grass clippings (not treated with weed killers), clean wheat straw, salt hay, wood chips, pine needles, or other organic materials. Organic mulches reduce soil compaction as you walk down the rows to care for the plants. There are many other choices of mulching materials to use. One of my favorites is old pine needles that knit together and won't blow away. Others include newspaper set down in heavy layers, old carpeting, or aged wood chips.

To mulch: cover all the bare soil over the root zone, but do not put mulch directly against the stems. A 2- to 3-inch layer of organic matter will prevent the rain and water from splashing on the foliage and thereby reduce plant diseases. This also keeps the fruit and vegetables clean.

If you use plastic mulches, cover them with organic mulch, too. Unless you have a drip irrigation system under the plastic mulch, poke several holes in the plastic to allow for air and water exchange to the roots.

Note any problem areas in your garden that may include drainage, weedy areas, or pests. As trees mature and cast shade on your vegetable garden, the lack of sunlight can often limit your production. At the close of the year, review your notes and plan solutions for the following season.

CONSTRUCTING RAISED BEDS

If you are limited for garden space or have poor soils, consider growing herbs and vegetables in raised beds. Prepared raised beds are perhaps the most successful for mountain gardeners since this allows the soil to warm faster and retain heat. They can also be covered with an ensuing frost. Start with small beds and enlarge them as you gain more experience.

A raised bed can be constructed from cinder blocks, landscape timbers, or dry stacked rocks. The bed should be about 3 to 4 feet wide and about 6 to 8 inches deep. If you have more than one raised bed, allow at least 2 feet between beds for an accessible pathway. Before planting, improve the soil by adding more compost and turning it in.

Once the soil is prepared, raised beds are very easy to maintain. You can garden intensively by planting many crops in close proximity to get the most use of the space. A drip irrigation system can be installed to make watering simple and to maintain uniform moisture. Raised garden beds are notorious for moisture fluctuations, so mulch as recommended and check the soil regularly. Use a timer with your automatic irrigation system to lower maintenance.

STARTING SEEDLINGS INDOORS

Planting seeds in trays or pots indoors can help you get a jump on our short growing season. Use a seed-starting mixture, and as seedlings sprout, place them in bright light or under the fluorescent lights of the seedling stand. Adjust the lights to 2 inches above the top leaves.

Before transplanting your seedlings outdoors, they must be hardened off to acclimatize them to the outside conditions. This process is often overlooked, and plants will be shocked if set directly outside after thriving in a warm home environment. Here's how to harden-off homegrown transplants:

1. Set the plants outdoors few hours each warm day (40 degrees Fahrenheit or higher). Place the transplants where they receive morning sun but not direct afternoon sun. A little wind will actually toughen them up.

2. At night, when temperatures start to dip below 40 degrees, bring the transplants back indoors.

3. Increase the outside exposure gradually over a week or two, but be sure to bring them in at night while it is still cold or freezing. Stick a note to the door to remind you daily.

4. If you have a cold frame, this would be the ideal place to keep hardier seedlings until planting time, as they will acclimate very nicely. Prop up the top when days are sunny and hot. Warm-season transplants, such as tomatoes, peppers, and eggplant, should have additional warmth. Use a heat mat or cable to keep the coldframe from getting too cold, which may stunt the plants.

GARDENING WITH AN ALTITUDE TIPS
Vegetables for Idaho

The planting dates in these charts are based on the approximate frost-free dates for Zones 4 to 5. For some parts of the region, particularly the mountain communities, dates may be up to two to three weeks later. For south and southwestern areas, dates may be as much as two weeks earlier.

Variety	Sow Seeds Indoors	Plant Outside	Spacing Inches In row	Between Rows
Asparagus	Purchase transplants	March 15 to April 15	10 inches	36 inches
Beans, Bush and Snap	Seed directly in garden	May 10	18	24
Beets	Sow directly in garden	April 20	3-4	12
Broccoli	February 25	April 25	18	36
Cabbage	February 25	April 25	12	18
Carrots	Sow directly in garden	April 25	2	12
Cauliflower	February 25	April 25	18	36
Chard, Swiss	Sow directly in garden	April 20	4-6	18
Chinese Cabbage	March 1	April 25	12	24
Corn, Sweet	Sow directly in garden	May 7	9	24-36
Cucumber	April 27	May 27	Plant in hills	36 inches apart
Eggplant	March 30	May 27	18	30
Endive	March 10	April 25	9	18
Garlic		Late August-Sept.	3	12
Lettuce	March 15 (or direct sow in garden)	April 15	2-4	12
Muskmelon (Cantaloupe)	April 15	May 27	Plant in hills	36 inches apart
Mustard	Sow directly in garden	April 15	2	12
Okra	April 20	May 27	12	36
Onion sets	Sow directly in garden	April 10	2-5	12
Parsnip	Seed directly in garden	April 20	2	12
Pea	Sow directly in garden	April 1	8-10	18
Peppers	March 15	May 27	18	24
Potatoes	Plant seed pieces in garden	April 15	12	24
Pumpkins	April 1 (or direct sow in garden)	May 27	Plant in hills	48 inches
Radishes	Sow directly in garden	April 10	2	12
Rhubarb	Plant transplants or roots	March 20	36	48
Rutabaga	Sow directly in garden	April 10	6	18
Spinach	Sow directly in garden	March 20	4	12
Squash, Bush or Vine	April 1 (or directly in garden)	May 27	Plant in hills	36-48 inches apart
Tomatoes	March 20	May 27	36	36
Turnip	Sow directly in garden	April 10	4	12
Watermelon	April 15 (or directly in garden)	May 27	Plant in hills	48 inches apart

BUILDING A SEEDLING STAND

The seedling stand can be placed in a basement or unused room and will free up valuable counter space elsewhere. Here's how to make your own:

1. Use a workbench or secure boards over sawhorses to make a stand that is about 4 feet long and 20 inches wide. This is a good size to accommodate several flats or pots.

2. Construct a frame to hold simple lighting fixtures above the growing shelf. An inexpensive shop light that holds two 40-watt fluorescent shop lights works well. Use two light fixtures to provide enough light to the growing surface. I recommend that you use one cool white tube and one warm white tube in each light fixture.

3. Hang the lighting setup so that the light fixtures can be suspended over the shelf or growing bench. The fixtures can be attached to chains that can be easily adjusted for height with pulleys.

4. Arrange the light setup so the light source can be raised and lowered as needed. Most seedlings do best with the light source 2 to 3 inches above the tips of the young seedlings as they grow and develop.

CONSTRUCTING A COLD FRAME

Making your own cold frame is simple and inexpensive. If you prefer, cold frames are available for purchase through mail-order or local garden supply stores. Here's how to make one:

1. Use redwood lumber or cedar that will not decay.

2. Find an old storm door for the cover.

3. Plan the size of the cold frame to match the dimensions of the storm door cover—about 30 inches wide and 60 inches long.

4. Construct the corners out of four pieces of two-by-fours.

5. Make the back wall at least 15 inches tall, the front wall 10 inches tall.

6. Hinge the old storm door to the back wall so it is easy to lift and prop open. This permits you to work on the plants and to let air circulation in.

PLANNING AN INDOOR HERB GARDEN

A sunny, south-facing windowsill and cool temperatures are a must for an indoor herb garden. If you are growing herbs under artificial light, set the plants about 1 to 2 inches below adjustable fluorescent lights to keep them growing strong. Oregano, thyme, parsley, sage, chives, onion plants, and garlic can be grown in small clay pots, and you can clip stems and leaves or harvest cloves as needed for culinary uses.

The mint family, including peppermint, spearmint, and lemon balm, are suitable for indoor gardening with bright light. They will need to be pinched or sheared regularly to keep the plants compact.

Use a well-drained potting soil because herbs don't like "wet feet." Water when the potting mixture gets dry to the touch. Overwatering may cause rot and invite fungus gnats. If the humidity in your home is too low, place the pots on pebble trays to add moisture. This will help to discourage pests like spider mites, too.

Remember, cool temperatures at night, (55 to 60 degrees Fahrenheit) will keep herbs growing their best.

To start your indoor herb garden, root cuttings from outdoor plants. Here's how:

• Pinch or cut off 4- to 6-inch-long cuttings of the tender stem tips or terminals.

• Remove all but the top three to five leaves.

• Place the stems into a shallow pot filled with moistened, sterile seed-starting mix. Cover the container with plastic to create a mini-greenhouse.

• Check after a few weeks for signs of root development. Gently tug on the stems to see if roots have anchored in the growing medium.

• After a month or so, pot the rooted cuttings in a quality soilless potting mixture and add slow-release granular fertilizer.

• Place the plants under fluorescent lights on a plant stand or grow on a sunny windowsill.

• Rotate potted herbs plants growing on the windowsill every week so they can receive sunlight on all sides and grow uniformly. Pinch back the leggy weak stems.

If you prefer, you can start herb seeds outdoors in the cold frame. Plant the seeds in 4-inch containers of seed-starting mix, and add slow-release granular fertilizer according to the manufacturer's recommendations. Bring the new herb plants indoors, and place them under fluorescent lights on your plant stand before the first fall frost.

Keep a watch for insect pests that may have piggybacked inside with the cuttings. If you detect them, rinse them off under the kitchen faucet. Minor pest outbreaks can be sprayed with a homemade soap spray (see page 283), but if infestations become severe, it is best to discard the plant.

BUILDING YOUR OWN TOMATO CAGES

Tomato cages can be used to support a variety of vegetables, and they're easy to make. Here is how:

1. Purchase concrete reinforcing wire which usually comes in 5-foot widths.

2. Cut pieces 5 feet wide and $3^1/2$ feet tall.

3. Carefully roll this stiff wire into cylinders.

4. Leave the wires sticking out at the bottom so they can be used to insert the cage about 6 inches into the ground to anchor the cage.

STORING ROOT CROPS AFTER THE FIRST FREEZE

Even when the weather turns frosty, root crops can be stored in place if you know how. Cover carrots and parsnips with straw or compost up to 6 inches

deep. This will protect the roots and make them even sweeter. When you need to harvest some, just pull away some of the mulch, and dig down to harvest what you need. Replace the mulch to protect the remainder from constant freezing.

An alternative to storing root crops in the ground is to bury a 5-gallon bucket in the soil, harvest the root crops, and place them in moistened sand in the bucket. Put the lid on the bucket, and set a bale of straw as mulch on top of the lid. You can access the bucket when you need to harvest vegetables for the kitchen.

DEALING WITH BLOSSOM-END ROT (BER)

Growing tomatoes and peppers can be rewarding, but dry, baked clay soils and moisture fluctuations can often pose a common problem to home gardeners. The problem: Blossom-End Rot or BER. You've probably seen the symptoms of this physiological problem on the tomato fruits. Dark, sunken, leathery spots will form on the ends of the tomato or pepper. Occasionally, spots will appear on the sides of the fruit.

The cause is calcium deficiency during the rapid growth of young tomato and pepper fruit. Tomato and pepper plant roots take up calcium and other nutrients in ionic forms dissolved in moisture. If soils are too dry, water and calcium uptake will be restricted.

Most soils throughout our region are generally high in calcium. Therefore, don't be fooled by out-of-region chemical companies recommending the application of lime or calcium additives to our already alkaline soils.

Blossom-end rot can occur in our area when calcium uptake is erratic due to alternating high and low soil moisture. It is important to keep soil conditions uniformly moist by applying mulches around plants, especially during the heat of summer.

GARDENING WITH AN ALTITUDE TIPS
Herbs for Idaho

The planting dates in these charts are based on the approximate frost-free dates for Zones 4 to 5. For some parts of the region, particularly the mountain communities, dates may be up to two to three weeks later. For south and southwestern areas, dates may be as much as two weeks earlier.

Variety Rows	Sow Seeds Indoors	Plant Outside	Spacing Inches In row	Between
Basil	April 1	May 27	12	18
Chives	March 1	March 30	Plant in clumps	12 inches apart
Cilantro/Coriander	March 1	March 30	2-6	20
Dill	March 1*	March 25	12	24
Fennel	March 1*	March 25	12	24
Horseradish	Plant divisions or roots	March	Plant in clumps	24 inches apart
Mints	Purchase transplants	March 20	12	12
Parsley	March 15	May 15	6	12
Oregano	Purchase transplants	March 25	12	12
Rosemary	Purchase transplants	April 27	18	18
Sage	March 1	April 15	18	18
Salad Burnet	February 20*	October or March	12	12
Savory, Summer	April 20*	May 20	6	12
Savory, Winter	March 1	May 1	24	24
Sorrel, French	March 1*	April 20	12	12
Sweet Cicely	Fall *	March 20	12	18
Sweet Marjoram	April 10	May 10	6	12
Sweet Woodruff	October 15 or direct sow or started plants	March 20	6	6
Tarragon	Buy transplants or divide in fall	March 20	12	18
Thyme	March 1 or buy transplants	March 27	12	12

*or direct sow in garden

Many other variables can restrict the availability of calcium. If garden soils become too cool and limit root growth, restricted nutrient uptake is restricted will cause the development of BER on young fruit. Overuse of high-nitrogen plant fertilizers will induce faster foliage growth, thereby increasing the plant's demand for calcium.

To control BER, keep soils warm by using organic mulches or black plastic. Raised beds with a good soil mix and drip irrigation are helpful. Some varieties of tomatoes that are said to have some resistance to BER include 'Early Girl', 'Duke', 'Doublerich', 'Floradel', 'Manalucie', 'Tropic', and 'Walter'.

January
VEGETABLES

PLANNING

As you begin to plan your vegetable garden, your local garden retailer or state university can provide you with a list of recommended varieties suited to your area. Draw a garden plan to scale, and browse through mail-order catalogs. Check out the newest All America Selections, and give them a try if you have space in your garden plot.

With limited space, consider growing vining plants such as **cucumbers, melons, pole beans, garden peas** and others on supports. You can construct a fence or put up garden netting to support plants that like to climb.

If you live in an area where deer, elk, and other creatures will share your garden, now is the time to plan a fence for the vegetable garden. Your local Division of Wildlife can help you with information on deer fencing and strategies to thwart wildlife. Lower fencing can be placed around the garden to keep out rabbits, dogs, cats, and other critters. If your municipality permits, a low-voltage electric fence will repel many animals if constructed properly.

If you are new to vegetable gardening, start with a small plan. Preparing and maintaining a large area can take a lot of time for beginners, so ease in to it first.

PLANTING

It's still a bit too early to start seeds indoors, but now is a good time to build a seed-starting stand (see page 205). Place seed orders as early as possible. Some seed varieties will sell out fast.

If weather conditions permit, and you can get outdoors into the garden, dig, pot, and force some **chive** plants. If you have herbs that have been spending the winter indoors, now is a good time to take cuttings and start fresh plants.

If you decide to start seeds indoors in the latter part of the month, organize your seed packets to create a sowing schedule for specific varieties. Follow the step-by-step information on the packets for suggested starting dates indoors. This can give you a head start on the short growing season.

CARE

If you have a cold frame to overwinter herbs, be sure the plants get proper ventilation. Heat can build up on sunny days, so prop up the glass cover slightly during the day, but close it at night. Snow on the cold frame cover is good insulation, so leave it in place. If there is no snow cover, you can cover the top with an old rug at night to buffer extremely cold temperatures.

WATERING

Water indoor vegetable plants carefully. Avoid daily watering because this may keep the soil too moist and lead to root rot. Check the soil moisture with your finger. When it feels dry to the touch, give the soil a good drink, and let the water drain out. Remove excess water with a turkey baster, or carefully pour into the sink or a plastic tub.

Outdoors: If we experience a prolonged dry period and the soil is unfrozen, perennial vegetables may need water. Apply water early in the day when temperatures are above 45 degrees. Disconnect the garden hose, drain, and return to storage.

FERTILIZING

Indoor herbs should be fertilized minimally because too much will cause them to grow spindly and to develop rapid succulent growth that dilutes flavor in the leaves. Some gardeners recommend seaweed (kelp) and fish emulsion for feeding indoor herbs and vegetable transplants. These organic fertilizers often contain other trace elements as well as the three major nutrients. Read and follow label directions for dilution rates and application.

GROOMING

A general rule of thumb is to pinch or trim off flowers that are developing on indoor herbs. Flowering takes energy away from the plants and will alter the flavor of the foliage as the plant is reaching a maturing stage. Grooming the plant allows you to have leaves and stems for culinary uses. Remove fallen leaves and other debris from the surface of the potting mixture to reduce problems with fungus gnats or diseases.

PROBLEMS

Be on the watch for aphids, spider mites, and whiteflies on plants that are spending the winter indoors. You can keep most of these pests at bay by washing them off with a homemade soap spray (see page 283) or rinsing off the foliage under the kitchen faucet. If infestations are severe, use an insecticidal soap. Read and follow label directions.

GARDENING WITH AN ALTITUDE TIPS
Grow Your Own Potatoes—in a Bed of Straw

Even if you're a couch potato, you can grow a great crop of potatoes with very little effort. You don't even need a large garden to succeed. It's a method we've used for years, and all it takes is a few bales of straw.

Always select disease-free potato seed pieces. Don't use supermarket potatoes because they're chemically treated to delay sprouting. Choose egg-sized tubers, or you may cut larger potato tubers into two or three seed pieces; make sure each seed piece has an "eye" or sprout. Make cuts a few days before planting which will allow the freshly cut surfaces to dry or "suberize" at room temperature.

Plant potatoes four to six weeks before the last frost, from early to late spring. Choose a location that receives at least six hours of sun, and provide well-drained soil with additional organic matter. Prepare the area with a generous amount of compost, working it in to a depth of six inches or more.

Once you've planned the length of your row, dig a trench 4 inches deep and 12 inches wide. Set the potato seed pieces in the trench with the cut side down or orient the small whole potatoes with the eyes facing upwards. Push the seed about 1/2 inch into the loosened soil in the bottom of the trench. Space the potato seeds 10 to 12 inches apart.

Now comes the easy part! Fill the trench with about 6 inches of clean, weed-free straw—don't cover the potatoes with soil. As the potato plants begin to emerge, add another 4 to 6 inches of straw. Water the soil as needed to keep the soil around the plants and straw evenly moist but not soggy. Avoid overwatering, as potatoes don't like soggy ground.

Straw promotes vigorous, healthy plant growth, reduces weed invasion and protects the tubers from turning green in the sunlight. It is also a great mulch that will keep the soil cool and help retain moisture. The best part: you won't expose your spuds to cuts from digging—in fact, you won't dig at all. Just scoop the potatoes out when you're ready to harvest.

FEBRUARY
VEGETABLES

 PLANNING

As the days begin to lengthen, our gardening urges stir. It is time to take an inventory of your supplies and make a shopping list for starting seeds indoors. Include seed-starting mixes, trays, covers, water-soluble fertilizer, seed inoculant, and fluorescent lights. Also, consider investing in new tools if necessary. Check you supplies of garden insecticides and other pest controls. Many products have a shelf life of only a few years and should be discarded once the container begins to shrink, leak, or show signs of degradation. Check with your local EPA office for disposal sites and dates of chemical pickup in your area. Do not dispose of pesticides in the trash.

Plan to visit your local garden stores to check out plastic flats and containers that are specially designed to start seeds successfully. Choose a proper seed-starting mix that has been pasteurized or sterilized to avoid damping-off diseases, which are fatal to emerging seedlings. Some seeds may germinate more rapidly with heating cables or heating mats.

Lack of light can be one of the most limiting factors in growing seedlings indoors. Plants tend to become spindly and weak before you can plant them. You can solve this problem by purchasing or building a seedling stand with artificial light. This way, you can control the amount and quality of light the plants receive. To build a seedling stand, see page 205.

 PLANTING

It's still a bit too early to start many vegetable and herb seeds indoors, but you can start the cool-season crops such as **onion** and **cabbage** that can be set out in the garden in April. If you have a small garden and don't have enough space or time to tend seedlings, you can buy young plants at the garden store.

You can plant herb seeds such as **chives, cilantro-coriander, dill, fennel, salad burnet, sage, winter savory, French sorrel,** and **thyme** at the end of the month or early March. Start these seeds in a sterilized seed-starting mixture to prevent damping-off.

Fill individual seed trays with moistened seed-starting medium. If it is too dry, it will float to the top with seeds and all when watered in. Sow the seeds at the recommended depth on the seed package. Cover them with a tiny bit of the mix, and mist to water them in. Record the name of the herbs on plant labels for each tray or container. Use a pen with moisture-resistant ink or a wax pencil. Then, gently cover the tray with a plastic bag to maintain humidity until the seedlings begin to sprout.

As soon as you see the seedlings, remove the plastic, and set them under the fluorescent lights so that the top leaves are just a few inches below the lights. The light fixtures should be adjustable so they can be raised as the seedlings grow. This will keep the plants growing vigorously.

Water new seedlings carefully so as to avoid waterlogging them and causing rot. Wait until the surface of the seed-starting mixture begins to dry out, then water either from the bottom or lightly from the top.

CARE

Watch newly planted seedlings so you can customize a watering schedule just for your indoor environment. As the seedlings sprout, remove the plastic cover to prevent them from pushing up against it. Condensation in the plastic that constantly covers the leaves can result in rot or other leaf diseases. Did you know that by gently brushing your hand over the tops of growing seedlings daily, you can flex their stems and help them grow stronger? Give it a try. It is good plant and human therapy.

 WATERING

Learning to water vegetable and herb seedlings indoors in an art. It is better to keep the plants a little too dry than too wet. If there is excess water in the drainage saucer, discard it after a half-hour to discourage fungus gnats and soil-borne diseases.

Watering too often from the bottom will increase the incidence of soluble salts. These will be noticed as a white crust on the rim of the trays or containers. Leach the soil with clean water from the top to flush salts out the growing medium.

 FERTILIZING

You don't need to fertilize young seedlings immediately after they sprout. This can do more damage than good. Wait until the stem growth begins and a **second set** of leaves emerges on the seedlings. Then, use a water-soluble plant fertilizer such as 10-10-10 or an equivalent at half the recommended strength.

 GROOMING

Continue to pinch or prune back herbs that are successfully growing indoors as needed. This will keep them compact and in shape. It will also promote denser foliar growth.

 PROBLEMS

Be on the watch for damping-off fungus disease, which will kill seedlings rapidly. The stems will turn black, flop over, and die. This is the reason to water sparingly. Always use a sterilized growing or seed-starting mixture, or sterilize regular outdoor garden soil by baking it in the oven to an internal temperature of 160 degrees Fahrenheit. Garden soil will need to be amended with sphagnum peat moss and perlite.

NOTES

_____
_____
_____
_____
_____
_____
_____
_____
_____
_____
_____
_____
_____
_____
_____
_____
_____
_____
_____
_____
_____
_____
_____
_____
_____
_____
_____
_____
_____

MARCH
VEGETABLES

PLANNING

If your plant stand is filling up, cool-weather seedlings can be moved outdoors to a cold frame until they are ready to plant. Make plans for getting the garden plot ready. Prepare your garden rakes, shovels, trowels, and cultivators, and tune up the small engines. Rake or till the garden when the weather is nice and the soil is not too wet.

Planting dates for specific crops will vary throughout the region. Check with your local weather reporting station or state university, or chat with experienced gardeners.

For early crops, it is important to warm up the soil prior to setting out transplants. Plan on covering the prepared garden bed with clear or black plastic several weeks in advance. This will absorb the sun's heat. Later, when planting time arrives, cut holes in the plastic, and plant through it so the plastic continues to warm up the soil for the young transplants.

Keep plant protectors on hand (cardboard boxes, fiber pots, hotkaps, 5-gallon plastic buckets) to cover plants if extreme cold is predicted.

PLANTING

If the soil is workable and not too wet, set out the bare-root **asparagus** plants, **rhubarb, horseradish,** and **onion** sets. Asparagus is one of my favorites and is hardy throughout the region. Considering the cost at the supermarket, why not grow your own? .

Although Saint Patrick's Day is the traditional time to plant **garden peas,** the soil in our region may be too moist and cold. Use your best judgment. I usually wait till early April.

Herbs that were started indoors should be hardened off for a few weeks before they are set outdoors later in the month. When nighttime temperatures are above freezing, let them spend the night outside.

Around the middle of the month, start warm-season vegetables including **tomatoes, peppers, eggplant,** and **okra. Spinach, Swiss chard, endive,** and **leaf lettuces** can be planted in late March.

CARE

If you have overwintered **carrots** and **parsnips,** and other root crops in the garden, dig them out before they start to grow.

To grow herbs in limited space, plant them in large containers such as strawberry pots or terracotta planters. Use a fresh, soilless potting mixture that has good drainage, and be sure the containers have drainage holes.

WATERING

When watering homegrown seedlings, use a spray bottle that will deliver water without knocking the plants over. Don't overwater, as this increases the chances for damping-off diseases and fungus gnats. Before setting transplants directly into the garden, water them a few hours ahead of time to reduce transplant shock.

FERTILIZING

Fertilize indoor seedlings weekly with a water-soluble fertilizer diluted to half strength. Apply the fertilizer to a moist soil, never to dry soil. Keep the plants in bright light so they utilize the nutrients.

To fertilize the outdoor garden for transplants, add a slow-acting fertilizer ahead of time, or add a water-soluble fertilizer at half strength as you plant. Do not add fresh manure to the garden prior to planting because its high soluble salts will burn the transplants. Add manure to the garden in the autumn, and till it so winter freezes will break it down.

 GROOMING

Pinch herbs that are growing leggy or floppy to keep them growing more compact. Thin out seedlings planted directly in the garden or raised beds to allow proper spacing for vigorous growth.

 PROBLEMS

Unexpected late frosts may threaten new transplants or tender seedlings. You can cover them with polyspun garden frost blankets, also known as floating row covers, or use cardboard boxes, burlap, buckets or wooden crates. Remove coverings during the day so the plants will get sunlight and air circulation.

Be on the watch for rabbits, and protect plants with a low fencing (see page 221) or garden netting.

Soil-inhabiting insects such as cutworms can clip off the stems at ground level, so place collars around vulnerable plant stems of plants. Use plastic cups with the bottoms cut out. Slip over the plant with 2 inches set into the ground.

GARDENING WITH AN ALTITUDE TIPS

Grow Your Own Asparagus

To enjoy the crunchy delicious vegetable right out of your garden year after year, follow these steps:

1. Soak the dry roots in moistened peat moss overnight before planting.

2. Dig a trench about a foot deep.

3. Set the crowns of the asparagus in the trench with the roots spread out over a mound of soil. Space as recommended on the package label.

4. Cover the asparagus roots with only a few inches of soil, maintaining the depth until the stems start to grow.

5. Gradually fill in the trench with soil as the stems grow taller until the soil is level with the surrounding ground.

Grow Your Own Horseradish

Horseradish is one of the hardiest medium-height perennials to grow throughout Idaho. Most gardeners will generally find the plant more difficult to get rid of than to establish. Horseradish plants can grow to a height of 2 to 4 feet.

The plant develops no seeds and must be propagated through root cuttings that are available in early spring or root sections can be taken in March.

1. Make 6-inch-long cuttings that include a bud from straight horseradish roots.

2. Work the soil to a depth of 2 feet, and then plant the cuttings a foot deep and a foot apart. Plant as early as possible, preferably in late February or early March, for a good fall crop.

3. Locate the cuttings in a corner of the garden where only horseradish will be grown. It is a long-lived perennial.

4. Choose clay soils that are fairly moist, supplemented with aged manure or compost, and a neutral pH of 7.0.

5. To keep the long taproots growing straight, dig around the plant in early spring and remove the side roots.

APRIL
VEGETABLES

PLANNING

To maximize the production from your garden, have young warm-weather transplants ready to go into empty spots after harvesting the cool-season crops. Successive planting with **snap beans, beets, carrots,** more **radishes, Swiss chard** and **spinach** will fill in the voids. If your home-grown transplants didn't fare so well, buy young, healthy transplants from a reputable garden store. You still have time to start more warm-season seedlings to fill in later blank spots. Get ready to set out **tomato** transplants by making your own tomato cages (see page 206). Consider drying some herbs and vegetables in a food dehydrator or home-made herb dryer, or do it the old-fashioned way by hanging up bundles of herbs.

PLANTING

Plant cool-weather crops early in the month. **Radishes, spinach, leaf lettuce,** and **green onions** thrive in cooler weather. In very high elevations, you may need to wait until late May or early June.

Transplant strong, vigorous transplants that you've hardened off, and make room for more seedlings indoors. Start **cucum-bers, melons, summer squash, pumpkins,** and **watermelons** in mid- to late April, and transplant then out-side in the latter part of May as the soil temperature warms up.

Continue to plant **asparagus, parsnips, rhubarb, salsify,** and **onion** plants. As mid-April approaches and the weather is milder, sow seeds of **beets, cabbage, lettuce, parsley** and **garden peas.** When available, transplant young seedlings of cole crops such as **broccoli** and **cabbage.** Plant **horseradish** roots at the same time as early **cabbage.**

Many herbs and vegetables can be combined with flowers in containers or raised beds for a handsome effect. Use a well-draining potting mixture, and be sure the containers have drainage holes. Shallow-rooted vegetables and herbs will grow well in containers. **Lettuce, radishes, onions, short carrot** varieties, **beets,** and herbs need a container that is at least 8 inches deep and 6 to 12 inches in diameter. When grouping plants together, use larger pots such as half whiskey or wine barrels, 5-gallon buckets, or an antique bathtub. Let your imagination guide you.

Indoor **tomato** seedlings should be hardened off outside before transplanting directly to the garden. You can transplant them into larger pots if it is still too cold to set them out permanently. They will continue to grow and develop and may even begin to set flowers.

As the soil warms up, plant **beans, cucumbers, melons, squash,** and **pumpkins** in the garden. If you live in a cold area, wait to plant these towards mid-May.

Plant **sunflowers** in late April or as soon as the soil temperature warms up. They add height to the garden and can provide support for **pole beans.** Later the seeds are a welcome food source for birds and squirrels.

CARE

As the seeds you've sown in garden rows or raised beds begin to sprout, be sure to thin out crowded plants. Refer to the spacing on the seed packets. Plants that are too thick will not perform to your expectations. Instead of pulling out plants, **snip off** the excess seedlings to avoid pulling out too many.

Discourage weeds, and help retain soil moisture by applying an organic mulch around plants that are 4 to 6 inches tall. If you prefer, lay down plastic and transplant seedlings through the plastic mulch, which in turn will warm the soil. This is especially good for warm-season crops. It is helpful to punch holes through the plastic mulch to allow for water and air to get to the root zone. Mulch the plastic with wood chips, dried grass clippings, or organic materials if weeds are a concern and this will keep the plastic anchored down, too.

To get an early crop of **tomatoes** and **peppers,** provide additional protection to warm the soil and air temperature at night. Set up clear plastic tunnels over raised beds, or surround plants with plant protectors to hold in the heat at night. There are many ingenious plant protectors on the market, so give some of them a try.

WATERING

Before setting transplants, moisten the root systems. This reduces transplant shock. Watering also helps settle transplants and seeds into the soil.

Vegetables and herbs may need daily watering if rainfall is scarce. The roots of transplants and germinating seeds are shallow and tend to dry out quickly until they develop. Once the plants are established, you can wean them off an everyday schedule.

For container gardens, water regularly to ensure germination of seeds and establishment of transplants. Soilless mixtures dry out rapidly and need more attention. Use a watering can or a gentle sprinkling from the garden hose.

FERTILIZING

Add a slow-release granular fertilizer as the garden beds are prepared. This saves time later and will provide nutrients for a more extended period. Some slow-acting fertilizers will last up to 12 weeks.

Fertilize container gardens more often because frequent watering leaches nutrients out of the soilless mixes. You can mix in a granular, slow-release vegetable fertilizer into the potting soil or purchase a soilless mix that already contains one.

If you use a water-soluble plant fertilizer, apply according to the manufacturer's recommendations. Do not overdo, because a soluble salt accumulation may damage plant roots.

GROOMING

Pinch or prune back woody herbs including **sage, rosemary,** and **lavender** that grew back from last year. This will help

them regenerate compact growth. Pinch the tips of **basil** and other herbs monthly to encourage compact branching.

PROBLEMS

Watch for cutworms and armyworms. These soil-inhabiting pests will chew through the stems of young seedlings overnight. Protect the stems with collars made from plastic or cardboard cups. Cut the bottoms out of the cups, and gently lower the collar over the plant, top down, twisting the rim into the soil around the plants' stems.

Protect young seedlings with a cover of netting to thwart hungry birds. Also, set out a bird feeder to divert the birds' attention to a bird feeding station.

NOTES

_____
_____
_____
_____
_____
_____
_____
_____
_____
_____
_____

MAY
VEGETABLES

PLANNING

May is the month for planting, growing, and harvesting cool-season vegetables. As the soil dries out and becomes more workable, plan to prepare garden soil by tilling or cultivating the clods and uneven ground. Even though you may have added organic amendments last fall, it is a good idea to loosen the soil in spring. Add more compost now. Compost is one of the secrets to successful vegetable gardens in Idaho. You can also add a slow-release organic fertilizer and work the granules into the soil prior to planting. Lay out your rows using twine, and designate pathways to work in the garden.

Plan to add trellises or other supports for crops that like to climb. This is also a good time to consider preparing a raised bed. Remember to keep notes in your garden journal.

PLANTING

May is an ideal time to direct seed many vegetable crops. Sow vegetable seeds according to directions on the seed packet regarding sun exposure, depth of planting, spacing, and days to harvest. Place labels in the row to identify specific crops and note the date planted. Some root crops such as **carrots** and **radishes** can be sown in the same row. By the time the carrots are ready to be thinned, the radishes are ready for harvesting.

Mid-May is a traditional time to sow **sweet corn.** Planting corn in blocks of nine to 12 plants rather than rows ensures better pollination and takes up less space.

Transplant **dill, sweet marjoram, basil, sage,** and other herbs into the garden now. If you like to grow **mint,** remember that is spreads by underground roots. Confine it by planting it in a 5-gallon bucket with the bottom cut out. Bury the bucket into the ground with the rim a few inches above ground level. This technique will usually restrict the roots from wandering over the rim to invade other areas of the garden.

At the end of the month, set out **tomatoes, peppers, eggplants** and **okra.** Some garden stores offer transplants of **squash, beans, cucumbers,** and **melons** that can also be transplanted. I prefer, however, to direct seed the latter as they are often fussy about being transplanted. These vegetables will germinate quickly and suffer less transplant shock when direct seeded in a prepared soil.

CARE

Even though the weather has mellowed, you can still to expect a late spring frost, so be prepared with plant protectors if the forecast calls for a freeze at night. Remove the covers during the day for the plants to receive sunlight and air circulation. Floating row covers work well, or 5-gallon buckets, fiber nursery pots, cardboard boxes, and other materials can be used to protect plants overnight.

Thin out the crowded rows of **carrots, beets, endive,** and **leaf lettuce.** Be careful when pulling out seedlings so as not to remove large clumps. Use tweezers to snip unwanted plants and space them accordingly.

Some vegetables can be grown vertically in the garden, especially those that grow as vines. **Cucumbers, squash, pole beans,** and **garden peas** will grow up fences and trellises. This will take up less space if your garden area is limited and the vegetables will grow more uniformly.

WATERING

Proper watering is essential to get new vegetable transplants started. Water young transplants before they are taken out of their containers. They tend to dry out quickly when set directly into the garden. This will prepare them for the transition.

During periods of dry weather, be sure to water the garden every few days to maintain sub-soil moisture so the root systems develop deeply. Use mulches when the plants are 6 inches tall to conserve water and help suppress weed growth.

Container gardens and raised beds will drain more rapidly and may require more attention to watering. To determine if the soil needs watering, dig down to a depth of 2 to 3 inches with a garden trowel to check whether the soil is beginning to dry out. If it is, give the garden a good soaking.

If time and your budget permits, consider installing a drip irrigation system to water the vegetable garden. Not only is this a time- and water-saver, but also it puts water at the root zone of the crops and will soak deeply. It reduces the chances of moisture staying on the foliage at night and thereby reduces the incidence of powdery mildew and other leaf diseases.

 FERTILIZING

If you did not add a slow-release fertilizer to the garden soil in the spring, you can supplement with a water-soluble plant fertilizer to give the plants a boost while they are establishing. I prefer to dilute soluble plant fertilizers to half strength to avoid the accumulation of soluble salts around the root zone. Read and follow label directions.

Too much nitrogen (the first number in the fertilizer analysis) will promote excessive vegetative growth and will often attract aphids and other insect pests. It will also delay flowering and fruiting of many vegetable crops.

 GROOMING

Keep herbs pinched or pruned to encourage branching and make the plants grow more compact. This will also delay premature flowering so you can enjoy harvesting and using the foliage for culinary purposes.

Pinch off excessive branch suckers on indeterminate **tomato** plants to develop stronger central stems that will support the plants throughout the season.

 PROBLEMS

Watch for hatches of aphids that attack the tender, succulent growth of vegetable and herbs. At the first sight of them, wash them off or use the homemade soap spray (see page 283). Ladybugs are Nature's best predators to keep these pests at bay.

White butterflies are a sign that cabbageworms are on the way. They chew holes in the leaves of cole crops. Use floating row covers to prevent the butterflies from depositing eggs on the foliage, or use *Bacillus thuringiensis* (Bt). This bacterial warfare will stop the larvae in their tracks.

NOTES

_____
_____
_____
_____
_____
_____
_____
_____
_____
_____
_____
_____
_____
_____
_____
_____

JUNE
VEGETABLES

PLANNING

Plan to harvest crops as they begin to reach their prime. Pinch herb blooms to delay flowering, encourage more branching, and sweeten the foliage.

Begin now to plan for the late-summer and autumn garden. You can start to decide what to plant in cool weather conditions after certain crops are finished. Some areas of the garden will be vacated after the harvest of **bush beans,** leaving room for a fall crop of **radishes** or **spinach.** Succession planting will keep the garden productive and prevent weed invasions.

Start cool-weather seedlings now so they will be ready to set out later in the season. Stock up on fresh seed-starting mixture and other supplies for new transplants. Purchase seeds of cool-weather crops now while they are still in supply. Look for **cabbage, broccoli, cauliflower,** and **Brussels sprouts.**

PLANTING

In higher elevations with shorter growing seasons, the soil temperatures are rising, and it's time to plant vegetables and herbs in containers or garden beds. Hardened-off plants of **tomatoes, peppers,** and **eggplants** should be put in their permanent summer homes. However, there can still be nights with frost, so be prepared to cover the tender plants or have the containers on rollers so they can be easily moved to the garage or indoors overnight.

It's last call for planting **pumpkins** and **watermelons** in early June to allow them sufficient time to grow and mature before fall frost. You can purchase seedlings, but my preference is to direct seed them in the garden the first week in June. Allow plenty of space for these crops as they vine. Bush varieties produce smaller fruits.

If space permits, plant more **sweet corn, beans,** and late **cucumbers.** Replant the **pea** patch with something else as soon as you have harvested all the pea pods. If you plant the early determinate **tomatoes,** you still have time to plant mid-season varieties now. These will grow and produce a fresh crop of tomatoes when the early ones are finished.

CARE

Apply mulch around vegetable rows. As vegetables finish off, pull out the bolted (seed-forming) **lettuce,** spent **broccoli** stems, and other cool-season crops to make room for the warm-season crops. Continue to thin root crops if they are growing too closely. Use the tops of **beets** and **turnips** as salad greens. If you like to grow tall **tomatoes** with a strong single stem, now is the time to train the plants onto a fence, trellis, stake, or tomato cage. Tomato fruit that is kept off the ground gets better air circulation, ripens more uniformly, and is less prone to insect and disease problems.

WATERING

Deep watering in summer is essential to encourage deeper rooting, drought-resistant vegetables. Provide at least an inch of water to the garden per week. Use either a drip irrigation system, soaker hoses between rows, or a frog-eye sprinkler that delivers water at a low arc over a larger zone. Set out rain gauges to measure the amount of water applied, and time how long it takes to put on 1 inch of water per garden area.

Tomatoes do best with a uniform supply of moisture, rather than going through a wet-dry cycle. Otherwise, **tomatoes** and **peppers,** will develop a condition known as blossom-end rot (see page 206).

Keep container-grown vegetables and herbs watered when soilless mixtures feel dry to the touch. Do not allow the plants to dry to the point of wilting because this will make them less productive and more prone to pests.

FERTILIZING

If you incorporated a slow-release granular fertilizer into the soil at planting time, you should not need additional fertilizer now. If you prefer a water-soluble plant fertilizer, dilute it to half strength, and apply at biweekly intervals to a moist—never a dry—soil. Plants that may have been slightly damaged by hail or wind early in the season will benefit from a light foliar feeding from a water-soluble plant fertilizer. Apply this early in the morning or later evening so the plants can absorb the nutrients directly through their leaves as well as roots.

GROOMING

Pinch and prune the tips of herbs to delay premature flowering and encourage more compact growth.

To grow indeterminate **tomatoes** with less suckering, break off side suckers at the point of origin. This will direct energy to the main stem. A few tomato suckers are acceptable and will eventually develop flowers and fruit. Note: Determinate tomato varieties grow multiple stems that are not suckers and that will develop flowers and fruit.

PROBLEMS

Insect season is in full swing. Watch for invasions of aphids on herbs and vegetables. At the first signs of invasion, wash them down with a spray of water or use a homemade soap spray (see page 283).

Flea beetles may invade the garden and puncture tiny holes in the foliage of many leafy crops. You can use insecticidal soap sprays or Neem oil to thwart these beasties. Repeat sprays after a rain shower or after overhead watering since this reduces the effectiveness of the control. Floating row covers are helpful to exclude these pests, too.

Colorado potato beetles can be spotted as oval, yellow and black striped beetles that will feed on potato foliage. Look for their eggs as masses of soft yellow spots underneath the leaves. Pick them off and discard, or spray with Neem oil on both the upper and lower surface of the leaves

Caterpillars of all sorts love the vegetable and herb garden. If you want to encourage the **black swallowtail butterfly**, be prepared to leave some of the parsley worms on the dill, parsley, and celery foliage. They will do minimal damage anyway. Otherwise, handpick off excess numbers if they strip the foliage badly. The use of Bt can also reduce the damage from caterpillars that develop into butterflies and moths. Read and follow label directions.

Weeds need to be pulled or dug as soon as they appear in the garden after a good watering or a nice rain.

NOTES

_____
_____
_____
_____
_____
_____
_____
_____
_____
_____
_____
_____
_____
_____
_____

JULY
VEGETABLES

PLANNING

In July, vegetable and herb gardens may be stressed by prolonged periods of heat and drought. Plan on regular watering to maintain healthy growth. If you haven't applied organic mulches around plants, do so now. Mulches help conserve water and maintain uniform moisture in the root zone. They also suppress weed growth that competes for water and nutrients.

Plan how you'll fill empty garden spots. You may choose a second crop of heat-tolerant vegetables, or you may prefer to mulch empty spots and wait until later to plant cool weather vegetables. Check the seed packets to determine how many days to harvest.

Plan on doing some insect and disease patrol, and clean up garden debris. If it is insect- and disease-free, add it to the compost pile. Keep the compost layers moist to hasten decomposition.

PLANTING

In mid- to late July, you can sow seeds of **beets, bush beans, chard, radishes, kohlrabi, kale, endive,** and **carrots.** When sown directly into prepared garden soil and watered, they will germinate quickly. You can also purchase and transplant seedlings of **broccoli, cauliflower,** and **late cabbage.**

CARE

Apply a 2- to 3-inch layer of mulch around the plants, leaving space for air circulation to discourage pests from nesting at the base of the plants. Organic mulches preserve soil moisture, discourages weed growth, and keep foliage, fruit, and vegetables clean.

Harvest maturing vegetables and fruit at their peak to stimulate more growth. This will also prevent the vegetables from over-maturing and rotting. **Sweet corn** can mature quite quickly, so pick it after the milk squirts from the top row of kernels. Have a pot of boiling water ready so you can enjoy this sweet harvest right from your own garden.

Dig early **onions** if the tops have naturally dried and flopped over. Let them dry for a day or two, then store in a cool, dry spot.

Continue to pinch and prune herbs to delay flowering and loss of flavor. You can use fresh herbs at twice the amounts recommended for dried, bottled ones. If you have time and space, freeze or dry extra herbs.

My Italian grandmother used cheesecloth to shade the herb garden during prolonged periods of heat and drought. She set sturdy wooden poles in the ground and stretched the cheesecloth over the crops so they would continue to grow and flourish.

WATERING

This is the time of year that plants use more moisture to sustain growth and develop fruit and vegetables. Water when the soil underneath the layers of mulch is beginning to dry out. Check moisture levels with a garden trowel or shovel to customize your own watering schedule. Gardens need 1 inch of water a week to keep growing and producing. Uniform moisture is a must for **tomatoes, peppers,** and **cucumbers.**

Water container gardens that are in full sun daily, unless you have incorporated moisture-holding polymers into the soil mix (then water as the soil begins to dry out). Again, you need to customize a watering schedule to fit your garden's exposure, soil type, wind, and various other environmental factors.

I prefer to water early in the morning to give the plants a good start for the day. Avoid overhead watering at night since this allows moisture to stay on the foliage and encourage mildew diseases. Vegetables that touch wet ground are more prone to rot.

FERTILIZING

Most vegetables and herbs that were fertilized earlier will not need additional applications now. For new plants, apply a water-soluble plant fertilizer to the foliage in early morning or late evening. A fish emulsion product or liquid kelp may prove helpful. If you are doing successive planting, mix compost or sphagnum peat moss into the empty spots before planting the next round of fall crops. This will ensure they get off to a good start.

GROOMING

As the fall crop of **carrots** and **beets** are growing, thin the plants to the correct spacing as recommended on the seed packets. Pinch suckers off indeterminate **tomato** plants if you are training them on a support. Once the stem is sufficiently strong and securely attached to the support, you can leave some to encourage additional side branches that will develop flowers and fruit.

PROBLEMS

Continue to monitor for insect pests including squash bugs, cucumber beetles, aphids, whiteflies, and a variety of caterpillars. You can control most pests early in the game by washing them off with a forceful spray of water from the hose. If this doesn't get them all, use a homemade soap spray (see page 283) in early morning or evening. Insecticidal soaps are also labeled for vegetables and herbs.

Squash bugs, cucumber beetles, slugs, weevils, and asparagus beetles can be handpicked if you're not squeamish about this kind of control. Just drop them into a bucket of soapy water. Read and follow label directions when using any kind of pesticide and observe waiting periods before harvest time.

Powdery mildew disease can appear almost overnight. Use the homemade mildew prevention control on page 285. Pick off the heavily infected leaves and discard. Do not compost diseased or insect-ridden plant parts.

GARDENING WITH AN ALTITUDE TIPS
Building Your Own Critter Barrier

If you live in an area where wildlife poses a problem to your vegetables, here's how to create a barrier to exclude voles, meadow mice, chipmunks, and rabbits.

String rabbit fencing around the garden perimeter, and set the lower portion snugly into the ground in a trench.

Dig a trench at least 6 inches deep and 6 inches wide. Set the fencing so that 6 inches stretches across the bottom full width of the trench, then bends up the side. Set the height of the fence above the top of the trench about 18 inches or more. This method creates a barrier to deter tunneling varmints from making their way into the garden. Note: It may not succeed against the deeper tunneling gophers and groundhogs.

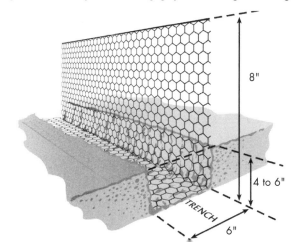

AUGUST

VEGETABLES

PLANNING

Now is the time to update your garden journal or notebook as the garden grows on. Take notes on which vegetables and herbs are performing well, and note those that are not living up to your expectations.

Plan on harvesting vegetables, fruits, and herbs on a regular basis so you can enjoy them at their peak. Pick **cucumbers** when they reach their mature size. Don't leave them on the vines too long or they will turn yellow, develop seeds, and get bitter. **Summer squash** should be harvested daily while they are still immature and tender. Nothing tastes better than a 6-inch zucchini fried in garlic butter. If you like, let a zucchini grow bigger and use it for stuffing.

PLANTING

Early in the month, there is still time for a second planting of **radishes, turnips, spinach, leaf lettuce, chard,** and **winter onions.** Be sure to check the maturity dates on the seed packets and count back from the first expected frost in your area. It's a good idea to sow the seeds a bit deeper during the heat of sum-

mer and sow them a little more generously so you get good germination. Keep the seedbed moist so it will have the opportunity to get started. A light misting two or three times a day may be needed for the first week or so after planting.

Sow **garlic** cloves so they can start growing. Once the ground has frosted, it can be mulched for the winter. Garlic plants overwinter, start growing again next spring, and are ready to harvest by next summer.

CARE

Top-dress the vegetable garden with fresh compost as needed to maintain soil moisture and suppress weed growth. Mulching around **tomatoes** will keep the fruit from contacting the ground and rotting or getting invaded by earwigs and other pests.

Gather bundles of herbs, tie together with rubber bands, and hang upside down in a warm, dark, dry garage or garden shed. You can start to harvest last year's crop of **garlic** when the tops have turned yellow and flopped over. Lift out the entire bulb and dry the garlic in a well-ventilated shed or garage.

To protect **pumpkins** and **winter squash** from rot, slip a roof shingle or a fragment of outdoor carpeting under ripening fruits to lift them off the moist soil. When winter squash is ready to harvest, the outer rind will be too hard to puncture with your thumbnail.

Temperatures that are above 90 degrees Fahrenheit can slow **tomato** production. You can shade them with cheesecloth or shade cloth, but patience will pay off, and they will start producing again as the weather begins to cool down.

WATERING

Keep monitoring the water needs of plants. Hot weather can deplete plants of needed energy and delay or stunt production. If it doesn't rain for a week or more, apply an inch of water to the garden, and let it soak in. This is where mulches are helpful to maintain the plants throughout the remainder of the growing season. Invest in soaker hoses and drip irrigation if time and water conservation are high on your garden wish list.

Regular watering is necessary to prevent **tomatoes** from splitting and cracking and will reduce the onset of blossom-end rot. Keep the bare soil mulched around the plants.

Keep newly planted seeds moist to ensure a vigorous root system. You may have to water both morning and early evening with a light sprinkling. Never allow the soil to get bone-dry, as this will surely kill newly germinating seeds or emerging seedlings.

Container gardens will require more attention in hot, windy weather. Reflecting heat from masonry walls, paved walkways, and driveways all contribute to faster drying of soilless mixtures. Check the soil regularly to customize your watering schedule.

FERTILIZING

Younger plants that were seeded for a successive crop will benefit from a side-dressing of granular fertilizer such as a 5-10-5. Lightly rake the fertilizer into the soil, and water it in. If you prefer, an application of soluble plant fertilizer can be sprayed on the foliage early in the morning or evening.

Herbs should be fertilized with a soluble plant fertilizer diluted at half strength. Too much fertilizer will stimulate lush, succulent top growth that lacks flavor.

GROOMING

Clean up any plants that have stopped producing, including **bush** and **pole beans,** early **cucumbers, summer squash,** and **peppers.** If the plant debris is insect- and disease-free, chop or grind it up and add it to the compost pile. Cover the bare soil where plants were removed to keep it from baking and to reduce weed invasions.

PROBLEMS

Watch for spider mites and whiteflies. Mites cause the leaves to look a sickly brown or silvery gray. Pinch off and discard the badly infested leaves. Spraying the upper and lower surfaces of the leaves with water will keep mites at bay temporarily. You must be persistent with natural controls. Natural populations of ladybugs will consume large quantities of aphids.

If virus diseases attack **tomatoes** and **peppers** in your garden, the best control is to remove and dispose of infected plants. There are no miracle treatments for viruses. Choose disease-resistant varieties for next year; and make a note in your garden journal to indicate which plants were infected the worst.

Powdery mildew is a sure bet this month and will show up on **melons, cucumbers, summer squash,** and other vegetables. Warm days and cool nights favor this disease. You can choose to ignore it on maturing plants or those that are nearing the end of the growing season. On newly planted fall vegetables, you can prevent mildew by applying the homemade mildew recipe on page 285. It will protect the plants from a severe infection so they can continue to produce foliage and a late crop.

Continue to pull or dig weeds before they have the opportunity to produce seeds.

To exclude wildlife including rabbits, raccoons, deer, and mice, fencing is the best defense, but in some cases, you can try repellents.

SEPTEMBER
VEGETABLES

 PLANNING

With the arrival of Labor Day, you may think it's time to hang up the garden hoe. Not so fast! With some planning, you can devise protective covers and extend the garden season, even after the first frost in September. Covers can be made from 5-gallon buckets, large fiber nursery pots, plastic or spun fabric tunnels, or cold frames. With this extra protection, cool-weather crops can continue to grow and produce for several weeks more.

Prepare the soil in the garden for next year's crops. If the weather remains mild for several weeks, you might consider planting a "green manure" or cover crop in early September. This will grow through the fall and can be turned under in the spring to improve soil fertility and structure. It will also hold topsoil in place, improve water retention, and suppress annual winter weeds.

 PLANTING

You can get a head start on spring **spinach** if you plant seeds in a prepared bed early this month. Sow the seeds and keep watered to allow them to germinate. The new young plants will overwinter in a mulched bed and resume growth in the spring.

There is not adequate time to plant cool-weather crops, unless you grow them under protection. However, you can increase your collection of indoor herbs by taking stem cuttings from outdoor plants.

Plant cover crops for "green manure" at least a month before the first killing frost. **Annual rye grass, oats, buckwheat,** and **crimson clover** can be planted in late August to early September.

 CARE

Harvest young **broccoli, cabbage,** and other cool-weather crops planted in July or early August. If they are not quite ready, mulch them so they can continue to grow through a light frost. Root crops can be left in the ground until after the first hard frost. This will actually sweeten their flavor. Try this with **carrots, turnips,** and **parsnips.**

Harvest **winter squash** and **pumpkins** as they mature. The outer skin will be too hard to penetrate with your thumbnail. If left in the garden and hit by a frost, the outer skin will decay. Cut the **pumpkins** and **winter squash** from the vines, but leave a short piece of stem on the vegetable. This way, they will last for several months in cool, dry storage.

Harvest any remaining **onions** and **garlic** when the tops turn yellow or brown and flop over. Cure the bulbs for a few weeks in a warm, dry shady, airy place. Then store them in a cool, dry location.

If **tomatoes** have not been killed by the first frost, you can encourage more fruit ripening by covering the plants at night with a frost blanket. Remove the cover during the warmth of the day. Also, try pulling the indeterminate tomato plants that still have clusters of green tomatoes attached and hang them upside down in a garage or garden shed where they won't freeze. These will eventually ripen.

Some gardeners harvest the last of green **tomatoes** and place them in single layers in cardboard boxes in a warm room. Do not place them in direct sunlight, or they will sunscald. Over a period of weeks, the green tomatoes will ripen.

 WATERING

Unless the autumn is extremely dry, there is no need to water the garden if cool-weather vegetables have been properly mulched. If you're uncertain, check underneath the mulch with a garden trowel or shovel to see what the soil moisture is like. Cool weather is a time to wean the garden off frequent waterings.

During dry spells, continue to water perennial vegetables, including **asparagus** and **rhubarb**. Keep the compost pile moist to help speed up the process of decomposition. The microorganisms will continue to work on warm days, and the pile may emit steam in the early morning, meaning things are in balance. Composting can continue deep in the pile even after the first few frosts.

 ## FERTILIZING

No fertilizer is needed at this time of year. As the garden is cleared of plants or raised beds readied for winter, it's time to add organic amendments such as aged manure, compost, or sphagnum peat moss. Or you can plant a "green manure" cover crop if you want to add a source of nitrogen for next spring. After amending and turning the soil, leave the ground rough to absorb winter's moisture. By spring, the clods will have broken down, and the soil will be mellow and ready to be raked and leveled.

 ## GROOMING

Weeds will continue to grow and produce seedheads, so keep pulling them. Remove dead and dying plants from the garden, and recycle disease- and insect-free plant debris to the compost pile. Do not compost weeds that have seedheads. The compost pile usually does not get hot enough to kill weed seeds, and you will be plagued by their growth next year. Clean out container gardens after herbs and vegetables are finished producing. This will remove nesting areas for insect pests and disease organisms.

 ## PROBLEMS

Insects will be looking for winter quarters this month. Cultivating the soil and exposing their eggs or other overwintering stages will keep bugs from becoming a problem.

Some rodents may try to overwinter in the compost pile or heavily mulched areas. Check for signs of their activity. To deter mice, voles, chipmunks, and other critters, delay spreading winter mulch until the ground has frozen hard. By this time, they will have found homes elsewhere.

 ## NOTES

_____
_____
_____
_____
_____
_____
_____
_____
_____
_____
_____
_____
_____
_____
_____
_____
_____
_____
_____
_____
_____
_____
_____
_____
_____
_____
_____
_____
_____
_____
_____
_____
_____
_____
_____

OCTOBER
VEGETABLES

 PLANNING

This is the month to amend the bare garden soil, so make plans to stockpile some well-rotted manure, compost, shredded leaves, or dried grass clippings. Leaves that have waxy cuticles like cottonwood should be shredded or sent through a grinder before adding to the garden soil. Otherwise, you'll have a mucky mess come spring.

Plan to spread the organic amendment over the bare soil to a depth of 2 to 3 inches, then turn it under to a depth or 6 to 8 inches. A rototiller or small disk attachment on a tractor will make this task easier. Do not over amend the soil, as too much organic material can build up soluble salts that will damage plant roots next year. The general rule of thumb is to add 3 to 5 cubic yards of organic amendment per 1,000 square feet in the autumn.

Leave the surface rough after working the soil so it receives the winter moisture and alternate freezing and thawing effects. This weathering process will mellow the soil and the organic amendments will keep the soil open for winter moisture to percolate down more deeply.

By spring, your garden soil will be ready for planting. Remove some of the old, tired soil and add a layer of compost so you can add fertility and refresh the garden bed.

' Designate an area for a compost pile if you don't already have one. It's a great source of free organic amendment and mulch for the vegetable garden.

 PLANTING

There is very little planting to do this time of year. Plants growing in cold frames are the exception, as you can control the environment. Prop open the lid on warm sunny days, and cover the cold frame in the evening. You can grow **leaf lettuce, endive, escarole,** and **radishes** for several weeks by this method.

If the frost has not killed back all the herbs in your garden, you can still dig up viable plants and pot them up in a soilless potting mixture or take cuttings to root indoors.

Herbs can be grown on a sunny windowsill or under bright artificial lights on a plant stand. Watch for insects that may piggyback indoors. Control the pests by washing them off the foliage and stems.

If the weather remains mild and the soil is workable, plant a crop of fall **garlic** if the bulbs are available at your local garden store. After the soil freezes, mulch the garlic with straw or coarse compost. Also, dig, sever, and replant the rooted suckers from **raspberries.**

 CARE

Some years, we experience an Indian summer, and **pumpkins, winter squash,** and **ornamental gourds** can continue to mature in the garden. Once a hard frost arrives, harvest them right away so they won't rot. When the **pumpkins** turn a solid orange, cut their stems with a knife. Cure them in a warm, dry location for a week or so. Then store in a cool, dry garage or barn at 55 to 60 degrees Fahrenheit.

Root crops can remain in the ground until after the first freeze.

Do you still have green **tomatoes?** They will require temperatures of 65 degrees Fahrenheit to ripen. Harvest the unblemished green fruits, set them in shallow cardboard boxes shoulder to shoulder, and store them in a cool spot to ripen. Bring the pinkish ones to ripen more quickly in the warmth of the kitchen. Enjoy!

 ## WATERING

Make sure that perennial vegetables are deeply watered before the ground freezes solid. Do this on a warm sunny day when temperatures are in the 50s or higher. Once a month is usually all that is needed during prolonged dry spells. Water when the soil is unfrozen.

Keep the compost pile moist to kept the microorganisms working. Check the interior of the compost pile with a piece of pipe to determine moisture needs. If the plant refuse and other garden debris was wet when added, you may not want to overwater the compost as this will inhibit decomposition. For your wish list: request a compost thermometer to check on how the compost is coming along.

 ## FERTILIZING

No fertilizer is required at this time of the year. You can add some well-rotted manure around **asparagus** plants and **rhubarb** so it will gradually break down over the winter months.

 ## GROOMING

Collect and grind or shred leaves and other garden debris that may blow in. Add to the compost pile. Keep weeds pulled or dug to prevent seed dispersal. Throw away plants that are suspect for diseases. Squash vine borers can overwinter in plant debris, so dispose of any plants that are likely to harbor these pests.

 ## PROBLEMS

Cultivate the soil to expose the larvae and cocoons of overwintering insect pests. The freezing and thawing effects over the winter will rid the garden of many soil-inhabiting insects and their eggs. Leave the soil rough so it will take the full brunt of winter freezing, thawing, wetting, and drying. Inspect areas around the compost pile for rodents, and set out traps if necessary.

NOTES

227

NOVEMBER

VEGETABLES

 PLANNING

This is a restful month for the vegetable gardener. You can add deciduous leaves to the garden soil, but don't overdo the application because it can "gum up" the soil. If you don't already have a compost pile, find an area in the corner of the yard where you can recycle leaves and other disease-free plant refuse. It will take six months to a year to achieve good compost, but who doesn't want to have this "black gold" for augmenting the soil?

Keep adding notes to your garden notebook or journal while things are still fresh in your mind. Remember specific things that happened over the garden season including weather, planting and harvesting dates, insect pests, disease problems, and any other environmental factors that may have made the gardening year interesting or challenging.

Plan to inventory your garden tools. Clean them up before putting them in storage. A wire brush will scrape off caked soil. Once the metal parts are cleaned, spray a coating of oil to prevent rust. If you have space, prepare a 5-gallon bucket of sharp sand, and mix in a quart of motor oil. Then insert the metal parts of rakes, hoes, shovels, trowels, and others into the oily sand. This will do a good job of cleaning and coating the metal surfaces.

Keep a hose handy to do some fall and winter watering should we experience prolonged dry spells. Perennial vegetables and fruits need supplemental moisture if there is little or no snow in your area.

This is also a good time to consider building a cold frame (see page 205). This handy structure is a great way to harden off seedlings in the spring as they make their transition from the indoor environment to the outside conditions. It's like a miniature unheated greenhouse, but can be transformed into a temporary hotbed if you add heating cables or a heat mat.

If your garden has performed poorly over the past few years, it may be time for a soil test. Vegetables, herbs, and fruit will deplete the soil of nutrients more than most ornamental plants or the pH may be affecting the availability of certain nutrients or elements. However, you don't need to have a soil test done every year. The test is only one instrument in the diagnosis of problems. There can be other problems including the evolvement of shade from maturing trees and shrubs, new buildings, poor soil drainage, chemical residues in the soil, and watering issues.

 PLANTING

Nothing should be planted directly outdoors this month, unless you have a season extender such as a cold frame or hot bed. Many short-season crops such as **spinach, leaf lettuce,** and **endive** can be grown with the protection of a cold frame and will provide fresh greens until a hard frost sets them back. A heating mat or cable can help protect plants within the cold frame on very cold nights, or you can cover the top with an insulated blanket or carpeting. Experiment and see what you can grow even though winter is approaching!

 CARE

If you haven't done the final garden cleanup, remove the last of the frozen, dead plants. Left in the garden, they can harbor insects and their eggs over the winter. Cut back the tops of maturing **asparagus** and **rhubarb** plants. Clean out fallen leaves, weeds, and other plant refuse. Turn the compost every few weeks while the weather remains open and warm. Lightly water the compost pile if rain or snow is scarce to help microorganisms break down the raw materials. You can also get a compost thermometer to monitor the internal temperature of your pile and "keep it cooking."

Prepare the soil for next spring by adding compost to the garden before the soil freezes. If you have a source of manure available, now is the time to spread it over the vegetable garden to a depth of 6 to 8 inches.

 ## WATERING

Very little watering is needed this month. The only exceptions are the perennial **asparagus** beds and **rhubarb.** Water them once a month when there is little or no moisture. Apply water early in the day to allow it to soak in. I use a frog-eye sprinkler and allow it to run 15 to 20 minutes to get needed moisture into dry soils. Once the ground is frozen, it is too late to water.

 ## FERTILIZING

No fertilizer applications are recommended now. The addition of organic materials such as compost and manure will provide nutrients as they begin to break down during winter.

 ## GROOMING

Continue to clean up any garden debris, old plants, and refuse that blows into your garden. Gather up and store old pots, plant stakes and other gardening items that are still hanging around outside.

 ## PROBLEMS

If you live in an area where wildlife poses a problem, consider building your own critter barrier described on page 221.

NOTES

_____
_____
_____
_____
_____
_____
_____
_____
_____
_____
_____
_____
_____
_____
_____
_____
_____
_____
_____
_____
_____
_____
_____
_____
_____
_____
_____
_____
_____
_____
_____

DECEMBER
VEGETABLES

 PLANNING

Winter is a cleansing process for the garden. Freezing, thawing and winter precipitation will mellow the soil to make it easy to work in spring. A long period of freezing weather also rids the soil of pests. Winter gives us pause to reflect.

As snow begins to fly through the air, seed catalogs begin to fly through the mail. Peruse them as your time permits. Look for new varieties of vegetables and herbs to try next growing season. It's easy to be persuaded by the colorful photographs and plant descriptions, but shop wisely and choose plants that are appropriate for your particular garden site. Add notes to your garden notebook or journal while thoughts are fresh in your mind.

 PLANTING

The only planting at this time of year is that of starting herbs indoors, or taking cuttings and rooting them in a sterile growing medium. Keep the seedlings in bright light to prevent them from becoming too leggy. Temperatures should be kept on the low side to discourage pests and diseases.

 CARE

Once the ground has frozen, it is time to apply mulch around perennial vegetables, herbs, and fruits, including **strawberries, rhubarb, sage, mint,** and **chives**. Use clean wheat straw, chopped leaves, or pine needles if they are available. Winter mulching helps insulate the plants from the cycles of freezing and thawing that can heave the crowns out of the ground. If you grow fall-bearing **raspberries**, this is a good time to cut them back to the ground as a final cleanup. Harvest herbs as they continue to grow indoors.

 WATERING

Indoor herbs need careful watering to avoid waterlogging the soil, especially those artificial mixes that can stay wet for longer periods. Allow the soil mix to dry out slightly between waterings to prevent root rot.

Outdoors: When we experience warm periods without snow or rain, check perennial vegetables and fruits to see if they need water. Apply the water early in the day when air temperatures are in the 45 to 50 degrees Fahrenheit range, and the ground is not frozen.

 FERTILIZING

Go easy on fertilizing indoor herbs since they are not receiving the quantity and quality of light they were used to outdoors. Use a soluble plant fertilizer, but dilute it to half strength and apply to a moistened soil. Never apply fertilizer to a dried out soil as the salts can damage the tender roots.

 GROOMING

Pick a warm day and get outside to enjoy the sunshine, and to clean up and check out the garden in winter. It will refresh your body and spirit.

 PROBLEMS

Watch for aphids, whiteflies, and spider mites on indoor herbs. Warm, dry indoor conditions favor these pests. Periodic rinsing of foliage under the kitchen faucet will keep most of these pests at bay.

Fungus gnats do not damage the plants, but the larvae will feed on organic matter in the potting soil and, rarely, on plant roots. Keep plant debris from accumulating on the soil surface, and allow the soil mix to dry out between waterings.

VINES, GROUND COVERS, & ORNAMENTAL GRASSES

VINES

Growing versatile vines, ground covers and ornamental grasses in Idaho can be rewarding—if you
understand their growth habits. Imagine a vine
spilling over a mailbox post, fence, old tree stump,
or large boulder. Many vines have handsome
foliage, beautiful flowers, and edible fruits, and
their clinging, twining or upright growth makes a
nice visual contrast with other plants. Vines can be
functional and ornamental at the same time. If a
redwood deck is too hot to sit on in summer, build
an arbor so a vine can shade it and provide a
wall of colorful blooms.

No matter where you live in our region, there
are many vines to choose from. Some vines are

herbaceous with soft stems, and some are
woody. Some are tender and may die back each
winter, while others are rather aggressive and
long-lived. Some vines are fast-growing, others
more restrained.

Annual vines live for just one growing season,
while perennials may last a lifetime. Annual vines
like scented sweet peas and morning glories
provide a delightful summer screen. They are
fast to grow but will have to be replaced each
year. Perennial vines will survive the winter and
grow thicker and stronger each year. Though
these may bloom for shorter periods, they may
produce berries or fruits later in the season for
birds and winter interest. One of my favorites is

GARDENING WITH AN ALTITUDE TIPS
How Many Ground Cover Plants Are Needed?

To determine how many ground cover plants you will need, refer to the following table. Note, the
table assumes that plants are spaced "on center," i.e. the center of one is measured to the center
of the next. The table is derived for this formula: Area in square feet x Spacing Multiplier =
Number of plants needed to plant the area.

For an area not found on the chart, use this simple formula: $N = A/D^2$. In this formula, N =
Number of plants in a given bed; A = the area of the bed in square inches, and D = distance in
inches between plants in the row and between rows. For example: If the area of the bed measures 50 square feet and you want a spacing of 18 inches between plants, the N = 50 sq. ft (1.44
sq. in./1 sq. ft) = 22 plants; 18 in. x 18 in.

Area to be Planted	4 in.	6 in.	8 in.	10 in.	12 in.	15 in.	18 in.	24 in.
25 Sq. Ft.	225	100	56	36	25	16	11	6
50 Sq. Ft.	450	200	113	72	50	32	22	12
100 Sq. Ft.	900	400	225	144	100	64	44	25
200 Sq. Ft.	1,800	800	450	288	200	128	89	50
300 Sq. Ft.	2,700	1,200	675	432	300	192	133	75
1,000 Sq. Ft.	9,000	4,000	2,250	1,440	1,000	641	444	250
Spacing Multiplier	9	4	2.25	1.44	1	0.64	0.44	0.25

GARDENING WITH AN ALTITUDE TIPS
Vines, Ground Covers, and Ornamental Grasses
for Idaho

VINES
- American Bittersweet, *Celastrus scandens*
- Clematis, *Clematis* spp. and hybrids
- Climbing Honeysuckle, *Lonicera* spp.
- Climbing Hydrangea, *Hydrangea anomala* subsp. *Petioilaris*
- Common Hop, *Humulus lupulus*
- English Ivy, *Hedera helix*
- Moonflower (annual), *Ipomoea alba*
- Morning Glory (annual), *Ipomoea purpurea*
- Porcelain Vine, *Ampelopsis brevipedunculata*
- Silver Lace Vine, *Polygonum aubertii*
- Sweet Pea (annual), *Lathyrus ordoratus*
- Trumpet Vine, *Campsis radicans*
- Virginia Creeper, *Parthenocissus quinquefolia*

GROUND COVERS
- Carpet Bugleweed, *Ajuga reptans*
- Creeping Oregon Grape, *Mahonia repens*
- Creeping Juniper, *Juniperus horizontalis*
- Creeping Phlox, *Phlox subulata*
- Creeping Veronica, *Veronica* spp.
- False Rockcress, *Aubrieta deltoidea*
- Hardy Iceplant, *Delosperma* spp.
- Heart-leafed Bergenia, *Bergenia cordifolia*

GROUND COVERS
- Kinnikinick, *Arctostaphylos uva-ursi*
- Lamb's Ears, *Stachys byzantina*
- Lily-of-the-Valley, *Convallaria majalis*
- Moneywort, *Lysimachia nummularia* 'Aurea'
- Periwinkle, *Vinca minor*
- Pussytoes, *Antennaria parvifolia*
- Snow-in-Summer, *Cerastium tomentosum*
- Spotted Dead Nettle, *Lamium maculatum*
- Stonecrop, *Sedum* spp.
- Sweet Woodruff, *Galium odoratum*
- Vinca/Periwinkle, *Vinca minor*
- Woolly Thyme, *Thymus pseudolanuginosus*

ORNAMENTAL GRASSES
- Blue Fescue, *Festuca glauca*
- Blue Oat Grass, *Helictotrichon sempervirens*
- Feather Reed Grass, *Calamagrostis* x *acutiflora*
- Fountain Grass, *Pennisetum alopecuroides*
- Hardy Pampas Grass, *Saccharum ravennae*
- Little Bluestem, *Schizachyrium scoparium*
- Maiden Grass, *Miscanthus sinensis*
- Northern Sea Oats, *Chasmanthium latifolium*
- Prairie Dropseed, *Sporobolus heterolepis*
- Switchgrass, *Panicum virgatum*

the American bittersweet with its orange-red seed capsules through fall and winter. Virginia creeper makes a beautiful autumn display. Honeysuckle attracts visiting hummingbirds and is excellent for the wildlife-friendly garden.

Annual vines are a good way to experiment because you can add colors and textures to your landscape without making a long-term commitment. Many are easy to grow from seed in spring such as morning glories, sweet peas, and moonflowers. At the end of the season, many of these annuals will self-seed and germinate the following spring, if conditions are right. Annual vines will produce the largest leaves and bear more flowers when planted in full sun.

Perennial vines will reward you with flowers, interesting foliage, and often ornamental stems and bark for winter interest. Select perennial vines thoughtfully, and consider the best location for them to grow and prosper, because many of them do not like to be disturbed.

Vines will vary in the way they climb. Clematis uses tendrils or leaf-like appendages that grow out from the stems and wrap themselves around things. Some vines, including Boston ivy, Virginia creeper and trumpet vine have non-coiling, clinging tendrils with a different mechanism called an adherent pad. Like a super-strength adhesive, their stems bond to rough surfaces or support structures. Other vines, such as English ivy and climbing hydrangea, have aerial rootlets called holdfasts that cement themselves to walls, trees, or other objects.

Most vines climb by twining themselves around a structure. In the wild, they use a tree for climbing, but in your landscape, they could use a post, pillar, downspout or dead tree. The vine will start to twine when it touches an object, producing growth faster on one side of the vine than the other. This causes the stem to curl around and around the object. Just as people are right- or left-handed, twining vines will twist around supports either clockwise (to the right) or counterclockwise (to the left). This growth habit is easy to see when you observe honeysuckle, which grows clockwise, and bittersweet, which grows counterclockwise. It helps to know this so when a vine starts to grow, you won't inadvertently twist it in the wrong direction. Instead, let nature take it course.

Matching the vine to the support is one of the secrets for success. A twining vine will not grow up a brick wall, and you can't expect a clinging vine like ivy to climb a wire. Vines can be trained on arbors, trellises, pergolas, gazebos, fence posts, lattices, and trees. Clematis vines are often at their best when climbing through trees and shrubs. Some vines can be left to grow as ground cover to hold the soil, and they are attractive when cascading over walls and embankments. Some vines will grow on chain-link fences, and many annual vines can easily grow along twine or string. You just have to know the difference.

Even with hardy vines, it's helpful to provide some protection when they're newly planted.

Apply winter mulch in late November or early December. I suggest applying evergreen boughs and coarse compost at the base of the vines to protect the roots and crown from frost heaving. In general, water vines monthly in the absence of rain or snow, as long as the soil remains unfrozen and the temperatures are above freezing.

VINE PLANTING PROCEDURES

- Remove the containerized plants from their pots, gently loosen the roots that are tangled, and spread them out a bit.
- Gently knock off the loose artificial soil mix from the balls without damaging the roots.
- Set the plants in the planting holes at the same depth at which they were growing.
- Using the prepared backfill soil, fill in around the rootball halfway full. Then water to settle the soil in.
- Once the water has drained, add more backfill soil to complete the planting, and gently firm the soil around the plant. Repeat watering.

LAYERING, THE EASY WAY TO START NEW VINES

- In mid- to late spring, select one or two dormant shoots off last year's wood.
- Using a sharp knife, make a cut about $1/2$ inch away from a node, slicing halfway into the underside of the stem toward the node. (A node is the point of attachment where leaves emerge.)
- To stimulate rooting, dust some rooting powder over the wound. Bury the wounded stem in loosened garden soil amended with sphagnum peat moss to a depth of 2 inches. A stiff U-shaped wire or landscape pin can be used to peg the stem into the ground so it won't pop up.
- Secure the growing tip to a cane or pole so it can't grow upward.

• Lightly mulch this layered stem with compost or more sphagnum peat moss to keep the soil uniformly moist.

• Every month or so, check the stem to see if it is forming roots at the wound. Gently tug the stem to see if it is rooting. When it has rooted, it can be severed from the mother plant.

• Transplant it to a new location in late summer or early autumn when the weather cools down.

GROUND COVERS

Ground covers are a broad category of plants that includes about anything that will cover the ground quickly. A major advantage of ground covers over grass is that many are colorful and ornamental. The varied decorative qualities of ground covers provide pleasing contrasts in color and texture. They may be vines, shrubs, herbaceous perennials, roses, or even annuals that reseed themselves.

Like lawn grasses, ground covers are grown primarily for their usefulness to hold the soil and for their inviting foliage. The most desirable ground covers are low-growing, perennial evergreens that require minimal maintenance. Your mission is finding the right ground cover for the right spot. Observe ground covers in private and public gardens. Take notes of their height, color, texture, and overall ornamental value. Then consider how much ground cover you'll need and where it can be obtained. Nothing looks so sulky as plants situated without regard to how much sun or shade they prefer, so choose the appropriate ground cover for your exposure and growing conditions. Plants selected specifically for a site will have the best chance to grow into a healthy, dense, weed-free ground cover.

Ground covers will reduce lawn maintenance on steep slopes, where mowing is an arduous chore. However, don't assume ground covers are without maintenance. They will need attention and grooming to keep them looking good. Ground covers perform other functions, too. Their foliage will disguise the ripening foliage of spring-flowering bulbs. Once established, they grow so densely that they are weed-free, which is good news for the lazy gardener. Evergreen ground covers provide year-round greenery even in the dreariest months of winter.

With a few exceptions, the procedures for planting ground covers are essentially the same as those for installing a lawn. Ground covers are meant to be permanent plantings, so considerations of soil drainage, exposure, irrigation and soil preparation are essential for growing them successfully. Once a ground cover becomes established, it may be difficult and costly to alter the situation.

PLANTING GROUND COVERS ON STEEP SLOPES

Kill all the existing vegetation including lawn with a non-selective herbicide that contains glyphosate, or cover the area with clear plastic and solarize the area to kill all plants. Solarization may take up to six weeks for a total kill, so plan accordingly.

• After the vegetation has been killed, lay down a landscape fabric, making sure to overlap the pieces of fabric to prevent any bare spots. Tack down the fabric with landscape pins or U-shaped stiff wire.

• Place the containerized ground cover plants on top of the fabric is staggered rows, spacing them according to the plant tag. I prefer to stagger the ground covers randomly rather than lining them up like rows of soldiers.

• Cut an "X" through the fabric with a linoleum knife, then dig a planting hole as deep as the container is high. Place the soil in a 5-gallon bucket to use for backfill as needed. Letting the soil fall on the fabric may introduce weed seeds.

• Gently fold the "X" back down after planting the ground cover. Try to avoid leaving any large open spaces that can be invaded by weeds.

• Water each plant thoroughly.

• Finish by spreading a 2- to 3-inch layer of mulch such as shredded cedar mulch, pole peelings, or pea gravel.

ORNAMENTAL GRASSES

Ornamental grasses are prized for the natural beauty and unique textural qualities they add to the landscape. When selected and sited correctly, their gentle rustling leaves and seedheads evoke sounds of the prairie. Plant ornamental grasses in drifts or swathes or as accent plants in a shrub or perennial flower garden, where the fine textures create dramatic contrasts.

When other landscape plants are killed by autumn frosts, ornamental grasses stand tall, displaying shades of tan, russet, brown, gold or red, providing color and form for winter interest. The foliage and flowers are usually more delicate than other plants. Their flowers are small and unobtrusive, creating a cloud-like effect in the landscape

Generally, they are well adapted to most garden situations, able to withstand a variety of soil conditions and weather, and have relatively few pests. They require minimal maintenance. If a clump becomes too large for an area, it can be lifted and divided every three to four years.

NOTES

JANUARY
VINES, GROUND COVERS, & ORNAMENTAL GRASSES

 PLANNING

Gardening catalogs are arriving almost daily in the mail. Think about problem areas in your garden, and browse your catalogs for unique and interesting vines, ground covers, and ornamental grasses to fill in these areas with background effects and accents. Utilitarian vines, ground covers, and grasses will serve many purposes, so consider which ornamental characteristics you desire. The foliage of evergreens provides year-round color. Deciduous plants offer attractive leaves and handsome fall colors to enhance the architectural features of a trellis or latticework. Some vines have fragrant flowers that attract hummingbirds, while others have colorful and edible fruit or unique seedpods.

Observe the winter landscape from the windows in various rooms to see what kinds of plants might add beauty. Maybe the vertical lift of a tall ornamental grass would accent an area or border. Perhaps woody vines wrapped around arbors or posts might add compelling texture.

Is there a need to replace an expansive lawn with an attractive and drought-enduring ground cover? Imagine the sound and movement of the wind stirring ornamental grass stems and seedheads. Where horizontal space is limited, vines can offer architectural interest, colorful foliage, flowers, berries for wildlife, seedpods, and shelter for birds. As you compile your list of favorites, remember to match the vine, ground cover, or ornamental grass to the site where it will be planted.

 **PLANTING**

This is not the time of year to plant vines, ground covers, and ornamental grasses. Be patient.

 CARE

Most vines, ground covers, and ornamental grasses are self-reliant. They can tolerate the cold of winter and the heat of summer. Check the list of vines, ground covers, and ornamental grasses in *My Rocky Mountain Gardener's Guide* for a selection that is hardy in your growing zone.

If you did not mulch the soil in late fall, it is helpful to do so where vines, ground covers, and ornamental grasses were planted last year. Doing this after the ground freezes will help to buffer extreme temperature fluctuations. This prevents the new plants from heaving to the soil surface as a result of alternate freezing and thawing. Do not pile the mulch against the vine and ornamental grass stems as it can encourage rodents and may result in rot if it stays too wet. Make sure vines are secured to their supports so they won't be damaged in high winds.

 **WATERING**

In dry winters, recently planted vines, ground covers, and ornamental grasses need supplemental watering. Choose a day when temperatures are above freezing and the ground is not frozen. Water for 10 to 15 minutes using a frog-eye sprinkler. Apply water early in the day so it can percolate to the roots. Don't forget to disconnect the hose, drain it, and put it back in storage for future use.

Mulched plants will not need to be watered as often. Evergreens continue to transpire through their foliage, and they can lose moisture even though it is winter.

FERTILIZING

Do not fertilize at this time of year.

GROOMING

Don't prune unless there are broken or damaged branches on vines. Cut back any stems or branches that are whipping in the wind, or provide them with support before they break. Ornamental grasses will continue to look attractive in the winter landscape, especially when they catch snow or ice crystals form on the stems and seedheads. Delay cutting them back until early spring, just as the new shoots begin to sprout.

PROBLEMS

Deer and elk can be damaging to vines, ground covers, and ornamental grasses when their natural food sources are scarce. They will nibble on the tender shoots, leaves, berries, and stems to sustain themselves during the cold, harsh winter. Spray vulnerable plants with the homemade critter repellent (see page 284) or a commercial product to keep them away. Repellents will need to be reapplied as they break down over a period of time.

Lay chicken or rabbit wire over beds of ground covers, or use it to fashion a temporary barrier around vines, and ornamental grasses to keep critters at bay.

In some situations, deer will avoid plants that have aromatic or fuzzy leaves. Two of my favorites are **lamb's ears** and **artemisia**. They grow as handsome ground covers and are not generally bothered by wildlife.

Smaller rodents can pose a problem by nibbling at the roots and crowns of plants. Avoid placing mulches directly at the base of vines, ground covers, and ornamental grasses as this creates a haven for meadow mice, voles, chipmunks, and pocket gophers. To forestall the problem, delay mulching until the ground is frozen, forcing rodents to nest elsewhere. You can install wire wraps crafted from hardware cloth around the stems of vines or spray them with a repellent.

NOTES

FEBRUARY
VINES, GROUND COVERS, & ORNAMENTAL GRASSES

 PLANNING

Winter is a good time to read *My Rocky Mountain Gardener's Guide* and make notes about the various vines, ground covers, and ornamental grasses that are suited to our region. Evaluate your landscape, and determine which areas need more winter plant interest. Ornamental grasses work especially well for vertical lift and texture, and vines will add cover and texture to arbors and fencing. Some are very attractive spilling over large stones or retaining walls. Be creative, and experiment. Sketch some of your ideas. Visit public gardens in winter to see what they use to make the landscape attractive.

If deer are a problem in your area, use this time to plan appropriate fencing.

 PLANTING

It's still too early to plant outdoors, but if you have space and time, start annual vines from seeds indoors. This should be done towards the end of the month so the seedlings won't become too leggy before planting time. Read the seed packet to determine how many days to plant ahead of the last killing frost in the spring.

If you start seeds indoors, use sterile containers or seed flats. Plant them in a clean, soilless growing mixture. A plant stand would be handy if you are growing many different kinds of plants indoors. Use fluorescent lights to make the seedlings grow strong and vigorously.

Steps for starting seeds indoors:

• Fill the containers or seed flats with moistened soilless potting mixture.

• Place one or two seeds in each pot and sow a row in the flat. Cover the seeds with the mixture. Plant at the depth recommended on the seed packets.

• Water each pot or the seed flat. Individual pots or containers should be placed in a tray for easier transport to the windowsill or plant stand.

• Cover the containers with a sheet of plastic or plexiglass to prevent the growing medium from drying out.

• Give the pots or seed flat warmth from a heat mat or heating cables to help germination.

• Remove the plastic or cover when the seeds have sprouted. Move them to bright light or artificial light that can be adjusted so they are consistently about 2 inches above the seedlings as they grow.

• Snip off the second or less vigorous seedling in pots so there is just one per container. Thin plants in the seed flat so they are 2 to 3 inches apart. This will make them easier to transplant later.

• Water the growing medium when it is getting dry to the touch. Do not keep it too wet, as this will cause damping-off disease or seedling rot.

Violets, violas, Johnny Jump-Ups, and **pansies** will be available by month's end and can be planted as a winter ground cover as the weather permits. Plant some in outdoor containers for a splash of winter color.

 CARE

Some hardy bulbs may soon be emerging from the soil and poking through ground covers like **vinca, veronica,** and **thyme**. They add welcome color to the landscape, and later the ground cover will mask their ripening foliage. Remove any accumulation of leaves, as these can smother ground cover growth.

WATERING

During periods of warm, windy, dry weather, it may be necessary to water vines, ground covers, and hardy ornamental grasses. Take advantage of the winter thaw, and water when the ground is not frozen. Water early in the day to allow the water to percolate into the root zone. Winter watering may need to be done every four to five weeks, depending upon local weather conditions.

FERTILIZING

Delay fertilizing until new growth emerges later in the spring.

GROOMING

Cut back ornamental grasses as their stems and seedheads collapse to the ground. Choose a warm, sunny day and sheer the clump to allow the new shoots room to grow. Cutting now will prevent you from cutting the tips of new shoots later when they start to emerge in spring. Chop or shred the clippings, and add them to the compost pile.

GARDENING WITH AN ALTITUDE TIPS
The When and How of Pruning Clematis

Pruning methods vary. Spring-blooming **clematis** that bloom on previous year's growth should be pruned after flowering (no later than mid-July) to allow for the production and ripening of the new growth. Remove dead wood or winterkilled tips. Deadheading can often stimulate new blooms later in summer and early fall. Summer-flowering and early fall-blooming varieties do best if cut back in early spring. Prune stems back to a pair of plump buds, and thin out weak and dead wood. Late-flowering cultivars and species produce flowers on the current season's growth, so prune in early spring, removing the previous season's stems down to a pair of plump, healthy buds, 6 to 12 inches above the ground.

PROBLEMS

Be on the watch for rabbits and deer. They will show up to nibble tender stems and new buds. Prevent damage by wrapping the exposed stems with chicken or rabbit wire. You can also spray vulnerable plants with a repellent as directed on the product label. Try the homemade critter repellent on page 284.

If mice or voles are a problem, you may have to set traps to eliminate them. Bait them with peanut butter. Also, keep mulches away from the base of the stems and crowns of plants to discourage critters from nesting there.

NOTES

_____
_____
_____
_____
_____
_____
_____
_____
_____
_____
_____
_____
_____
_____
_____
_____

MARCH
VINES, GROUND COVERS, & ORNAMENTAL GRASSES

 PLANNING

Can you feel and smell the arrival of spring? As the days get longer, our garden urges stir. Consider eliminating large expanses of lawn. Are there slopes that are difficult to mow and just "a pain in the grass?" Consider one of my favorite ever-green ground covers, *Juniperus horizontalis* or **Blue Rug juniper,** as an alternative to tur-fgrass. Once established, it is a very hardy and reliable ground cover for difficult slopes, with year-round visual appeal.

For shady areas, consider *Vinca minor* or **periwinkle**, one of the most adaptable covers for areas under tree canopy. See *My Rocky Mountain Gardener's Guide* for more plant selections. Plan where you'll plant ornamen-tal grasses as accents in your yard. They are virtually foolproof, and once established, can be very drought-tolerant. Leave them standing in the autumn and winter for added texture in the winter landscape.

 PLANTING

As the **pansies** and **violas** arrive at local garden stores, plant them in flower beds to pro-vide early spring color. They love the cool weather and will grow and bloom with gusto.

Bare-root vines and ground covers that arrive via mail-order can be planted anytime the soil can be worked. I like bare-root plants since they are economical and acclimate so well to our native soil conditions.

Divide ornamental grasses as soon as the soil can be worked. Lift the clump with a heavy-duty spading fork. Begin by cutting back last year's old stems if you haven't already done so. Here are the steps to divide and con-quer hardy ornamental grasses:

• Dig down around the out-side of the clump until you begin to feel the clump dislodge from the ground.

• Lift the entire rootball out of the ground to expose the mas-sive amount of roots and crown.

• Cut the clump into manage-able rooted divisions by slicing down with a sharp spade or machete.

• Replant each division as needed to other parts of the land-scape, or share extra clumps with friends and neighbors.

An alternative way to divide grasses is to split them right where they grow:

• Use a sharp spade to slice down through the grass clump while it is still planted.

• Pry apart chunks or wedges of the grass as if cutting a piece of pie.

Remove the divisions by dig-ging under and around them, leaving the main rootball in place.

• Fill in the empty holes with garden soil.

• Replant the grass divisions to new areas or give them away.

 CARE

Some perennial vines awaken from winter dormancy this month. Check their supports to be sure they are secure when growth really gets going. There's an old adage about perennial vines: "The first year they sleep, the sec-ond year they creep, and the third year they leap!"

Check newly planted ground covers, and mulch around them to suppress weed growth early in the season. It can be a real challenge to control weeds in ground covers once the weeds get a stronghold. Spread a 2- to 3-inch layer of pine needles, shredded cedar chips, pole peel-ings, or chopped leaves over the soil between the ground cover plants.

Cultivate the soil around vines, ground covers, and ornamental grasses if it has become compacted over the winter season. This will loosen the soil so it can more easily absorb water and will also eliminate any new weed seedlings.

WATERING

Hopefully we have a wet spring, but this may not always be the case. If we experience a dry, windy spell of weather, water newly planted ground covers, vines, and ornamental grasses. The soil moisture is essential to sustain the root system. **Pansies** and **violas** will need regular watering during their peak blooming season. Mulched plantings will need less frequent watering and will survive the drier conditions more favorably.

FERTILIZING

Once ground covers are established, they require minimal fertilizing, unlike turfgrasses. You can scatter a slow-release granular fertilizer around the plants and water in well. This will provide nutrients for the entire growing season. Organic matter worked into the soil will also encourage microbial activity and help break down sloughing foliage and other plant debris that eventually turns into nutrients.

GROOMING

Later in the month, you can begin to prune back **Jackmanii clematis** and other clematis that bloom on new wood. Spring-blooming varieties that bloom on the previous year's wood should be pruned after flowering, no later than mid-July.

Finish cutting off the old tops of ornamental grasses, and recycle the clippings to the compost pile. Be careful not to damage any new green shoots if they are emerging.

Gently rake over ground covers to remove any accumulation of leaves and other debris that may have blown in. Prune out dead tips and broken branches, if needed.

PROBLEMS

Control weeds in ground cover plantings while they are still accessible. Once ground covers grow dense enough, weeds will not be as aggressive. Handpull or dig young weeds when the soil is moist. You can also apply pre-emergent weed control products over the soil around ground covers to stop the germination of annual weed seeds. Read and follow label directions when using herbicides.

Grasses in ground covers are the most difficult to control. The "cowboy way" of hand-digging or pulling works when the grasses are young and not well anchored in. However, established grass clumps are harder to eliminate. A product that contains Fusilade can be used on some ground covers, but not all. It is used as a spot treatment. Read label instructions and precautions.

NOTES

_____
_____
_____
_____
_____
_____
_____
_____
_____
_____
_____
_____
_____
_____
_____

APRIL
VINES, GROUND COVERS, & ORNAMENTAL GRASSES

PLANNING

If you plan to renovate your landscape with drought-enduring ground covers and ornamental grasses, now is the time to get started. Cut out sections of sod, or design areas that are suited for these plantings. This can make landscape maintenance easier while adding special accents and providing a year-round carpet.

One of my favorite ground covers for shade to semi-shady areas is *Ajuga* **'Burgundy Glow'**. The eye-catching variegated foliage is especially handsome near rocks, retaining walls, and pathways. **Pansies** and **violas** are also dependable as ground covers.

If you have arbors, pergolas, or latticework in your landscape, get some vines growing on them. They add interest throughout the year. You can even hang a songbird nesting house from an arbor, and the vine will provide extra protection as it leafs out. Use vines to break the monotony of a wood fence or to screen a chain-link fence.

Consider ornamental grasses to provide accent in the center of a flower bed, or use them as a living screen to block the sounds from the street. Use your imagination to create something original and enticing.

PLANTING

April is the prime time to plant ornamental grasses, vines, and ground covers. These plants need sufficient time to get established before the heat of summer. Bare-root plants are more economical, but many can be purchased already growing in containers. Plant the bare-root plants as early as possible before they fully leaf out to reduce transplant stress.

Here are some planting tips:

• To prepare the planting area, dig out the weeds and turn the soil with a shovel or rototiller. Add a generous supply of compost to improve drainage and hold nutrients.

• Rake the area smooth, and stake the spots where the grasses are to be planted. With ground cover plants, make sure they are spaced equidistant from each other to allow them to spread to their mature width as indicated on the plant tag.

• Dig a hole for each plant as deep as its pot is tall. If you are planting on a slope, dig the hole straight up and down so the plant will be sitting vertically.

• Remove the plant from the nursery pot. Tease any tangled roots and set the plant in the hole. Fill in with the backfill soil you set aside.

• Water the plants in thoroughly for good root-to-soil contact.

• Mulch new plantings to maintain uniform moisture and suppress weed growth.

CARE

Well-established ground covers need very little maintenance other than cleaning out debris in the spring. If winter winds have desiccated the tips of the plants, a light pruning will give them a fresher look.

WATERING

April showers are usually adequate for most ground covers, vines, and ornamental grasses to survive, but if has been dry, it's time to bring out the hose and water.

Use a frog-eye or similar sprinkler set at the drip line of the plants, and water for 10 to 15 minutes. This will allow uniform coverage of the root zone and sustain the plants during dry spells. If you have installed a drip irrigation system, use it to give the plants a deep soaking.

Remember, mulched plantings will need less frequent watering than those that are growing on bare ground. As ground cover plants begin to mature they naturally shade the soil and this attribute makes them more drought tolerant.

FERTILIZING

Newly planted areas that have not yet filled in can be top-dressed with compost to improve the soil. Lightly lift the ground cover plants, and scatter the compost over the soil around the plants. At the same time, you can add slow-release granular fertilizer around the plants. Water thoroughly to settle in the organic matter and fertilizer. This feeding will last for the growing season.

As established plants begin to show signs of active growth, you can incorporate slow-release granular fertilizer over the root zone. Lightly scratch it in with a cultivator, and then water the fertilizer in thoroughly. One application in spring is all that is needed. It will provide consistent, uniform nutrition over several weeks to months. Check label of the fertilizer package to determine how often it needs to be applied.

GROOMING

Buds will begin to expand and leaves emerge on **clematis, honeysuckle, Virginia creeper, trumpet vine,** and others as the temperatures warm up. You can tell how healthy a vine is by its annual growth. To stimulate more vigorous growth and flowering buds, cut back the vines by 30 to 50 percent. This process will rejuvenate the vine and make it grow more prolifically. Thin out dead and damaged stems and branches that may have suffered "winterkill." If you have a hardy **wisteria**, cut back the excess growth along the main stem; prune back to the already formed flower buds on the spurs of last year's wood.

PROBLEMS

As landscapes mature, shade can pose a problem for some vines, especially if they are not blooming as well as they did in past seasons. You may need to prune deciduous shade trees to increase available light to the vine or ground cover. Thinning out lower branches and raising the skirt on the tree can be helpful in some cases.

If ground covers develop brown or yellow dead patches, especially at the edges and corners, this could be a sign of salt damage or that "Rover went all over." It is not unusual for dogs and even cats to visit ground covers to relieve themselves. Their urine will burn the foliage. Clip off dead and brittle portions, and water the area well to leach out the soluble salts. To repel stray dogs and cats, spray with a repellent or exclude them from the area by constructing a fence.

Keep weeds from invading ground covers and areas around vines and ornamental grasses. Pull weeds while they are young after a rainstorm or watering. Perennial weeds that are tough to pull can be **spot-treated** with a herbicide that contains glyphosate. Read and follow label directions and precautions.

NOTES

_____
_____
_____
_____
_____
_____
_____
_____
_____
_____

MAY
VINES, GROUND COVERS, & ORNAMENTAL GRASSES

 PLANNING

Garden stores are well stocked with potted plants by now, and you can find a great variety of ground covers, vines, and ornamental grasses. Grasses and vines are available in 1-, 2-, 3-, and 5-gallon sizes, so let your budget guide you on what you want to spend. I recommend the smaller plants since they are fast to start up and will often outgrow the bigger rootbound specimens. Ground covers are available in packs or in smaller 2- to 4-inch pots. Walk around your landscape and make a shopping list.

 PLANTING

Since most potted plants are grown in an artificial soilless mixture, the roots are "pampered" to grow faster, so they become rootbound faster. If the plants are set into our unmodified native soils, the roots remain within the artificial soil and are slow to grow outward from the original rootball. I refer to this as the "bathtub effect." To minimize this problem, modify your native soil by adding compost, sphagnum peat moss, or a combination of both (a 50/50 mix is what I prefer). Add one-third by volume to the backfill soil.

 CARE

Newly set-out plants should be mulched to reduce weeds and water loss. Use a 2- to 3-inch layer of compost, shredded bark or cedar, pine needles, or chopped leaves over the soil around the ground cover, vine, or ornamental grass.

Check trellises and other vine supports to make sure they are securely fastened to a wall or post. This will prevent them from falling over when the vines start growing vigorously. Ensure adequate air circulation behind trellises and other supports so vines will not bake in the heat of the sun. Air circulation will also reduce the incidence of foliar diseases later in the season. Construct trellises, arbors, and other supports so they sit about 12 to 18 inches away from a solid wall.

Check some of the more established ground cover plants that are becoming crowded. It may be time to lift them up and do some plant division. This will renew the bed and stimulate healthier, more vigorous growth. **Daylilies, hostas,** and **irises** will benefit from lifting and dividing every three years.

 WATERING

Keep newly planted ground covers, vines, and ornamental grasses watered deeply if the weather is dry and windy. Dig down and check soil moisture with a garden trowel. If it is beginning to dry out 3 to 4 inches down, it is time to water the plants thoroughly. The first growing season is critical so the plants can become well established and drought-tolerant.

 FERTILIZING

My preference is to add a granular slow-release fertilizer at the time of planting so it can be done once in the spring, then you can "forget about it" for the rest of the year. If however, you prefer to use a soluble plant fertilizer, use it sparingly according to the manufacturer's recommendations. It is better to fertilize less often than is recommended on the label. Once a month is adequate. Ground covers, vines, and ornamental grasses are not big feeders.

GROOMING

As perennial vines are growing vigorously, prune off straggly stems and shoots to encourage more fullness. Help direct the stems to the supports as needed.

Prune out dead and damaged twigs injured by winter desiccation or windstorms.

Trailing vines such as **vinca** and **ivies** should be growing vigorously, too. Cut back any unruly stems that creep out into the lawn or perennial garden. This will direct their growth where it should be. **Boston ivy, English ivy, Virginia creeper,** and **trumpet vine** can encroach on gutters, windows, and chimneys. Don't be afraid to cut them back when they grow so aggressively.

PROBLEMS

As the weather warms, it is time for slugs to make their sneak attacks on vines and ground covers. These creatures are active at night. You can make the homemade slug trap on page 285 to capture hoards of them. Since they overwinter in moist, organic debris and under mulch, lightly cultivate the mulch to expose them to sunlight and heat. Commercially prepared slug

baits are also available, but must be used with caution as they are a threat to wildlife, pets and small children. Read and follow label directions and observe safety precautions.

Other insects may find vines and ground covers attractive, too. Aphids will feed on the new tender growth and flower buds. Until there are beneficial insects to prey on the aphids, wash them off with a forceful stream of water. Insecticidal soap sprays or the homemade soap spray can also control aphids. Read and follow label instructions when using any pesticide.

Weevils may feed on the foliage of vines and ground covers. They chew pieces of the leaves and buds. If you can spot them early in the morning or late evening, handpick them off the plant and drop them in a can of soapy water and discard later.

A disease known as *Phomopsis* twig blight can often attack ground cover junipers and other upright types. The fungus affects the branch tips in the spring, eventually killing them back. Prune out the dead, grayish-brown branches to eliminate the fungus spores before they spread to other branches. Keep the plants healthy by proper watering and pruning.

Keep weeds from invading new plantings of ground covers, vines, and ornamental grasses. A light cultivation when the weed seedlings are young is a good cultural control. Once weeds become more fully established, they are harder to pull or control.

NOTES

JUNE
VINES, GROUND COVERS, & ORNAMENTAL GRASSES

PLANNING

Summer begins on June 21, and some planning for the landscape will be helpful. Have you been making entries in your garden journal or notebook? We all tend to forget which plants we planted, if they were good or bad, and if any were plagued by pests or diseases. Jot down these observations so you can refer to them as needed.

Vines will need sturdy support to hold them in place for a good display. Take time to check the bolts, nails, eyehooks, or other types of fasteners holding a wire matrix or wooden trellis out from a wall. Make sure they are secure. Check the footings of arbors and pergolas that must bear the weight of heavy **grape vines, trumpet vine, wisteria,** or **climbing hydrangea.** It's a good idea to have twist ties or soft twine handy for securing the stems of vines that tend to wander. Proper training early in their growth will save time and prevent damage to the stems.

Think about ordering hardy bulbs for interplanting with existing ground covers. Pre-season discounts from mail-order catalogs should entice you to act soon. As the spring segues into summer, take photographs of

your landscape, and record when plants are in bloom.

PLANTING

You still have plenty of time to plant containerized vines, ornamental grasses, and ground covers. These are available at garden retailers and nurseries throughout the region. Get them into the ground as soon as possible, before the heat really turns on.

Ornamental grasses do best if planted early in the season so they have time to establish before they begin to set flower stalks. This will allow them to develop a strong root system and survive the winter.

If you have tender tropical vines indoors and like to bring them outside to a covered patio or deck, now is the time. Acclimate them gradually to the outside conditions and sunshine. **Bougainvillea, California ivy, mandevilla,** and **angel's trumpet** are a few that can be summered outdoors in filtered sunlight.

This would be a good time to repot indoor vines that are outgrowing their containers. Use a soilless potting mixture and choose a pot that is an inch or two larger in diameter. Carefully

remove the vine and support when doing the transplanting, and replace the stake or support into the new container.

CARE

Keep newly transplanted ground cover beds, vines, and ornamental grasses mulched with compost, pole peelings, or shredded cedar. This will help conserve moisture and suppress weed growth. Do not pile mulch on the stems of the plants or they can stay too wet and succumb to rot, insect pests, or rodent damage.

Some ground cover plants will do best if they are periodically pinched back to maintain colorful foliage. Routinely pinch off the flowers from **lamb's ears, artemisias,** and the shade-loving **coleus.**

Pansies are starting to lose their vigor as the heat arrives. They often become yellow and leggy. You can replace them with other annuals such as **nasturtiums, portulaca, salvias, marigolds,** and **creeping zinnias.**

WATERING

When rainfall is scare, newly planted vines, ground covers,

and ornamental grasses will need supplemental irrigation. Mulched plants will need to be watered less frequently, but check underneath the mulch by digging down 4 inches or so with a garden trowel. When the soil is getting dry to the touch, it is time to do some deep watering. Most of these plants prefer deep, infrequent watering rather than frequent light sprinklings.

Vines in containers or pots will need checking often to make sure they are not stressed to the point of wilting. Most potting mixtures dry out quickly in the hot sun and wind. Use a water-saving polymer in the soil mix to help retain moisture longer.

FERTILIZING

The application of a slow-release granular fertilizer earlier in the year should suffice for most ground covers, vines, and ornamental grasses. If you did not apply a slow-release product, apply a water-soluble plant fertilizer using the manufacturer's recommendations. Remember, it is better to underfertilize than it is to feed plants too often. Blooming vines will not appreciate high doses of high-nitrogen plant fertilizers and often fail to bloom well.

GROOMING

Once the **wisteria** has finished blooming, it is known to produce leafy stems with gusto. Prune any excess growth back before the buds for next year start to develop. This should be done by mid-July to ensure you don't inadvertently cut off the next year's buds. Now is the time to control the spread, size, and direction of the vine.

Pinch back the faded flowers from **clematis** and **honeysuckle** unless you want them to produce seedpods. Prune spring-flowering **clematis** as soon as it finishes blooming. Cut back woody ground cover plants anytime you need to tidy them up. This will allow them to produce fresh, new growth.

PROBLEMS

Aphids may be on the rampage now, so take action to wash them off infested plant parts. Once they fall to the ground in a shower of water "they can't get up." Pick off heavily infested tips or leaves and dispose in the trash. If you prefer, use a homemade soap spray (see page 283) or appropriate insecticide. Read and follow label directions.

Keep trapping the slugs that make their sneak attacks at night. Slugs and their kin are a nuisance, particularly in the shady areas of the yard.

Black vine weevil can be a serious pest to ground covers such as **euonymus** and **vinca.** Applying a soil insecticide may help eliminate these pests. Read and follow label directions and observe precautions when using any pesticide on ground covers and vines. Trapping these pests can be effective, too.

NOTES

_____
_____
_____
_____
_____
_____
_____
_____
_____
_____
_____
_____
_____
_____
_____
_____
_____
_____

JULY
VINES, GROUND COVERS, & ORNAMENTAL GRASSES

 PLANNING

July is a time of vacations, and you will appreciate the beauty and relatively low maintenance offered by ground covers, vines, and ornamental grasses. There will be less lawn to mow and water. Ornamental grasses are starting to come into their own glory, and vines are blooming.

Plan to have someone take care of your new plantings while you're away. This not only ensures the survival of your plants, but also keeps your property from looking vacated.

It's a time to enjoy the beauty of flowering vines that attract hummingbirds. You can spot them around **honeysuckles, trumpet vine,** and **morning glory.** These tiny flying gems love the tubular flowers that provide a source of sweet nectar. Get the camera out and take photos. Record what's blooming and when, identify plants of particular interest, and note which ones are not performing well.

 PLANTING

You can still plant container-grown plants from the nursery, but special precautions are urged. Choose a cloudy, cool day to plant, as summer heat discourages root growth and

wilts topgrowth. Shade new plants with cardboard boxes or burlap for a few days after transplanting to help them acclimate to the hot weather. Spread an organic mulch around the root zone to keep the soil cool and reduce evaporation.

Be prepared to water as the soil dries out and mist the foliage on hot days to cool the plants and reduce scorch and wilting. A fine mist nozzle that attaches to the garden hose is a handy tool for this purpose.

 CARE

Many perennial ground covers planted in May will be growing steadily and knitting together. Keep them well watered during the heat of summer, and if you didn't mulch them earlier after planting, do so now. Gently spread mulch over the bare spots of the soil to conserve water and maintain uniform moisture. As the plants mature, they will shade the ground themselves.

Clean up fallen leaves and other debris that have blown into your yard. This will keep the garden looking tidy and reduce the onset of plant diseases that may be harboring on plant debris. Vines should be checked periodically to make sure they are secure to their supports. You may

need to tie rapidly extending stems to supports before they try to embrace neighboring plants. In some cases, pinch off excess growth to keep the vine in bounds.

 WATERING

During the summer as temperatures rise and humidity is low, the stress on plants increases. Vines, ground covers, and ornamental grasses will appreciate a deep watering every week or two. Mulched plantings can go longer between waterings as the mulch cools the soil and reduces evaporation.

Look for signs of wilt. Even though this is normal during the day, the wilting should subside by evening. If it does not, the plant is in need of a good watering. Use a frog-eye sprinkler to water at a low angle and cover a larger area. Water each section 10 to 15 minutes, then move the sprinkler to cover the planting area. Water in early morning, or early evening if necessary, so the foliage will be dry by nightfall.

 FERTILIZING

Fertilizer is not needed now, with the exception of potted vines that are flowering on the patio or deck. Use a water-soluble plant fertilizer diluted to half strength, and apply to a moistened potting mixture every other week.

GROOMING

Once the large-flowered **clematis** have finished blooming, you may cut them back 30 to 50 percent to stimulate repeat bloom later in the summer. Even a light clipping will tidy up the vines and leave some handsome seedpods for summer and fall interest.

Cut back the branches of **climbing hydrangea** that extend more than a foot from the main stem. Otherwise, this vine can become top-heavy and pull itself away from its support. Snip the overgrown branching stems individually back to a point where some leaves are emerging.

Annual ground covers may begin to get leggy and will benefit from a light pruning to stimulate more side branching. They will resume blooming in a few short weeks. This works well on **trailing petunias, impatiens, creeping zinnia,** and others.

PROBLEMS

Aphids seem to thrive in hot weather and feed on the new tender growth of vines and ground covers. Wash them off with a stream of water, or use a homemade soap spray (see page 283). Rinse after applying the soap spray; during the heat of summer soap sprays may burn the foliage. If infestations are severe, you may have to resort to using an insecticide. Read and follow label directions for dilution rates and timing of applications.

Spider mites can wreak havoc in the garden during hot, dry spells. They target stressed plants including **ivies, creeping junipers,** and **Virginia creeper.** Mites cause a pale yellow or tan stippling on the leaves; sometimes you can detect a fine webbing among the stems and branches. Disrupt the mites' life cycle by hosing down the upper and lower surfaces of the foliage. Insecticidal soap sprays and homemade soap sprays are effective for heavy infestations. Read and follow label directions.

Keep weeds controlled before they go to seed. Handpull or dig weeds when the soil is moistened after a rain or irrigation. Some of the more difficult perennials weeds such as Canada thistle and bindweed may need to be spot-treated with a nonselective herbicide. **Follow label instructions, and observe precautions when using herbicides.**

NOTES

AUGUST
VINES, GROUND COVERS, & ORNAMENTAL GRASSES

 PLANNING

August is a bouquet of infinite variety of color and form in the landscape. Ground covers, vines, and ornamental grasses are perhaps at their finest now. These plants are reliable and once established, are quite drought-tolerant. Enjoy their beauty.

Take photographs of how these plants accentuate specific areas with their colorful foliage, flowers, fruits and berries, and vertical lift. Continue ordering hardy bulbs to plant among ground covers and around ornamental grasses.

The heat of summer can take its toll on plants. Now would be a good time to evaluate changes that may be necessary to fill in gaps. Consider soil conditions, wind, exposure to sunlight or shade, and other variables that affect plant growth and performance. Watch the ornamental grasses as they unfold their seedheads. It's a great time to pick a bouquet of feathery grass tassels to dry for winter-long indoor arrangements.

 PLANTING

As the weather begins to cool down in mid- to late August, you can start to plant container-grown plants again. Prepare the planting site by adding some compost or sphagnum peat moss. Incorporate at least one-third by volume into your native soil. This will help improve drainage, hold nutrients, and enhance root development.

Dig the planting holes two to three times wider than the container, and only as deep as the pot is high. Set the plants in the planting hole at the same depth as they were originally growing. If the roots have become pot-bound, tease them apart so they will intermingle with your native soil and start growing.

 CARE

Refresh the mulch under vines if it has dwindled. Fluff up the mulch with a rake where it has become compacted. This will allow air, water, and nutrients to reach the root zone.

Secure vine stems and branches that are growing out of bounds, being careful not to damage the plants. Training wayward vines now will save you time later. **Boston** and **English ivy** are notorious for growing along the ground when there is no support. Train them as you desire.

If your ornamental grasses are beginning to topple over, they may be getting too much nitrogen or water, or not enough sun. Give them support, such as a tomato cage, to keep standing tall, and plan to treat them differently next year. Relocate them to a sunnier location if light is the problem.

 WATERING

Water plants as needed to prevent wilting. Early August can be hot and dry, so water deeply, but not frequently. Take advantage of mulching to help conserve water, keep the soil from baking, and suppress weed growth.

Ground cover plants can be watered efficiently with a drip irrigation system. It's best to install the system before newly transplanted ground covers intertwine, making it more difficult to lay down the irrigation tubes.

If you are growing hardy **ferns** as ground cover in shady exposures, the summer heat can be harsh on them. They prefer cool, moist conditions and will often show signs of scorch during heat and prolonged drought. Water them weekly to maintain more uniform moisture, and add organic matter to bare areas to enrich the soil and help retain moisture.

FERTILIZING

There is no need to fertilize vines, ground covers, and ornamental grasses this month. If you incorporated a slow-release granular fertilizer at planting time, it is likely that it is still providing some nutrition to the plants.

GROOMING

Continue to cut back the faster-growing vines to direct their growth and control their spread. Vines are resilient and can recover from several light prunings throughout the year. Keep them from pulling down gutters and covering the windows. Prune out dead, damaged, or overly long twigs that are rambling aimlessly.

Annual ground covers such as **impatiens** and **creeping zin-**

nias continue to bloom until the first hard frost. You can stimulate more flower buds and new branching if you deadhead or pinch off the old flowers. After cutting them back, fertilize these annuals with a water-soluble plant fertilizer sprayed on the foliage.

PROBLEMS

Wilting is not always an indication that plants are thirsty. If the foliage recovers when evening arrives, the problem is just plain heat. Water plants only if wilted foliage does not recover in the cool of evening. If watering does not do the trick, it may be a sign of a virus or wilt disease. In this situation, pull the infected plant and discard it in the trash. Do not compost diseased plant materials.

Foliar diseases, including leaf spot and powdery mildew, may show up this month. You can prevent many of these fungal diseases by providing good air circulation around vines and ground covers. This is where pruning is necessary to thin out crowded and crossing branches. For powdery mildew, try using the homemade mildew control to prevent a severe outbreak of this disease. See page 285 for

the recipe.

Insect invasions may still be evident on ground covers and vines. Be on the watch for mites, aphids, and caterpillars. These pests can be controlled by hosing them down with a forceful spray of water.

NOTES

_____
_____
_____
_____
_____
_____
_____
_____
_____
_____
_____
_____
_____
_____
_____
_____
_____
_____
_____
_____
_____
_____

September
VINES, GROUND COVERS, & ORNAMENTAL GRASSES

 PLANNING

Labor Day signals the end of summer, though it is not officially over for a few more weeks. "Jack Frost" is lurking behind the corner waiting to finish off the annuals and give the signal for autumn to arrive. Plan to have some plant protectors handy (cardboard boxes, 5-gallon plastic buckets, frost blankets, and the like) if you desire to extend the growing season a bit longer.

The hardy ornamental grasses are in their glory now, putting on a show with changing colors in foliage, feathery seed plumes, and the soothing sounds of wispy stems in the wind. Fly-fishing isn't so bad this time of year either!

Take photographs of plants in your landscape to capture the subtle changes. Make notes in your journal of vines, ground covers, and ornamental grasses that did especially well, and note those that may need rejuvenating. Maybe you could change an area from lawn to ground cover if the light conditions are making it difficult for turf to grow. Note this now, so you can sketch plans and prepare to do the project next spring.

Cooler weather makes it an ideal time to catch up on landscape projects that were left undone. Trellises may need repair or painting. Reinforce trellises and fences if the vines are pulling them down or sideways. In larger masses of ground covers, steppingstones for a walkway will make it easier to maintain the plants and lead you through the garden. Add more compost to bare spots to improve soil structure and drainage.

American bittersweet and **euonymus** should be loaded with colorful fruit. Plan to harvest some of the branches for indoor fall arrangements. If they are not yet fully dry, hang them upside down in a cool, dry place for a few weeks. Once thoroughly dry, they will last quite a long time as unique accents.

 PLANTING

This is the time to plant spring-flowering bulbs. They make wonderful ground cover by themselves or can be underplanted with perennial ground covers. Once the bulbs have finished blooming, the ground covers help mask the ripening bulb foliage. Use a bulb planter to set bulbs within ground covers. Plant the bulbs at the appropriate depth and water in well. **Minia-ture daffodils, crocus, snowdrops, wood hyacinths,** *Iris reticulata,* **grape hyacinths** and others are good to plant among established ground covers. Study the bulb catalogs and experiment with different kinds.

You can still plant container-grown ground covers and vines while the soil remains unfrozen. Ornamental grasses, however, are best planted in the spring and early summer.

Prepare the planting sites with a generous supply of compost or a mix of compost and sphagnum peat moss. I like to use a 50/50 blend at the rate of one-third by volume to my native soil.

 CARE

Bring in the tender vines that were summering out on the patio or deck as night temperatures get too cold. Check these plants for insects and spider mites that would have a field day if they piggyback inside. If you discover any pests, wash them off with a forceful spray of water, or use the homemade soap spray (see page 283).

WATERING

If we are experiencing prolonged periods of dry, windy conditions, water new plants at least every two weeks. This will protect your investment and insure root survival. Established plantings can get along with a deep watering once a month. Mulched areas will not need to be watered as frequently because the mulch helps to maintain soil moisture and reduce evaporation.

If you haven't done so earlier, this would be a good time to install a drip irrigation system to save time and water. It is relatively easy to snake or pull soaker hoses through ground cover plants after the first frost. Cover the hoses with mulch if you like to camouflage them. Next spring, the ground covers will hide them naturally.

Check the soil around ornamental grasses. If it is beginning to dry out, give it a deep watering about once a month. The same goes for perennial vines. The soil should be watered thoroughly before it freezes.

 GROOMING

When "Jack Frost" leaves his calling card, it's time to clean up the garden. Remove frost-blackened annual vines from their trellises or other supports. As the foliage of some ground covers matures and ripens, snip off the dead leaves, and put them in the compost pile. This will help improve the appearance of the bed and reduce the areas where insects and diseases may spend the winter.

Unless vines are extremely top-heavy or damaged by wind and storms, delay pruning until late winter or early spring. Pruning can stimulate latent growth during a possible Indian summer. This tender new growth is vulnerable to frost injury, which stresses the plant. It is okay to prune off dead, dying, or damaged branches or stems.

 PROBLEMS

It's the season for critters to scout out winter nesting sites, and rodents like to construct winter homes in heavily mulched areas. Keep mulch away from the base of vines and ornamental grasses. A good rule of thumb is to wait to apply more mulch around plants until after the ground freezes. Meadow mice, voles, chipmunks, and other critters will have already nested elsewhere.

Continue to pull up weeds or dig them out before they go to seed. It can be challenging to get weeds out of ground covers, but after a good rain or irrigation, slip on a pair of leather gloves, and start pulling. Otherwise, you may need to spot-treat weeds. Remember to shield the ground cover before spraying the weed's foliage.

 FERTILIZING

Most vines, ground covers, and ornamental grasses are best fertilized in the spring, not now. Unnecessary fertilizer applications will build up the soluble salt levels in the soil and result in root injury.

Spot-treating to control weeds

OCTOBER
VINES, GROUND COVERS, & ORNAMENTAL GRASSES

PLANNING

If the first fall frost has not visited your garden, it won't be long. Enjoy the mild autumn days, and photograph your landscape to capture the essence of fall. Make notes in your garden journal as the season winds down, and note the date when the first frost arrives for future reference. October is the time to plan the color of your next year's autumn.

When other perennials are finished, fall bulbs like **meadow saffron** (*Colchicum autumnale*) bloom among your ground covers with wonderful lavender to purple blossoms. Look for the bulbs at the local garden store or nursery, and plant some now for next season. They grow their foliage in the spring, die back in summer, and emerge with flowers in the autumn.

Lamb's ears (*Stachys byzantina*) is a handsome, drought-tolerant perennial that works well as a ground cover, adding both texture and color. Children and adults like to stroke the soft, silvery leaves.

If your landscape lacks red fall foliage, consider planting **Virginia creeper** next spring. Its leaves transform to shades of purple, red, and scarlet. Most other vines display yellow fall color. The many types of **sumac** can also add flaming red to the autumn landscape.

There are a few evergreen ground covers that transform from green to purplish-red in fall. One of my favorites that I've planted for many years is *Juniperus horizontalis* **'Wiltonii'.** A deciduous ground cover that holds its foliage through the fall and winter remarkably well is *Ajuga* **'Burgundy Glow'.**

Cranberry cotoneaster is a hardy deciduous shrub that works well as ground cover as it spills over rocks and retaining walls. The foliage turns a plum purple in fall covered with bright red berries. The seed capsules on vines such as **bittersweet** and **euonymus** can be quite outstanding, so if you have an appropriate location, plan to add these colorful touches to your landscape for next fall.

PLANTING

If planting must be done this month, get containerized nursery stock in the ground by midmonth. After that, you are gambling with Nature. Plants need at least four to six weeks of time with unfrozen ground to establish a strong root system. Keep them watered as the soil dries out, and mulch around the plants (not directly at the base of the vine or ground cover), to help maintain soil moisture and prevent the soil from freezing early.

Snow cover will help insulate the soil in some parts of the region, but at lower elevations, snow is not a long-lasting commodity in the autumn landscape.

Plant hardy, spring-flowering bulbs as they arrive through the mail or in local gardening stores. Some bulbs are good for naturalizing; see Bulb Section. They can serve as a ground cover or be mixed in with other ground covers. Over the years, bulbs will spread to form drifts or patches of color in spring.

CARE

Mulch newly set plants after the ground freezes. Voles and meadow mice will get into heavy mulch now and nest around the plants, eventually feeding on the bark and roots, so keep mulch away from the plant bases and stems. After the ground freezes, these critters will have already found winter quarters elsewhere, and there will be less chance that they will come back to live next to your plants.

As leaves fall from deciduous trees, you might find it handy to lay wire or nylon netting over ground covers to catch the leaves that often mat together and get stuck among the plants. Once leaf fall is over, just roll up the leaf-laden netting and carry the accumulated leaves to the compost pile. Store the netting until it's time to protect the **strawberry** and **raspberry** patch from the birds next year.

 WATERING

Water new plantings monthly when weather conditions are windy and dry. Mulched plants will need less frequent watering than those with bare ground. Check the soil moisture by digging down with a garden trowel. If it is dry to a depth of 4 inches or more, apply water on a warm day. Do not allow your vines, ground covers, and ornamental grasses to go into winter without a good drink.

 FERTILIZING

It is too late in the season to apply fertilizer to ground covers, vines, and ornamental grasses. Wait until spring when you observe the new growth emerging.

 GROOMING

Plan to clean up the frosted annuals, remove other plant debris, and build your compost pile. Tidying up the garden will remove nesting areas for insects, diseases, and rodents.

Cut back dead or damaged branches or stems. Otherwise, delay pruning until late winter or early spring. Secure stems of vines that have been loosened by the wind or ties that have disintegrated.

 PROBLEMS

As weeds continue to grow despite the cool weather, keep them pulled. Do not let them disperse their seeds. Some weeds are "winter annuals," which germinate in the fall and survive the winter. When spring arrives, they continue to grow and compete with your landscape plants. Get rid of these young seedlings while they are vulnerable to hoeing or cultivation.

Rodents are scouting for winter quarters, so be on the watch for their nesting sites. Delay mulching until after the ground freezes. To prevent the spread of diseases and rid the wintering places for insects, rake up and remove fallen leaves.

NOTES

255

NOVEMBER
VINES, GROUND COVERS, & ORNAMENTAL GRASSES

PLANNING

November can be mild and dry, or it can be cold and snowy. High Country gardeners have their plants covered by a blanket of snow. The outdoor landscape will have subtle changes in colors against the cobalt blue sky, and vines with berry-laden branches will show off their beauty.

Keep your binoculars handy to watch for wild birds visiting your landscape. They'll be hunting for berries and other seedpods as a food source. Squirrels may visit the garden, too. Dried seedheads and bleached stems of ornamental grasses hang on through fall and early winter. A light frost on the branches of vines and ornamental grasses gives the landscape a special touch.

Take some time to photograph Nature's wonders, take an inventory of the plants that performed well, and make notes in your garden journal. Did that new ground cover fill in as promised? Would you like to add more ornamental grasses to accentuate the landscape and add a living screen for the summer months? Are there areas in the yard that may need a redesign?

Enjoy the bare branches of vines as they cling to trellises and arbors. Even **Boston ivy** leaves its tracings of dried stems to stand out on the walls and old tree trunks.

Appreciate the ornamental grasses as they glow in the autumn light and rustle in the wind. There is much to be thankful for when the winter garden glistens with vines, ground covers, and ornamental grasses.

PLANTING

If you forgot to plant your ground cover bulbs earlier, it's better to plant them now than to store them over the winter in their packages. Dig into the slightly frozen ground, and set them under trees and around shrub borders. Try minor bulbs around steppingstones.

Water new plantings to ensure that the roots can start to grow before the bulbs undergo their dormancy. Then, once the water has soaked in, mulch the areas to maintain uniform moisture and protection from fluctuating temperatures.

CARE

Fasten the stems of older established perennial vines such as **climbing hydrangea, trumpet vine, honeysuckle,** and **hardy wisteria.** This will prevent them from suffering from winter storm damage.

Remove fallen leaves that accumulate on ground covers since they can smother the plants and block the passage of air and water to the root zone. As mentioned earlier, you can rig up a nylon or wire netting over ground covers under trees to capture the falling leaves. Once leaf drop has finished, lift up the netting, carry the leaves to the compost pile, or shred them to make soil amendment. If you prefer, use a power vacuum or blower to dislodge leaves from ground cover foliage.

If you have a wildlife-friendly garden, set up a winterproof birdbath to provide a source of water for the birds. It is essential for them since natural water supplies may be frozen. Some birdbaths have built-in heaters that will keep the water from freezing.

WATERING

Watering should be done on a limited basis now. However, if it has been a dry fall without snow or rain, new plants will benefit from a deep watering while the ground remains unfrozen. Do not let evergreen ground covers go into the winter with dry soil. This will result in more winter desiccation to their foliage. Some of the broadleaf evergreens such as **euonymus** will hold on to their foliage and need winter watering when conditions are dry.

Ornamental grasses also suffer from desiccation during prolonged dry periods. Even though the leaves dry up in autumn and winter, the crowns can be killed by continual exposure to drying winds and dry soil. Keep the root systems moist by watering before the ground freezes solid. Apply water early in the day so it can soak down to the root zone. Disconnect the hose and return to storage.

 ## FERTILIZING

Do not fertilize ground covers, vines, and ornamental grasses during this month. Delay that activity for early spring when growth resumes.

 ## GROOMING

It is time to do a final cleanup of the yard to prevent overwintering insects and disease spores. Cut back dead plant stems and seedheads. Pull up the support stakes or tomato cages that provided temporary support for new plants, and place them in storage. Limit your pruning to removal of dead, damaged, or overly long branches that pose a hazard to nearby structures.

 ## PROBLEMS

During the late fall and early winter, deer, elk, rabbits and other critters will feed on landscape plants if they can gain entry to your yard. The best defense against elk and deer is exclusion; construct a deer-proof fence 10 feet high to keep them out. Some areas allow the use of electric fences with two sets of wire to keep deer from jumping over into your property. Repellents will work temporarily, but must be reapplied after they begin to break down from sunlight, heat, and moisture. Try the homemade repellent on page 284.

Rabbits and other small rodents can be deterred by placing wire cages around or over individual plants and ground covers.

 ## NOTES

_____
_____
_____
_____
_____
_____
_____
_____
_____
_____
_____
_____
_____
_____
_____
_____
_____
_____
_____
_____
_____
_____
_____
_____
_____
_____
_____
_____
_____
_____
_____
_____
_____
_____
_____
_____

DECEMBER
VINES, GROUND COVERS, & ORNAMENTAL GRASSES

 PLANNING

As the winter solstice approaches, the holiday season begins to take up our time and energy. But if you can find a quiet moment, this is a good time to re-read the year's garden journal and reflect on the beautiful seasons that have just passed. Make lists of what kinds of ground covers, vines, and ornamental grasses you would like to try next year. The mail-order catalogs are full of enticing pictures, but study them carefully before making final decisions. Will the plants grow in your area? What is its hardiness rating? Do they need special soil conditions? Will they tolerate drought? Making the right choices will save you time, energy, and money.

Plan your holiday shopping list. Gardeners always appreciate a gift certificate to a special nursery or garden store. For friends who love vines, give the gift of an arbor or pergola. No matter how the season turned out, we gardeners are always optimistic that next year will be even better!

 PLANTING

In areas where the ground has not yet frozen, plant bulbs that are on final closeout. This is the best way to store bulbs rather than keeping them in their packages. The bulbs will grow roots and come up in spring with a riot of color.

 CARE

After the ground freezes, spread a 2- to 3-inch layer of mulch around new plantings to protect them from temperature fluctuations and hold in moisture. For the High Country, a blanket of snow is Nature's best insulator to protect plants from wind and winter sun.

 WATERING

If you have been watering regularly throughout the fall, vines, ground covers, and ornamental grasses should be fine. It is important that these plants have adequate moisture before the ground freezes, especially the newly planted ones.

When there's no snow or rain for a prolonged period, you can apply water on a warm day. Temperatures should be above freezing, and the ground should not be frozen. Otherwise, the water will run off.

 FERTILIZING

Do not fertilize in this month. Bake holiday cookies instead!

 GROOMING

Prune only to remove storm damaged stems, twigs, and branches. If vines have come loose from supports, tie them back up with a twist tie or soft twine.

 PROBLEMS

One drawback of persistent snow are critters known as voles. They can tunnel under the snow to the roots and tender bark of vines and ground covers. Be on the watch for them. Trapping may be necessary, or you can check out the homemade repellent recipe on page 284. If deer are a continual problem, consider investing in a deer-proof fence around your property.

Beware of road salt that is spread on the street to melt ice and snow. If the snowplow splashes this onto your ground covers or other plants, the soluble salts can damage the roots. Shovel salt-laden snow and ice off plants, and leach the soil with copious amounts of water as soon as the ground thaws.

WATER GARDENS

Maybe it's because our higher elevation sunlight is more intense. Because we average more than 300 days of sunshine annually, water garden plants will grow and flower with beautiful and brilliant colors. Warm days and cool nights during the primary growing season make an ideal environment to grow water and bog plants. It just takes the right planning to locate the water feature in an appropriate site.

With the right conditions, lotus, water poppies, rushes, sedges, cattails water lilies, water hyacinths, and many more aquatic plants can thrive and provide a peaceful retreat. Water gardening should be considered an extension of terrestrial gardening. It sharpens your skills to grow a whole new world of plants. Once you get hooked on water gardening, it often becomes a favorite pastime. You'll indulge yourself with new and unusual water plants. Add fish, and you're on your way to having a wildlife habitat to soothe a gardener's soul.

Those who plan and maintain a water garden relate the serenity they experience when they work near their ponds or water features, nurturing the plants and observing the wildlife that this garden environment attracts. It is a place where all kinds of creatures will want to visit, prey and predator alike. It is not unusual for a blue heron to be perched high above the water garden, eyeballing the pond for a meal of koi or goldfish.

You will soon discover that a water garden will become its own complex ecosystem with dragonflies, toads, tadpoles, frogs, snails, turtles, birds, and bees. And with a balance of Nature, these residents of the water garden will help to consume the many pests that may annoy you.

Before you decide on digging and planting a water garden, you should make a plan. Consider the time you have to tend to this specialized garden and the amount of space you have to accommodate a water feature. Even with limited space, you can grow water plants in a plastic tub or half-whiskey barrel that can be moved from one end of the patio or deck to the other.

A larger, underground water garden or pond, on the other hand, cannot be moved or changed so easily. You may want to contact a landscape contractor who specializes in designing and installing a larger water garden that will include waterfalls and bog areas.

An ideal site will receive at least six hours of sunlight daily. The location should be near your home so you can enjoy the benefits through a window. It is amazing what you will see and hear once this becomes a part of your landscape. Safety will be an issue, too, particularly if small children will be around. You and I know how water can attract kids of all ages.

Avoid putting a water garden beneath large trees. Falling leaves mean higher maintenance. Even though you can put a net over the water, it is still a hassle to deal with cleanup. Remember that excavating to install a pond can damage tree roots. If you want to have a water feature near trees, consider an aboveground water garden.

A belowground water garden can be constructed from a variety of materials:

• Natural clay-lined mud bottoms will form an almost waterproof seal. There may still be some leakage, though, so be aware of the site's drainage patterns.

GARDENING WITH AN ALTITUDE TIPS
Aquatic Plants for Water Gardens

SUBMERGED PLANTS (Oxygenators)
- Myriophyllum (*Myriophyllum ceratophyllum*)
- Cabomba (*Cabomba caroliniana*)
- Anacharis (*Elodea canadensis* var. *gigantea*)
- Vallisneria (*Vallisneria spiralis*)

FLOATING AQUATIC PLANTS
- Water Hyacinth* (*Eichhornia crassipes* var. *major*)
- Water Lettuce* (*Pistia stratiotes*)
- Parrot Feather (*Myriophyllum aquaticum*)
- Azolla (*Azolla* spp.)
- Duckweed* (*Lemna minor*)
- Salvinia* (*Salvinia* spp.)

DEEP WATER AQUATIC PLANTS
- Water Snowflake (*Nymphoides indica*)
- Water Poppy (*Hydrocleys nymphoides*)
- Floating Heart (*Nymphoides peltata*)

HARDY WATER LILIES
- *Nymphaea* 'Carnea' – very light pink
- *N.* 'Mayla' – double deep pink
- *N.* 'Colorado' – salmon
- *N.* 'Escarboucle' –red
- *N.* 'Joey Tomocik' – yellow
- *N.* 'Texas Dawn' – rich yellow

TROPICAL WATER LILIES
- *Nymphaea colorata* – blue flowers
- *N. micrantha* – purple, viviparous reproduction
- Dauben' – light blue, viviparous reproduction
- *N.* 'St. Louis Gold' – yellow, fragrant
- *N.* 'Tina' – deep, violet purple, semidwarf growth habit, viviparous reproduction
- *N.* 'Albert Greenberg' – pink and yellow
- *N.* 'Panama Pacific' – violet, fragrant
- *N.* 'Antares' – crimson, night blooming

SMALLER WATER LILIES
- *Nymphaea* ' Helvola' – yellow blooms
- *N.* 'James Brydon' – rose-red flowers

- *N.* 'Lucida' – tolerates less light
- *N.* 'Fabiola' – floriferous, pink flowers
- *N.* 'Fulgens' – red flowers
- *N.* 'Pink Laydekeri' – white flowers
- *N. tetragona* – smallest white

LOTUS
- *Nelumbo* 'Momo Botan' – small rose double
- *N.* 'Mrs. Perry Slocum' – large, pink, fading to yellow

MARGINAL AND BOG PLANTS
- Canna (*Canna* hybrids) Hybrid water cannas
- Corkscrew Rush (*Juncus effusus* 'Spiralis')
- Horsetail (*Equisetum hyemale*)
- Iris (*Iris* spp. and hybrids)
- Yellow Water Iris (*Iris pseudacorus*)
- Purple Water Iris (*Iris laevigata*)
- Dwarf Cattail (*Typha minima*)
- Sweet Flag (*Acorus calamus*)
- Dwarf Cyprus (*Cyperus haspan*)
- Chameleon Plant (*Houttuynia cordata*)
- Bulrush (*Scirpus*)
- Arrowhead (*Sagittaria* spp.)
- Zebra Grass (*Scirpus* 'Zebrinus')
- Dwarf Umbrella Palm (*Cyperus haspan*)
- Umbrella Palm (*Cyperus alternifolius*)
- Cardinal Flower (*Lobelia cardinalis*)
- Aquatic Mint (*Mentha aquatica*)
- Water Clover (*Marsilea quadrifolia*)
- Prairie Cord Grass (*Spartina pectinata*)
- Watercress (*Nasturtium officinale*)
- Water Celery (*Oenanthe javanica*)
- Pitcher Plant (*Sarracenia* spp.)
- Taro Plant (*Colocasia* spp.)
- Variegated Taro (*Alocasia* spp.)
- Horsetail Rush (*Equisetum hyemale*)
- Spider Lily (*Hymenocallis liriosome*)
- Pickerel Rush (*Pontederia cordata*)
- Japanese Willow (*Salix* 'Hakuro Nishiki')
- Mosaic Plant (*Ludwigia sedioides*)

*Note: these water plants may be restricted in some parts of the region. Check with your local nursery or garden retailer.

• Durable plastic liners can be used to create various shapes and styles of water gardens and pools.

• Polyvinyl chloride (PVC) liners are more flexible and will last longer than the less expensive poly-ethylene type materials (35 mil or thicker). Depending upon the gauge of the liner, they may last from five to 10 years before breaking down from sunlight and temperature fluctuations.

• Rubber and synthetic liners can be even more durable and flexible than PVC (45 mil or thicker). Two common materials are butyl rubber and EPDM (ethylene propylene diene monmer) rubber. They can last up to 50 years.

• Rigid pre-formed liners made of fiberglass or plastic are available in a variety of shapes and sizes. If you want to keep fish in these pre-formed ponds, be sure the liners are at least 3 feet deep.

• For a more elaborate and larger water garden, concrete pools are well suited for a larger landscape. Just keep in mind that in colder parts of the region, freezing and thawing during the winter can result in more cracking unless the concrete is properly reinforced. Consult a professional land-scape contractor experienced in construction.

Once you have decided on the location, shape and size of your water feature, you will be ready to have it installed. Water garden plants can be divided into four general groups:

1. Floating plants such as lotus, water lilies, and water snowflakes are rooted on the bottom and produce leaves and flowers on the water's surface.

2. Marginal or bog plants include cannas, rushes, cattails, and water irises. These will grow and thrive in shallow water along the edges of the pond or water feature. Some will produce showy flowers. Some of the marginal plants can be grown in deeper water on ledges. Most appreci-ate 2 to 6 inches of water over their crowns. Bog and marginal plants differ from moisture-loving plants, which will languish if their roots are water-logged for any length of time.

3. Free-floating plants such as water hyacinth and duckweed will float on the surface with their roots suspended in the water. They are very capable of spreading rapidly, so use free-floaters with caution.

4. Submerged or oxygen-producing plants such as hornwort or *Ludwigia* help to maintain the health of the water garden. These underwater "oxygenating" plants release oxygen into the water and absorb nutrients and carbon dioxide produced by fish, other aquatic life, and decaying plants. They also provide food and shelter for fish.

Some tropical water lilies are propagated via viviparous reproduction. Tiny plant clones emerge at the center connection between the two lobes of a leaf. Some water lilies such as *Nymphaea* 'Dauben' will produce these tiny clones on every leaf.

CARE FOR YOUR WATER GARDEN AND BOG PLANTS
See pages 263 and 265 for tips on the proper care of your water garden and bog plants.

GARDENING WITH AN ALTITUDE TIPS
Planting at the Margins

Some plants will grow in water but do not need to be submerged. They will add accents to the margins of your water garden. Plants typically grown in soil that don't mind a little water over their "feet and ankles" include canna, creeping Jenny, chameleon plant, sedges, purple water iris, zebra grass, and cardinal flower, to name a few. Check with local water gardening experts for more plant choices.

JANUARY
WATER GARDENS

PLANNING

Whether you are new to growing a water garden or have experience with a water feature, now is the time to plan a water garden that features your lifestyle and time. Water gardens can be planned for a large pond, a waterfall, or even a small half-whiskey barrel.

Look over the many mail-order catalogs and books on water gardening, and develop a list of plants that may be suited for your particular needs. Learn about the ornamental features, optimum growth depth, mature spread, and hardiness rating of each plant. If size is going to be a limitation, consider dwarf cultivars, plan for fewer plants, or consider designing a larger area for a more extensive water garden.

A good recipe for your pond for every 100 to 500 gallons of water you will need:

1. One **water lily** (tropical or hardy variety)

2. Two **bog** or **marginal plants** (make sure one of them is a rush like a **cattail** or **bull rush**, as they are natural cleaners)

3. Two floaters (**water hyacinth** or **water lettuce;** they are fast-growers unless you have large fish which can consume many of them)

4. One oxygenating plant per square foot of water surface; usually a clump of five will cover 5 square feet.

A properly designed water garden has a special appeal in winter when it will be covered by shimmering ice. Landscape lighting can highlight a water feature in the winter landscape and add another interesting dimension.

Many hardy plants can remain submerged in a pond that is 18 or more inches deep and survive. If you include fish like **koi**, the pond will need to be 3 or more feet deep for them to survive in a dormant winter mode. Their cold-blooded systems react to low water temperatures by stalling their metabolism until conditions are favorable for them to return to action.

If frost is a concern in your area, causing freezing to a depth of 18 inches or more, consider installing a de-icer or pond heater for water gardens, or have the water re-circulating year-round. This will protect vulnerable plants and fish.

Caution: Some water plants may become invasive weeds if they escape your water garden. Some to be aware of include:

- **Water Hyacinth** (*Eichhornia crassipes*)
- **Water Clover** (*Marsilea quadrifolia*)

- **Elephant Ear** (*Colocasia antiquorum*)
- **Mosquito Fern** (*Azolla pinnata*)
- **Parrot's Feather** (*Myriophyllum aquaticum*)
- **Primrose Creeper** (*Ludwigia arcuata*)
- **Dollar Weed** (*Hydrocotyl umbellata*)
- **Duckweed** (*Lemna minor*)
- **Yellow Flag Iris** (*Iris pseudacorus*)
- **Cattails** (*Typha latifolia*)
- **Horsetail** (*Equisetum hyemale*)

These plants should be grown with care in confined locations and should never be released into natural waterways where they may get out of control and cause serious problems in the environment. **Check with your local municipalities for a list of invasive water plants determined by federal and state agencies.** They can provide you with an updated list or direct you to an appropriate agency that has jurisdiction over invasive plants.

PLANTING

This is not the time of year to plant a water garden unless you have an a large atrium with room for a water feature. If you are overwintering water plants in a sun porch or basement, take cuttings from the tender aquatic plants and start them under bright artificial lights. Stem sections from **parrot's feather, water mint**, and offshoots of **taro** can be started in an aquarium where they will root. Once roots are developed, pot the individual plants in soil, and re-immerse in water.

 CARE

Check any **tropical water lilies** you are overwintering indoors. Discard any tubers showing signs of rot. Make sure the sand is damp and has not dried out.

GARDENING WITH AN ALTITUDE TIPS
Caring for Your Water Garden and Bog Plants

Like all plants, aquatic plants need attention during the growing season to grow healthy and strong. Prune and trim away dead and dying foliage and spent flowers on a regular basis. Any fallen leaves and other debris that accumulates in the water should be scooped up with a net or removed by other means. Divide or remove plants when they become too numerous. Tropical water lilies and other tender plants that are not winter hardy will have to be lifted and overwintered indoors.

Various methods are available for fertilizing water garden plants. Some specialists recommend making a sachet of fertilizer (15-30-15 or 20-20-20) by wrapping a granular plant fertilizer in cheesecloth or paper towel and placing it in the garden soil in which the plants are potted. Too much fertilizer can "burn" the plants or cause the water to become foul, however. Slow-release fertilizers in pellet form are specially designed for water plants and are much safer. Simply follow the manufacturer's recommendations, and use a fertilizer designed for aquatic plants.

 WATERING

Water lilies overwintering indoors should be covered with water and not allowed to dry out. If needed, cover the tops of the storage containers with plastic to maintain humidity, but leave the sides open for air circulation.

 FERTILIZING

None needed!

 GROOMING

To maintain winter interest in the water garden, leave the stems of **cattails** and other hardy perennials planted near the water's edge uncut. If snow or ice tends to make them blow over into the garden, those that are broken can be cut back.

 PROBLEMS

Freezing will prevent oxygen exchange between the air and water in your garden. This can kill fish and plants at the bottom of the pond. Install a de-icer device, or melt a portion of the ice by gradually pouring boiling water over it to open up an area for air exchange. Keep a bubbler or waterfall running to keep the water moving. Also, a large hollow log can be set in the pond to provide a port for air to move to the bottom of the water garden.

FEBRUARY
WATER GARDENS

PLANNING

Look through the various water gardening magazines and journals that provide an array of information about aquatic plants and how to grow them. The color photographs are enticing and offer descriptions of each type of plant. Some companies will offer detailed instructions for creating a water garden, constructing a pond, or growing water plants in containers. There are many dwarf varieties of traditional water plants that are well suited for container gardening.

Consider pre-formed garden pools that make installation easier for creating a water garden. They are very good for maintaining fish if the water depth is adequate. Now is the time to pick a site for a water garden that will be visible from a window, the patio, or deck. Draw a plan to scale on graph paper to be sure the water feature will fit the location.

Water gardens can range from a foot to several feet deep. A water garden that is a least 3 feet deep will not freeze completely and will allow overwintering fish and hardy water plants to survive the winter. Shallow ponds require extra work since plants and fish will have to be removed to indoor conditions.

Take time to check out water gardening equipment before installing it in the pond. Test all pumps, connectors, pipes, hoses, tubing clamps, electrical wires and boxes. Clean filters so debris won't interfere with water uptake. It is easier to make repairs early in the season before installation in the water garden. Once the water garden is planted and running, disturb it only in an emergency. Each time the pond is upset it must undergo an adjustment period that can take two years.

PLANTING

It's still too early to do much planting, other than propagating new plants by division or rooting cuttings. Check any tender aquatic plants that are wrapped or stored in a soil medium. The soil should remain moist with temperatures in the 40- to 50-degree Fahrenheit range so they won't freeze.

By the end of the month, as temperatures rise and the days get longer, many stored plants may initiate growth by sending out shoots. As they begin to grow and crowd their pots, transplant them into larger containers. If you have a rather large plant, it may be divided and the individual divisions repotted.

CARE

Outdoor water plants need lots of good light to survive. Provide good air circulation to prevent the plants from becoming rancid. Plants and fish in the water garden should be safe if they are resting below the freeze line and there is open water to release gases and provide oxygen to the water. If you live in an area where a heavy snowfall covers the pond, clear away an area of the snow so that the plants can continue to photosynthesize on sunny days. This helps them absorb the carbon dioxide and releases oxygen to the plants.

Check your water heater or de-icer regularly to be sure it is working properly. If the water should freeze, you can open a hole by melting the ice in one area with hot water. Or set a bucket of boiling water on the ice, which should eventually melt its way through. Tie a rope on the bucket to haul it out if it falls through the ice. Do not chop or hammer the ice. Shock waves can harm the fish and damage the pond liner.

Remove fallen leaves, twigs, and branches, or any other debris that may have blown in and accumulated on the ice over the pond. Do this before the ice melts because it is easier to clear it now than to sieve it out of the water later.

If your indoor storage area is becoming too warm, relocate the plants to a spot where temperatures are in the range of 40 to 50 degrees Fahrenheit.

 ## WATERING

Do not allow outdoor water plants to either dry out or become a rotted mass of slime. **Bog plants** and most tropical types don't need to be completely submerged in water. Just be sure the pot is sitting in a little water so the roots are kept moist.

 ## FERTILIZING

None needed!

 ## GROOMING

Toward the end of the month, it's time to tidy up the water garden. Areas around the edge of the pond may need to be cleaned up by clipping off dead stems of **cattails, ornamental grasses,** and other **marginal**

> ## GARDENING WITH AN ALTITUDE TIPS
> ### More About Caring for
> ### Your Water Garden and Bog Plants
>
> Maintain water levels throughout the season. Some water will naturally evaporate, and rain will sometimes replenish the water garden to the proper level. When needed, top off with a garden hose. Caution: If you have fish, don't add treated municipal water directly to your water garden. Fill a container, and use a de-chlorinator, or let it sit for a day. Aerate the water to boost oxygen levels, especially during the heat of the summer. Bubbling filters, fountains, and waterfalls can be useful.
>
> Relatively few pests bother aquatic plants, except for aphids on water lilies in the late summer and fall. Most pests can be controlled by scavengers and by carefully monitoring the water environment. It is not recommended to use pesticides around water features that harbor fish and other aquatic life. These materials will disrupt the natural ecosystem and kill dragonflies, snails, frogs, fish, and other wildlife that live around the water garden. You can use mint oil or diatomaceous earth to help control insect pests on water garden plants.

plants. With the right planning, you may have planted some early spring-blooming bulbs that will add color around the water feature. **Crocus** and **snowdrops** add a special accent to the water feature and attract birds.

 ## PROBLEMS

Be aware that aquatic plants overwintering indoors can attract insect pests. The tender growth may be vulnerable to aphids and scale. If you notice them, wash them off with a forceful spray of water. Avoid applying too much

fertilizer to the plants, which tends to make them more succulent and attractive to indoor pests.

Safety Note: If you have small children or infants in the household, they may fail to detect the water garden when playing outdoors when it is semi-frozen and covered with snow. To prevent accidents, construct a low fence or barrier around the water garden to let them know to stay out of bounds. Otherwise, have someone outside to supervise the playing area.

March
WATER GARDENS

 PLANNING

The signs of spring are all around us this month, so pick a comfortable day to install your water garden. Here are some steps to follow:

• Outline the shape of a flexible liner with rope or garden hose. Mark the border with spray paint or builder's chalk. When using a pre-formed pond, set it on the ground and mark its outline with the same marking materials.

• Start digging from the edges to create a permanent outline, and excavate toward the center. Dig the sides steeply sloped at a about a 20-degree angle from the vertical to create a good volume relative to the surface area. This is important to avoid algae problems in the future.

• Check the edge of the pond frequently as you dig to make sure it is level. The edge should be even all around to prevent water from overflowing before it is completely full. Set a carpenter's level on top of a long, straight two-by-four laid across the hole.

• Create an underwater shelf along the inside wall to hold potted marginal or bog plants and rocks, if desired. The shelves can be 10 to 12 inches long and about 18 inches wide. You can still grow **marginals** in shallow water by placing them on clean bricks or upside down on clay flower pots.

• Dig the hole at least 2 feet deep, deeper in the mountain communities, allowing for a 1- to 2-inch layer of sand. When using a performed liner, dig the hole about 2 inches deeper and 3 inches wider on the sides.

• For flexible liners, apply a one to 2-inch layer of damp sand, old indoor-outdoor carpeting, or any other soft material to prevent the liner from being pierced by sharp rocks or other debris.

To calculate the size of the pond liner you will need, determine the inside area and depth by following these steps.

• Measure the length and width of the pond. If it is circular or irregularly shaped, draw a square or rectangle around it and use the length and width of that figure for your calculations.

• Use this equation to calculate the length and width of your pond liner:

Length = Maximum length of pond + (2 x maximum depth) + (2 x edging allowance)

Width = Maximum width of pond + (2 x maximum depth) + (2 x edging allowance)

• Center the flexible liner over the hole and weight down its edges with bricks or smooth stones. Slowly fill the pond with water. As the pond fills, gradually take the weights off the edges so the water will fill into the crevices. When the water comes to within 1 inch of the top, shut it off and cut away any excess material, leaving about a foot beyond the rim.

• Line the edges of the pond with flagstone rock, pavers, bricks, stones, or other suitable materials.

• For pre-formed ponds, spread an inch or two of sand on the bottom of the hole. Set the form in the hole so that the rim is just above ground level. Take it out and make any adjustments. When it is level, firmly pack soil around its edges. Fill the pond with water. Hide the rim with stones, flagstones, or plant a spreading ground cover.

PLANTING

If you ordered aquatic plants via mail, it will be necessary to pot these up. Divide plants in storage if they are becoming overgrown. I find it easier to plant aquatic plants in clay pots or plastic containers since they are easier to check and maintain. Also, pots hold plants inbounds, and potted plants are easier to remove from the water garden for maintenance. Heights of plants can be adjusted to assure correct water depth over the root systems.

Water temperatures need to reach a certain level before you reintroduce fish and plants that were overwintered indoors. Check the water temperature about a week after the ice melts. At 35 degrees Fahrenheit, you can remove the heater. At 45 degrees Fahrenheit, start the pumps. As the temperatures approach 50 degrees, release the last of the overwintering fish into the water garden.

 CARE

Continue to monitor the condition of overwintering aquatic plants indoors. It will soon be time to set them outside in the water garden. If you haven't already cleaned up around the periphery of the water garden, get this task accomplished. Prune back **marginal plants, ornamental grasses, cattails,** and others that may flop over in the water. Send this plant debris to the compost pile. Remove any debris that may have blown into the water as well.

 WATERING

Keep overwintering aquatic plants cool and sufficiently cov-ered with water to maintain their indoor health.

 FERTILIZING

None needed!

 GROOMING

Cut back **grasses** and **sedges** at the water's edge to make way for new foliage to sprout. Dig up and divide overgrown clumps. Prune **shrubs,** small **ornamental trees,** and **evergreens** that may have suffered winterkill so the dead branches won't end up in the water garden.

 PROBLEMS

Sanitation is the key to a clean and healthy water garden. It is the best defense against diseases and pest problems. When a water garden is new, it is common for the water to become clouded and dirty-looking. This is because the water has not yet reached a biological balance. Resist the urge to drain the water garden and refill it with fresh water. Give the water several weeks to mellow and become ecologically balanced. A small amount of algae is an essential part of a healthy water feature.

Animal predators include raccoons, blue herons, feral cats, and other wildlife that may find a water garden enticing, especially when water levels are low. Great blue herons love to feed on **koi** where there is little or no foliage to camouflage the fish. You can place unobtrusive bird netting over the water to foil birds until plant foliage begins to cover the water's surface.

NOTES

_____
_____
_____
_____
_____
_____
_____
_____
_____
_____
_____
_____
_____
_____
_____
_____
_____
_____
_____
_____
_____

APRIL
WATER GARDENS

 PLANNING

A water garden is not maintenance-free; it is considered a specialty garden that requires attention to be successful. If you plan to install a water garden, be prepared to make an effort to keep the plants healthy. Otherwise, they will probably succumb to pests, diseases, or environmental injury.

As a pond becomes properly balanced, aquatic life does most of the work to maintain water quality. Fish will feed on mosquito larvae, while oxygenating plants will offer food, shelter, and oxygen for fish and allow for gas exchange for plant root growth. Consider adding snails and other scavenger fish to feed on algae and other debris from the bottom of the pond.

Remember that a water feature attracts small children and can pose a potential danger. If this is the case in your landscape, consider constructing decorative fencing around the pond or water garden to keep the small ones from falling in.

Review earlier plans, schedules, or lists of plants that you wish to add to the water garden. Local garden retailers will soon have their water garden supplies ready for sale. Shop around to see who has the best selections.

 PLANTING

As the water temperatures rise to 50 degrees Fahrenheit, it's time to lift, divide and repot marginal plants that have overwintered at the bottom of the water garden. If you received plants via mail-order, pot them up for their transition to the pond. Here are some tips on repotting plants that wintered at the bottom of the pond:

• Lift them out of the water and trim off all dead and winter-damaged portions.

• Before discarding dead plants, check for new growth at the base of the crowns.

• If no new growth is forthcoming, replant the container with new plants. Use new soil and add fertilizer tabs if needed.

• Cover the surface with pea gravel to ensure that the soil does not float from the pot into the water.

Water lily rhizomes should be planted in heavy soil or commercial aquatic planting mixture to make sure they don't float to the top. A mulch of pea gravel on top of the soil will help prevent this problem. Use a wide, shallow rectangular container that will accommodate the narrow, rooted rhizomes. Orient the rhizomes at a 45-degree angle so the crown (where the new leaves emerge) will be sprouting

upwards. Spread the roots over the soil.

At least an inch or two of soil should cover the rhizome's cut end (if it has just been divided) and the roots. Allow the growing tip and crown to protrude from the soil, which should reach to within an inch of two of the container rim. Make sure you don't plant too deep.

Firm the soil over the planted rhizome, and water it in. Then you're ready to immerse the pot in the pond so the air bubbles have a chance to escape. The container may be a bit heavy until it is completely under water. **Water lily** pans or pots can sit at the bottom of the water garden at a maximum depth of 18 inches. In deeper water, set the pots on ledges, overturned clay pots, or bricks.

 CARE

Clean up storm debris, spills, and other damage that may occasionally occur. Don't allow the water to foul and upset the ecological balance. Too much organic debris accumulating in the bottom of the pond will cause anaerobic decomposition. This will deplete the available oxygen in the water. Cleaning is usually done in autumn, but can be done in spring if necessary. You can dredge the bottom of the pond with a net to remove any excess decaying leaf matter, plant refuse or sludge. Then continue to remove dead leaves, twigs, and other debris as it accumulates.

As the water warms, overwintering fish will venture to the surface to feed. In an established water garden there is vegetation for them to nibble on, so they don't need to be fed right away. In a new water garden with little or no aquatic plants, you will have to provide food regularly. Feeding the fish provides an opportunity to check their general color and health.

Set immersed water plants back on their ledges later in the month, when there is no danger of a severe frost. You can also use bricks, overturned clay pots, overturned laundry baskets, or flat rocks to set the plants at the correct depth.

 WATERING

As water temperatures rise, don't be alarmed if the water quality becomes somewhat murky. Soil from newly potted plants, pollens in the air, seeds from **elms** and other trees, and other debris are sure to make the water dirty. Skim off the pond if needed. Just remember, biological reactions are adjusting the natural balance of the water.

Filters can be used to help circulate water and maintain clarity. Biological filters are set outside the pond and require less-frequent cleaning. Check out which kind of filter will best suit your conditions.

 FERTILIZING

None needed!

 GROOMING

If submerged plants were not thinned and pruned earlier, clean out the matted bunches from the water, and recycle them in the compost pile. Leave a few to oxygenate the water and provide shelter for any fish while other plants become established.

 PROBLEMS

Be on the watch for wildlife. As the water garden becomes active, it will attract an array of critters. Sometimes it will be necessary to install netting over the pond or fencing around it to keep out predators.

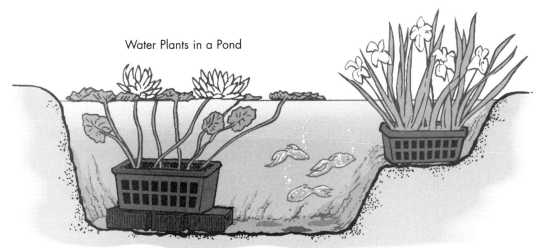
Water Plants in a Pond

MAY
WATER GARDENS

 PLANNING

The new water garden constructed last year will be ready for planting as soon as the plants are ready, but an established water garden or pond may need some draining and cleaning every few years to eliminate silt accumulation and to check for leaks. However, don't replace more than one-third at any one time as this will disrupt the pond's balance.

Clean an older pond in the spring with a few precautions. Have a holding tank ready to house overwintering plants and fish until the job is done. This is a good time to divide and thin overgrown plants and discard those that are waning. Cleaned and repotted plants will have plenty of time to become established before the onset of hot weather.

Assemble materials you need to do the job properly. These will include:
- Tubing to drain the water
- Garden hose
- Buckets
- Plastic dustpan
- Soft broom
- A pump for draining larger volumes
- A soft net with a sturdy handle
- A bowl

- A children's wading pool or several large plastic garbage cans
- Netting or towels to cover the containers
- Water treatment chemicals for chlorine and ammonia
- Newspapers

Here are the steps for cleaning a water garden:
- Drain the pond by two-thirds, and reserve this pond water in a holding container.
- Remove the containerized plants.
- Wrap the containers in wet newspaper, and set them in shade.
- Protect scavenger species that may be trapped in the plants.
- Capture the fish with the net and bowl, and put them in the holding pool.
- Move floating plants into buckets of water.
- Check for tadpoles and frogs in the mud, and transfer them to the holding pool.
- Cover the pool with netting so they won't escape.
- Recycle the remaining water by pouring it onto the lawn or garden.
- Carefully shovel out accumulated mud and silt with the plastic dustpan. Reserve one bucket of mud to repopulate the pond later. Add excess mud to the compost pile.

- After most of the mud has been scooped out, scrub the bottom and sides of the liner with a soft brush. Add a little fresh water if needed. Rinse, and bail out the dirty water.
- This is a good time to examine the liner. Patches or masonry repairs are easy to install while the pond is empty.

PLANTING

Once the pond has been cleaned and repaired, you are ready to replant:
- Fill the pond one-third full with the garden hose. If using treated municipal water, let the chemicals evaporate for one day.
- Unwrap **lilies** and other containerized plants. Divide them if necessary, and replant them in containers. Set the containers in the deepest part of the pond on bricks, overturned laundry baskets, or flat rocks to the proper heights so that the leaves are at the surface when the pond is full.
- Once the larger plants have been set in the water, add the saved bucket of mud and the reserved pond water. This will reestablish fish and other organisms more quickly.
- Plant sprigs of oxygenators in small containers, a dozen or so bunches per container, and set on the bottom of the pond.

• If the danger of frost has passed, add **tropical water lilies** and **water hyacinths.** The water temperature must be 60 degrees Fahrenheit or higher, so monitor the temperature. Each spring is different. I usually recommend setting them out in late May, around Memorial Day, when the days are consistently warm.

• Set marginal plants at the right depth, leaving an opening to get into the pond.

• Carefully transfer the fish from the holding wading pool. Examine them for diseases or pests, and treat them if needed. Transfer all other beneficial organisms and scavengers.

• Finish filling the pond. Add any water treatments, and install the pump.

• Finish replacing the marginal plants, and enjoy the water garden for another season.

 ## CARE

Periodically check to see that the pots have not shifted or fallen over in the water. Sometimes aggressive fish, a wildlife visitor, or water currents from the pump or waterfall can upset containerized plants from their original positions.

Check **bog plants** at the pond's edge to make sure they are getting adequate moisture to establish. **Marginal plants** on the water garden's shelves should be inspected to make sure they are at the correct water level.

 ## WATERING

Algae will cloud a newly cleaned pond after about 10 days, and it will take about a month for the pond to reach a balance and clear. Adding natural bacteria and barley bales will help to control excessive algae growth. If you desire, you can add an algicide to temporarily clear the water, but this is not always necessary.

Most municipalities treat water with chlorine or fluorine, which can be harmful to fish. If you use treated water, wait a day before adding fish. These chemicals will dissipate, and the water will be safe. If you like, you can add drops of de-chlorinating products as directed on the package label if fish are already in the water garden. This is important when you top off the pond with more water.

Cloudy or murky water may persist for a few weeks as warm weather accelerates the biological activity. Don't become alarmed and add chemicals. Brown, furry algae on containers and liner surfaces is a sign of the pond reaching a biological balance, which is healthy for both plants and fish. If filamentous algae becomes excessive, gently rake it out with a plastic leaf rake.

 ## FERTILIZING

As your water plants begin to show signs of growth, it's time for the first application of fertilizer designed for aquatic plants. Read and follow manufacturer's recommendations.

 ## GROOMING

Remove faded or dying stems and foliage from **water lilies, lotus,** and **bog plants.** Thin oxygenators if they are getting too thick.

 ## PROBLEMS

Continue to watch for great blue herons and other critters that may visit your water garden for a meal of fish. Install netting over the pond, or set netted clothes baskets upside down in the water as a retreat for fish.

JUNE
WATER GARDENS

 ## PLANNING

This is the time when water gardens are beginning to look their best. The water should have stabilized and cleared somewhat with a proper balance. Now is a good time to add notes to your garden journal about your experiences with this phase of gardening. Record how the plants are doing, what kinds of complications you may have encountered, and how the cleaning process went. Sometimes a water garden can require more maintenance than you anticipated. I live in an area of high winds and often dread the duty of cleaning out all those tumble weeds and other debris that blow in. Place netting over your water garden to make cleanup less tedious.

Consider installing a pump and filter in your water garden if you have fish. Fish will generate nutrient-dense waste that can make the water murky. Choose a pump powerful enough to move up to one-half of the total volume of water in your pond each hour. If combined with a biological filter set up outside the pond, the pump needs to move one-sixteenth to one-fourth of the pond's total volume of water per hour. Besides powering the filter, a pump can operate a waterfall or fountain to keep oxygen levels

high and discourage mosquito larvae.

If you don't have space for an in-ground water garden, consider starting small with a containerized water garden. Growing aquatic plants above ground is a way to have a water garden on the patio, deck, or balcony near the house. Aboveground water gardens are also easier to work, especially for gardeners with bad backs. Here's how to begin:

• Use a watertight container at least 18 to 20 inches in diameter and a foot or two deep.

• Fill the container with water.

• Let it sit for a day to warm the water to air temperature and to allow chlorine and other chemicals to dissipate.

• Use a bubbler to circulate the water and add soft, soothing, trickling sounds to the area.

• Choose plants such as **water lilies,** oxygenating plants, and **marginals** that perform well in warm water. **Lotus** plants are good candidates.

 ## PLANTING

Tender **tropical water lilies** grow best when temperatures are 65 to 70 degrees Fahrenheit. A good rule of thumb is to set tropical aquatic plants outdoors about the same time you plant **tomatoes** and **pep-**

pers, around Memorial Day weekend, or later in the mountains.

Plant **tropical water lilies** in wide dishpan-type pots, about five gallons in capacity, similar to those used for **hardy water lilies.** Drill drainage holes in the containers if they do not have them. Fill each pot one-third full with moist heavy garden soil (do not use compost or peat moss in the soil mix), and place fertilizer tabs into the soil according to manufacturer's recommendations.

Add a bit more soil, then lay the horizontal tuber on its surface, the roots splayed out over the soil. Be sure the growing tip is pointed upward. Cover it with more soil up to the crown where some green buds are visible at the growing tip. Look for a pale line or ridge at the tip. The soil should be an inch or two below the rim of the container after you press it gently over the tuber. Water it in until is settles. Spread a layer of pea gravel mulch over the soil to avoid muddying the water.

 ## CARE

Blooming **water lilies** will benefit from periodic deadheading after the flowers are finished. It's easy to tell the **hardy water**

lilies apart from the **tropical water lilies;** most tropical water lilies hold their flowers above the water. Leave the spent flowers on **lotus** because they form ornamental pods that can be used in dried-flower arrangements.

Remove any foliage that may become infested by insects, and clean out debris that blows in. Keep track of the water pH, ammonia, and nitrate levels, especially if you have the water garden stocked with fish.

For the aboveground water feature, remember that mosquitoes can breed in the water if it is not moving or does not have fish to consume the wigglers. You can prevent this by adding a few briquettes of mosquito larvae killer that contain Bt (*Bacillus thriingiensis* var. *israelensis*). One briquette can treat 100 square feet of water regardless of its depth.

Remove, rinse, and replace the pads from submersible filters every week.

WATERING

Top off the water garden to maintain the proper level. Add the water slowly. Topping with water once a week is usually adequate.

FERTILIZING

If you desire, fertilize **water lilies** with aquatic fertilizer tablets according to the package recommendations, usually once a month. **Bog plants** can be fertilized based on how well they are growing. I recommend that you apply fertilizer at half strength to avoid promoting a lot of soft, floppy growth.

GROOMING

Prune off dying or hail-injured foliage of **water lilies** and other plants. You can use a pole pruner to reach and clip leaves in the center of the pond. Do not let the prunings fall down into the water because they will decay and foul it. Tall **bog plants** at the pond's edge or tall **marginal plants** in shallow water may get floppy. Stake the plants as needed, or tidy them up with pruning.

PROBLEMS

Water lily aphids can disfigure leaves and distort flowers. Remove them with a forceful spray of water. You can also submerge the infested leaves and give them a shake. Spider mites can show up on the underside of raised **water lily** leaves and **lotus.** Clip off heavily infested leaves and discard.

Predator birds may find it more difficult to hunt when aquatic plants hide the fish. A plastic milk crate or clothes basket placed upside down in the pond where plants are not sufficient will help to shelter fish from predators. Set pots of water plants on the crate or clothes basket to keep it weighted down and camouflaged.

NOTES

_____
_____
_____
_____
_____
_____
_____
_____
_____
_____
_____
_____
_____
_____
_____
_____
_____
_____
_____

JULY
WATER GARDENS

PLANNING

The summer water garden is a relaxing retreat as the heat intensifies. The sound of water will attract birds, butterflies, squirrels, and other wildlife. You have created an ecological niche that brings in my favorites— dragonflies, plus toads, frogs, tadpoles, spiders, and a resident snake. These are all a gardener's best friends.

If you are concerned about a mosquito problem, don't fret. A living pond with the right balance of colorful **koi** and **mosquito fish** will keep these pests at bay. Plus, if you set up bat houses, bats will help control hundreds of mosquitoes in just one night. For water gardens without fish or moving water, plan to add the mosquito larvae killer briquettes that contain *Bacillus thuringiensis* var. *israelensis*. This bacterial larvicide will kill the wigglers; one briquette can treat up to 100 feet of water regardless of depth.

Take time to record your water gardening experiences in your garden journal or notebook. Clip out articles from local garden writers who feature water gardening.

Visit local and regional water gardens to see the various designs and plants. You can glean many ideas to use in your water garden next season. Consider installing some lighting in or around your pond. This will enhance your enjoyment of the water garden at night.

July is a good month to take photographs of the water garden at its peak when plants are in bloom. Add these to your journal to remind you which plants performed best, and note which plants that may have turned out to be less than favorable. Then you can make appropriate changes next spring.

PLANTING

You can continue to add water plants to the pond or ornamental containers anytime during the summer. If more than 60 percent of the water's surface is not yet covered by foliage, you can add more plants to prevent algae problems.

Conversely, if too many plants are overrunning the water garden, remove some of them and put them in pots or barrels filled with water. Maybe you can share them with other water gardening enthusiasts.

Check to see if the **lotus** plants start blooming when temperatures are consistently above 80 degrees Fahrenheit. Their foliage is unique, but don't be surprised if they don't bloom the first year after transplanting.

Add floating plants to the water garden to provide texture and color contrast to the larger leaves of **water lilies, water hyacinth,** and **lotus.**

CARE

Continue to clean debris from the water garden, and check to see that the pots have not shifted or fallen over. Return any displaced containerized plants to their original positions. Check **bog plants** at the pond's edge to make sure they are getting adequate moisture. The soil should stay moist just below the surface. Water these plants with the hose if needed.

WATERING

As the water in your water garden clears up, this is a good indication that all elements are in a balance. Water that becomes too rich in food sources can encourage filamentous algae or planktonic algae that turns the water pea-soup green. To prevent this:

- Limit food for fish
- Reduce the number of fish in the pond, especially if they are multiplying
- Discontinue fertilizing the plants
- Add more submerged plants
- Shade more of the water surface from the direct sun
- Remove organic debris regularly
- Add barley and lavender bundles to control string algae

Don't allow the water level in the water garden to drop more than an inch or two. The liner should not be exposed to sunshine because this shortens its life span. It there is no rain, and warm weather is causing the water to evaporate, top off the garden with a hose. You may need to add de-chlorinating drops if you have fish and your water provider treats the water with chlorine.

FERTILIZING

If you find that your water plants are growing too fast and the stems are weak and floppy, it may mean they are getting too much fertilizer. Cut back on the feeding. Plants receive some nutrients from water and fish

waste, so you don't always need to fertilize as often as recommended. **Water lilies** that are not blooming may need to be fertilized to coax them to flower.

GROOMING

Remove spent flowers to encourage the production of new blooms. You may want to allow some **lotus** flowers to remain so you can harvest the fruits or sow the seed to produce your own homegrown plants. Yellow leaves should be trimmed off and discarded.

PROBLEMS

Be on the watch for aphids and mites on the foliage of water plants. Mites feed primarily on the underside of the leaves. Dislodge and remove them with a forceful spray of water.

To prevent foliar diseases, remove discolored or spotted leaves. This cultural method will remove disease spores that can spread to other plants.

Filamentous algae can become a weedy pest during the summer. Skim off the floating plants with a plastic leaf rake. Remove the algae from the pond and retire it to the compost pile. You can also spread it underneath perennials as a mulch.

Watch for herons as they discover your water garden in search for a fishy treat. Use netting or a wire covering to discourage them, or place a heron decoy nearby since herons are solitary feeders and don't like company.

NOTES

_____
_____
_____
_____
_____
_____
_____
_____
_____
_____
_____
_____
_____
_____
_____
_____
_____
_____
_____
_____
_____
_____
_____
_____

AUGUST
WATER GARDENS

 PLANNING

If you are planning a vacation, clean your filters and make sure your water garden or pond is filled to capacity before you go away. There is likely to be some evaporation in the heat of summer, and rain can be scarce this month. If small children live in the neighborhood, consider having the water garden covered or fenced while you are gone to prevent accidents. Plants and fish will be able to survive a few weeks while you are away. Arrange with a neighbor or fellow gardener to check the pond if a storm should come up or if you have any special concerns.

August is a good time to choose fish for your water garden if you haven't already. Fish are fun to observe because they can be trained to come on demand for feeding. They are also important to the pond ecology. They consume oxygen, release carbon dioxide for the plants, and control algae. And fish will consume hoards of insects including mosquito larvae.

Planning is necessary before stocking the pond with fish. Various kinds of fish require special conditions to survive. Some fish, like **goldfish**, are very tolerant, while others are sensitive to conditions and will require more care. Some species are carnivorous and will eat the smaller fish. Some are happy in shallow ponds, while others, like **koi**, need water that is at least 3 feet deep.

Deeper ponds allow some fish to overwinter. A shallow pond means that fish will need to be captured and kept in a water-holding tank over the winter. Visit your local library to study up on the various fish species for water gardening in your area.

 PLANTING

Divide and repot potbound water plants in midseason. As plants outgrow their containers, their health and flowering can be diminished. Bulging tubers and restricted, matted roots can actually split the thin nursery pots. **Water lilies** usually need to be repotted every three to four years. Here's how:

• Remove the plant from its potbound container, and lay it on a rock or other hard surface.

• Use a sharp knife or spade to slice through the crown and stems to make rooted halves or quarters, depending upon its size.

• Trim excessively long roots from each chunk, and plant each division in heavy garden soil in its own pot.

• Return one newly potted division to the water garden. You can place the others in an aboveground auxiliary garden or give them to a friend.

CARE

Continue to monitor the water levels in the water garden, and check bog areas for moisture. If necessary, remove a few floating plants, and prune trailing stems of submerged plants to open up space in a crowded water garden. Submerged oxygenating plants should take up only one-third of the total volume of the water.

 WATERING

Continue to check the water level to make sure it doesn't drop too rapidly. Check for leaks in the pond liner and make repairs. Tap water from the hydrant should not be added directly to the garden if your water provider treats the water with chlorine or other chemicals, as this can harm fish. A de-chlorinating additive should be used according to package directions.

FERTILIZING

This is the last month to fertilize **water lilies** if they need it. As the daylight hours decrease, the plants will start to reduce flowering. There are generally enough nutrients in the water to keep them going through the rest of the summer.

 ## GROOMING

As **water lilies** mature with blossoms and lots of foliage, they can become overcrowded. If there is no room for them to spread, correct the situation by repositioning the pots, and prune off excess foliage to thin the plants and reduce disease problems. Remove yellow, dying, or hail-torn leaves promptly from water plants. This will not only improve their appearance but also prevent an outbreak of foliar diseases. Do not let the stems of **bog plants** flop into the water.

Allow the **lotus** flowers to form seedpods. When they are dried and the plant goes dormant, cut the stems and use these ornamental pods for floral arrangements or other craft projects.

GARDENING WITH AN ALTITUDE TIPS
Net the Leaves

Before the leaves fall from deciduous trees and shrubs, cover the surface of your water garden with netting. Fallen leaves will eventually decompose in the water, releasing minerals and gases that are toxic to fish. This decay will also encourage more algae growth.

Use netting or knitted fabric to capture the leaves. After the leaves have collected on the net, carefully drag it off the water's surface, and roll it up so it can be moved to the compost pile. Shred the leaves with a grinder or shredder so they will decompose more rapidly. Replace the netting to collect any late-falling leaves and to thwart predators from feeding on fish that are staying in the pond for winter.

 ## PROBLEMS

Aquatic plants can be attacked by a myriad of insects, particularly aphids in summer and early fall. Cut off the worst of the infested portions. Trim away any dead, damaged, or diseased leaves. Preventing the spread of insects and disease is the best defense.

NOTES

_____
_____
_____
_____
_____
_____
_____
_____
_____
_____
_____
_____
_____
_____
_____
_____
_____
_____
_____

SEPTEMBER
WATER GARDENS

 PLANNING

A water garden can be the focal point in the landscape, but it should blend harmoniously with your terrestrial plants including trees, shrubs, perennials, ground covers and bulbs. Plan to grow perennial ground covers such as *Juniperus horizontalis* about 3 to 4 feet from the water garden's edge. As this evergreen grows and spreads, it will make a transition and fill in to create a natural look at the edge of the water. This is a good time to visit public water gardens to see how professionals create special interest. Take along a notebook or your garden journal to jot down ideas.

As the temperatures begin to cool down by mid-month, it's time to think about overwintering the tender tropical plants. Do you have space, light, and time to do this yourself? If not, treat them as annuals, or give them to other water gardening enthusiasts.

If your water garden is in an aboveground container, your plants will need special attention. You can either put them storage or allow them to die when the hard frost arrives.

Take photographs of the water garden before the season is finished, and add them to your garden journal. Which plants did best? What were the problems? Note any major events such as hail or flooding that may have caused concern. Were critters a nuisance? This will help you plan for future water gardening seasons.

 PLANTING

Dividing and repotting overgrown water plants is best done in spring when they are about to emerge from dormancy. However, if you have time and space for their storage, it may be more convenient to do some transplanting in the early autumn before they enter dormancy. (See April for details.)

Early autumn is a good time to plant the outside edge of the water garden with ground cover plants and hardy bulbs. These will provide early spring interest. Use bulbs that will tolerate moisture such as **Siberian iris, marsh marigold, Japanese primrose, ornamental skunk cabbage,** various **sedges, rushes,** and **ferns.** Check local garden retailers for special sales on water plants. You can add more plants now, especially when you can purchase them at discounted prices.

 CARE

Continue to trim off spent flowers and ripening foliage to prevent them from sinking to the bottom of the pond. Plant debris will quickly deteriorate and foul the water. Allow the plants to gradually die back with the cooler weather. **Marginals** on the pond shelf and **bog plants** along the edge will begin to form seedheads, and their stems will dry and turn brown. Some of the nearby **ornamental grasses** will remain decorative, so allow them to stand through the fall and early winter. This will help soften the edge and add fall and winter interest. As the grasses begin to die back and get floppy, they can be cut to keep the area tidy.

Continue to feed fish while the weather remains mild and water temperatures are 50 degrees Fahrenheit or higher. They will feed voraciously, loading up on food to help them survive the winter. Do not feed more than they can collectively devour within five to 10 minutes. More than that will just dissolve and foul the water.

If frost is predicted in your area before the end of the month, dismantle ornamental containers that hold water plants. Lift the plants, and cut them back for storage at the bottom of the pond, or place them in an unheated area for winter storage. Drain the water from large containers, and bring those indoors that are susceptible to cracking from alternate freezing and thawing. Some tropicals such as **cannas, cypress, bamboo,** and **taro** can be brought indoors and treated like houseplants.

 ## WATERING

Autumn can often have prolonged dry periods. Maintain the water level in the water garden or pond to protect the liner and sustain the plants and fish.

 ## FERTILIZING

There is no need to fertilize water plants this late in the season, because they will not be growing for several months. It is best to add fertilizer tablets in spring.

 ## GROOMING

With the first frost soon approaching, prune off dead stems from the **marginal plants** and **bog plants** to prevent them from flopping over into the water. Treat them as you would any other

perennial, and cut them back within reason to keep the garden neat. Trim away any damaged, dead, diseased, or pest-infested leaves, and discard them in the trash barrel. To plan for the upcoming leaf drop from deciduous trees, be ready to cover the water garden with bird or leaf netting.

GARDENING WITH AN ALTITUDE TIPS
Plan Ahead for Winter

To keep the water from freezing solid in your outdoor water garden, consider installing a heater or di-icer while the weather is still mild. When the temperatures get low enough for ice to form over the water at night, your heater will be in place and ready.

The heater is important, not to keep the pond water heated but to maintain an open area in the ice at all times. Air exchange and release of toxic gases from decaying plants must not stop, or the fish and plants will be harmed.

Open water also reduces the pressure on the pond lining from the ice. As the surface of the pond freezes, it can exert pressure on the pond. You may want to float some old driftwood logs in the pond to relieve some of the pressure.

In some parts of the region where winters get particularly cold and severe, added protection may be warranted to get plants and fish through the winter. If all the plants can be submerged in the deepest end of the pond, cover that area with a large plank extending from one side of the pond to the other. Cover the boards with an additional foot of straw, and cover the straw with a plastic tarp. Anchor the tarp down with bricks or stones.

Be ready for winter by planning ahead now and having the materials you need.

 ## PROBLEMS

Predator birds will have a better chance of getting to the fish when the plant foliage no longer covers the water surface to provide shelter. Set up bird netting, or string monofilament fishing line over the water's surface to foil the blue heron and other opportunistic predators.

OCTOBER
WATER GARDENS

 PLANNING

Now is the time to add thoughts to your garden journal before the memories of the season grow dim. Keep a record of this year's water gardening events, clippings from your local paper or magazines, ideas, problems, and successes of the year. This is helpful so you won't repeat the same mistakes next year.

Evaluate the plants in your water garden and decide which ones to keep; those that have become too invasive or troublesome should be eliminated, while the more expensive **water lilies** will need to be overwintered. If you desire, some of the floating or marginal plants can be treated as annuals and replaced every spring if you don't have the space or proper area to keep them over the winter.

 PLANTING

No planting is done at this time of year. **Tropical water lilies** will have to be lifted and stored in a tank indoors in a cool spot. Some plants including **water hyacinths** are difficult to keep indoors over the winter unless the water temperature is maintained at 65 to 70 degrees Fahrenheit. If needed, lift and divide overgrown plants before they go completely dormant. This may save time next spring.

 CARE

Before freezing weather damages the **marginal plants** and other tender **tropical plants,** bring them to an indoor storage area. Continue to trim away the spent flowers and yellow foliage that is ripening or maturing on the plants. Clean up any leaves that may have sloughed off into the water, and add them to the compost pile.

If needed, clean the pond this month (see cleaning instructions in May). Dredge the bottom of the pond with a net that has a long handle to remove excess sludge. Add a sludge remover such as **Boderia** to help reduce the buildup of this material.

 WATERING

Maintain the water level in the water garden.

 FERTILIZING

As the water temperature drops, most aquatic plants will cease growth and will be getting ready for dormancy. They do not have to be fertilized.

 GROOMING

Deadhead the faded flowers from **water lilies** and other aquatic plants. Trim back the foliage for the deep water and emergent plants. Trim back submerged plants significantly since they will soon die back during the winter months. This reduces the buildup of excess debris at the bottom of the pond where it decays the next season to foul the water. If these plants are in containers, they can be lifted to make the cleanup easier.

 PROBLEMS

Wildlife, including deer, elk, raccoons, herons, squirrels, and other critters, may find the water garden a retreat and a place to feed. Without the cover of floating leaf plants, any remaining fish are fair game if they have no place to hide. Provide the fish with stones, upside-down netted laundry baskets, or sections of PVC pipe 3 to 6 inches in diameter so they can swim to a protected area when predators arrive.

NOVEMBER
WATER GARDENS

 PLANNING

The snow will soon be falling and the water garden is at rest. As the water garden is quiet, the frost has killed back the perennials, and just a few ornamental grasses remain to give height and interest around the pond. I hope you had a pleasant experience growing water plants and adding fish.

To learn more about this specialty gardening, join a water gardening society in your area or read more books about the subject. Surf the Internet for water gardening information to learn about various approaches and techniques. There are several water gardening magazines from which you can glean ideas.

 PLANTING

No planting is recommended at this time of year, unless you have a greenhouse and wish to try to grow seeds from some of the seedpods you salvaged from the summer and fall.

 CARE

Shallow ponds should be drained and cleaned. Cover them with a large sheet of plywood or landscape fabric to keep debris from blowing in. **Hardy water lilies** will need to be lifted out of a shallow pond. Cut away the leaves, and move them to a cool location (40 to 50 degrees Fahrenheit is ideal). Keep the soil damp. This storage technique will work for **marginal plants,** too.

Tropical water lilies and other floating plants can be expensive to replace. If you have space, you can bring them into a storage pool in a sunroom, and keep them there over the winter. Have a bubbler to keep the water moving.

Aboveground water gardens such as half whiskey barrels will freeze during extended cold and dry periods. Move them into a greenhouse or sunroom, or indoors to a cool room with moderate light where the plants can receive full sun for four hours or more.

To prevent ice from forming on the surface of the water garden, trapping carbon dioxide and other gases that can kill fish, keep a water pump running. This water movement prevents at least a small area from freezing solid. In the past, I have placed a hollow log into the pond to introduce oxygen. Do this carefully so as not to injure the fish.

If the water does freeze solid, set a kettle of hot water on the ice to melt an opening. Tie a rope around the kettle or bucket to retrieve it.

 WATERING

Maintain the water level in the water garden to prevent the liner from being exposed to sunlight. Add water slowly, and if it is treated with chlorine, add de-chlorinating drops as recommended on the package label.

 FERTILIZING

None needed!

 GROOMING

Keep leaves, twigs, and other garden debris cleaned off the pond, and recycle these materials to the compost pile.

 PROBLEMS

Trim away any damaged, diseased, or pest-infested leaves on plants that are overwintering indoors. Discard infested foliage in the trash.

December

WATER GARDENS

 PLANNING

Water gardening in December includes poring over catalogs and books, making lists, and planning for next year's garden endeavors. It's a good idea to review your garden journal and note areas where you need to make changes. If there were problems with too much algae or fish that didn't thrive, look back over your notes to see what may have caused these problems. As with most water gardening, monitoring the garden on a regular basis will help prevent many serious problems from occurring in the first place.

You may want to add a fountain or waterfall to your water garden, both for beauty and functionality. Use this dormant period to decide what kind will work best for you and do comparison shopping.

Water garden specialty nurseries are introducing new forms and colors of **water lilies, marginals,** and edge-of-the-pond plants with variegated leaves and stems. For the water garden in containers, there are selections of **dwarf lilies** and more compact marginal plants. Study the catalogs during the cold, dreary days, and jot down some ideas you would like to implement. Take pictures of the water garden before and after the first snow, and observe how a water garden adds accent at all seasons.

 PLANTING

No planting at this time of year. Just decide on what new things you would like to try.

 CARE

The aquatic plants you are storing indoors must be covered with water and should not be allowed to dry out. Cover the containers with plastic wrap to maintain moisture. Leave the sides open so that there is good air circulation. If air is completely excluded, the soil can become rancid and the plants may rot.

 WATERING

If we have a dry winter with little or no rain or snow, it may be necessary to raise the water level of the pond on a warm day. Maximum depth is critical to keep fish alive, salvage the plants, and protect the liner. If you use water treated with chemicals, add de-chlorinating drops if there are fish in the water.

 FERTILIZING

No fertilizer is needed now.

 GROOMING

Check that pots of hardy plants are at least 2 feet deep in the water at the bottom of the pond. **Cattails** and **water iris** should be kept in a shallow area of the pond to spend the winter. They will not bloom if they do not experience a cold treatment. No plant stems or foliage should protrude above the water surface. If some have started to send up shoots because of a prolonged mild winter, cut them back to the soil level in their pots; otherwise, they will freeze.

 PROBLEMS

Voles can dig around water features and wreak havoc. When you inspect the water garden, check for critter damage. If you detect any, you may need to set traps. Baiting the traps with peanut butter will help capture voles and meadow mice.

JOHN'S HOMEMADE REMEDIES

Compiling this book of advice and personal observations has led me into closer contact with our horticultural past, which is a combination of science and art. It has added to my respect for the experience and wisdom of the Gardeners Who Have Gone Before, those who were willing to experiment with natural ways to combat pests and diseases.

Twenty-six years of hosting a garden talk radio show in the Rocky Mountain region has led me to discover the strong sense of nature's enduring patterns and the forces that guide gardeners to work the earth and to achieve a sense of accomplishment. I've learned that the old fashioned traditions can be not only quite effective but also less meddlesome and less destructive to our earth's resources.

I hope you find these homemade recipes and remedies useful in your gardening endeavors. You may be creative and discover some of your own safe, natural methods of dealing with the various pests that invade your yard.

May your garden grow and prosper!

SOAP SPRAY FOR APHIDS, SPIDER MITES, AND OTHER PESTS
Household dishwashing soaps and liquid hand soaps have been used for generations to control insect pests in both indoor and outdoor gardens. Many are effective insecticides when used as a diluted spray. As products change or are "improved," be cautious that they do not contain additives such as bleach or degreasers that may be more caustic to the plant foliage. The old-fashioned, biodegradable soaps or liquid detergents are generally the safest to use.

Ingredients:
- 1 to 2 tablespoons liquid soap, with no bleach or degreaser additives.
- 1 gallon water

Pour the mixture into a spray bottle, and apply to the underside of the foliage, on infested stems, or directly to the insect pest.

Used at a diluted rate, soap sprays are generally safe for most plants. Some plants with waxy leaves may be more sensitive to soap sprays, so test the dilution on a small amount of foliage first to check for damage. **Caution:** Do not apply to the foliage during the heat of the day. Always apply soap sprays in the coolest part of the day or on an overcast day.

HOMEMADE HORTICULTURAL OIL
Make your own horticultural oil from familiar household products. Use this spray to reduce invasions of aphids, whiteflies, soft scale, and spider mites.

Ingredients:
- 1 tablespoon liquid dishwashing detergent, preferably lemon-scented (The soap is needed to emulsify the oil in water)
- 1 cup corn, peanut, safflower, soybean, or sunflower oil

Add 1 to 2½ teaspoons of this stock solution to 1 cup of water. Pour solution into a plastic pump-handled bottle. Agitate the mixture and spray onto the undersides and topsides of infested leaves.

TIRED AND ACHING ROSES? TRY EPSOM SALTS!
Did you know that **rose bushes** like some Epsom salts?

Epsom salts can be used as a supplemental fertilizer on your rose bushes. American Rose Society members in Portland, Oregon, found that applying Epsom Salts led to higher growth rates, increased basal breaks, stronger stems and improved color and foliage.

Epsom salts are suggested for use on magnesium-deficient soils. Use at the rate of one tablespoon per rose bush each month throughout the growing season. Stop applications by mid-August.

ROSE TONIC

One of my favorite and most effective fertilizers for all roses is this homemade rose tonic:

Ingredients:
- 5 tablespoons of Epsom salts
- 1/2 cup fish emulsion
- 1/3 cup Sequestrene™ Chelated Iron
- 5 tablespoons Bloom-promoting fertilizer (15-30-15 or 10-60-10) soluble plant food

Combine above ingredients in 5 gallons of warm water, and mix thoroughly.

This homemade fertilizer mixture will "perk up" your **roses, flowering shrubs, perennials** and **annual flowers.** It is especially good to use after transplanting bedding plants and vegetables.

How to apply Rose Tonic to your **roses, ornamental trees,** and **shrubs:**

1. Start applying this fertilizer to rose bushes soon after leaf emergence in mid to late spring.

2. Water the rose garden prior to the application of the Rose Tonic.

3. Use 2 quarts of tonic for each rose bush.

4. Water the fertilizer into the soil with an additional 2 quarts of plain water.

5. You can apply fertilizer to the rose garden every four to six weeks throughout the growing season; stop applications after mid-August.

How to apply Rose Tonic to flowers:

Apply this homemade plant fertilizer to annual and perennial flowers early in the spring to get them off to a happy and healthy start. Follow up with applications on a monthly basis throughout the growing season.

CRITTER REPELLENT AND NATURAL INSECTICIDE

If you've been searching for an effective and non-toxic spray that will zap pesky bugs, and repel rabbits, dogs, cats, deer, chipmunks, and other critters, this one really works.

Ingredients:
- Dry, crushed hot cayenne peppers
- Liquid detergent
- Vegetable oil
- 1 quart water

Steep 3 tablespoons of dry, crushed hot peppers in 1/2 cup of hot water, covered, for an hour. Strain out the particles of peppers, and set this solution aside.

In a separate container, mix 2 to 3 teaspoons liquid detergent (Murphy's Oil Soap™ or a lemon-scented dishwashing liquid) with 1 cup of vegetable oil. Shake vigorously to emulsify. Add this mixture to 1 quart of warm water.

Add the pepper solution to the liquid detergent formulation. Pour into a tank sprayer or spray bottle, and apply at 10-day intervals as an all-purpose insect spray for whiteflies, aphids, flea beetles, spider mites, and various insects on **vegetables, herbs, evergreens,** and other ornamentals. The odor will repel other critters, too.

Note: It is wise to test this spray on a single plant, because it may cause tip burn in hot weather. This acts like a contact insecticide, so spray the mixture directly on pests. Avoid breathing fumes, which may be irritating to the nose and eyes.

SPICY SQUIRREL, CHIPMUNK, MEADOW MOUSE, AND PORCUPINE STOPPER

After planting your spring-flowering **bulbs** in autumn, you can spray this homemade mixture over the soil. This will thwart squirrels from digging the bulbs up for their dinner. Young **trees** and **shrubs** with tender bark can be protected from nibbling meadow mice, voles, and porcupines if you spray this mixture around the base of the plants. Many critters are fond of fruit tree bark, so use it in the home orchard.

As winter turns to spring, mix more of this spicy mixture to apply to the edges of **bulb** beds to stop squirrels and chipmunks in their tracks.

Ingredients:
- 3 tablespoons hot pepper sauce
- 1 quart water
- 1 teaspoon lemon-scented dishwashing detergent
- 1 teaspoon cayenne pepper
- Spray bottle

Mix all ingredients together, and pour the mixture into the spray bottle for application.

POWDERY MILDEW REMEDY

Ingredients:
- 1$1/2$ teaspoons baking soda
- 1 teaspoon vegetable oil
- 1 quart water

Mix together thoroughly. Pour into a spray bottle or tank sprayer. Apply to infected plants; spray both upper and lower surfaces of the leaves.

This spray is particularly effective to control powdery mildew on **lilacs, Virginia creeper (woodbine), zinnias, dahlias, asters, honeysuckle, crabapples, bee balm**, vegetables, and other plants that are susceptible to this fungus. Repeat applications after overhead irrigation or a heavy rain.

ECO-FRIENDLY CONTROL FOR GARDEN SLUGS

They hide during the day and make their sneak attacks at night. They munch on the new and succulent leaves of flowers, vegetables, even lawns, and they can demolish whole plants with their voracious appetites. They are slugs!

You've most likely heard that beer attracts slugs. It does. They crawl to containers filled with beer, glide down into the brew, and drown. But I'm not fond of sharing my beer with slugs. Here's a homemade remedy that works better than beer and discourages intoxicated cats!

Ingredients:
- 1 cup water
- 1 teaspoon raw sugar
- $1/4$ teaspoon yeast

Warm water in microwave for one to two minutes. Add one teaspoon sugar, and stir until dissolved. Add $1/4$ teaspoon of yeast, and mix thoroughly. Put this liquid slug bait in shallow containers, like empty tuna cans or yogurt cups cut in half. Bury the containers in the ground to their rims. The slugs will crawl in and drown. Repeat as often as necessary.

Traps should be checked each morning, and any slugs collected should be destroyed or cooked up for "Rocky Mountain escargot."

STALK SLUGS WITH AMMONIA-WATER SOLUTION

If you like adventure, become a slug slayer with a squirt bottle filled with a 10-percent solution of household cleaning ammonia and water. Take a good flashlight out in the garden at night to search for the slimy creatures. One squirt with this homemade remedy will cause quick death while at the same time adding a bit of fertilizer—the ammonia is a nitrogen compound that can be used by plants.

SPEARMINT INSECTICIDE

Herbs are not only useful for spicing up food, making teas, and concocting poultices; some can be used to zap pesky bugs outdoors and indoors. Here's a fragrant recipe my Italian grandma used to control aphids, spider mites, fungus gnats, caterpillars, weevils, and ants.

Ingredients:
- 1 cup chopped spearmint leaves
- 1 cup green onion tops
- $1/2$ cup chopped hot cayenne pepper
- $1/2$ cup water
- $1/2$ cup liquid soap (Murphy's oil soap or a lemon-scented dishwashing detergent)
- 1 gallon water

Combine spearmint leaves, green onion tops, and hot red pepper in a blender. Add water to assist in the blending process. Once blended, pour this solution into 1 gallon of water. Add the liquid soap. Strain and store this concentrated solution. Before use in a pressure tank or hose-end sprayer, dilute by adding $1/2$ cup of concentrated spearmint spray mixture to 1 quart of water.

For small houseplants, you can dunk the plant foliage in the diluted solution. Place a newspaper or cardboard cover over the soil. It is very effective on aphids, caterpillars, and mites.

For outdoor use, strain the mixture as indicated, and spray on infested foliage and stems. It is effective on a broad range of chewing pests.

TOMATO TONIC FOR INSECT AND DISEASE CONTROL

One of our favorite fruits from the garden, the **tomato,** is the target of aphids, psyllids, and whiteflies during this season. Here is an old-fashioned, homemade remedy that can prevent and reduce an outbreak of insect pests. The baking soda will assault plant diseases too!

Ingredients:
- 1 tablespoon baking soda
- 1 tablespoon antibacterial liquid hand soap
- 1 tablespoon tomato and vegetable food (5-10-5)
- 1 tablespoon Epsom salts
- 1 tablespoon soy or canola oil
- 3 tablespoon rubbing alcohol
- 1 gallon water

Mix until ingredients are thoroughly dissolved in the water. Warm or tepid water can help speed up the process. Pour this homemade remedy in a $1 1/2$ or 2 gallon tank sprayer, and close the lid tightly. Pressurize the tank, and you're ready to spray the tomato plants. Apply during the cool of the day, early morning or late evening. Repeat every 7 to 10 days depending upon weather conditions, more often after a heavy rainfall.

Old-timers claim this tomato tonic will also help prevent powdery mildew on foliage.

WEED BUSTER

The most natural way to get rid of weeds in your garden is the "cowboy way," hand-pulling or digging. If you're getting tired of this method, you can thwart them with a shot of this homemade vinegar spray. Grandma used this to kill weeds growing in driveway and sidewalk cracks. This spray has a short residual presence in the soil, too, and can keep weeds from coming back for several months.

Ingredients:
- $1 1/2$ cups vinegar (as close to 10% acidity as possible)
- $1/2$ cup dishwashing soap like Ivory or Joy
- Pump spray bottle

Fill a spray bottle with the mixture of vinegar and dishwashing soap. Spot-spray weeds by dousing the foliage and crown (the area at the base of the weed). Be careful not to splash any vinegar solution on plants that you want to keep.

Tip: To shield desirable plants, cut the bottom out of a plastic milk jug, and place it over the weed. Apply the spray through the top opening.

Note: If using a metal tank sprayer, rinse the sprayer with water because vinegar is corrosive.

SOIL SOLARIZATION FOR SOILBORNE DISEASE AND PEST CONTROL

If you've been plagued by recurring soil-inhabiting pests or diseases, here's a simple and inexpensive way to sterilize the soil without chemicals. Cover moist soil with transparent polyethylene plastic for six to eight weeks during the late summer and early fall. The process, known as soil solarization, also improves yields and crop quality.

During the process, radiant heat from the sun raises soil temperatures to levels lethal to plant pathogens such as *Verticillium* and *Fusarium*, weed seeds and seedlings, nematodes, and some soil-inhabiting mites. For effective treatment, the area should be moist, level, and free of weeds, debris or large clods. Air pockets will slow the heating process, so press the plastic to the soil surface, and anchor it by burying the edges under soil. Moisture conducts heat faster and makes organisms more sensitive. Irrigate the area before laying the plastic. Or, soak the area afterward by inserting hoses under one end of the tarp.

Polyethylene plastic of 1 mil thickness is the most efficient and economical for soil heating. Patch holes as they occur. Thicker plastic up to 2 mils can withstand higher winds, but it reflects more solar energy away, which results in lower soil temperatures.

Killing of pathogens and pests is related to time and temperature. Although some pests and organisms are killed within days, allow at least four to six weeks of treatment in full sun during the summer and early fall for maximum effectiveness.

Research has shown that soil solarization can increase yields and result in earlier crops, possibly by promoting the presence of beneficial micro- and macroorganisims such as *mycorrhiza* and by destroying phytotoxic substances in the soil.

FUNGI KILLER TO CLEAN AND DISINFECT CONTAINERS

When I was a young boy, Grandma would periodically clean flower pots with a household solution prepared from liquid bleach. Even with today's technology of fungicides, this homemade remedy remains one of the most effective and least expensive ways to disinfect containers and gardening tools. **CAUTION:** Wear rubber gloves to protect your hands.

1. Scrub dirty clay and plastic pots with a brush to remove caked on soil and other debris.

2. Soak them in a solution of one part liquid bleach to ten parts water.

3. Allow the pots to soak for 20 to 30 minutes, remove from solution and let dry.

4. If you clean garden tools with this solution, remember that bleach can hasten rust formation on metal parts. Rinse metal parts thoroughly, and dry with a cotton cloth.

PRESERVE WINTER SQUASH AND GOURDS

Bleach can make winter squash and gourds last longer. Add 1 tablespoon of bleach to a quart of water. Wash dirt and other solids from the squash and gourds with the bleach solution, then dry with cloth or paper towel. Now your squash and gourds are ready to be put into storage in a cool, dry storage area till you need them.

FOUNTAIN OF YOUTH FOR SEEDS

Heat and humidity will shorten the life span of seeds. Specialists gently dry bulk seeds and seal them in moisture-proof containers with a desiccant to absorb moisture and keep them dry. Next, the seeds are placed in cool, air-conditioned storage. These precautions prolong seed vigor for three to five years. Now you can utilize a similar but inexpensive method of storing leftover garden seeds, using powdered milk as a desiccant. Here's how:

1. Unfold and stack four facial tissues.

2. On one corner of the stack, place 2 heaping tablespoons of powdered milk from a freshly opened pouch or box to guarantee dryness.

3. Fold and roll the facial tissue to make a small pouch. Secure with tape or a rubber band. The tissue will prevent the milk from sifting out and will prevent seed packets from touching the desiccant as it absorbs moisture.

4. Place the desiccant pouch in a wide-mouthed jar, and immediately drop in packets of leftover seeds.

5. Seal the jar tightly using a rubber ring to exclude moist air. Store the jar in the refrigerator, not the freezer.

6. Replace the desiccant once or twice yearly. Dried milk is "hygroscopic" and will quickly soak up moisture from the air when you open the bottle. Therefore, be quick about it when you remove seed packets, and recap the jar quickly.

7. Use seeds as soon as possible.

CUT FLOWER COCKTAIL

When you buy a bouquet of flowers, the florist will usually include a packet of floral preservative. It's formulated with sugar to feed the rootless flowers, citric acid to lower the water's pH, and disinfectant to inhibit microorganisms that will clog up the "plumbing system of the flower stem." You should already have most of these components to make your own floral preservative.

Ingredients:
- 1 tablespoon light corn syrup
- 1/2 teaspoon liquid chlorine bleach
- 2 tablespoons lemon or lime juice
- 1 quart warm water

Combine ingredients in the water, and mix thoroughly. Before placing the flowers in the vase, strip off the lower leaves that would otherwise be underwater. Excessive foliage in the water increases bacteria, contaminates the water, and shortens the shelf life of your cut flowers.

GARDEN STORAGE IN A MAILBOX

If you're tired of making trips between your garden and tool shed, here's a nifty short cut. Install a large mailbox close to the garden. A mailbox is a great place to store gloves, pruners, scissors, and various other small garden tools. Your equipment will be close at hand and still protected from the elements.

Visit your local hardware store, and purchase a wooden fencepost (4 inches x 4 inches or 6 inches x 6 inches). Set the post with about one-third of the total length buried in the ground. In clay soils, dig the posthole twice the diameter of the post. If you prefer, anchor the post with a concrete collar (a layer of concrete placed in the posthole around the post and extended slightly above ground to shed water). Once the post is set, secure a mailbox to the top for tool storage. You can be creative and decorate it to match your gardening style.

GREEN TOMATO ROUNDUP

If a hard freeze is on its way, you can either pick all your **tomatoes** or, if you have space, pull whole plants. If you harvest the whole plants, hang them upside down in a garage or basement, and let the tomatoes ripen gradually. Check them frequently to get the ripe ones before they hit the floor and splat!

If you pick green tomatoes, sort them by size. Use the smaller ones in recipes that call for green tomatoes. Those about three-fourths of full size will ripen. Place them in a shallow cardboard box, stem-end facing upwards, and cover them with newspaper. You don't need to wrap each fruit individually. Store in the basement or warm area of the garage. Lift the newspaper cover every day, and check for ripe tomatoes. Remove any that show signs of rotting.

THISTLE AND BINDWEED ELIMINATOR

To eliminate tough weeds like Canada thistle and bindweed (wild morning glory) once and for all, weedkillers such as glyphosate or 2,4-D are more readily absorbed translocated throughout the plant and root system in autumn. You can safely use 2,4-D in autumn lawns without harming grasses. In areas beyond the lawn, use glyphosate. **As with all weed control products, read the label, and follow directions explicitly.** Do not allow weedkillers to contact plants other than target weeds.

REPLANTING TIME-SAVER

When replanting any woody plant, ignore recommendations to cut back the branches to "balance" a reduced root system. There is no justification for this advice. Prune only damaged or overlong branches, or those with very narrow angles and weak attachment points that may break under heavy snow or fruit loads.

The more leaf surface a newly-moved plant has, the more food energy it can make for itself, and the more roots it can regenerate. This is exactly what you want to happen, and it will ensure a more vigorous and healthy plant.

COMPOSTING: TRANSFORM HOUSEHOLD WASTE INTO 'BLACK GOLD'

All organic matter will eventually decompose. Composting speeds the process by providing an ideal environment for bacteria and other decomposing microorganisms. The final product, humus or compost, looks and feels like fertile garden soil. This dark, crumbly, earthy-smelling stuff works wonders on all kinds of soil and provides vital nutrients to help plants grow and stay healthy.

Decomposing micro-organisms need four key elements to thrive: nitrogen, carbon, moisture, and oxygen. For best results, mix materials high in nitrogen, such as fresh grass clippings and clover, with those high in carbon, such as dried leaves and shredded wood products. If there is not a good supply of nitrogen-rich material, a handful of general lawn fertilizer will help the nitrogen-carbon ratio. Moisture is provided by rain, but you will usually have to sprinkle the compost to keep it damp. Be careful not to saturate the pile. Oxygen is supplied by turning or mixing the pile. More turning will yield faster decomposition.

Getting Started

Many materials can be added to a compost pile, including leaves, grass clippings, straw, woody stems, vegetable and fruit scraps, coffee grounds, livestock manure, sawdust, and shredded paper. Avoid using diseased plants, meat scraps that may attract flies and animals, or dog and cat manure which may carry disease.

Composting can be as simple or as involved as you would like. It depends on how much yard waste you have, how fast you want results, and how much effort you're willing to invest.

Cold Composting

Cold composting requires no maintenance. You just pile grass clippings and dry leaves on the ground or in a bin. Since you're doing nothing to speed the process, you'll have to wait a year or more for the materials to decompose. Cold composting works well if you're short on time or have little yard waste. Keep weeds and diseased plants out of the mix. Add yard waste as it becomes available.

Hot Composting

Hot composting requires more work, but with the right ingredients and a little daily effort, you can have finished compost in a few months. Hot piles can be built all at once in a 4- to 5-foot cube and turned regularly. As the decomposition occurs, the pile will begin to shrink. A 3-foot cube is needed to maintain necessary heat. Hot piles can reach 110 to 160 degrees Fahrenheit, which kills most weed seeds and plant diseases.

1. On a level site, lay down a base of bricks or prunings to promote air circulation.

2. Spread several inches of the high-carbon material, then mix high-carbon and high-nitrogen material together. Water periodically.

3. Punch holes in the sides of the pile for aeration.

4. The pile will heat up and then begin to cool. Start turning when the pile's temperature begins to drop.

5. Move materials from the center of the pile to the outside and vice versa. Turn every day or two, and you should get compost in a few months. Turning compost every other week will give compost in four to six months. Finished compost will smell sweet and be cool and crumbly to the touch.

FOR YOUR GARDEN'S HEALTH

PLANT DAMAGE: CAUSE AND CURE

To preserve an ecological balance in your landscape, take time to accurately identify the insects in your lawn and garden before you turn to an arsenal of chemical pest killers. Many times in our efforts to control pests, we also destroy beneficial insects and ultimately upset the natural balance in our own backyards. We strongly urge that you take steps to preserve the local ecosystem.

A safer and often more reliable concept in lawn and garden management to control pests, while reducing the use of chemicals, is known as Integrated Pest Management or IPM. IPM combines a variety of eco-friendly methods to control insects, diseases, and weeds, including natural, physical, mechanical, cultural and biological tactics.

Treatments are made only when and where monitoring has determined that the pest problem will cause significant damage. Timing of treatments is critical to insure the most effective control that is least disruptive to natural predators.

Knowing what a pest feeds upon, what feeds upon the pest, and what other factors are favorable or unfavorable to its survival will help to determine a multitude of control strategies.

Numerous pests inhabit the landscapes, and we will discuss a few of the major pests you should watch for. By monitoring the life in your lawn and garden, you will be better equipped to allow beneficial organisms to do their job of natural control.

Aphids

Aphids are among the most common landscape pests, attacking trees, shrubs, and flowers at the beginning and end of the growing season. Some 4,000 species of aphids have been described, and more are likely to be discovered and named. Aphids of assorted sizes and colors suck the life out of plants. They stunt growth, deform buds and flowers, and distort leaves. Some aphids produce fine filaments of wax around their bodies and are known as woolly aphids. As they feed, aphids excrete a sticky, shiny honeydew on leaf surfaces, which attracts ants. The honeydew is a good medium for the development and growth of sooty mold fungus.

Natural enemies: Many predators feed on aphids. Among them are the familiar ladybird beetles, lacewings, and syrphid flies. The disadvantage of using aphid predators outdoors is that they often move to find more abundant colonies of aphids as populations begin to decrease. Whenever possible, we suggest that you encourage native predators.

Physical controls: Grandma's old-fashion method of washing aphids off infested plants with a strong stream of water is a good method of control. Many can be killed by this method, while spiders and other insect predators will devour others once the aphids hit the ground. The disadvantage of this procedure is that water-washing must be repeated every three to four days, until natural enemies come into the garden and start to take over.

Chemical controls: When natural enemies and physical controls are not effective, the use of insecticides may be warranted. Insecticidal soap sprays, pyrethrins, and other products labeled for aphid control may be used. Follow label directions and precautions.

Leafhoppers

This group of insects has the ability to transmit diseases such as curly top virus and aster yellows. Leafhoppers are about $1/8$-inch, elongate insects that fly and jump away quickly when disturbed. The young run sideways or forward and backward. Both adults and young will feed on the undersides of leaves, which soon become stippled with tiny white dots. "Hopperburn" is a type of injury that can be a result from leafhopper infestation. Leaves look scorched as they begin to die back.

Natural controls: Green lacewings, hunting wasps, and damsel bugs are predators of leafhoppers. Parasitic wasps and diseases are also natural enemies of some leafhopper species.

Physical and cultural controls: Hose off plants to dislodge many of the leafhoppers that are attacking plants. Late winter and early spring pruning will remove overwintering eggs under the bark.

Chemical controls: Insecticidal soap sprays, the new horticultural oils, and carbaryl can effectively control newly hatched young. Follow label directions and precautions.

Caterpillars

This varied group of insects represents the immature stages of moths and butterflies. They come in all shapes and colors. Some are named for their appearance or life cycle, such as leaf roller, webworm, cutworm, armyworm, leaf tier, cabbage looper, skeletonizer, and hornworm. They chew portions of leaves, and some cut off plant stems. Tent caterpillars spin masses of webs intertwined among the branches and stay grouped together as they feed on the foliage. When full-grown, tent caterpillars will leave the web tent and find places to pupate.

Natural and biological controls: Many naturally occurring predators and parasites reduce severe caterpillar infestations. Bacterial sprays of *Bacillus thuringiensis* (Bt) can control many types of caterpillars.

Mechanical and physical methods: Handpicking is effective in small plantings, and periodic hosing with a forceful jet of water can destroy many caterpillars. Floating row covers will help to exclude adult butterflies and moths from laying eggs. Removing the visible tent can easily destroy tent caterpillars by exposing them to predators. Constructing barriers around vulnerable plants can control cutworms and armyworms that inhabit the soil. You can cut yogurt containers, cardboard milk cartons, paper cups, or strips of roofing paper to create a barrier around plant stems. Bury the cup an inch beneath the soil, with an inch above ground to protect the plant stem from damage.

Chemical controls: Pyrethrums, new horticultural oils, neem oil extracts, insecticidal soaps, and various insecticides can control caterpillars. Follow label directions and precautions.

Slugs

They make sneak attacks at night, chew leaves, devour succulent stems, and infest lawns. Signs of their invasion can be found in the morning as shiny, dry slime trails leaving the ravaged area.

Slugs are not insects but mollusks, related to shellfish such as clams, and they feed by rasping or scraping plant tissues. They can cause significant damage and lots of frustration for vegetable, fruit, and flower gardeners. Slugs creep along a cushion of mucous or "slime," and they primarily come out at dusk to feed during the night, avoiding hot, drying conditions. They can also be active during rainy, cloudy weather.

Natural enemies: If you live on a farm or ranch, peacocks, ducks, and geese roaming the landscape will devour these delicacies. Toads and snakes will also feed on slugs. Even larvae of some fireflies and parasitic flies will seek out, attack, and parasitize young slugs.

Physical controls: Conscientious handpicking where slugs are a problem is an important control and can be combined with other tactics. If you're squeamish about picking up slugs, wear plastic gloves, or use tweezers to capture them. Put them in a container of half vinegar and half water to finish them out.

Trapping slugs in shady areas of the garden can be effective. Overturn clay pots, and leave openings under the rims to lure slugs into cool, shady retreats during the early morning hours. Inverted grapefruit and orange halves (after you've eaten the contents) are excellent lures. Just pick up the collection of slugs the following day. Slugs are attracted to fermenting liquids, so beer works well as bait, that is if you're willing to share the brew. Shallow containers (such as empty tuna or cat food cans) can be buried with rims level to the ground and filled with beer. A mixture of one teaspoon sugar and $1/4$ teaspoon yeast dissolved in a cup of water is another homemade recipe that will attract slugs. Traps should be checked each morning, and any slugs collected should be destroyed.

Barriers against slugs are becoming more popular. Slugs will avoid crossing copper barriers since the metal is toxic to them. Copper strips at least $2^1/2$ inches wide can be placed around vulnerable garden areas. To be effective, make sure no leaves or stems bridge the copper strips allowing slugs to cross over and invade.

Diatomaceous earth, sawdust, and hardwood and softwood ashes are good barriers if kept dry. They become less effective, however, when wet from rain or irrigation.

Chemical controls: In damp protected spots, chemical baits can be placed. To prevent children, pets, and wildlife from getting to the bait, be creative in applying the material. Place it underneath stones, boards, or in sections of PVC pipe. The slugs will crawl to the baited areas, feed, and die.

Insecticides are not effective against slugs and their relatives. You should use molluscicides containing metaldehyde, available in a variety of solid and liquid formulations. Read and follow the label and all precautions.

Spider Mites
Summer's heat and dry conditions favor the activity of tiny creatures known as spider mites. Populations can explode since new generations appear every 10 days. Spider mites are not insects; they are more closely related to spiders and ticks. Though tiny, the damage they inflict makes them mighty.

Symptoms of spider mite damage include: leaves stippled with tiny yellow or white dots; silvery streaking; and fine webbing between leaves and stems. Ornamental landscape plants such as evergreens (**spruce, pine, juniper**) and deciduous trees and shrubs can be targets of spider mites. Flowers, vegetables, herbs, and fruit plants are also attacked.

How to check for Spider mites: If foliage shows any of the above symptoms, turn the leaves over, and use a magnifying glass to look for minute ($1/16$-inch or less) specks and eggs. Tap or shake leaves or needles of a suspect branch over a sheet of white paper. If tiny specks appear and start to crawl, you've got spider mites.

Natural and biological controls: Tiny pirate bugs and predatory species will feed on spider mites. Under conditions of adequate humidity, fungi can kill mites.

Cultural controls: Hose down infested plants with water to dislodge and even kill mites. Maintain plant health and vigor by providing adequate water during the summer. This prevents stress and helps to reduce a severe outbreak of mites.

Chemical controls: Be careful when selecting pesticide controls. Some such as carbaryl can aggravate spider mite problems by killing their natural enemies. Insecticidal soaps, sulfur dusts, and homemade soap sprays can suppress spider mite infestations. Various products claiming to control mites are available. Always read and follow label directions and heed precautions.

Flower Thrips
These pests are very small but can be extremely destructive to developing flowers such as **gladiolus, roses, dahlias, lilies,** and **irises.** Thrips are typically yellowish-brown to amber-colored insects. They damage flowers by rasping the tissues and sucking up the sap that oozes out. Rosebuds often become discolored and fail to

open. Flowers are distorted as if poisoned. Thrips also act as vectors to introduce and spread diseases such as necrotic spot viruses and tomato spotted wilt.

Natural and biological control: Watering overhead and heavy rains that crust the soil serve as abiotic controls of flower thrips. Predatory mites are used in greenhouse situations to control infestations of thrips. Minute pirate bugs, ladybugs, lacewings, and big-eyed bugs will often feed on thrips. The fungus *Beauveria bassiana* will infect these pests and reduce populations.

Cultural controls: Yellow and blue sticky traps are very effective in luring and capturing winged thrips before they can cause injury. Regularly "deadhead" flowers and flower buds that show symptoms of thrip damage, and discard in the trash. This will prevent them from developing in the blossoms and will reduce a severe outbreak in your garden. Severely diseased plants should be pulled up and promptly destroyed. To prevent tomato spotted wilt, select disease-free transplants early in the season.

Chemical controls: Controlling thrips with pesticides is difficult and often not very effective. Those with systemic activity are generally the most effective but must be used with care. Read and follow label directions.

Whiteflies

These common summer garden pests can also be a problem on houseplants. The young nymphs and adults cause damage by sucking plant juices from the underside of the leaves. They excrete sticky "honeydew" that is often colonized by a sooty mold. If you brush up against a plant and see a cloud of tiny white moth-like pests flying about, you are dealing with whiteflies. Many generations can continue throughout the growing season as long as temperatures remain warm.

Natural and biological controls: Whiteflies cannot survive freezing temperatures and will generally die out in unprotected areas of the garden. However, if you bring houseplants indoors, they can continue to survive and breed. Parasitic

wasps have been effective in greenhouse conditions. Check garden catalogs and suppliers that specialize in distributing biological control agents.

Cultural controls: Yellow sticky traps are very effective in keeping populations of whiteflies down to a minimum. The flies can also be repelled from plants by using light-colored mulches such as newspaper or aluminum foil.

Chemical controls: Most whitefly controls are for the adult stages and include pyrethrins or closely related insecticides. Some may not be appropriate for edible crops. Always read and follow the label instructions before applying any insecticide. Refined horticultural oils, neem oil, and homemade soap sprays are effective against the nymphs. Repeated applications are necessary since egg and adult stages often escape these treatments. Be sure to spray the leaf undersides thoroughly to destroy the nymphs.

Blister Beetles

Most blister beetles emerge in June and July and feed on leaves and flowers, often stripping a plant of its foliage and causing serious damage. These pests often attack **potatoes, beans, peas,** and other **legumes**, but other vegetables and ornamental trees and shrubs can be attacked as well. Blister beetles feed in packs, massing in a small area of the garden or on a tree or shrub. They appear and then disappear quickly.

Mechanical controls: Blister beetles can be excluded from susceptible plants by placing a shade cloth or a floating row cover over the plants. Beetles can be handpicked, too, but they do produce a chemical that can be injurious to skin (hence the name), so don a pair of gloves before picking.

Borers

The grub-looking larval stages of the shothole borer will make tunnels underneath the bark of fruit trees such as **cherry, peach,** and **plum**. They will also attack ornamental trees and shrubs of similar species. Constant attacks and girdling wounds can eventually cause sections of the branch or twig to die. Trees and shrubs that are already in a stressed state are more vulnerable than vigorous, healthy plants. When it's time for the adult beetles to emerge through the bark, they chew exit holes that look like holes made from a shotgun. Branches often will ooze a sticky sap from these tunnels.

Another serious pest of the *Prunus* family is the peach tree borer. The larvae will tunnel under the bark of **peaches, apricot, plum,** and **cherry trees**. Damage is usually most evident at the base of the tree, and the tunneling and chewing injuries will weaken and often kill trees. The adult moths fly from June through August, and female moths lay their eggs on the lower branches or in the soil near weak or previously wounded trees. Larvae will feed through spring and will produce deep, gouging wounds that ooze sap that may contain chewed wood fragments.

Cultural controls: Shothole borers rarely attack and will not thrive in trees that are growing vigorously. Trees stressed by drought, winter injury, trunk wounds, poor site conditions, or other factors are at greater risk to borer damage. Prune out dead or dying branches and limbs in which borers breed. Since many borers can continue to develop in freshly pruned wood, remove and destroy it before the adult beetles emerge.

Peach crown borers lay eggs around wounds or cracks at the base of the tree. Avoid wounding the trunk; trim weeds and grass away from the trunk with a grass clipper, not a "weed whacker." Also, an organic mulch around the base of the tree seems to reduce borer invasions. White latex paint applied to cracks will deter the female moths from depositing eggs.

If you have time, larvae can be dug out and destroyed using an ice pick or stiff piece of clothes hanger wire. Do this with care, however, to avoid creating a larger wound and causing further damage to the tree.

Chemical controls: These are not effective once borers have tunneled underneath the bark. Preventative treatments of insecticides can be applied to the trunk and branches while the female adults are active and laying eggs. Read and follow label directions carefully.

For peach crown borers, the application of mothballs or paradichloro-benzene crystals can fumigate larvae within the trunk. Apply these crystals around the base of the tree, and temporarily mound soil over the crystals to help retain the fumigant gas in the region of borer infestation. Do not place the crystals directly on the trunk or bark of the tree.

Voles, Meadow, and Field Mice

These critters can severely damage ornamental trees and shrubs, fruit trees, ground covers, and perennial flowers. They cause damage by gnawing bark and roots. Voles are noted for tunneling through lawns covered by snow.

Controls: Barriers constructed of hardware cloth are effective. When planting a new tree, make a cylinder to fit around the tree trunk, but not snug against the bark. Bury the bottom edge at least 8 inches below the surface. Note: To avoid injuring the roots, remove the barrier after one of two years, or re-install another barrier farther away from the trunk.

Reduce the numbers of these prolific reproducers by various trapping methods. Snap traps are effective in the fall and winter seasons.

Mousetrap tips: Locate the vole tunnels by probing with a wooden dowel or an old ski pole. Open them at 8-foot intervals, removing enough soil to allow a mousetrap to sit crosswise on the bottom of the tunnel. Bait the trap with peanut butter. It is very important that light not reach the trap site or the critters won't wander there. Cover the trap site with an inverted flowerpot or a piece of plywood or strong cardboard.

Rodenticides: These poisons must be applied with great care because they can enter the food chain and harm pets, predatory birds, fish, andother nontarget creatures. **Read and follow the label directions exactly.** Place bait in the runways next to the tunnels or in burrow entrances. Replace bait every week or so to take care of a severe problem because rodenticides are slow acting and must be available until the pest population is controlled.

Lilac Bacterial Twig Blight

Be on the watch for a disease that attacks **lilacs**. It is often misdiagnosed as frost injury or fire blight. The culprit is lilac bacterial twig blight or shoot blight caused by the bacterium *Pseudomonas syringae*. This bacterial disease affects various woody plants including **apple, cherry, peach, pear,** and **plum trees**. All varieties of lilacs are susceptible if conditions are right.

The bacteria overwinter in previously infected twigs. During the spring, as wet weather persists and temperatures are mild, the bacteria will spread to plants via rain splash, wind, and insect vectors. Bacteria will enter the plant through natural openings in the leaves, tender shoots, and bark.

Symptoms of this disease closely resemble fire blight, but don't waste your time applying a fire blight spray. The appearance of infected shoots can also resemble frost injury, so check recent weather conditions to confirm if this may be the problem. If the plants are infected with the bacterial twig blight, black spots will occur on foliage, shoots, and blossoms. As these spots enlarge, leaves and twigs become blackened, and twigs will crook over and gradually die.

Controls: Infected shoots and branches should be promptly pruned out and discarded. The best time to prune diseased portions is during dry weather. Since this is a bacterial disease, it is important that pruning tools be disinfected after each pruning cut. Use Lysol solution or equivalent, or ethyl alcohol. Avoid using bleach because it will rust the metal parts of your pruning equipment.

Chlorosis

Many trees, shrubs, and herbaceous perennials throughout Idaho suffer from iron deficiency. This condition is commonly induced by poorly drained or compacted soils or by soils with a high calcium content. Our soils are characterized by pH levels above 7.5. (Note: The relative acidity or alkalinity of soil is commonly expressed in terms of the symbol "pH". The neutral point in the pH scale is 7. Soil below a pH of 7 is acid; soil above a pH of 7 is alkaline.) This makes iron unavailable to the plants. Symptoms include yellow leaves, slow growth, and branch dieback.

Iron deficiency generally discolors the newest foliage. The leaf veins remain green while the tissue between the veins turns a pale yellow. This creates a network of darker green veins on a light green or yellow background. When chlorosis is severe, the entire leaf may become cream-colored, while the leaf tips and margins turn brown. Eventually, numerous dead spots speckle the leaf surface. It is not uncommon to have an affected and healthy plant of the same species growing side by side.

Though iron deficiency is one of the most common problems, manganese and zinc deficiencies may occur as well and will mimic the symptoms of iron deficiency. **Maple trees,** especially **red maples**, are sensitive to manganese deficiency. Here's a homemade method to find out which micronutrient deficiency you are dealing with: Spray solutions of iron, manganese and zinc sulfate on separate branches of an affected tree. Mix $1\frac{1}{2}$ tablespoons per gallon of water, and apply to the foliage. Observe whether any of the treatments correct the chlorosis.

Correcting iron chlorosis: A severe case of chlorosis can cause decline in shade trees and shrubs and is rarely reversible. The following treatments are useful for cases of moderate iron deficiency, and depending upon the treatment selected, may need to be repeated yearly or every few years. Some of the commonly used methods to treat for iron chlorotic plants are 1) altering soil pH; 2) applying a chelated iron compound to the soil and root zone; or 3) spraying the foliage with a solution of iron (ferrous) sulfate or iron chelate. However, the most effective way to prevent iron chlorosis is to plant species or cultivars that can do well in our alkaline soil conditions without special treatments. **Northern red oak**, for example, is very similar to **pin oak**, but is generally less prone to iron chlorosis.

Soil acidification with sulfur or aluminum sulfate can be effective for small shrubs or herbaceous plants in localized planting beds. It can be difficult, if not impossible, to acidify large areas of soil such as found within a tree's feeder root system. The amount of material required per unit area will depend upon type and existing pH.

Where it is not feasible to acidify the soil region, iron chelates can be applied to the soil. Chelated materials are less affected by soil pH. Work the chelate into the top 2 inches of soil throughout the root zone, and water in well. One of the best sources of chelated iron formulations for our region is "Sequestrene." **Follow label directions on the package for rates of use and methods of application.**

Spraying the foliage with an iron chelate or ferrous sulfate solution usually results in a quicker but temporary response, and several sprays are often required. To mix ferrous sulfate, use 2 ounces in 3 gallons of water, plus a few drops of mild dishwashing soap. Use a very fine mist so the leaves will not be burned by the solution. Treated foliage should green up in about 10 days if the treatment is successful. To prevent iron stains, be sure to rinse equipment and hose off any spills immediately after applying iron products.

"Lawnmower-itis"

One of the biggest killers of trees in landscapes is a manmade disease coined "lawnmower-itis". It begins with careless mowing practices as the lawn mower whips around tree trunks and nicks off pieces of bark. Additionally, weed trimmers with the strong nylon string will scar the bark and cause injury to the trunk. These wounds will predispose the tree to diseases and insect invasion.

You can prevent the scraping of your tree trunks by placing inexpensive plastic drainpipe collars around the base of small, vulnerable trees. Buy 10-foot lengths of 4-inch diameter plastic drain-

pipe. Cut the pipe in 1-foot sections, and slit each section so you can easily slip it around the tree base. These homemade guards will protect the tree trunks from "lawnmower-itis," gnawing rodents, and sunscald damage, too.

Another method to protect trees from lawn mowers and weed trimmers is to recycle automobile tires. You can make two tree guards from one old tire.

To make a tire trunk protector, you'll need to poke a heavy-duty sharp knife through the middle of the tire tread. Start cutting the tire in half, cutting away from you. Once the tire is cut, turn each tire half inside out. Carefully slit the tire open on one side of each tire half so you can easily separate the tire for placement around the tree trunk.

If you desire, fill the tire guard with shredded cedar mulch, but leave the 2 inches closest to the tree trunk bare so pests won't have a place to hide.

Tomato Problems

Two tomato blights can give gardeners problems in Idaho. One called early blight is caused by a fungus that lives on plant refuse or in the soil. It usually infects the oldest leaves with small, irregular, brown spots. These spots will get larger in a concentric, target-like pattern, and the tissue surrounding them is usually yellow. Later in the season, large target-pattern spots will develop on maturing fruit, usually somewhat water-soaked in appearance.

If this begins to show up on your tomatoes, it's very important to begin a spray program using a fungicide labeled for vegetables. Also, when the season is over, be sure to destroy all the plants and fruit that showed symptoms.

Late blight is the other fungus that can cause serious harm to your tomatoes. This one comes on during cool and wet weather. Unlike early blight, this one hits stems, usually with brown or black blotches (there is no definite target pattern). The fruit will develop brownish, wrinkled areas which eventually may become mushy. Use the same kind of treatment for late blight, especially during humid periods, and avoid overhead watering.

Blossom-end rot is not a fungus disease, but a physiological problem. Using a fungicide will not help. The aberrations on tomatoes are caused by improper watering practices while the young fruit are developing.

During this developmental stage, the young fruit need readily available water to take up sufficient calcium. If water is inadequate, the blossom end of the fruit (farthest from the stem) will develop a black or brown leathery lesion which becomes somewhat flattened. This can happen to all or only some of the tomatoes on the plant and to green as well as ripening fruit.

The best way to avoid this problem is to make sure your tomato plants don't suffer drought stress. Water them thoroughly and deeply once a week. Don't just lightly sprinkle them. On the other hand, don't water them daily since overwatering is just as bad. Use a mulch to help maintain uniform moisture in the soil.

Don't remove tomato leaves. You may have heard or read in magazines that pruning plants and removing leaves will hasten ripening of tomatoes. Contrary to this popular suggestion, removing leaves does not hasten ripening or do anything positive for the plant. It cuts down on the amount of food energy the plant can manufacture and will open the developing fruit to sunscald injury. Tomatoes do not need to be in the sun to ripen.

Sunscald injury appears as white or yellowish spots on green fruit. This is bound to happen when gardeners remove leaves and expose the immature fruit to sunlight.

Yellow Jackets, Wasps, and Hornets

Sharing your garden with pesky yellow jackets, hornets, and wasps requires a combination of diplomacy and knowledge. Many of these stinging pests share our tastes in barbecue and picnic foods. They are social insects. They start nesting in April and May and reach their peak in August and September.

In the overall balance of nature, these insects are highly beneficial as pollinators and predators of harmful insect pests. They can become a serious nuisance and safety issue though, particularly during outdoor entertaining activities.

Wasps feeding at outdoor tables are not especially aggressive and often will flee when bothered. But yellow jackets may sting if swatted or disturbed while feeding. Some people have been stung in the mouth while they and a yellow jacket were taking a bite of the same food.

Some yellow jackets are ground nesters, while others nest in cavities of trees and buildings. Paper wasps and some hornets build paper nests on tree branches. All of them do an excellent job of hiding their nests, and it is often difficult to ferret them out. Finding the nests in June or July can save you a lot of grief later in the season.

Insect repellents that are formulated to ward off biting insects such as deer flies and mosquitoes will do little to stop a stinging insect in search of food. If you fear being stung, wear light-colored clothing, which repels the pests. Rough, dark clothing appears to antagonize wasps, and suede and leather are especially a problem. As in the case with other biting insects, the stinging types appear to be irritated by human perspiration.

If you use perfume and scented soaps, you may find yourself more attractive to these uninvited picnic guests. Many people are stung when wasps become entangled in their hair. People who fear being stung are advised to cover as much of their bodies as is reasonable.

When stung by a honeybee, the stinger is usually left behind. Carefully remove the stinger so the small, attached poison sac is not squeezed, which would force more venom into the wound. Other bees and wasps do not leave a stinger. Stings should be treated with an antiseptic.

First Aid for Stings

1. Apply an antiseptic, cool lotion, or compress to relieve pain and swelling.

2. Crushed aspirin or powdered meat tenderizer also helps to reduce pain.

3. If you are stung numerous times, oral antihistamines can reduce swelling and itching.

4. Symptoms generally disappear in a few hours.

5. Contact a medical doctor immediately if you develop a severe allergic reaction, which may include difficulty breathing, dizziness, nausea, and hives.

More Pest Management Tips

Good planning can put you a step ahead of unwanted insects, weeds, and diseases. Healthy, vigorous plants minimize pest damage. Regular monitoring of your lawn or garden is the best way to stay on top of potential plant health and pest problems. If you see minimal damage, it is often easiest to just tolerate it and continue monitoring, If pests begin to cause serious damage, there are a number of treatment methods.

Preventing Pests

1. Plant disease- and pest-resistant species.

2. Select a variety of hardy plant species, and space them properly.

3. Select plants that bloom and bear fruit at different times of year.

4. Plant flowers, herbs, and vegetables together, and change the location of annuals every year to prevent buildup of certain pests.

5. Clean up plant litter, and remove weeds before they go to seed.

6. Add bird and bat houses to the garden.

7. Provide habitat for beneficial insects that prey on pests.

8. Water and add nutrients properly to increase plant vigor.

Physical Pest Control

1. Remove insects by hand.

2. Wash pests away using a spray nozzle.

3. Set traps.

4. Make physical barriers around plants, such as a wire mesh fence partially sunk into the ground for rabbits, aluminum foil wrapped around vegetable plants for cutworms, and solid barriers to prevent weeds from invading flower beds or vegetable gardens.

Beneficial Insects

Having the right insects in your garden or backyard can keep pests and weeds in check. Beneficial insects, such as ladybugs, assassin bugs, and praying mantises, prey on insects that can harm your plants. The following insects can help control pests in your backyard:

1. Ladybugs and lacewing larvae for controlling aphids and a wide variety of other insects

2. Preying mantises for controlling many insects

3. Seedhead weevils and other beetles for controlling weeds

4. Predatory mites for controlling spider mites, thrips, and many others

5. Ground beetles for controlling caterpillars that attack trees and shrubs

Chemical Controls

If the methods listed above fail to solve your pest problem, use chemicals of low toxicity and rapid decomposition. **Always read the label, follow directions, wear protective clothing, and spot-spray.** Some of these chemicals are:

1. Pesticidal soaps for aphids, scale crawlers, white flies, and thrips

2. Insecticidal dusts for aphids, beetles, fleas, ticks, ants, and crickets

3. Horticultural oils for aphids, mites, leafhoppers, mealybugs, scales, plant lice, and mosquito larvae

4. Botanicals for leafminers, fleas, and ticks

Before you apply pesticides, make sure they will not harm beneficial insects or be hazardous to humans, pets, or wildlife. **Read and follow label directions exactly as prescribed.**

BIBLIOGRAPHY

Bailey Hortorium. *Hortus Third*. Macmillan Publishing Company, 1976.

Ball, Liz. *Month-By-Month Gardening in Pennsylvania*. Cool Springs Press, A Division of Thomas Nelson, Inc. 2001.

Bryan, John E. *John E. Bryan on Bulbs*. Macmillan Publishing, 1994.

Clausen, Ruth Rogers and Nicolas H. Ekstrom. *Perennials For American Gardens*. Random House, 1989.

Crandall, Barbara and Chuck. *Flowering, Fruiting & Foliage Vines*. Sterling Publishing Company, 1995.

Cranshaw, Whitney. *Pests of the West*. Fulcrum Publishing, 1998.

Cretti, John. *Colorado Gardener's Guide*. Cool Springs Press. 1998.

Darr, Shelia and Helga and William Olkowski. *Common-Sense Pest Control*. The Tauton Press, Inc., 1991.

Dirr, Michael A. *Manual of Woody Landscape Plants*. Stipes Publishing Company, 1998.

DiSaabato-Aust, Tracy. *The Well-Tended Perennial Garden*. Timber, Press, 1998.

Evison, Raymond J. *Making the Most of Clematis*. Burall Floraprint Ltd., 1991.

Fairchild, D. H. and J. E. Klett. *Woody Landscape Plants for the High Plains*. Colorado State University, 1993.

Greenlee, John. *The Encyclopedia of Ornamental Grasses*. Michael Friedman Publishing Group, 1992.

Griffiths, Mark. *Index of Garden Plants: The New Royal Horticulture Society Dictionary*. Timber Press, 1994.

Harper, Pamela. *Designing with Perennials*. Macmillan Publishing Company, 1991.

Jimerson, Douglas A. *Successful Rose Gardening*. Meredith Books, 1993.

Kelly, George W. *Trees For The Rocky Mountains*. Rocky Mountain Horticultural Publishing Company, 1976.

Kelly, George W. *Rocky Mountain Horticulture*. Pruett Publishing Company, 1957.

Meyer, Mary Hockenberry. *Ornamental Grasses*. Charles Scribner's Sons, 1975.

Olson, Marsha. *A Garden of Love and Healing*. Fairview Press, Minneapolis, 2002.

Pesman, M. Walter. *Meet the Natives*. Pruett Publishing, 1988.

Phillips, Roger and Martyn. *Perennials*. Volume 1 and 2. Random House, 1991.

Polomski, Bob (Edited by Felder Rushing). *Gardening in Mississippi*. Cool Springs Press, a Division of Thomas Nelson, Inc. 2002.

Shigo, Alex L. *A New Tree Biology*. Shigo and Trees, Associates, 1986.

Still, Steven. *Manual of Herbaceous Ornamental Plants*. Stipes Publishing Company, 1994.

Strauch, Jr., J. G., and J. E. Klett. *Flowering Herbaceous Perennials for the High Plains*. Colorado State University, 1989.

Thomasson, Joseph R. *Growing Vegetables in the Great Plains*. University Press of Kansas, 1991.

Turgeonn, A. J. *Turfgrass Management*. Prentice Hall, Inc., 1991.

Wyman, Donald. *Ground Cover Plants*. Macmillan Company, 1976.

Wyman, Donald. *Shrubs and Vines for American Gardens*. The Macmillan Company, 1969.

Winger, David and Connie Lockhart Ellefson. *Xeriscape Colorado: The Complete Guide*. Westcliffe Publishers, Inc, 2004.

INDEX

INDEX

INDEX

MEET THE AUTHOR

John Cretti is a highly regarded horticulturist and award-winning gardening expert whose multimedia approach to reach gardeners includes television, radio, print, and world wide web. His motto is, "To grow plants successfully the way nature intended, you have to *think* like a plant."

John shares his down-to-earth Rocky Mountain and High Plains gardening expertise weekly at the web site: www.nationalgardening.com. His numerous awards include the Quill & Trowel Award from the Garden Writers Association of America. He has been hosting a call-in radio talk show since 1981.

His regional garden features and articles have been published in *Flower & Garden Magazine*, *Horticulture Magazine*, *Homes and Lifestyles*, *Boulder County Home & Garden Magazine*, and regional newspapers and newsletters. He also publishes online at www.yardcare.com.

John is radio talk-show host of the weekly "Gardening with an ALTITUDE" on radio stations KHOW-AM 630 and KOA 85. He can also be heard weekly on radio station 850 KOA's Saturday morning news, which reaches across Colorado and the Rockies. He has been a long-time host of "The Winter Gardener" television show on HGTV, and he also does regional television features of "Gardening with An ALTITUDE" during the gardening season.

Gardeners who live in the unique and challenging climate of the Rocky Mountain Region, where extremes of temperature, wind, soil, and critters are the norm, will enjoy John's practical wit and wisdom. He is author of *The Colorado Gardener's Guide* and *My Rocky Mountain Gardener's Guide* (Cool Springs Press, A Division of Thomas Nelson, Inc.).